Doll Values

ANTIQUE TO MODERN

NINTH EDITION
Linda Edward

OUR #1 BESTSELLING DOLL BOOK!

COLLECTOR BOOKS
A Division of Schroeder Publishing Co., Inc.

Cover design by Beth Summers
Book design by Holly C. Long

COLLECTOR BOOKS
P.O. Box 3009
Paducah, Kentucky 42002-3009

www.collectorbooks.com

Copyright © 2007 Linda Edward

The current values in this book should be used only as a guide. They are not intended to set prices, which vary from one section of the country to another. Auction prices as well as dealer prices vary greatly and are affected by condition as well as demand. Neither the author nor the publisher assumes responsibility for any losses that might be incurred as a result of consulting this guide.

Searching for a Publisher?

We are always looking for people knowledgeable within their fields. If you feel that there is a real need for a book on your collectible subject and have a large comprehensive collection, contact Collector Books.

Proudly printed and bound in the
United States of America

ACKNOWLEDGMENTS

Thank you to the following collectors for sharing their dolls and those of their friends for this edition of *Doll Values*: Alderfer Auctions, Carole Barboza, Ruth Cayton, Margo Delaughter, Lucy DiTerlizzi, Maxine Evans, McMasters-Harris Auctions, Ursula Mertz, Susan Mitchell, Morris Musem, George & Cynthia Orgeron, Marilyn Parsons, Mimi Salzman, Louise Scala, Skinner Inc., Shelly Smith, Louise Stevens, Turn of the Century Antiques, Richard Withington Inc., and Yakety Yak dolls.

I would also like to thank every doll researcher and collector who has generously shared their dolls and knowledge through the many fine reference books, articles, seminars, special exhibits, and doll club programs. Without this constant exchange of information we would all be searching in the dark for answers.

Finally, I must thank my husband, Al Edward, for his encouragement, support, and belief in me and the work I pursue.

HOW TO USE THIS BOOK

This book is a tool for the collector, a place to start in a journey of study that can enrich a life. The best piece of advice this collector ever received was "buy every doll reference book you can find." Each volume, be it old or new, contains some piece of information that will be of aid to the collector. Building a reference library of your own will pay you back many times over in the knowledge it will bring you, knowledge which will ultimately allow you to make better decisions when purchasing a doll for your own collection. In addition to building a reference library I would also suggest that you take every opportunity to look at dolls wherever you go. Nothing beats first hand examination. Visit every doll museum and special display you can find. Go to shows and really look at the dolls that interest you most. Join a doll club to learn more and share your discoveries with others. All of these experiences will put you in a better position to understand and evaluate a doll when you are considering a purchase.

When evaluating any doll there are several questions to ask oneself. These relate to identification, quality, originality, condition, rarity, and value. Each component is important to the overall picture of any doll. All dolls should be thoroughly examined before making a purchase.

Identification — What is this doll? A doll is classified by the material from which its head is made, therefore a doll with a composition head on a cloth body will be considered a composition doll or a doll with a papier-mâché head on a leather body will be considered a papier-mâché doll and so on. Look for and learn about makers' marks. These will be of invaluable aid in identifying the doll you are looking at. Many manufacturers marked their dolls on the back of the head or on the torso. An appendix of makers' initials and an appendix of known mold numbers are included in the back of this book to assist you.

Quality — As stated by Patsy Moyer in the first edition of this book, "all dolls are not created equal." Any model of doll made by any particular manufacturer can range vastly in quality depending on the conditions on the day it was made. Remember these dolls were produced in factories which in many cases turned out thousands of dolls a year. How worn was the mold when this doll was poured, what weather conditions affected the materials it was made from, how tired was the worker who cleaned or painted a particular doll that day? If you line up six AM 390s you will be looking at six different degrees of quality of finish. Therefore when preparing to make a purchase consider each doll carefully from a standpoint of quality. A sharply molded, evenly textured, well painted doll will always be of more value than an example of the same doll with blurry molding, uneven texture, or poor quality painting.

Originality is another important component of a doll evaluation. Does the doll have the correct eyes, wig, body type, clothing? Each of these parts adds value to the doll and dolls on incorrect bodies or with replaced clothing or wigs should not bring the same amount in the marketplace as examples in all original condition.

Condition — What is the overall condition of the doll? Check carefully to look for damage or repair to the doll. In most cases a damaged or repaired doll will not be worth as much as a perfect example.

Rarity is perhaps one of the most important aspects of doll evaluation. How unusual is this doll? How many were made and survive? How difficult would it be to find another example of this doll today? Sometimes rarity can cause us to forgive problems of originality or condition that would in a more common doll deter us from adding a particular example to our collection.

Value takes into account all of the aforementioned qualifications and combines them with somewhat more elusive components such as collector demand and trends. At various points in time collectors tend to favor certain dolls. A good example of this can be seen in the value of the Bye-Lo Baby. Every generation of collectors tends to start out collecting the dolls they had or wanted as children. In the 1950s and 1960s many adult collectors eagerly sought the Bye-Lo Baby from the 1920s and the dolls achieved comparatively high market price. In the past 20 years the value of the Bye-Lo has changed very little compared to other antique dolls because collector demand for them has quieted down.

After evaluating each of the aforementioned aspects of any doll, this book will assist you in figuring out the current market value of the doll. Unless otherwise noted the values stated in this volume represent dolls in good overall condition with original or appropriate clothing. When looking at the values presented here gauge the particular doll you are considering accordingly. Allow a lower value for dolls which do not meet the standard for the values listed here. This is especially important in judging vintage collectible or modern dolls. These must be in perfect and completely original condition with appropriate hang tags to attain the values listed in this guide. For example, an all original #3 Barbie in good condition will bring approximately half the price of the same doll mint in box.

This book is laid out in alphabetical order. You will notice that it is not divided into "antique" and "modern" sections as some other books are. The reason for this choice is threefold; firstly, the line between antique and modern is not as clear cut in doll collecting as it is in other areas. In furniture for instance a piece must be at least 100 years old to be considered antique whereas in car collecting a vehicle that is 25 years old is considered antique. In doll collecting the line is blurry although it generally falls somewhere in the neighborhood of 75 years. Dolls 30 to 75 years old are most often referred to as "collectible vintage" and dolls 30 years old or less are usually referred to as modern. Secondly, many doll-making companies were in business for such long periods of time that they produced dolls which would now be considered antique as well as dolls that fall into the collectible vintage and modern categories.

Thirdly, it is the belief of this author that by not creating barriers between dolls of different ages we see a more complete picture of the doll world and promote a better understanding of the history of the dolls we love and of our fellow collectors.

As stated previously, this book is laid out in an alphabetical order by the manufacturer's name or general type. Most dolls are marked in some way which indicates their maker. Wherever possible those markings have been included for reference. The general type headings include dolls made of like materials. Under these headings you will find dolls made by small companies, or about which little is known, as well as unmarked and as yet unattributable dolls.

The values listed in this book are complied from several sources including auction prices, online auction prices, dealer asking prices, dealer prices realized, as well as other sources. These values are then compiled, analyzed, and averaged. Although the collecting world is now much more global than it was even just a few years ago, there are still some regional differences in value which are generated by collector interest and doll availability in certain areas. This book is meant as a guide and is not the "definitive" word on doll values. Ultimately a doll is worth whatever a particular collector wishes to pay for it. Neither this author nor the publisher of this book take any responsibility for any decision or actions taken by an individual on the basis of the information presented here. As stated earlier, this book is one more tool for the collector to use in their decision-making process.

Finally I will say that study, evaluation, and value, although important, are not the bottom line in doll collecting. Ultimately we each need to "follow our bliss" as it were, and buy dolls that mean something to us and enrich our lives and collections.

Collectors seeking to learn more about dolls and exchange doll knowledge can turn to a national organization whose goals are education, research, preservation, and enjoyment of dolls. The United Federation of Doll Clubs can tell you if a doll club in your area is accepting members or tell you how to become a member-at-large. You may write for more information at:

United Federation of Doll Clubs, Inc.
10900 North Pomona Avenue
Kansas City, MO 64153
816-891-7040
fax: 816-891-8360
www.ufdc.org

CODES

RED (ALL CAPS)	Main category ex: **ADVERTISING DOLLS**
Red (Roman)	First subcategory, usualy a name of the doll, company, or material ex: **Gerber Baby**
Blue (Italic)	Second subcategory ex: *1979 – 1985*
Black (Roman)	Third subcategory ex: **Talker**
Black (Indented, Italic)	Fourth subcategory

* at auction

ADVERTISING DOLLS

Dolls of various materials, made by a variety of manufacturers, to promote commercial brands or specific products. Doll in good condition with original clothing and accessories.

14½" printed cloth Buster Brown made by Knickerbocker and his dog Tige (9½"). $225.00. *Courtesy of The Museum Doll Shop.*

Uncut printed cloth Uncle Mose for Aunt Jemima Pancakes, made by Arnold Printworks. $110.00. *Courtesy of The Museum Doll Shop.*

Cream of Wheat, Rastus, printed cloth doll
   16" $90.00 – 100.00
Gerber Baby, 1936 to present. An advertising and trademark doll for Gerber Products, a baby food manufacturer located in Fremont, Michigan. More for black or special sets with accessories.
1936, cloth one-piece doll, printed girl or boy, holds can
   8" $450.00 – 500.00

13" Gerber Baby, vinyl head, c. 1990s. $20.00. *Courtesy of The Museum Doll Shop.*

Aunt Jemima, cloth, Aunt Jemima, Uncle Moses, Diana, and Wade Davis
   16" $85.00 – 95.00
Bell Telephone "Pioneers of America" Bell
   15" $65.00 – 75.00
Buster Brown Shoes
Composition head, cloth body, tag reads "Buster Brown Shoes"
   15" $256.00*
Capezio Shoes
"Aida, Toe Dancing Ballerina Dolls"
                              $125.00 – 150.00
Colgate Fab Soap Princess Doll, ca. 1951
   5½" $12.00 – 18.00

15" pair of cloth Campbell Kids. $40.00. *Courtesy of The Museum Doll Shop.*

1955 – 1958, Sun Rubber Company, designed by Bernard Lipfert, vinyl
    12" – 18" $100.00 – 125.00
1965, Arrow Rubber & Plastic Co., vinyl
    14" $125.00 – 150.00
1972 – 1973, Amsco, Milton Bradley, vinyl
    10" $75.00 – 90.00
    14" – 18" $55.00 – 65.00
1979 – 1985, Atlanta Novelty, vinyl, flirty eyes, cloth body
    17" $90.00 – 100.00
Talker
    17" $90.00 – 100.00
Collector Doll, christening gown, basket
    12" $90.00 – 100.00
Porcelain, limited edition
    17" $275.00 – 325.00
1989 – 1992, Lucky Ltd., vinyl
    6" $12.00 – 18.00
    11" $35.00 – 40.00
    14" – 16" $35.00 – 40.00
1994 – 1996, Toy Biz, Inc., vinyl
    8" $12.00 – 15.00
    15" $20.00 – 25.00
Battery operated
    12" – 13" $20.00 – 25.00
Talker
    14" $35.00 – 40.00
    17" $45.00 – 50.00

Green Giant, Sprout, 1973
    10½" $18.00 – 25.00
Jolly Joan, Portland, Oregon, restaurant
    11" $100.00 – 125.00
Kellogg's cereals
Corn Flakes Red Riding Hood, printed cloth
    13½" $125.00 – 150.00
Goldilocks & Three Bears, set of four, printed cloth
    12" – 15" $200.00 – 225.00
Korn Krisp cereal
Miss Korn-Krisp, ca. 1900, cloth marked body
    24" $200.00 – 225.00
Lustre Crème, original dress, patterns
    7½" $85.00 – 100.00
Mr. Peanut, ca. 1970s
    19" $15.00 – 20.00
Pangburn Chocolates
Hard plastic, gold foil label
    7" $10.00 – 15.00
"The Selling Fool," 1926, made by Cameo, wood segmented body, hat represents radio tube, composition advertising doll for RCA Radiotrons
    16" $750.00 – 850.00
Too few in database for a reliable range.

ZuZu Ginger Snap advertising doll, made *by* Ideal. $250.00. *Courtesy of The Museum Doll Shop.*

ZuZu, 1916, composition doll made by Ideal advertising ginger snaps made by the National Biscuit Co.

14"	$250.00 – 30.00

ALABAMA BABY

1900 – 1925, Roanoke, Alabama. Ella Gauntt Smith, cloth over plaster doll, stitched on skull cap, painted features. Tab jointed at shoulders and hips, painted feet may be bare with stitched toes or have shoes painted pink, blue, black, brown, or yellow.

Two Alabama Babies, by Ella Smith. $1,200.00 and 2,000.00. *Courtesy of The Museum Doll Shop.*

Earlier model with applied ears

11" – 14"	$1,450.00 – 1,550.00
18" – 22"	$2,500.00 – 3,600.00
Wigged	
24"	$2,800.00 – 3,500.00
Black	
14" – 18"	$5,500.00 – 6,000.00
20" – 22"	$6,200.00 – 6,800.00

Later model with molded ears, bobbed hairstyle

14" – 16"	$1,000.00 – 1,200.00
18" – 22"	$1,800.00 – 2,200.00
Black	
14" – 18"	$2,800.00 – 3,000.00
20" – 22"	$3,200.00 – 4,000.00

MADAME ALEXANDER

1912 – present, New York City. In 1912 in New York City, Beatrice and Rose Alexander, known for making doll costumes, began the Alexander Doll Co. They began using the "Madame Alexander" trademark in 1928. Beatrice Alexander Behrman became a legend in the doll world with her long reign as head of the Alexander Doll Company. Alexander made cloth, composition, and wooden dolls, and eventually made the transition to hard plastic and vinyl. Dolls are listed by subcategories of the material of which the head is made.

With Madame Alexander dolls, especially those made from 1950 on, condition as it relates to value is extremely important. **For the values listed here the doll must be in perfect condition with complete original clothing and tags. Dolls with incomplete or soiled costumes will bring one-fourth to one-third of the value of perfect examples.** Unusual dolls with presentation cases, trousseaux, or rare costumes may bring much more.

Cloth, 1930 – 1950 on

All-cloth head and body, mohair wig, flat or molded mask face, painted side-glancing eyes

Storybook characters such as Little Women, Dickens characters, Edith, and others

16"	$600.00 – 700.00

Alice in Wonderland

Flat face	$775.00 – 850.00
Mask face	
10" – 20"	$575.00 – 950.00

Animals

$225.00 – 275.00

Baby

13"	$300.00 – 325.00
17"	$450.00 – 500.00
24"	$525.00 – 575.00

Funny, 1963 – 1977

18"	$70.00

Little Shaver, 1940 – 1944, yarn hair

7"	$375.00 – 400.00
10"	$275.00 – 300.00
15"	$325.00 – 375.00
22"	$400.00 – 450.00

Muffin, ca. 1963 – 1977

14"	$75.00 – 95.00

So Lite Baby or Toddler, 1930s – 1940s

20"	$375.00 – 425.00

Suzie Q, 1940 – 1942

$475.00 – 550.00

Teeny Twinkle, 1946, disc floating eyes

$525.00 – 800.00

Dionne Quintuplets, various materials

Cloth, 1935 – 1936

16"	$825.00 – 875.00
24"	$1,100.00 – 1,200.00

Composition, 1935 – 1945, all-composition, swivel head, jointed toddler or baby body, molded and painted hair or wigged, sleep or painted eyes. Outfit colors: Annette, yellow; Cecile, green; Emilie, lavender; Marie, blue; Yvonne, pink. Add more for extra accessories or in layette.

10" Little Shaver, c. 1940. $275.00.
Courtesy of The Museum Doll Shop.

17" Bobby Q, cloth mask face doll. $500.00.
Doll courtesy of Louise Scala.

Baby

8"	$225.00 – 275.00
Complete set	$1,400.00 – 1,600.00

Set of five with wooden nursery furniture

8"	$2,000.00 – 2,250.00

Toddler

8"	$275.00 – 300.00
Complete set	$1,400.00 – 1,500.00
11"	$325.00 – 375.00
Complete set	$2,000.00 – 2,200.00
14"	$525.00 – 575.00
Complete set	$2,600.00 – 2,900.00
20"	$700.00 – 750.00
Complete set	$3,800.00 – 4,200.00
On cloth body	
22"	$650.00 – 750.00
Complete set	$3,400.00 – 3,700.00

Vinyl, 8", in carousel

Set of 5	$325.00 – 375.00

Dr. Dafoe, 1937 – 1939

14"	$1,200.00 – 1,400.00

Nurse

13"	$850.00 – 900.00*

Composition, 1930 – 1950

Babies, cloth body, sleep eyes, marked "Alexander," dolls such as Baby Genius, Butch, Baby McGuffy, Pinky, and others

10" – 12"	$150.00 – 200.00
16" – 22"	$425.00 – 475.00

Baby Jane, 1935

16"	$900.00 – 1,100.00

Child

Alice in Wonderland, 1930s, swivel waist

7" – 9"	$250.00 – 300.00
11" – 14"	$425.00 – 500.00
18" – 21"	$750.00 – 1,000.00

Babs Skater, 1948, marked "ALEX" on head, clover tag

18"	$1,000.00 – 1,250.00

Carmen (Miranda), 1942, black hair, painted eyes

9"	$325.00 – 375.00
14"	$450.00 – 550.00

Fairy Queen, ca. 1939 – 1946, clover wrist tag, tagged gown

14"	$650.00 – 700.00
18"	$750.00 – 800.00

8" Dionne Quintuplets in original wicker hamper. $2,200.00.
Courtesy of The Museum Doll Shop.

16" composition Flora McFlimsey, c. 1938. $650.00. *Courtesy of Alderfer Auction Co.*

Flora McFlimsey, 1938, freckles, marked "Princess Elizabeth"

13"	$400.00 – 500.00
16"	$600.00 – 750.00
22"	$800.00 – 1,000.00

Happy Birthday, set of 12, side-glancing eyes

7", all original	$2,700.00

Jane Withers, 1937 – 1939, green sleep eyes, open mouth, brown mohair wig

12" – 13½"	$900.00 – 1,000.00
15" – 17"	$1,100.00 – $1,300.00
18" – 19"	$1,400.00 – 1,550.00
20" – 22"	$1,600.00 – 1800.00

Jeannie Walker, tagged dress, closed mouth, mohair wig

13" – 14"	$675.00 – 750.00
18"	$950.00 – 1,100.00

Judy, original box, wrist tag, Wendy Ann face, eye shadow

21"	$3,100.00 – 3,300.00

Karen Ballerina, blue sleep eyes, closed mouth, "Alexander" on head

15"	$900.00 – 1,000.00
18"	$1,400.00 – 1,600.00

Kate Greenaway, yellow wig, marked "Princess Elizabeth"

13" – 15"	$650.00 – 750.00
18"	$800.00 – 900.00
24"	$900.00 – 1,000.00

Little Betty, 1939 – 1943, side-glancing painted eyes

9" – 11"	$325.00 – 400.00

Little Colonel

11" – 13"	$625.00 – 700.00
17"	$750.00 – 825.00

Little Genius, blue sleep eyes, cloth body, closed mouth, clover tag

12"	$250.00 – 300.00
16"	$325.00 – 375.00

Little Women, Meg, Jo, Amy, Beth

7"	$300.00
Set	$1,400.00
9"	$325.00
Set	$1,500.00

Madelaine DuBain, 1937 – 1944

14"	$550.00 – 600.00
17"	$675.00 – 700.00

Marcella, 1936, open mouth, wig, sleep eyes

24"	$700.00 – 900.00

Margaret O'Brien, 1946 – 1948

14½"	$700.00 – 775.00
17" – 19"	$925.00 – 1,000.00
21" – 24"	$1,150.00 – 1,300.00

McGuffey Ana, 1935 – 1937, sleep eyes, open mouth, tagged dress

11" – 13"	$475.00 – 550.00
14" – 16"	$550.00 – 625.00

17" – 20"	$650.00 – 725.00
21" – 25"	$750.00 – 775.00
28"	$800.00 – 850.00
Painted eyes, 9"	$375.00 – 450.00

Marionettes by Tony Sarg

12"	$425.00 – 475.00

Princess Elizabeth, 1937 – 1941

Closed mouth

13"	$500.00 – 625.00

Open mouth

13" – 16"	$400.00 – 500.00
22" – 24"	$625.00 – 825.00
28"	$950.00 – 1,000.00

Scarlett, 1937 – 1946, add more for rare costume

11"	$850.00 – 900.00
14"	$750.00 – 900.00
18"	$1,200.00 – 1,350.00
21"	$1,600.00 – 1,750.00

13" Snow White, composition, marked "Princess Elizabeth." $450.00. *Courtesy of Richard Withington Inc., Nashua, New Hampshire.*

Snow White, 1939 – 1942, marked "Princess Elizabeth"

14"	$450.00 – 475.00
18"	$750.00

Sonja Henie, 1939 – 1942, open mouth, sleep eyes

13", twist waist, MIB	$1,000.00
13" – 15"	$900.00 – 1,100.00
17" – 18"	$950.00 – 1,200.00
20" – 23"	$1,200.00 – 1,400.00

Tiny Betty, 1934 – 1943, side-glancing painted eyes

7"	$200.00 – 350.00

W.A.A.C. (Army), W.A.A.F. (Air Force), W.A.V.E. (Navy), ca. 1943 – 1944

14"	$725.00 – 800.00

Wendy Ann, 1935 – 1948, more for special outfit

11" – 15"	$475.00 – 550.00
17" – 21"	$850.00 – 950.00

Painted eyes

9"	$375.00 – 400.00

Molded hair

14"	$625.00 – 675.00

Swivel waist

14"	$475.00 – 550.00

Hard Plastic and Vinyl, 1948 on

Alexander-kins, 1953 on

1953, 7½" – 8", straight leg nonwalker

Nude	$250.00 – 300.00
Dressed	$500.00 – 700.00

1954 – 1955, straight leg walker

Nude	$250.00 – 300.00
Dressed	$450.00 – 650.00

1956 – 1965, bent-knee walker, after 1963 marked "Alex"

Nude	$150.00 – 200.00

1965 – 1972, bent-knee non-walker

Nude	$100.00 – 125.00
Dressed	$300.00 – 500.00

1973 – 1975, straight leg

Ballerina	$60.00 – 80.00

Bride	$75.00 – 100.00

1976 – 1994, straight leg non-walker, marked "Alexander"

Ballerina	$65.00 – 85.00
Bride	$75.00 – 100.00

Babies

Baby Angel, #480, tagged tulle gown

8"	$950.00

Too few in database for a reliable range

Baby Brother or Sister, 1977 – 1982, vinyl

14"	$75.00 – 85.00

Baby Clown, #464, seven-piece walker, leashed dog, Huggy

8"	$1,100.00 – 1,200.00

Baby Ellen, 1965 – 1972, vinyl, rigid vinyl body, marked "Alexander 1965"

14"	$100.00 – 125.00

Baby Precious, 1975, vinyl, cloth body

14"	$75.00 – 100.00

Bonnie Toddler, 1954 – 1955, vinyl

19"	$100.00 – 125.00

Happy, 1970 only, vinyl

20"	$175.00 – 225.00

Hello Baby, 1962 only

22"	$150.00 – 175.00

Honeybun, 1951, vinyl

19"	$150.00 – 200.00

Huggums,

   Big, 1963 – 1979

25"	$75.00 – 100.00

   Lively, 1963

25"	$125.00 – 150.00

Little Bitsey, 1967 – 1968, all-vinyl

9"	$125.00 – 150.00

Little Genius, 1956 – 1962, hard plastic, varies with outfit, nude

8"	$85.00 – 100.00

Littlest Kitten, vinyl

8"	$175.00 – 200.00

Mary Cassatt, 1969 – 1970, vinyl

14"	$100.00 – 125.00
20"	$175.00 – 200.00

Cissette bride from the 1950s. $450.00. *Courtesy of The Museum Doll Shop.*

Pussy Cat, 1965 – 1985, vinyl

14"	$50.00 – 65.00

   Black

14"	$65.00 – 75.00

Rusty, 1967 – 1968 only, vinyl

20"	$250.00 – 300.00

Sweet Tears, 1965 – 1974

9"	$75.00 – 100.00

   With layette, 1965 – 1973

	$150.00 – 175.00

Victoria, 1967 – 1989

20"	$75.00 – 100.00

Bible Character Dolls, 1954 only, hard plastic, original box made like Bible

8"	$7,000.00+

Cissette, 1957 – 1963, 10", hard plastic head, synthetic wig, pierced ears, closed mouth, seven-piece adult body, jointed elbows and knees, high-heeled feet, mold later used for other dolls. Marks: None on body, clothes tagged "Cissette." Doll in good condition with original clothing — value can be doubled for mint in box.

Basic doll in undergarments

	$175.00 – 225.00

In street dress	$275.00 – 350.00
In formal wear	$350.00 – 450.00
Gibson Girl	$800.00 – 900.00
Jacqueline	$800.00 – 900.00
Margot	$525.00 – 625.00
Portrette	$375.00 – 450.00

Sleeping Beauty, 1959 only

	$375.00 – 450.00
Tinkerbell	$475.00 – 525.00

Cissy, 1955 – 1959, 20", hard plastic, vinyl arms, jointed elbows and knees, high-heeled feet. Clothes are tagged "Cissy."

In undergarments	$350.00 – 400.00
In street dress	$600.00 – 800.00
In formalwear	$1,000.00 – 2,200.00

With trunk and trousseau

	$1,500.00 – 1,800.00

Miss Flora McFlimsey, 1953 only, Cissy, vinyl head, inset eyes

15"	$600.00 – 650.00

Secret Armoire Trunk Set

	$900.00 – 1,500.00
Princess	$800.00 – 900.00

Hard plastic Binnie Walker. $300.00. *Courtesy of The Museum Doll Shop.*

Queen	$900.00 – 1,100.00

Scarlett, rare white organdy dress

	$2,000.00+

Others

Alice in Wonderland, 1949 – 1952, Margaret and/or Maggie

15"	$500.00 – 700.00
18" – 23"	$900.00 – 1,000.00

American Girl, 1962 – 1963, #388, seven-piece walker body, became McGuffey Ana in 1964 – 1965

8"	$375.00 – 425.00

Annabelle, 1952, Maggie head

18" – 20"	$950.00 – 1,000.00

Aunt Pitty-Pat, 1957, #435, seven-piece body

8"	$1,700.00 – 1,900.00

Babs Skater, 1948 – 1950, hard plastic, Margaret

15"	$950.00 – 1,100.00
18"	$1,250.00 – 1,350.00

Bill/Billy, 1960, seven-piece walker body

8"	$475.00 – 525.00

Binnie Walker, 1954 – 1955, Cissy

15"	$375.00 – 400.00
18"	$475.00 – 525.00
25"	$625.00 – 675.00

Bitsey, 1950, cloth body, molded hair, more for wigged version

11"	$275.00 – 325.00

Brenda Starr, 1964 only, 12" hard plastic, vinyl arms, red wig

In street dress	$250.00 – 275.00
In formalwear	$250.00 – 350.00

Caroline, 1961, #131, vinyl

15"	$375.00 – 425.00

Cinderella

1950, Margaret face, 14", hard plastic Ballgown

14"	$650.00 – 800.00
18"	$1,150.00 – 1,250.00

Poor Cinderella, gray dress, original broom

14"	$600.00 – 650.00

1966, Lissy

12"	$500.00 – 600.00

1970 – 1986, vinyl body, ball gown (pink and blue)

14"	$100.00 – 125.00

Cynthia, 1952 only, hard plastic

15"	$850.00 – 1,000.00
18"	$1,200.00 – 1,400.00
23"	$1,400.00 – 1,600.00

Davy Crockett, 1955, hard plastic, straight leg walker, coonskin cap

8"	$650.00 – 750.00

Edith, The Lonely Doll, 1958 – 1959, vinyl head, hard plastic body

8"	$700.00 – 750.00
16"	$325.00 – 375.00
22"	$425.00 – 450.00

Elise

1957 – 1964, 16½", hard plastic b o d y, vinyl arms, jointed ankles and knees

Ballerina	$350.00 – 400.00
Ballgown	$500.00 – 700.00
Street dress	$225.00 – 275.00

1963 only, 18", hard plastic, vinyl arms, jointed ankles and knees

Riding habit	$350.00 – 400.00
Bouffant hairstyle	$375.00 – 425.00

1966 – 1972, 17", hard plastic, vinyl arms, jointed ankles and knees

Street dress	$250.00 – 275.00
Trousseau/Trunk	$750.00 – 900.00

1966 – 1987

Bride	$160.00 – 180.00

Fairy Queen, 1948 – 1950, Margaret face

14½"	$750.00 – 775.00

Fashions of a Century, 1954 – 1955, Margaret face, hard plastic

14" – 18"	$1,800.00 – 1,900.00

8" Cousin Grace, Wendy face, c. 1956. $450.00.
Courtesy of Alderfer Auction Co.

First Ladies, 1976 – 1990

Set 1, 1976 – 1978
$65.00 – 90.00 each

Set 2, 1979 – 1981
$65.00 – 90.00 each

Set 3, 1982 – 1984
$50.00 – 75.00 each

Set 4, 1985 – 1987
$50.00 – 75.00 each

Set 5, 1988
$50.00 – 75.00 each

Set 6, 1989 – 1990
$50.00 – 75.00 each

Fischer Quints, 1964 only, vinyl, hard plastic body (Little Genius), one boy, four girls

7"	$65.00 – 75.00
Set of five	$400.00 – 475.00

Flower Girl, 1954, hard plastic, Margaret

15"	$550.00 – 600.00

Glamour Girl Series, 1953 only, hard plastic, Margaret head, auburn wig, straight leg walker

18"	$1,000.00 – 1,400.00

Godey Bride, 1950 – 1951, Margaret, hard plastic

14"	$850.00 – 950.00
18"	$1,000.00 – 1,200.00

Godey Lady, 1950 – 1951, Margaret, hard plastic
    14" $1,400.00 – 1,600.00

Godey Groom, 1950 – 1951, Margaret, hard plastic
    18" $900.00 – 1,100.00

Gold Rush, 1963 only, hard plastic, Cissette
    10" $1,500.00 – 1,600.00

Grandma Jane, 1970 – 1972, #1420, Mary Ann, vinyl body
    14" $180.00 – 200.00

Groom
    1949 – 1951, Margaret, hard plastic
    14" – 16" $750.00 – 850.00
    1953 – 1955, Wendy Ann, hard plastic
    7½" $425.00 – 475.00

Jacqueline, 1961 – 1962, 21", hard plastic, vinyl arms
    Formalwear $850.00 – 900.00
    Riding habit $725.00 – 775.00
    Street dress $650.00 – 700.00

Janie, 1964 – 1966, #1156, toddler, vinyl head, hard plastic body, rooted hair
    12" $200.00 – 250.00

Jenny Lind, 1969 – 1970, hard plastic head
    14" $250.00 – 300.00
    21" $1,100.00 – 1,200.00

John Robert Powers Model, 1952, with oval beauty box, hard plastic
    14" $1,700.00 – 2,000.00

Kathy, 1949 – 1951, Maggie, has braids
    15" – 18" $1,050.00 – 1,300.00

Kelly
    1959 only, hard plastic, Lissy
    12" $575.00 – 625.00
    1958 – 1959, hard plastic, Marybel
    15" – 16" $325.00 – 400.00

Leslie (black Polly), 1965 – 1971, 17", vinyl head, hard plastic body, vinyl limbs, rooted hair
    Ballerina $375.00 – 425.00
    Bride $350.00 – 400.00

Lissy, 1956 – 1958, 12", jointed knees and elbows, hard plastic
    Ballerina $450.00 – 500.00
    Bridesmaid $675.00 – 725.00
    Formalwear $600.00 – 650.00
    Street dress $400.00 – 500.00

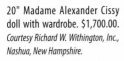

20" Madame Alexander Cissy doll with wardrobe. $1,700.00.
Courtesy Richard W. Withington, Inc., Nashua, New Hampshire.

Little Shaver, 1963 – 1965, painted eyes, vinyl body

12"	$250.00 – 300.00

Little Women

1947 – 1956, Meg, Jo, Amy, Beth, plus Marme, Margaret and Maggie faces

14" – 15"	$475.00 – 525.00

1955, Meg, Jo, Amy, Beth, plus Marme, Wendy Ann, straight-leg walker

Set of five	$1,500.00 – 1,800.00

1956 – 1959, Wendy Ann, bent-knee walker

Set of five	$1,200.00 – 1,300.00

1974 – 1992, straight leg, #411 – #415

Set of five	$350.00 – 375.00

1957 – 1958, Lissy, jointed elbows and knees

12"	$275.00 – 325.00

1959 – 1968, Lissy, one-piece arms and legs

12"	$225.00 – 250.00

Lovey-Dove Ringbearer, 1951, hard plastic, five-piece toddler body, mohair wig, satin top, shorts

12"	$450.00 – 650.00

Maggie Mixup, 1960 – 1961, hard plastic, freckles

8"	$450.00 – 500.00

15½" Maggie Mixup, hard plastic and vinyl. $575.00.
Courtesy of Richard Withington Inc., Nashua, New Hampshire.

Angel	$750.00 – 850.00

Maggie Teenager, 1951 – 1953, hard plastic

15" – 18"	$575.00 – 600.00

Margaret O'Brien, 1949 – 1951, hard plastic

14"	$900.00 – 1,000.00
18"	$1,200.00 – 1,400.00

Margot Ballerina, 1953 – 1955, Margaret and Maggie, dressed in various colored outfits

14"	$750.00 – 800.00
18"	$800.00 – 900.00

Mary Ellen, 1954 only, rigid vinyl walker

31"	$675.00 – 775.00

Mary Ellen Playmate, 1965 only, bendable vinyl body

17"	$250.00 – 300.00

Mary Martin, 1948 – 1952, South Pacific character Nell, two-piece sailor outfit, hard plastic

14"	$850.00 – 900.00
18"	$950.00 – 1,000.00

Marybel, "The Doll That Gets Well," 1959 – 1965, rigid vinyl, in case

16"	$300.00 – 325.00

McGuffey Ana

1948 – 1950, hard plastic, Margaret

14"	$1,100.00 – 1,200.00
18"	$1,300.00 – 1,400.00
21"	$1,400.00 – 1,500.00

1956 only, hard plastic, #616, Wendy Ann face

8"	$675.00 – 750.00

1963 only, hard plastic, rare doll, Lissy face

12"	$1,700.00 – 1,900.00

Melanie, 1966, "Coco," #2050, blue gown

21"	$2,200.00 – 2,400.00

Melinda, 1962 – 1963, plastic/vinyl, cotton dress

14" – 22"	$350.00 – 50.00

Nancy Drew, 1967 only, vinyl body, Literature Series

12"	$225.00 – 275.00

14" hard plastic Little Women. $500.00 each.
Courtesy of Alderfer Auction Co.

Nina Ballerina, 1949 – 1951, Margaret head, clover wrist tag

14"	$850.00 – 950.00
18"	$1,000.00 – 1,100.00
21"	$1,500.00 – 1,600.00

Peter Pan, 1953 – 1954, Margaret

15"	$400.00- $450.00

1969, 14" Wendy (Mary Ann head), 12" Peter, Michael (Jamie head), 10" Tinker Bell (Cissette head)

Peter, Wendy	$200.00 – 225.00
Michael	$225.00 – 250.00
Tinkerbell	$300.00 – 350.00
Set of four	$1,000.00

Pink Champagne/Arlene Dahl, hard plastic, red hair, pink lace, rhinestone bodice gown

18"	$4,500.00 – 5,500.00

Polly, 1965 only, 17"

Street dress	$225.00 – 275.00

Polly Pigtails, 1949 – 1951, Maggie, hard plastic

14"	$650.00 – 750.00
17"	$750.00 – 850.00

Portraits, 1960 on, marked "1961," Jacqueline, 21", early dolls have jointed elbows, later one piece

Agatha, 1967 – 1980

#2171	$550.00 – 650.00

Cornelia, 1972

#2191	$400.00 – 450.00

Gainsborough, 1968 – 1978

#2184	$400.00 – 475.00

Godey, Coco, 1966

#2063	$2,100.00 – 2,300.00

Godey, Jacqueline, 1969

#2195	$475.00 – 550.00

Goya, 1968

#2183	$450.00 – 550.00

Jenny Lind, 1969 – 1970

#2193	$1,200.00 – 1,400.00

Lady Hamilton, 1968

#2182	$425.00 – 475.00

Madame, 1966

#2060	$2,200.00 – 2,400.00

Madame Alexander,

1985 – 1987	$225.00 – 275.00

Madame Pompadour, 1970

#2197	$1,100.00 – 1,200.00

Melanie (Coco), 1966

#2050	$2,200.00 – 2,300.00

Melanie, 1970

#2196	$425.00 – 525.00

Magnolia, 1977	
#2297	$475.00
Queen, 1965 – 1968	
#2150	$650.00 – 750.00
Renoir, 1965	
#2154	$650.00 – 700.00
Scarlett, green satin gown, 1965	
#2152	$1,400.00 – 1,900.00
Scarlett (Coco), white gown	
2061	$2,700.00 – 2,900.00
Southern Belle, 1965	
#2155	$1,100.00 – 1,200.00
Southern Belle, 1967	
#2170	$575.00 – 625.00

Prince Charles, 1957 only, #397, hard plastic, blue jacket, cap, shorts

8"	$750.00 – 800.00

Prince Charming, 1948 – 1950, hard plastic, Margaret face, brocade jacket, white tights

14"	$700.00 – 775.00
18"	$825.00 – 875.00

Princess Margaret Rose

1949 – 1953, hard plastic, Margaret face

14"	$750.00 – 800.00
18"	$875.00 – 925.00

1953 only, #2020B, hard plastic, Beaux Arts Series, pink taffeta gown with red ribbon, tiara, Margaret face

18"	$1,700.00 – 1,900.00

Queen, 1953, Margaret

18"	$1,400.00 – 1,700.00

Quiz-Kin, 1953, hard plastic, back buttons, nods yes or no

8"	$400.00 – 500.00

Renoir Girl, 1967 – 1968, vinyl body, Portrait Children Series

14"	$100.00 – 125.00

Shari Lewis, 1958 – 1959

14"	$600.00 – 650.00
21"	$800.00 – 850.00

Sleeping Beauty, 1959, Disneyland Special

10"	$375.00 – 425.00

16"	$600.00 – 650.00
21"	$850.00 – 900.00

Smarty, 1962 – 1963, vinyl body

12"	$225.00 – 300.00

Snow White, 1952, gold vest, Walt Disney edition

14"	$750.00 – 850.00
21"	$1,200.00 – 1,300.00

Sound of Music, 1965 – 1970 (large), 1971 – 1973 (small), vinyl

Brigitta

10"	$100.00 – 150.00
14"	$125.00 – 150.00

Friedrich

8"	$125.00 – 150.00
10"	$150.00 – 175.00

Gretl

8"	$100.00 – 150.00
10"	$125.00 – 150.00

Liesl

10"	$250.00
14"	$125.00 – 150.00

Louisa

10"	$100.00 – 150.00
14"	$125.00 – 150.00

Maria

12"	$200.00 – 250.00
17"	$250.00 – 300.00

Marta

8"	$100.00 – 150.00
10"	$145.00 – 175.00

Southern Belle, hard plastic

1956 – 1963

8"	$500.00 – 550.00

1968 – 1973

10"	$325.00 – 375.00

Timmy Toddler, 1960 – 1961, vinyl head, hard plastic body

23"	$125.00 – 150.00

1960 only

30"	$200.00 – 250.00

Tommy Bangs, 1952 only, hard plastic, Little

Men Series

11" $625.00 – 825.00

Wendy, Wendy Ann, Wendy-kin:
See Alexander-kins section.

Winnie Walker & Binnie Walker, 1953 – 1955, hard plastic

15" $375.00- $400.00
18" $400.00 – 450.00
25" $500.00 – 550.00

Souvenir Dolls, UFDC, Limited Edition
Little Emperor, 1992, limit 400

8" $450.00 – 475.00

Miss Unity, 1991, limit 310

10" $375.00 – 400.00

Sailor Boy, limit 260

8" $700.00 – 750.00

Turn of Century Bathing Beauty, 1992, R9 Conference, limit 300

10" $250.00 – 275.00

Columbian 1893 Sailor, 1993

12" $250.00 – 300.00

Gabrielle, 1998, limit 400

10" $300.00 – 325.00

HENRI ALEXANDRE

1888 – 1891, Paris. Succeeded by Tourrel in 1892 and in 1895 merged with Jules Steiner.

Incised HA model, bisque socket head, paperweight eyes, closed mouth with space between lips, straight wrist body

17" – 20" $5,500.00 – 6,900.00

Bébé Phénix, trademarked in 1895, bisque socket head, paperweight eyes, pierced ears, composition body

Child, closed mouth

10" – 14" $1,500.00 – 2,800.00
16" – 18" $3,400.00 – 4,200.00
20" – 24" $4,900.00 – 5,500.00

Child, open mouth

16" – 18" $1,900.00 – 2,200.00
20" – 24" $2,300.00 – 2,600.00

ALL-BISQUE FRENCH

1880 on, made by various French and German doll companies. Sold as French products. Most are unmarked, some have numbers only. Allow more for original clothes and tags, less for chips or repairs.

Glass eyes, swivel head, molded shoes or boots

2½" – 3½" $800.00 – 900.00
4" – 5" $1,700.00 – 1,900.00
6" – 7" $3,500.00 – 4,500.00
10" $6,600.00 – 6,800.00

Five-strap boots, glass eyes, swivel neck

5" – 6" $1,900.00 – 2,100.00

Painted eyes

2½" $200.00 – 250.00
4" $900.00 – 1,000.00

Bare feet

5" $2,300.00 – 2,600.00
6" $2,900.00 – 3,100.00

Later style, 1910 – 1920, glass eyes, molded socks, swivel neck, long stockings

5" – 6" $575.00 – 675.00
7" $700.00 – 725.00

ALL-BISQUE GERMAN

1880s onward, made by various German doll companies including Alt, Beck & Gottschalk; Bähr & Pröschild; Hertel Schwab & Co.; Kämmer &

4" all-bisque with molded clothing. $145.00.
Courtesy of The Museum Doll Shop.

Reinhardt; Kestner; Kling; Limbach; Bruno Schmidt; Simon & Halbig. Some incised "Germany" with or without numbers, others have paper labels glued onto their torsos. More for labels, less for chips and repairs.

All-Bisque, Black or Brown: See Black or Brown Section.

Painted eyes, 1880 – 1910, stationary neck, molded painted footwear, dressed or undressed, all in good condition

2"	$75.00 – 85.00
4" – 5"	$190.00 – 225.00
6" – 8"	$275.00 – 350.00

Black or brown stockings, tan slippers

4" – 5"	$375.00 – 450.00
6"	$475.00 – 525.00

Ribbed hose or blue or yellow shoes

4" – 5"	$275.00 – 325.00
6"	$425.00 – 475.00
8"	$825.00 – 875.00

Molded hair

4 ½"	$150.00 – 175.00
6"	$325.00 – 350.00

Early very round face

7"	$2,100.00 – 2,300.00

Molded clothing, 1890 – 1910, jointed at shoulders only or at shoulders and hips, painted eyes, molded hair, molded shoes or bare feet, excellent workmanship, no breaks, chips, or rubs

3½" – 4"	$115.00 – 145.00
5" – 6"	$225.00 – 275.00
7"	$300.00 – 325.00

Lesser quality

3"	$75.00 – 85.00
4"	$90.00 – 100.00
6"	$120.00 – 140.00

Molded on hat or bonnet

5" – 6½"	$365.00 – 395.00
8" – 9"	$500.00 – 550.00

Stone bisque (porous)

4" – 5"	$115.00 – 135.00
6" – 7"	$145.00 – 165.00

Glass eyes, 1890 – 1910, stationary neck, molded painted footwear, excellent bisque, open-closed mouth, sleep or set eyes, good wig, nicely dressed, molded one-strap shoes. Allow more for unusual footwear such as yellow or multi-strap boots.

3"	$275.00 – 325.00
5"	$300.00 – 350.00
7"	$400.00 – 475.00
9"	$750.00 – 800.00

4½" all-bisque with sleep eyes, stationary neck and yellow boots, c.1890s. $375.00.
Courtesy of The Museum Doll Shop.

6¾" all-bisque Kestner mold 150. $475.00. *Doll courtesy of Ruth Cayton.*

Early style with unjointed hips, ribbed stockings or elaborate style shoes

3"	$325.00 – 350.00
4½"	$350.00 – 400.00
6" – 7"	$575.00 – 850.00
8" – 8½"	$1,200.00 – 1,300.00

Mold 100, 125, 150, 225 (preceded by 83/), Rigid neck, fat tummy, jointed shoulders and hips, glass sleep eyes, open-closed molded black one-strap shoes with tan soles, white molded stockings with blue band. Similarly molded dolls, imported in 1950s by Kimport, have synthetic hair, lesser quality bisque. Add more for original clothing. Mold number appears as a fraction, with the following size numbers under 83; Mold "83/100," "83/125," "83/150," or "83/225." One marked "83/100" has a green label on torso reading, "Princess// Made in Germany."

100, 5½"	$300.00 – 325.00
125, 6½"	$325.00 – 350.00
150, 7½"	$400.00 – 425.00
225, 8½"	$450.00 – 475.00

Swivel neck and glass eyes, 1880 – 1910, molded painted footwear, pegged or wired joints, open or closed mouth. Allow more for unusual footwear such as yellow or multi-strap boots.

3"	$325.00 – 350.00
4"	$425.00 – 450.00
5½"	$525.00 – 550.00
7"	$725.00 – 825.00
8"	$1,000.00 – 1,100.00
9"	$1,300.00 – 1,550.00
10"	$1,700.00 – 1,900.00

Simon & Halbig or Kestner types, closed mouth, excellent quality. Molds 130, 150, 160, 184, 208, 602, 881, 886, 890, and others

4" – 5"	$1,700.00 – 1,900.00
6"	$1,800.00 – 2,000.00
8"	$2,500.00 – 2,600.00
10"	$3,100.00 – 3,400.00

Jointed knees

6"	$3,500.00 – 4,000.00
8½"	$7,800.00 – 8,200.00

7" Kestner all-bisque with closed mouth, swivel neck, and sleep eyes. $2,000.00. *Courtesy Richard W. Withington, Inc., Nashua, New Hampshire.*

8½" Kestner swivel-neck doll with jointed knees. $8,000.00. *Courtesy of Skinner Inc., Boston and Bolton, Massachusettes.*

Bare feet

5"	$1,700.00 – 1,800.00
7½"	$2,400.00 – 2,600.00

Early round face

6"	$800.00 – 900.00
8"	$1,200.00 – 1,300.00

Mold 102, Wrestler (so called), fat thighs, arm bent at elbow, open mouth (can have two rows of teeth) or closed mouth, stocky body, glass eyes, socket head, individual fingers or molded fist

6"	$2,100.00 – 2,200.00
8"	$3,100.00 – 3,200.00
9"	$3,800.00 – 4,000.00

Slender dolls, 1900 on, stationary neck, slender arms and legs, glass eyes, molded footwear, usual wire or peg-jointed shoulders and hips. Allow much more for original clothes. May be in regional costumes. Add more for unusual color boots, such as gold, yellow, or orange, all in good condition.

3" – 4"	$175.00 – 225.00
5" – 6"	$275.00 – 325.00

Swivel neck, closed mouth

4"	$275.00 – 300.00
5" – 6"	$450.00 – 500.00
8½"	$800.00 – 900.00
10"	$1,100.00 – 1,300.00

Jointed knees and/or elbows with swivel waist

6"	$1,950.00 – 2,050.00
8"	$3,000.00 – 3,200.00

Swivel waist only

6"	$2,000.00 – 2,200.00

Santa Claus, molded beard

2½"	$1,450.00*

Baby, 1900 on, jointed at hips and shoulders, bent limbs, molded hair, painted features

2½" – 3½"	$80.00 – 90.00
5" – 6"	$175.00 – 200.00

Character Baby, 1910 on, jointed at hips and shoulders, bent limbs, molded hair, painted features

4" German painted all-bisque. $110.00. *Courtesy of The Museum Doll Shop.*

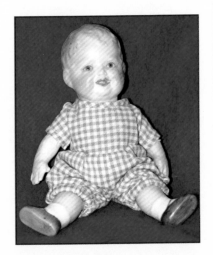

4½" all-bisque Bonnie Babe by Alt, Beck & Gottschalk. $800.00. *Doll courtesy of Ruth Cayton.*

Glass eyes, molds 391, 830, 833, and others

4" – 5"	$275.00 – 375.00
6"	$400.00 – 450.00
8"	$625.00 – 650.00
11"	$850.00 – 950.00

Painted eyes

3½"	$90.00 – 100.00
4" – 5"	$200.00 – 225.00
7"	$300.00 – 350.00
8"	$400.00 – 450.00

Swivel neck, glass eyes

5" – 6"	$575.00 – 650.00
8" – 10"	$1,000.00 – 1,100.00

Swivel neck, painted eyes

5" – 6"	$325.00 – 350.00
7" – 8"	$550.00 – 600.00

Baby Bo Kaye, mold 1394, designed by Kallus, distributed by Borgfeldt

5"	$1,300.00 – 1,500.00
7" – 8"	$1,700.00 – 1,800.00

Baby Bud, glass eyes, wig

6" – 7"	$1,100.00 – 1,300.00

Baby Darling, mold 497, Kestner, 178, one-piece body, painted eyes

6"	$850.00 – 950.00
8"	$950.00 – 1,000.00
10"	$1,100.00 – 1,200.00

Baby Peggy Montgomery, made by Louis Amberg, paper label, pink bisque with molded hair, painted brown eyes, closed mouth, jointed at shoulders and hips, molded and painted shoes/socks

3½"	$325.00 – 375.00
5½"	$525.00 – 575.00

Bonnie Babe, 1926 on, designed by Georgene Averill, glass eyes, swivel neck, wig, jointed arms and legs

5"	$850.00 – 1,000.00
7"	$1,400.00 – 1,500.00
8"	$1,600.00 – 1,700.00

Bye-Lo: See Bye-Lo Section.

Mildred (The Prize Baby), mold 880, 1914 on, made for Borgfeldt; molded, short painted hair; glass eyes; closed mouth; jointed at neck, shoulders, and hips; round paper label on chest; molded and painted footwear

5" – 7"	$3,000.00 – 4,000.00

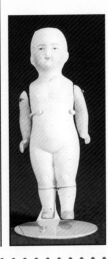

4" all-bisque with stationary neck and painted eyes, c. 1920s. $110.00. *Courtesy of The Museum Doll Shop.*

4½" all-bisque character by Heubach, c. 1913. $300.00.
Courtesy of The Museum Doll Shop.

5" glass-eyed Orsini character girl. $2,650.00. *Courtesy of The Museum Doll Shop.*

Our Darling, open mouth with teeth, glass eyes

5½"	$160.00 – 200.00

Tynie Baby, made for E.I. Horsman. Wigged or painted hair, glass eyes

8" – 10"	$1,600.00 – 2,200.00

Mold 231 (A.M.), toddler, swivel neck, with glass eyes

9"	$1,300.00 – 1,400.00

Mold 369, 372

7"	$650.00 – 725.00
9"	$1,000.00 – 1,100.00
11"	$1,400.00 – 1,500.00

Character Doll with glass eyes, 1910

Molds 155, 156

5" – 6"	$400.00 – 500.00
7"	$625.00 – 650.00

Mold 602, swivel neck

5½" – 6"	$575.00 – 650.00

Heubach, Ernst, 1913 – 1920s, jointed at shoulders and hips, molded painted hair, some with ribbons etc., intaglio eyes, Our Golden Three, molds such as 9557, 9558, 10134, 10490, 10499, 10511, others

8" – 8½"	$1,000.00 – 1,200.00

Orsini, 1919 on, designed by Jeanne Orsini for Borgfeldt, produced by Alt, Beck & Gottschalk, Chi Chi, Didi, Fifi, Mimi, Vivi

Glass eyes

5"	$2,500.00 – 2,800.00
7"	$4,000.00 – 5,000.00

Painted eyes

5"	$1,100.00 – 1,200.00

Our Fairy, mold 222, glass eyes

5"	$650.00 – 700.00
8½"	$875.00 – 900.00
11"	$1,700.00 – 1,800.00

Jointed animals, 1910 on, wire jointed shoulders and hips, crocheted clothing. Makers such as Kestner, others.

2" – 3½"

Rabbit	$475.00 – 525.00
Bear	$450.00 – 500.00
Frog, Monkey, Pig	$600.00 – 700.00
Puss in Boots	$350.00 – 400.00

Character Dolls, painted eyes, 1913 on

Campbell Kids, molded clothes, Dutch bob

5"	$210.00 – 245.00

Chin-chin, Gebruder Heubach, 1919,

jointed arms only, triangular label on chest

4"	$275.00 – 300.00

Happifats, designed by Kate Jordan for Borgfeldt, ca. 1913 – 1921

4"	$275.00 – 300.00

HEbee, SHEbee

4" – 5"	$750.00 – 825.00
7"	$850.00 – 875.00

Max, Moritz, Kestner, 1914, jointed at the neck, shoulders, and hips, many companies produced these characters from the Wilhelm Busch children's story

pair, 4½"	$2,300.00 – 2,500.00

Mibs, Amberg, 1921, molded blond hair, molded and painted socks and shoes, pink bisque, jointed at shoulders, legs molded to body, marked "C.//L.A.&S.192//GERMANY"

3"	$250.00 – 275.00
5"	$400.00 – 425.00
8"	$550.00 – 600.00

Peterkin, 1912, one-piece baby, side-glancing googly eyes, molded and painted hair, molded blue pajamas on

8½" mold 10499 from Gebruder Heubach's Our Golden Three series. $1,200.00. *Courtesy of The Museum Doll Shop.*

All-bisque pair by Hertwig, 2½" and 3", c. 1920s. $300.00. pair *Courtesy of The Museum Doll Shop.*

chubby torso, arms molded to body with hands clasping stomach

5" – 6"	$275.00 – 350.00

September Morn, jointed at shoulders and hips, Grace Drayton design, George Borgfeldt

4" – 5"	$2,100.00 – 2,500.00
6" – 7"	$2,600.00 – 3,200.00

Later issue with painted eyes, 1920 on, painted hair or wigged, molded painted single strap shoes, white stockings, makers such as Limbach, Hertwig & Co, others.

3½"	$75.00 – 85.00
4" – 5"	$110.00 – 125.00
6" – 7"	$175.00 – 225.00

So-called Flapper, 1920, tinted bisque, molded bobbed hairstyle, painted features, molded single strap shoes

Child

3"	$95.00 – 125.00

Adult

5½"	$300.00 – 350.00

Molded loop for bow

5"	$300.00 – 325.00
6 – 7"	$450.00 – 475.00

Molded hat

4"	$225.00 – 250.00

4" all-bisque Shebee. $750.00. *Courtesy Richard W. Withington, Inc., Nashua, New Hampshire.*

Aviatrix

5"	$225.00 – 250.00

Swivel waist

4½"	$375.00 – 400.00

Molded cap with rabbit ears

4½"	$375.00 – 400.00

Wigged

3½"	$95.00 – 125.00

Nodders, 1920 on, immobile body, head attached with elastic, makers such as Hertwig & Co., others, when their heads are touched, they "nod," molded clothes

Animals, cat, dog, rabbit

3" – 5"	$100.00 – 150.00

Child/Adult

3" – 4"	$50.00 – 75.00

Comic characters

3" – 5"	$75.00 – 125.00
Santa Claus or Indian	$200.00 – 225.00
Teddy Bear	$200.00 – 225.00

Immobiles, 1920, one-piece doll with molded clothing, top layer of paint not fired on and the color can be washed off, some have molded hats

Baby

3½"	$40.00 – 50.00
5"	$50.00 – 60.00

Adults and Children

3"	$50.00 – 60.00
5"	$65.00 – 70.00

Bathing Beauties, 1910 – 1930s, various German porcelain factories made these bisque figures, painted features

3"	$275.00 – 300.00
6"	$550.00 – 600.00

Reclining woman, lying on stomach

2½"	$135.00 – 165.00
4"	$375.00 – 425.00

Mermaid tail

4"	$300.00 – 325.00

Two figures molded together

4½" – 5½"	$1,500.00 – 1,700.00

Wigged

5"	$700.00 – 750.00

Wigged, seated, playing mandolin, molded stockings

4"	$1,225.00

Too few in database for a reliable range.

3½" German nodder. $65.00. *Courtesy of The Museum Doll Shop.*

ALL-BISQUE JAPANESE

1915 onward, made by a variety of Japanese companies. Quality varies widely, stationary dolls or jointed at shoulders and/or hips. Marked "Made in Japan" or "Nippon."

Immobiles, painted, top layer of paint not fired on and the color can be washed off, usually one-piece figurines with molded hair, painted features, including clothes, shoes, and socks. Some have molded hats.

5" Japanese all-bisque with molded bows in hair. $40.00. *Courtesy of The Museum Doll Shop.*

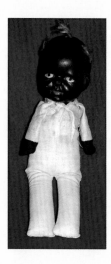

6" Black painted bisque doll made in Japan. $55.00. *Courtesy of The Museum Doll Shop, Newport, RI*

Child with molded clothes

4½"	$25.00 – 35.00
6"	$40.00 – 50.00

Child, 1920s – 1930s, pink or painted bisque with painted features, jointed at shoulders and hips, has molded hair or wig, excellent condition

3"	$15.00 – 20.00
4"	$35.00 – 40.00

Betty Boop, bobbed hair style, large eyes painted to side, head molded to torso

4"	$30.00 – 40.00
6"	$50.00 – 60.00

Bride & Groom, all original costume

4"	$75.00 – 100.00

Characters, Indian, Pirate, etc.

5"	$20.00 – 25.00

Skippy

6"	$110.00 – 135.00

Snow White

5"	$90.00 – 110.00

Baby

3" – 5"	$20.00 – 35.00
5" – 7"	$35.00 – 45.00

Black baby, with pigtails

4"	$40.00 – 45.00

Bye-Lo Baby-type, fine quality

3½"	$70.00 – 85.00
5"	$120.00 – 140.00

Child

3" – 4"	$18.00 – 22.00

3" Japanese immobile with cold painted clothing. $28.00. *Courtesy of The Museum Doll Shop.*

Boxed with Dwarfs $450.00 – 650.00
Three Bears/Goldilocks, boxed set
   $325.00 – 400.00
Nippon mark
   5" $75.00 – 85.00
Occupied Japan mark
   4" $30.00 – 35.00
   7" $50.00 – 55.00

4½" Baby Belle character doll by Morimura Brothers. $50.00. *Courtesy of The Museum Doll Shop.*

ALT, BECK & GOTTSCHALCK

1854, Nauendorf, Thüringia, Germany. Produced bisque and china headed dolls for a variety of companies including Bergmann and Borgfeldt.

Shoulder Heads, China, 1880 on. Mold 639, 698, 784, 870, 890, 912, 974, 990, 1000, 1008, 1028, 1032, 1044, 1046, 1064, 1112, 1123, 1127, 1142, 1210, 1222, 1234, 1235, 1254, 1304, cloth or kid body, bisque lower limbs, molded hair or wig, no damage, and nicely dressed. Allow more for molded hat or fancy hairdo.

15" – 18"	$350.00 – 375.00
19" – 22"	$425.00 – 450.00
23" – 26"	$500.00 – 525.00
28"	$625.00 – 650.00

18" china shoulder head child 1880s. $375.00. *Courtesy of The Museum Doll Shop.*

Shoulder Heads, Bisque, 1880. Cloth or kid body, bisque lower arms, closed mouth, molded hair or wig. Molds such as 784, 911, 912, 916, 990, 1000, 1008, 1028,

1044, 1046, 1064, 1127, 1142, 1210, 1234, 1254, 1304. Allow more for molded hat or fancy hairdo.

Glass eyes, closed mouth

9" – 11"	$400.00 – 450.00
15" – 17"	$550.00 – 750.00
18" – 22"	$1,000.00 – 1,250.00

Painted eyes, closed mouth

14" – 18"	$375.00 – 400.00
21" – 23"	$600.00 – 650.00

Turned Bisque Shoulder Heads, 1885, solid dome head or plaster pate, kid body, bisque lower arms, glass eyes, wigged, all in good condition, nicely dressed. Dolls marked 639, 698, 870, 1032, 1123, 1235, "DEP," or "Germany" after 1888. Some have Wagner & Zetzsche marked on head, paper label inside top of body. Allow more for molded bonnet or elaborate hairdo.

Closed mouth, glass eyes

16" – 18"	$700.00 – 800.00
20" – 22"	$850.00 – 950.00

Open mouth

16" – 18"	$375.00 – 450.00
20" – 22"	$475.00 – 550.00

Character Baby, 1910s on. Open mouth, sleep eyes, bent limb body. Allow more for toddler body or flirty eyes. Molds such as 1322, 1342, 1346, 1352, 1361.

10" – 12"	$375.00 – 425.00
16" – 19"	$575.00 – 650.00
22" – 24"	$875.00 – 950.00

Child, All-Bisque: See All-Bisque Section. Child, 1880 onward, bisque socket head, ball-jointed composition body, glass eyes, wig, closed mouth

Mold 630, glass eyes, closed mouth, ca. 1880

20" – 22"	$2,000.00 – 2,200.00

Mold 911, 916, swivel head, closed mouth, ca. 1890+; Mold 915, shoulder head, closed mouth, ca. 1890

23" pair of open mouth dolls by Alt, Beck and Gottschalck. $650.00. each *Courtesy of Skinner Inc., Boston and Bolton, Massachusetts.*

16" – 18"	$1,600.00 – 1,800.00
20" – 22"	$2,000.00 – 2,250.00

Mold 938, closed mouth

20" – 22"	$4,200.00 – 4,500.00

Too few in database for a reliable range.

Mold 1362, ca. 1912, Sweet Nell, more for flapper body

14" – 16"	$400.00 – 450.00
18" – 20"	$500.00 – 550.00
22" – 24"	$600.00 – 675.00
26" – 28"	$725.00 – 850.00

Character Child, ca. 1910 onward, bisque socket head, composition ball-jointed body.

Mold 1357, ca. 1912, solid dome or wigged, painted eyes, open mouth; Mold 1358, ca. 1910, molded hair, ribbon, flowers, painted eyes, open mouth

15" – 20"	$975.00 – 1,700.00

Mold 1322, 1342, 1352, 1361, glass eyes

10" – 12"	$325.00 – 400.00
14" – 16"	$425.00 – 500.00
18" – 20"	$550.00 – 650.00

Mold 1367, 1368, ca. 1914

15"	$450.00 – 475.00

LOUIS AMBERG & SONS

1878 – 1930, Cincinnati, Ohio, and New York City. Importer, wholesaler, and manufacturer. First company to manufacture all American-made composition dolls.

Newborn Babe, Bottle Babe, 1914 on, bisque head on cloth body, hands of celluloid, bisque, or rubber, sleep eyes, painted hair, closed or open mouth, molds such as 886, 371

Closed mouth

8" – 10"	$300.00 – 325.00
12" – 14"	$350.00 – 400.00
16" – 18"	$500.00 – 550.00

Charlie Chaplin, 1915, composition head with molded moustache, cloth body, composition hands, cloth label on sleeve

14"	$625.00 – 650.00

AmKid, 1918, composition shoulder head, kidolene body, composition arms, sleep eyes, wig

22"	$100.00 – 150.00

Happinus, 1918, all-composition with head and torso molded in one piece, coquette-style, brown painted hair molded with hair ribbon

10"	$275.00 – 325.00

Baby Peggy, portrait of child-actress Peggy Montgomery, composition, 1923, composition head, arms, and legs, cloth body, molded bobbed hair painted brown, painted eyes

18" – 20"	$500.00 – 750.00

Bisque Baby Peggy, 1924, bisque socket head, composition or kid body, sleep eyes, brown mohair wig

Molds 972, 973, socket head

18" – 22"	$2,000.00 – 2,200.00

Molds 982, 983, shoulder head

18" – 22"	$1,500.00 – 1,800.00

Baby Peggy, All-Bisque: See all-Bisque, German Section.

Mibs, 1921, composition turned shoulder head, designed by Hazel Drukker, cloth body with composition arms and legs, painted eyes, molded painted hair, molded painted shoes and socks or barefoot mama-style leg

16"	$1,000.00 – 1,200.00

Mibs, All-Bisque: See all-Bisque, German Section.

Sunny Orange Maid, 1924, composition shoulder head, cloth body with composition arms and legs, head has molded "orange" bonnet

14"	$800.00 – 1,000.00

Vanta Baby, 1927 on, sold through Sears, advertising for Vanta baby clothes, bent-limb composition body, sleep eyes, open mouth with two teeth, painted hair

Bisque head

18" – 22"	$1,100.00 – 1,275.00

Composition head

10" – 14"	$125.00 – 175.00
18" – 23"	$300.00 – 400.00

Composition Baby Peggy, c. 1923. $750.00. *Courtesy Otto and Ursula Mertz.*

Edwina, Sue, or It, 1928, all-composition, painted features, molded side-part hair with swirl on forehead, body twist construction

14"	$450.00 – 500.00

Tiny Tots, Body Twists, 1929, all-composition, swivel waist attached to torso with a ball, molded hair, painted features, boy or girl

7½" – 8½"	$125.00 – 175.00

Peter Pan, 1928, all-composition, round joint at waist, wearing original Peter Pan fashion dress

14"	$400.00 – 500.00

AMERICAN CHARACTER DOLL COMPANY

1919 – 1963, New York City. Made composition dolls, in 1923 registered the trademark "Petite" for mama and character dolls, later made cloth, rubber, hard plastic, and vinyl dolls. In 1960 the company name was changed to American Character Doll & Toy Co.

"A.C." or "Petite" marked composition doll, 1923, composition heads and limbs, cloth body

Baby

14"	$150.00 – 200.00
18"	$200.00 – 275.00

Mama doll, sleep eyes, human hair wig

16" – 18"	$250.00 – 300.00
24"	$350.00 – 375.00

Petite girls, 1930s, all-composition

16" – 18"	$275.00 – 325.00
24"	$350.00 – 375.00

Toddler

13"	$200.00 – 225.00

Bottletot, 1926, composition head and bent limbs, cloth body, painted hair, open mouth, one arm molded to hold molded celluloid bottle

13"	$200.00 – 225.00
18"	$300.00 – 325.00

Puggy, 1928, all-composition, character face with frown and side-glancing painted eyes, molded painted hair, jointed at neck, shoulders, and hips, original outfits included baseball player, boy scout, cowboy, and newsboy, mark: "A // Petite // Doll," clothes tagged "Puggy // A Petite Doll"

13"	$475.00 – 525.00

Sally, 1930, Patsy-type, all-composition, molded hair or wig, marks: "Petite" or "American Char. Doll Co.," painted or sleep eyes

12"	$200.00 – 250.00
14" – 16"	$250.00 – 350.00

Mary Make-up by American Character. $65.00. *Courtesy of The Museum Doll Shop.*

20" Sweet Sue Sophisticate, vinyl. $325.00.
Courtesy of The Museum Doll Shop.

Sally, Shirley-type wig
24"	$350.00 – 375.00

Sally-Joy, composition head on cloth body
18"	$300.00 – 325.00
21"	$325.00 – 350.00
24"	$350.00 – 375.00

Carol Ann Beery, 1935, portrait doll of child-actor, daughter of Wallace Beery, all-composition, mohair wig with two braids drawn up across top of head, marks: "Petite Sally" or "Petite"
13"	$450.00 – 550.00
16"	$650.00 – 750.00
20"	$750.00 – 800.00

Tiny Tears, 1950s, hard plastic head with tear ducts, drink and wet doll

Rubber body
11½"	$225.00 – 275.00
13½"	$275.00 – 335.00
16"	$325.00 – 425.00
18"	$450.00 – 500.00

Clothing and accessories
Bottle	$35.00
Bubble pipe	$25.00
Bracelet	$30.00

Plastic cradle	$200.00
Romper	$35.00

All- vinyl, 1963
11½"	$100.00 – 150.00
13½"	$150.00 – 175.00
16"	$175.00 – 225.00
20"	$225.00 – 250.00

Sweet Sue, 1953 – 1961, all-hard plastic or hard plastic and vinyl, saran wig, some on walker bodies, others fully jointed including elbows, knees, and ankles, marks: "A.C.", "Amer. Char. Doll," or "American Character" in a circle
15"	$225.00 – 300.00
18" – 20"	$250.00 – 300.00
22" – 25"	$300.00 – 350.00
31"	$425.00 – 475.00

Sweet Sue Sophisticate, vinyl head, earrings
20"	$325.00 – 400.00

Annie Oakley, 1953, hard plastic walker
14"	$400.00 – 450.00

Ricky Jr., 1954 – 1956, personality doll based on character from I Love Lucy television show, baby

Hard plastic with rubber body, 1952
14" – 16"	$350.00 – 500.00

15" Tiny Tears, hard plastic head, rubber body. $325.00. *Courtesy of The Museum Doll Shop.*

15" Tiny Tears, vinyl, c. 1963. $175.00. *Courtesy of The Museum Doll Shop.*

All-vinyl, 1953 – 1956

13"	$275.00 – 350.00
21"	$275.00 – 350.00

Toodles, 1956, hard rubber drink and wet doll

18" – 20"	$250.00 – 300.00
29"	$325.00 – 350.00

Teeny Toodles

11"	$225.00 – 275.00

Toodles Toddler, 1960, vinyl and hard plastic, "Peek-a-Boo" eyes

24"	$325.00 – 400.00
30"	$375.00 – 400.00

Eloise, 1955, cloth with molded mask face, yarn hair

22"	$475.00 – 550.00

Toni, 1958, vinyl head with rooted hair

10½"	$175.00 – 200.00
14"	$400.00 – 500.00
20"	$375.00 – 525.00
25"	$575.00 – 625.00

Whimsies, 1960, all-vinyl characters

Dixie the Pixie, Hedda Get Bedda (three face), Miss Take, Tiller the Talker, Wheeler the Dealer, and others

19" – 20"	$225.00 – 325.00

Whimettes, 1963, smaller doll modeled after the whimsies

7½"	$200.00 – 275.00

Little Miss Echo, 1964, vinyl, recorder mechanism in torso

30"	$250.00 – 300.00

Miss America, 1963

	$50.00 – 65.00

Tressy, 1963 – 1965, vinyl, grow hair doll, marks: "American Doll & Toy Corp. // 19C.63" in a circle

11"	$115.00 – 135.00
Black	$300.00 – 400.00

Pre-teen Tressy, 1963

15"	$150.00 – 200.00

Tressy family and friends

Cricket

9"	$50.00 – 75.00

Mary Make-Up, non-grow hair

11½"	$55.00 – 75.00

Cartwrights, Ben, Hoss, Little Joe, 1966, personality dolls based on characters from the Bonanza television show.

9"	$100.00 – 125.00

10" Toni, vinyl. $175.00. *Courtesy of The Museum Doll Shop.*

Tressy grow-hair doll. $120.00. *Courtesy of The Museum Doll Shop.*

ANNALEE MOBILITEE DOLL CO.

1934 to present, Meredith, New Hampshire. Dolls originally designed by Annalee Thorndike, cloth with wire armature "mobilitee" body, painted features.

Early dolls, 1934 – 1960
Golfer, 1966

10½"	$200.00 – 225.00

Snow Bunny 1961

	$350.00 – 375.00

Later dolls
10" Folk Hero doll
Robin Hood, 1983 – 1984

	$150.00 – 200.00

Johnny Appleseed , 1983 – 1984

	$150.00 – 200.00
Annie Oakley, 1985	$150.00 – 200.00
Mark Twain,1986	$150.00 – 200.00

Ben Franklin, 1987	$150.00 – 200.00
Sherlock Holmes, 1988	$150.00 – 200.00
Abraham Lincoln, 1989	$150.00 – 200.00
Betsy Ross, 1990	$150.00 – 200.00
Christopher Columbus, 1991	
	$150.00 – 200.00
Uncle Sam, 1990	$150.00 – 200.00
Pony Express, 1993	$150.00 – 200.00
50s Style Bean Nose Santa, 1994	
	$150.00 – 200.00
Pocahontas, 1995	$150.00 – 200.00

Logo Kid Dolls

Milk & Cookies, 1985	$675.00
Sweetheart, 1986	$75.00 – 100.00
Naughty, 1987	$75.00 – 100.00
Raincoat, 1988	$75.00 – 100.00
Christmas Morning, 1989	$75.00 – 100.00
Reading, 1990	$75.00 – 100.00
Clown, 1991	$75.00 – 100.00
Back to School, 1992	$35.00 – 50.00
Ice Cream, 1993	$35.00 – 50.00
Dress-Up Santa, 1994	$35.00 – 50.00
Goin' Fishin', 1995	$35.00 – 50.00
Little Mae Flowers, 1996	$18.00 – 22.00
Tea for Two?, 1997	$18.00 – 22.00
15th Anniversary Kid, 1998	$18.00 – 22.00
Mending My Teddy, 1999	$18.00 – 22.00

Dalmatian and felt man, 1960s. $225.00 and $300.00. *Courtesy of The Museum Doll Shop.*

Precious Cargo, 2000 $18.00 – 22.00
Mother's Little Helper, 2001 $18.00 – 22.00

MAX OSCAR ARNOLD

1877 – 1930, Neustadt, Thüringia, Germany. Made dressed dolls and mechanical dolls including phonograph dolls.
Baby, bisque socket head, composition body

12"	$145.00 – 145.00
16"	$265.00 – 285.00
19"	$450.00 – 500.00

Child, bisque socket head, composition body, glass sleep eyes, wigged, molds such as 200, 201, 250, or MOA

High quality bisque

12"	$225.00 – 275.00
15"	$300.00 – 325.00
21" – 24"	$475.00 – 525.00
32"	$900.00 – 950.00

Low quality bisque

15"	$145.00 – 165.00
20"	$250.00 – 300.00
24"	$400.00 – 450.00

ARRANBEE DOLL CO.

1922 – 1958, New York City. Sold to the Vogue Doll Company who continued to use their molds until 1961. Some bisque heads used by Arranbee were made by Armand Marseille and Simon & Halbig. The company also produced composition, rubber, hard plastic, and vinyl dolls.

My Dream Baby, 1924
Bisque head, made by Armand Marseille

11" – 13"	$200.00 – 225.00
14" – 16"	$250.00 – 300.00
22" – 24"	$375.00 – 425.00

Composition head, 1927, composition lower arms and legs, cloth body, metal sleep eyes

11" – 13"	$150.00 – 200.00
17" – 19"	$275.00 – 375.00

Composition
Baby

14"	$100.00 – 125.00
23"	$250.00 – 275.00

Bottletot, 1926, all-composition, molded bottle in hand

13"	$175.00 – 195.00

Child, 1930s and 1940s, all-composition, mohair wig, marks: "Arranbee" or "R & B"

9"	$100.00 – 125.00
15"	$225.00 – 275.00

Debu 'Teen, 1938 on, all-composition

11"	$275.00 – 300.00
14"	$325.00 – 350.00
17"	$400.00 – 425.00
21"	$450.00 – 475.00

10" Dream Baby, bisque head by Armand Marseille. $200.00. *Courtesy of The Museum Doll Shop.*

Skating costume

14"	$225.00 – 250.00
17"	$250.00 – 275.00
21"	$350.00 – 375.00

WAC

18"	$500.00 – 525.00

Kewty, 1934 – 1936, all-composition, mohair wig, marks: "Kewty"

14"	$275.00 – 300.00

Little Angel Baby, 1940s, composition head, cloth body, molded painted hair

11"	$150.00 – 160.00
16"	$275.00 – 300.00
18"	$325.00 – 350.00

Hard Plastic

18"	$325.00 – 350.00

Nancy, 1930s, Patsy-type, all-composition, marks: "Arranbee" or "Nancy"

14" Arranbee Deb'Teen, original clothing. $350.00. *Courtesy of The Museum Doll Shop.*

10" Littlest Angel. $175.00. *Doll courtesy of George and Cynthia Orgeron.*

Molded hair, painted eyes

12"	$200.00 – 225.00
19" – 21"	$425.00 – 500.00

Nancy Lee, all-composition, mohair wig, sleep eyes

12"	$250.00 – 275.00
16"	$350.00 – 375.00

Storybook dolls, 1935, composition dolls dressed as storybook charactors

8½" – 10"	$175.00 – 195.00

Little Bo Peep with papier-mâché lamb

	$150.00 – 175.00

Hard Plastic & Vinyl

Cinderella, 1952, hard plastic

14"	$450.00 – 500.00
20"	$400.00 – 475.00

Coty Girl, 1958, vinyl, high heel fashion doll

10½"	$160.00 – 180.00

Lil Imp, 1960, vinyl with red hair and freckles

10"	$75.00 – 100.00

Littlest Angel, 1956, hard plastic, bent knee walker, mark: "R & B"

| 11" | $175.00 – 200.00 |

My Angel, 1961, hard plastic and vinyl

17"	$35.00 – 45.00
22"	$60.00 – 70.00
36"	$155.00 – 165.00

Walker, 1957 – 1959

| 30" | $130.00 – 150.00 |

Vinyl head on oilcloth body, 1959

| 22" | $50.00 – 60.00 |

Nanette, 1949 – 1959, hard plastic, synthetic wig, sleep eyes, closed mouth

| 14" | $350.00 – 375.00 |
| 17" | $350.00 – 375.00 |

Nanette Walker, 1957 – 1959

| 17" | $350.00 – 400.00 |
| 20" | $400.00 – 450.00 |

Nancy, 1951 – 1952, vinyl head with hard plastic body, wigged

| 14" | $125.00 – 150.00 |
| 18" | $170.00 – 190.00 |

Nancy Lee, 1950 – 1959, hard plastic

| 14" | $425.00 – 450.00 |
| 17" | $450.00 – 475.00 |

Nancy Lee Baby, 1952, painted eyes, crying face

| 15" | $125.00 – 145.00 |

Taffy, 1956, Cissy-type

| 23" | $145.00 – 165.00 |

ARTIST DOLLS

Original artist dolls may be one-of-a-kind pieces or limited edition pieces made by the designing artist. Production artist dolls are artist series produced in workshop or factory settings, worked on by people other than the designing artist, often limited edition.

7½" ceramic doll by Muriel Bruyere. $200.00.
Courtesy of The Museum Doll Shop.

Original Artist Dolls

Armstrong-Hand, Martha, porcelain

| **Babies** | $1,200.00 – 1,300.00 |
| **Children** | |

Brandon, Elizabeth $450.00 – 500.00

Baker, Betsy

| **Sculpey or Paperclay** | $450.00 – 500.00 |

Barrie, Mirren, cloth

| **Historic Children** | $95.00 – 120.00 |

Beckett, Bob and June, wood

| **Children** | $325.00 – 400.00 |

Blakeley, Halle, high-fire clay

| **Lady dolls** | $650.00 – 750.00 |

Bringloe, Frances, wood

Pioneer Children

| 6¼" | $350.00 – 400.00 |

Bruyere, Muriel, low-fire porcelain

Little Vie

| 8" | $125.00 – 145.00 |

Bullard, Helen, wood

| **Original artist dolls** | $350.00 – 450.00 |

10" Holly doll by Helen Bullard. $175.00. *Courtesy of The Museum Doll Shop.*

George and Martha Washington produced by Emma Clear, c. 1940s. $650.00. pair *Courtesy of The Museum Doll Shop.*

Production artist dolls
Holly, Barbry Allen $150.00 – 200.00
Tennessee Mountain Kids $50.00 – 60.00
Campbell, Astry, porcelain
   Children $425.00 – 450.00
Clear, Emma, porcelain
   China or bisque ladies
                  $400.00 – 500.00
   George & Martha Washington
            $550.00 – 650.00 pair
Cochran, Dewees, various media: cloth, black characters, wood, latex composition
Grow Up Series
   18" $2,500.00 – 2,600.00
Look Alikes, portrait children
   15" – 16" $900.00 – 1,100.00
   18" – 20" $1,500.00 – 1,800.00
Dengel, Dianne, cloth
   20" – 24" $225.00 – 275.00
Florian, Gertrude, ceramic, composition
Ladies $275.00 – 300.00

Dewees Cochran portrait doll, latex. $1,100.00. *Courtesy of The Museum Doll Shop.*

Cloth dolls by Dianne Dengel, painted features. $225.00 – 275.00 each. *Courtesy of Skinner Inc., Boston and Bolton, Massachusetts.*

Goodnow, June, resin
Indian, cernit, one-of-a-kind
   14" $3,000.00
The Quilter
   18" $475.00 – 500.00
Hale, Patti, wood
               $200.00 – 300.00
Heizer, Dorothy, cloth
Alice in Wonderland (15"),
three doll set $8,000.00*
Historic Figures
   10" – 11" $1,200.00 – 1,600.00
20th Century Fashion Ladies
          $1,600.00 – 2,000.00
Kane, Maggie Head, porcelain
          $400.00 – 450.00
Oldenburg, Maryanne, porcelain
Children $200.00 – 250.00
Park, Irma, wax
Wax over porcelain miniatures
          $150.00 – 175.00
Ravca, Frances & Bernard, various media
Crepe paper
   6" – 7" $90.00 – 120.00

Cloth, needle sculpted
   Peasants
   10" – 14" $100.00 – 150.00
   Other figures
   10" – 14" $125.00 – 175.00
Composition, cloth, and paper
   Historical figures
   10" – 14" $75.00 – 125.00
Redmond, Kathy, porcelain
Henry VIII $550.00 – 600.00
Ladies $400.00 – 450.00

10" Dorothy Hiezer, Queen Isabella. $1,500.00. *Courtesy of The Museum Doll Shop.*

Sandreuter, Regina, wood
          $550.00 – 650.00
Saucier, Madeline, cloth
   15" $300.00 – 350.00
Smith, Sherman, wood, 5" – 6"
Simple style $250.00 – 325.00
More elaborate $375.00 – 500.00
Sorenson, Lewis, wax
Father Christmas $1,100.00 – 1,200.00
Toymaker $750.00 – 800.00

Thompson, Martha, porcelain
Betsy $850.00 – 900.00
Little Women $650.00 – 750.00 each
Princess Grace $1,500.00 – 1,800.00
Thorpe, Ellery, porcelain
Children $400.00 – 500.00
Vargas, wax
Ethnic figures
     10" – 11" $600.00 – 700.00
Wick, Faith, porcelain
     $2,500.00 – 2,700.00
Zeller, Fawn, porcelain
One-of-a-kind
     $2,000.00 – 2,500.00
US Historical Society
     Holly $500.00 – 600.00
     Polly II $200.00 – 225.00
Production Artist Dolls
Good-Krueger, Julie, vinyl
     20" – 21" $150.00 – 200.00

Julie Good-Krueger's Seaside II, vinyl. $175.00.
Courtesy of The Museum Doll Shop.

Martha Thompson's Grace Kelly doll. $1,700.00.
Courtesy of The Museum Doll Shop.

Gunzel, Hildegard, various media
Wax-over-porcelain
     28" – 31" $1,400.00 – 1,800.00
Vinyl
     For Madame Alexander
     17" $45.00 – 55.00
     27" $100.00 – 125.00
     Classic Children
     24" – 30" $100.00 – 150.00
Hartmann, Sonja, various media
Porcelain
     20" $275.00 – 300.00
Vinyl
     23" $150.00 – 200.00
Heath, Philip, vinyl
World of Children Collection
     $375.00 – 450.00
Heller, Karin, cloth
Children $200.00 – 250.00
Himstedt, Annette, 1986 on, distributed by Timeless Creations, a division of Mattel, Inc., swivel rigid vinyl head with

shoulder plate, cloth body, vinyl limbs, inset eyes, real lashes, molded eyelids, holes in nostrils, human hair wig, bare feet, original in box

Barefoot Children, 1986, 26"

Bastian	$425.00 – 475.00
Beckus	$550.00 – 650.00
Ellen	$425.00 – 475.00
Fatou	$550.00 – 650.00
Kathe	$425.00 – 475.00
Lisa	$425.00 – 475.00
Paula	$425.00 – 475.00

The World Children, 1988, 31"

Friederike	$450.00 – 500.00
Kasimi	$650.00 – 750.00
Makimura	$550.00 – 600.00
Malin	$700.00 – 800.00
Michiko	$625.00 – 700.00

Reflections of Youth, 1989 – 1990, 26"

Adrienne, 1989	$450.00 – 475.00

17" Hanna & Peter by R. John Wright. $1,200.00 each. *Courtesy of Carole Barboza.*

Jule, 1992, 26"	$600.00 – 650.00
Kai, 1989	$350.00 – 400.00
Mia Yin, 1999	$650.00 – 750.00
Neblina, 1991, 27½"	
	$525.00 – 550.00
Tara, 1993	$325.00 – 350.00

Iacono, Maggie, cloth
Children $500.00 – 650.00
Kish, Helen, vinyl
Ballerinas
    12" $90.00 – 110.00
Middleton, Lee, vinyl
Babies & Toddlers $75.00 – 85.00
Bubba Chubbs, 22" $175.00 – 200.00
Roche, Lynn & Michael, porcelain and wood
Children
    17" – 22" $800.00 – 1,000.00
Spanos, FayZah, vinyl
Baby $75.00 – 125.00
Children $150.00 – 175.00
Tonner, Robert, vinyl
Fashion Models
    19" $175.00 – 225.00

37" Nkike by Philip Heath from an edition of 500 pieces. $450.00. *Courtesy Richard W. Withington Auction, Inc., Nashua, New Hampshire.*

Wright, R. John, cloth
Children $750.00 – 1,200.00
Christopher Robin and Pooh, 1st edition, 1985
18" $1,200.00 – 1,500.00
Early adult peasant characters
$1,100.00 – 1,500.00
Kewpies $450.00 – 500.00
Raggedy Ann $500.00 – 525.00

ASHTON-DRAKE

Located in Niles, Illinois. Ashton-Drake is a division of Bradford Industries. Manufactures dolls designed by a number of well-known artists. Sells its doll lines through distributors or via direct mail-order sales to the public. Doll in perfect condition with original clothing and tags.

Yolanda Bello
Picture Perfect Babies
Jason, 1985 $150.00 – 200.00
Heather, 1986 $45.00 – 50.00
Jennifer, 1987 $50.00 – 60.00
Matthew, 1987 $40.00 – 50.00
Amanda, 1988 $45.00 – 50.00
Sarah, 1989 $35.00 – 40.00
Jessica, 1989 $35.00 – 40.00
Michael, 1990 $45.00 – 50.00
Lisa, 1990 $40.00 – 45.00
Emily, 1991 $35.00 – 40.00
Danielle, 1991 $35.00 – 40.00
Playtime Babies, 1994
Lindsey $25.00 – 30.00
Shawna $25.00 – 30.00
Todd $25.00 – 30.00
Lullaby Babies $20.00 – 25.00
Brigitte Duval
Fairy Tale Princesses
18" $40.00 – 50.00
Diana Effner
Heroines of Fairy Tale

Cinderella, Snow White, Goldilocks, Red Ridinghood, Rapunzel
16" $30.00 – 35.00
What Little Girls are Made Of
Sunshine & Lollipops, Peaches & Cream, Christmas & Candy Canes
15" $30.00 – 35.00
Mother Goose
Mary Mary, Girl with a Curl, Curly Locks, Snips & Snails
14" $30.00 – 35.00
Julie Good-Krueger
Amish Blessings
Rebeccah, Rachel, Adam $40.00 – 50.00
Joan Ibarolle
Little House on the Prairie, 1992 – 1995
Laura, Mary, Carrie $95.00 – 115.00
Ma & Pa $150.00 – 175.00
Wendy Lawton
Little Women, set of 5
16" $250.00 – 300.00
Mary Had a Little Lamb $25.00 – 30.00
Little Bo Peep $25.00 – 30.00
Little Miss Muffet $25.00 – 30.00
Jenny Lundy
Simple Pleasures
Gretchen, Molly $50.00 – 60.00
Mel Odom
Gene, 1995
Premier, 1st
1995 $350.00 – 450.00
Monaco, 2nd
1995 $75.00 – 100.00
Red Venus, 3rd
1995 $70.00 – 80.00
Other Genes
Bird of Paradise
1997 $110.00 – 130.00
Breathless
1999 $80.00 – 100.00
Iced Coffee
$45.00 – 55.00

15" Gene Red Venus. $75.00. *Courtesy of The Museum Doll Shop.*

Midnight Romance
1997 $150.00 – 175.00
Song of Spain
1999 $80.00 – 100.00
Gene Specials
Atlantic City Beauty, convention
1996 $850.00 – 950.00
Broadway Medley, convention
1998 $250.00 – 300.00
Covent Garden, NALED
1998 $55.00 – 65.00
Dream Girl, convention
1998 $225.00 – 250.00
Holiday Benefit Gala, LE 25
1998 $245.00 – 265.00
King's Daughter, NALED
1997 $75.00 – 100.00
Las Vegas Showgirl, limited edition of 50
1997 $1,700.00 – 2,000.00
Madra, Gene convention centerpiece,

limited edition of 100
2005 $300.00 – 320.00
Moments to Remember, MDCC 250
2000 $250.00 – 300.00
My Favorite Witch, convention
1997 $1,000.00 – 1,200.00
Night at Versailles, FAO Schwarz
1997 $200.00 – 250.00
On the Avenue, FAO Schwarz
1998 $160.00 – 180.00
Santa Fe Celebration, limited edition of 250
1999 $550.00 – 600.00
Gene Convention pack
2002 $400.00 – 500.00
Gene's green flight outfit, limited
2002 $710.00*
Titus Tomescu
From This Day Forward
1994 $60.00 – 70.00
Barely Yours Series
Snug as a Bug in a Rug $60.00 – 70.00
Cute as a Button
1993 $60.00 – 70.00
Pretty as a Picture
1996 $55.00 – 60.00
Good as Gold
1997 $55.00 – 65.00
Disney dolls
Snow White $40.00 – 50.00
Dopey $40.00 – 50.00
Disney Babies $40.00 – 50.00
Disney World Girl
16" $35.00 – 45.00

AUTOMATONS

Various manufacturers used many different mediums including bisque, wood, wax, cloth, and others to make dolls that performed some action. More complicated models performing more or complex actions bring higher prices. The unusual one-of-a-kind dolls in this category make it difficult to provide a good range. All these auction prices are for mechanicals in good working order.

Autoperipatetikos, 1860 – 1870s

Bisque, china, or papier-mâché by American Enoch Rice Morrison, key wound mechanism

12"	$1,000.00

Ballerina

Bisque Simon & Halbig mold 1159, key rotates head and arms lower, leg extends, Leopold Lambert, ca. 1900

23"	$4,250.00

Bébé Cage

Bisque Jumeau mold 203, key wound, turns head, hand gives berry to bird, bird flies, one tune, Leopold Lambert, ca. 1890

19"	$13,500.00

18" violin player made by Vichy, Jumeau head. $10,000.00. *Courtesy of The Museum Doll Shop.*

Bébé Eventail

Bisque Tété Jumeau, key wound, moves head, lifts flower and fan, plays "La Mascotte," blue silk costume, Leopold Lambert, ca. 1890

19"	$12,500.00

Bébé Piano

Bisque Jumeau, socket head, carton body, plays piano with four tunes, key wound, Leopold Lambert, ca. 1886

20"	$31,000.00

Bébé with Fan and Flowers

Bisque Tété Jumeau, key wound, moves hand, fans herself, sniffs flower, plays "Le Petit Bleu," Leopold Lambert, ca. 1892

19"	$16,500.00

Clown Équilibriste

Roullet et Descamps, Jumeau head, clown raises his body to do a handstand on the back of the chair, turns head, lifts one arm

25"	$8,812.50

16" Autoperipatetikos, key wound walking doll, untinted bisque head. $1,000.00. *Courtesy of The Museum Doll Shop.*

Edison Phonograph Doll
Simon Halbig or Jumeau bisque head doll with mechanism in torso of composition body
Simon Halbig head mold 719
   23" $4,900.00 – 5,400.00
Garden Tea Party
Three bisque children, painted eyes, move head and arms at tea table on 9" x 9" base
   12" $3,050.00
Laughing Girl with Kitten
Bisque laughing Jumeau socket head, carton torso, key wound mechanism, turns head, smells flower, kitten pulls ribbon, Leopold Lambert, ca. 1890
   20" $10,000.00
Little Girl with Marionette Theater
French bisque socket head, key wound, head moves, lifts curtain, stage rotates, shows five different players, Renou, ca. 1900
   16½" $16,500.00
Négre Buveur
Roullet et Descamps, papier-mâché head, boy drinking brandy while holding a monkey on his lap.
   30" $28,200.00

6" German key wound Indian Rider. $500.00.
Courtesy of The Museum Doll Shop.

Riding Toy, key wound, fur covered horse with doll, metal with German bisque head, when wound the horse gallops across the floor, heads such as Cowboys, Indians, George Washington
   6" $450.00 – 500.00
Waltzing Lady with Mandolin
Bisque socket head, carton body, rotates, turns head, strums mandolin, key wound, Alexandre Theroude, ca. 1865
   15" $8,000.00

GEORGENE AVERILL

1913 – 1960s, New York City. Georgene and James Averill began their doll business dressing dolls. Georgene was the designer, James the businessman. They began as Averill Manufacturing Company. In 1915 they trademarked the name "Madame Hendren" for doll designs. In 1923 the Averills ended their association with Averill Manufacturing which continued to make dolls designed by other artists. The Averills also continued to manufacture their own dolls under the name Georgene Novelties.

Allie Dog, bisque head by Alt, Beck & Gottschalk, glass eyes, open mouth with tongue and teeth, mold 1405
   12" – 15" $7,000.00 – 7,500.00
Baby Dawn, 1950, vinyl with cloth body
   19" $325.00 – 350.00
Baby Georgene or Baby Hendren, composition head, arms, and legs, cloth body, marked with name on head
   16" $250.00 – 275.00
   20" $325.00 – 340.00
   26" $525.00 – 575.00

18" composition baby, marked Madame Hendren. $300.00. *Courtesy of The Museum Doll Shop.*

Body Twists, 1927, composition with bale swivel joint in torso.
Dimmie & Jimmie
14½" $425.00 – 475.00

22" open mouth Bonnie Babe, marked 7005/3652. $1,550.00. *Courtesy Richard W. Withington, Inc., Nashua, New Hampshire.*

22" Baby, designed by Maude Tousey Fangel. $900.00. *Courtesy of The Museum Doll Shop.*

Bonnie Babe, 1926 – 1930s, bisque heads made in Germany by Alt, Beck, and Gottschalk, cloth bodies made in the USA by K&K toys.
Bisque head, open mouth with two lower teeth, composition or celluloid lower arms and legs, cloth body, molds 1368, 1402

12"	$900.00 – 1,000.00
15"	$1,100.00 – 1,200.00
18"	$1,300.00 – 1,400.00
22"	$1,500.00 – 1,600.00

Celluloid head

10"	$450.00 – 500.00
16"	$625.00 – 675.00

All-bisque Bonnie Babe: See All-bisque, German Section.
Brownies, Girl Scouts: See Girl Scout Section.
Character animals such as Uncle Wiggley, Nurse Jane, Krazy Kat, and others
          18" $650.00 – 750.00
Character or ethnic doll, 1915 on, composition head, cloth or composition

body, character faces, painted features
Indian, Sailor, Dutch Boy, etc.
12"	$150.00 – 175.00
16"	$275.00 – 300.00

Black
14"	$425.00 – 450.00

Cloth, 1920s on, molded mask face, painted features, sometimes inset hair eyelashes, yarn hair, cloth body, many dressed in International costumes
12" – 15"	$125.00 – 150.00
18"	$200.00 – 225.00

Comic Characters, 1944 – 1965, cloth, molded mask face, cloth body, appropriate character clothing
Alvin, Nancy, Sluggo, Little Lulu, etc.
14"	$500.00 – 550.00

Becassine, 1950s, French character doll
13"	$650.00 – 700.00

Dolly Reckord, 1922 – 1928, composition head, arms, and legs, cloth body with record player inside, human hair wig, sleep eyes, open mouth with teeth
26"	$650.00 – 675.00

Grace Drayton designs, 1923, flat faced cloth dolls with painted features, some with yarn hair

Cloth mask faced Nancy & Sluggo. $550.00. each *Courtesy of The Museum Doll Shop.*

Chocolate Drop
10"	$350.00 – 400.00
14"	$500.00 – 550.00

Dolly Dingle
11"	$375.00 – 400.00
15"	$525.00 – 550.00

Maude Tousey Fangel designs, 1938, flat faced cloth dolls with painted features
Sweets, Snooks, etc.
12" – 14"	$600.00 – 700.00
15" – 17"	$725.00 – 775.00
21"	$850.00 – 900.00

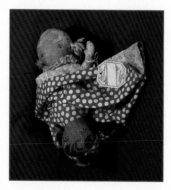

10" Topsy Turvy made by Averill Manufacturing. $300.00. *Courtesy of The Museum Doll Shop.*

13" cloth mask face Becassine. $650.00. *Courtesy of The Museum Doll Shop.*

16" Little Cherub, designed by Harriet Flanders. $400.00. *Courtesy Otto & Ursula Mertz.*

16" Sunny Girl, celluloid shoulder head, c. 1927. $400.00. *Courtesy of The Museum Doll Shop.*

Kris Kringle, cloth mask face
    14" $175.00 – 200.00
Little Cherub, designed by Harriet Flanders, composition with painted eyes
    16" $300.00 – 400.00
Mama doll, 1918 on, composition head, arms, and swing style legs, cloth body, voice box in torso, molded hair or mohair wig, painted or sleep eyes
    15" – 18" $275.00 – 325.00
    20" – 22" $475.00 – 525.00
Peaches, 1928 on, Patsy-type, all-composition, jointed at hips and shoulders, molded hair or wigged, painted or glass eyes, open or closed mouth.
    14" $325.00 – 350.00
    17" $400.00 – 425.00
Snookums, 1927, child actor at Universal-Stern Brothers studio, composition, laughing mouth with two rows of teeth
    14" $350.00 – 375.00
Sunny Girl, 1927, celluloid head, cloth body, turtle mark
    15" $375.00 – 425.00

Tear Drop Baby, designed by Dianne Dengel, cloth mask face, molded tear on cheek
    16" $275.00 – 300.00
Whistling doll, 1925 – 1929, doll made a whistling noise when its head was pushed down
Whistling Dan, etc.
    14" – 15" $350.00 – 450.00

Digital Tear Drop Baby, designed by Dianne Dengel. $275.00. *Courtesy of The Museum Doll Shop.*

BABYLAND RAG DOLL

Babyland Rag dolls were a line of dolls sold by Horsman from 1893 to 1928. The actual manufacturer of these dolls is still unknown. The dolls were originally marked with paper tags which read "Genuine // Babyland // Trade // Mark." Dolls had flat cloth faces, cloth bodies, some had mohair wigs. Dolls listed are in good, clean condition with original clothing. Faded, stained or worn examples can bring ½ the values listed.

Painted face

12" – 15"	$750.00 – 850.00
18" – 22"	$1,100.00
30"	$2,000.00 – 2,100.00

Black

15" – 17"	$750.00 – 850.00
20" – 22"	$1,100.00 – 1,300.00

Babyland Topsy-Turvy doll with lithographed features. $675.00. *Courtesy of The Museum Doll Shop.*

Topsy-Turvy

13" – 15"	$700.00 – 800.00

Lithographed face, 1907 on

12" – 15"	$550.00 – 600.00
24"	$650.00 – 700.00

Topsy-Turvy

14"	$650.00 – 700.00

BADEKINDER

1860 – 1940. Most porcelain factories made china and bisque dolls in one-piece molds with molded or painted black or blond hair, and usually undressed. Sometimes called Bathing Dolls, they were dubbed "Frozen Charlotte" from a song about a girl who went dancing dressed lightly and froze in the snow. They range in size from under 1" to over 19". Some were reproduced in Germany from the 1970s to the present. Allow

12" Babyland rag doll with painted features. $750.00. *Courtesy of The Museum Doll Shop.*

more for pink tint, extra decoration, or hairdo.

All china

2" – 3"	$150.00 – 200.00
4" – 5"	$215.00 – 230.00
6" – 7"	$245.00 – 265.00
9" – 10"	$275.00 – 300.00
14" – 15"	$500.00 – 575.00

Black china

5" – 6"	$190.00 – 250.00

Blond hair, flesh tones head and neck

9" – 12"	$500.00 – 800.00
14" – 15"	$800.00 – 1,000.00

Molded boots

4"	$225.00 – 225.00
8"	$275.00 – 300.00

Molded clothes or hats

3"	$250.00 – 375.00
6"	$300.00 – 350.00
8"	$425.00 – 475.00

2½" Badekinder. $150.00. *Courtesy of The Museum Doll Shop.*

Pink tint, hairdo

3"	$250.00 – 375.00
5"	$400.00 – 425.00

Pink tint, bonnet-head

3"	$400.00 – 425.00
5"	$500.00 – 550.00

Bisque

Good quality

5"	$200.00 – 275.00

Fancy hair, molded boots

4" – 5"	$275.00 – 300.00

Stone bisque, molded hair, one piece

3"	$18.00 – 25.00
6"	$30.00 – 40.00

Parian-type, 1860

5"	$200.00 – 225.00
7"	$250.00 – 275.00

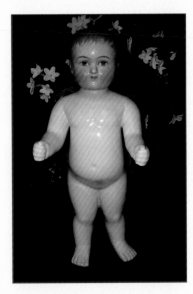

16" china Badekinder with pink tinted face. $1,100.00. *Courtesy of Turn of the Century Antiques, Denver, Colorado.*

BÄHR & PRÖSCHILD

1871 – 1930s, Orhdruf, Thüringia, Germany. Porcelain factory that made its own dolls as well as providing heads for companies such as Kley & Hahn, Bruno Schmidt, Heinrich Stier, and others.

Belton-type, 1880, on, solid dome head with flat crown with small stringing holes in it. Closed mouth, paperweight eyes, pierced ears, straight wrists, composition or kid body, molds in the 200 series

12"	$1,700.00 – 1,800.00
14" – 16"	$1,900.00 – 2,100.00
18" – 20"	$2,500.00 – 2,800.00

Child, 1888, bisque head, open or closed mouth, human hair or mohair wig, composition body in German or French style or kid body, molds: 204, 224 239, 246, 252, 273, 275, 277, 286, 289, 293, 297, 309, 325, 332, 340, 379, 394

11"	$950.00*
12" – 14"	$475.00 – 575.00
16" – 18"	$700.00 – 800.00
22" – 24"	$950.00 – 1,050.00

Kid body

13" – 16"	$250.00 – 375.00
24"	$625.00 – 675.00

Mold 224, with dimples

14" – 16"	$850.00 – 900.00
22" – 24"	$1,200.00 – 1,300.00

Character Child

Mold 247, open/closed mouth

26"	$2,100.00

Mold 520, closed mouth

13"	$2,500.00*

Mold 531

19"	$2,600.00*

Mold 536

18" – 20"	$3,750.00 – 3,800.00*

Mold 592

12"	$2,800.00*

Mold 604

11"	$1,400.00 – 1,500.00
20" – 22"	$1,200.00 – 1,500.00

Mold 624, open mouth

17"	$2,700.00

Too few in database for a reliable range.

Character Baby, 1909 on, bisque socket head, solid dome or wigged, sleep eyes, open mouth, bent limb body, molds: 585, 586, 587, 602, 604, 619, 620, 624, 630, 641, 678

9"	$100.00 – 125.00
12" – 14"	$425.00 – 450.00
17" – 19"	$575.00 – 625.00
22" – 24"	$725.00 – 800.00

Toddler body

11"	$1,100.00 – 1,200.00
18" – 20"	$1,300.00 – 1,400.00

BARBIE®

1959 to present, Hawthorne, California, 11½ inch fashion doll manufactured by Mattel Inc. Values listed are for perfect condition dolls in original clothing and bearing all appropriate tags. Played with and undressed dolls should be valued at ¼ to ⅓ the value of perfect. Mint-in-box examples will bring double the values listed here.

#1 Barbie®, 1959, heavy, solid vinyl torso, faded to pale white color, white irises, pointed arch eyebrows, soft texture ponytail hairstyle, black and white swimsuit, gold hoop earrings, metal lined holes in bottom of feet and shoes to accept doll stand.

Blonde	$3,500.00 – 3,700.00
Brunette	$4,000.00 – 4,300.00

#2 Barbie®, 1959, doll same as previous doll, but with no holes in feet, some wore pearl earrings

Blonde	$3,000.00 – 3,200.00

Brunette $3,500.00 – 3,700.00

#3 Barbie®, 1960, same as previous doll, but now has blue irises and curved eyebrows

Blonde $550.00 – 600.00

Brunette $600.00 – 650.00

#4 Barbie®, 1960, same as previous doll, but torso now has a flesh-tone color

Blonde or brunette $200.00 – 250.00

#5 Barbie®, 1961, same as previous, but now has a hollow, hard plastic torso, hair is now firmer texture saran

Blonde or brunette $225.00 – 250.00

Redhead $325.00 – 350.00

#6 Barbie®, 1962, same as previous, but now the doll is available in many more hair and lipstick colors and wears a red swimsuit $275.00 – 300.00

Swirl Ponytail, 1964, smooth bangs swirled across forehead and to the side instead of the curly bangs of the previous ponytail dolls $250.00 – 300.00

Bubblecut Barbie®, 1961, same doll as others of this year but with new bubble cut hairstyle

Brown $450.00 – 500.00

White Ginger $300.00 – 350.00

Others $200.00 – 250.00

Side-part bubblecut $300.00 – 350.00

Barbie® Fashion Queen, 1963, doll has molded hair with a hair band and three interchangeable wigs, gold and white striped swimsuit and turban $125.00 – 150.00

Miss Barbie®, 1964, doll has molded bendable legs, hair with a hair band and three interchangeable wigs, sleep eyes $900.00 – 1,000.00

American Girl Barbie®, 1965, bobbed hairstyle with bangs, bendable legs $500.00 – 700.00

#3 Barbie $575.00. #1 Skipper $100.00. *Courtesy Richard W. Withington, Inc., Nashua, New Hampshire.*

Color Magic Barbie®, 1966, dolls hair can change color

Blonde $500.00 – 550.00

Midnight to ruby red $700.00 – 800.00

Twist N' Turn Barbie®, 1967, swivel jointed at waist $200.00 – 250.00

Talking Barbie®, 1968, doll now has pull-string talker $130.00 – 150.00

From left: Swirl Ponytail Barbie, $300.00. Miss Barbie, $950.00. #5 Ponytail Barbie, $225.00. Brunette Bubble Cut Barbie, $475.00. *Courtesy Richard W. Withington, Inc., Nashua, New Hampshire.*

Living Barbie®, 1970, joints at neck, shoulder, elbow, wrist, hip, knee, and ankle $120.00 – 140.00

Other Barbie® dolls. Dolls listed are in excellent condition, wearing original clothing. Mint-in-box dolls can bring double the values listed.

Angel Face
1983 $16.00 – 20.00
Ballerina
1976 $35.00 – 45.00
Barbie Baby-sits
1974 $20.00 – 40.00
Beach Party
1980 $25.00 – 45.00
Beautiful Bride
1976 $95.00 – 120.00
Beauty Secrets
1980 $20.00 – 30.00
Bicyclin'
1994 $15.00 – 20.00
Busy Barbie
1972 $95.00 – 130.00
Dance Club
1989 $15.00 – 20.00

Buffy and Mrs. Beasley. $200.00. *Courtesy of The Museum Doll Shop.*

Day-To-Night
1985 $25.00 – 35.00
Doctor
1988 $22.50 – 30.00
Dream Barbie
1995 $20.00 – 30.00
Fashion Jeans, black
1982 $16.00 – 22.00
Fashion Photo
1978 $22.50 – 28.00
Free Moving
1975 $55.00 – 75.00
Gold Medal Skater
1975 $32.50 – 40.00
Golden Dream w/coat
1981 $35.00 – 50.00
Growin' Pretty Hair
1971 $125.00 – 175.00
Hair Fair
1967 $75.00 – 100.00
Hair Happenin's
1971 $375.00 – 550.00
Happy Birthday
1981 $17.50 – 25.00

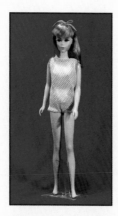

Twist N' Turn Barbie. $225.00. *Courtesy of The Museum Doll Shop.*

Francie, c. 1966. $125.00. *Courtesy of The Museum Doll Shop.*

Ice Capades, 50th
1990 $15.00 – 20.00
Kellogg Quick Curl
1974 $25.00 – 32.00
Kissing
1979 $15.00 – 20.00
Live Action on Stage
1971 $100.00 – 140.00
Loving You
1983 $25.00 – 32.00
Magic Curl
1982 $17.50 – 25.00
Magic Moves
1986 $25.00 – 32.00
Malibu (Sunset)
1971 $25.00 – 32.00
My First Barbie
1981 $10.00 – 15.00
My Size
1993 $55.00 – 75.00
Newport the Sport's Set
1973 $62.50 – 82.00

Peaches 'n Cream
1985 $15.00 – 20.00
Pink & Pretty
1982 $15.00 – 20.00
Rappin' Rockin'
1992 $22.50 – 30.00
Rocker
1986 $20.00 – 24.00
Roller Skating
1980 $22.50 – 30.00
Secret Hearts
1993 $12.50 – 18.00
Sensations
1988 $25.00 – 30.00
Sun Lovin' Malibu
1979 $16.00 – 22.00
Sun Valley, The Sport's Set
1973 $32.50 – 42.00
Super Fashion Fireworks
1976 $45.00 – 62.00
Super Size, 18"
1977 $100.00 – 130.00
Superstar Promotional
1978 $32.50 – 45.00
Talking Busy
1972 $130.00 – 162.00
Twinkle Lights
1993 $25.00 – 30.00
Walking Lively
1972 $90.00 – 122.00
Western (3 hairstyles)
1981 $25.00 – 30.00
Gift Sets
Mint-in-box prices; add more for NRFB (never removed from box), less for worn or faded
Barbie Hostess
1966 $4,750.00
Beautiful Blues, Sears
1967 $3,300.00
Color Magic Gift Set, Sears
1965 $2,000.00

Fashion Queen Barbie & Friends	
1963	$2,250.00
Fashion Queen & Ken Trousseau	
1963	$2,600.00
Little Theatre Set	
1964	$5,500.00
On Parade	
1960	$2,350.00
Party Set	
1960	$2,300.00
Pink Premier	
1969	$1,600.00
Round the Clock	
1964	$5,000.00
Sparkling Pink	
1964	$2,500.00
Travel in Style, Sears	
1964	$2,400.00
Trousseau Set	
1960	$2,850.00
Wedding Party	
1964	$3,000.00

#1 Ken. $90.00. *Courtesy of The Museum Doll Shop.*

Store Specials or Special Editions, Mint-in-Box

Avon Winter Velvet	
1996	$60.00
Billy Boy Feelin' Groovy	
1986	$290.00
Bloomingdales	
Savvy Shopper	
1994	$165.00
Donna Karan	
1995	$75.00
Bob Mackie	
Gold	
1990	$450.00
Platinum	
1991	$575.00
Starlight Splendor, black	
1992	$550.00
Empress	
1992	$725.00
Neptune Fantasy	
1992	$675.00
Masquerade Ball	
1993	$325.00
Queen of Hearts	
1994	$200.00
Goddess of the Sun	
1995	$175.00
Moon Goddess	
1996	$125.00
Madame du Barbie	
1997	$175.00
Classique Series	
Benefit Ball	
1992	$70.00
City Style	
1993	$45.00
Opening Night	
1994	$55.00
Evening Extravaganza	
1994	$50.00

Living Fluff. $130.00. *Courtesy of The Museum Doll Shop.*

Uptown Chic

1994	$45.00

Midnight Gala

1995	$50.00

Disney

Euro Disney

1992	$70.00

Disney Fun

1993	$55.00

FAO Schwarz

Golden Greetings

1989	$225.00

Winter Fantasy

1990	$235.00

Night Sensation

1991	$200.00

Madison Avenue

1991	$245.00

Rockette

1993	$260.00

Silver Screen

1994	$275.00

Jeweled Splendor

1995	$335.00

Great Eras

Gibson Girl

1993	$130.00

Flapper

1993	$200.00

Southern Belle

1994	$125.00

Hallmark

Victorian Elegance

1994	$115.00

Sweet Valentine

1996	$75.00

Hills

Party Lace

1989	$45.00

Evening Sparkle

1990	$45.00

Moonlight Rose

1991	$60.00

Blue Elegance

1991	$55.00

Holiday Barbie

1988, red gown	$550.00
1989, white gown	$150.00
1990, fuchsia gown	$125.00
1991, green gown	$145.00
1992, silver gown	$120.00
1993, red/gold gown	$90.00
1994	$50.00
1995	$25.00
1996	$20.00
1997	$20.00
1998	$20.00
1999	$20.00
2000	$20.00
2001	$20.00

Hollywood Legends

Scarlett O'Hara, red

1994	$70.00

Dorothy, Wizard of Oz

1995	$260.00

Glinda, Good Witch
1995 $105.00
Home Shopping Club
Evening Flame
1991 $160.00
J.C. Penney
Evening Elegance
1990 $105.00
Enchanted Evening
1991 $105.00
Golden Winter
1993 $70.00
Night Dazzle, blond
1994 $65.00
K-Mart
Peach Pretty
1989 $40.00
Pretty in Purple
1992 $35.00
Little Debbie
1993 $35.00
Mervyns
Ballerina
1983 $75.00

Ricky. $90.00. *Courtesy of The Museum Doll Shop.*

Fabulous Fur
1986 $70.00
Montgomery Ward
#1 Replica, shipping box
1972 $710.00
#1 Replica, pink box
1972 $840.00
Nostalgia Series
35th Anniversary
1994 $50.00
Solo in the Spotlight
1994 $30.00
Busy Gal
1995 $40.00
Enchanted Evening
1996 $35.00
Poodle Parade
1996 $30.0
Fashion Luncheon
1997 $45.00
Prima Ballerina Music Box
Swan Lake, music box
1991 $205.00
Nutcracker, music box
1992 $285.00
Sears
Celebration, 100th Anniversary
1986 $90.00
Star Dream
1987 $70.00
Blossom Beautiful
1992 $315.00
Ribbons & Roses
1995 $60.00
Service Merchandise
Blue Rhapsody
1991 $185.00
Satin Nights
1992 $80.00
City Sophisticate
1994 $110.00

Spiegel	
Sterling Wishes	
1991	$140.00
Regal Reflections	
1992	$250.00
Royal Invitation	
1993	$120.00
Theatre Elegance	
1994	$180.00
Target	
Gold 'n Lace	
1989	$40.00
Party Pretty	
1990	$30.00
Cute 'n Cool	
1991	$30.00
Golden Evening	
1991	$45.00
Timeless Creations, Stars & Stripes Collection	
Air Force	
1990	$30.00
Navy	
1991	$40.00
Marine	
1992	$35.00
Army Gift Set	
1993	$40.00
Air Force Gift Set	
1994	$40.00
Toys 'R Us	
Dance Sensation	
1985	$60.00
Pepsi Spirit	
1989	$80.00
Vacation Sensation	
1989	$80.00
Radiant in Red	
1992	$70.00
Moonlight Magic	
1993	$90.00
Harley-Davidson, #1	
1997	$475.00

Firefighter	
1995	$55.00
WalMart	
Pink Jubilee, 25th Anniversary	
1987	$75.00
Frills & Fantasy	
1988	$55.00
Dream Fantasy	
1990	$50.00
Wholesale Clubs	
Party Sensation	
1990	$65.00
Fantastica	
1992	$70.00
Royal Romance	
1992	$115.00
Very Violet	
1992	$75.00
Season's Greetings	
1994	$75.00
Winter Royale	
1994	$75.00

Uptown Chic Barbie. $45.00.
Courtesy of The Museum Doll Shop.

After the Walk, Sam's Club
1997 $75.00
Country Rose, Sam's Club
1997 $100.00
Woolworths
Special Expressions, white
1989 $30.00
Sweet Lavender
1992 $25.00
Family and other related dolls. Doll in excellent condition, wearing original clothing, mint-in-box can bring double the values listed
Alan, 1964 – 1967
Straight leg $100.00 – 125.00
Bendable leg $150.00 – 175.00
Casey, Twist 'N Turn
1967 $75.00 – 85.00
Chris, brunette, bendable leg
1967 $90.00 – 100.00
Francie
Bendable leg
1966 $125.00 – 150.00
Straight leg
1966 $125.00 – 150.00
Twist 'N Turn
1967 $150.00 – 165.00
Black
1967 $850.00 – 950.00
Malibu
1971 $20.00 – 25.00
Growin' Pretty Hair
1971 $100.00 – 125.00
Jamie, Walking
1970 $150.00 – 170.00
Julia, Twist 'N Turn
1969 $110.00 – 125.00
Talking
1969 $95.00 – 105.00
Kelly
Quick Curl
1973 $70.00 – 80.00

Yellowstone
1974 $125.00 – 145.00
Ken, #1, straight leg, blue eyes, hard plastic hollow body, flocked hair, 12" mark: "Ken® MCMLX//by//Mattel//Inc."
1961 $100.00 – 140.00
Molded hair
1962 $65.00 – 75.00
Bendable legs
1965 $150.00 – 175.00
Midge
Straight leg
1963 $85.00 – 100.00
No freckles
1963 $170.00 – 190.00
Bendable legs
1965 $225.00 – 250.00
P.J. Talking
1970 $90.00 – 110.00
Twist 'N Turn
1970 $110.00 – 130.00
Live Action/Stage
1971 $110.00 – 125.00
Ricky, straight legs
1965 $85.00 – 95.00
Skipper
Straight leg
1964 $95.00 – 105.00
Bendable leg
1965 $100.00 – 125.00
Twist 'N Turn
1968 $90.00 – 100.00
Skooter
Straight leg
1965 $55.00 – 65.00
Bendable leg
1966 $130.00 – 150.00
Stacey
Talking
1968 $125.00 – 150.00
Twist 'N Turn
1968 $140.00 – 160.00

Todd, bendable, posable
  1966 $80.00 – 90.00
Tutti, bendable, posable
  1967 $65.00 – 75.00
Twiggy, Twist 'N Turn
  1967 $150.00 – 160.00
Barbie Accessories
Animals
All American (horse)
  1991 $35.00
Blinking Beauty (horse)
  1988 $25.00
Champion (horse)
  1991 $40.00
Dancer (horse)
  1971 $100.00
Fluff (kitten)
  1983 $20.00
Ginger (giraffe)
  1988 $30.00
Prancer (horse)
  1984 $35.00
Prince (poodle)
  1985 $35.00
Snowball (dog)
  1990 $35.00
Tahiti (bird w/cage)
  1985 $20.00
Cases
Fashion Queen, black, zippered
  1964 $150.00
Fashion Queen, round hatbox
  1965 $250.00
Miss Barbie, zippered
  1964 $160.00
Vanity, Barbie & Skipper
  1964 $200.00
Clothing
Name of outfit, stock number; price for
mint in package, much less for loose
Aboard Ship
  1631 $550.00

All That Jazz
  1848 $350.00
Arabian Knights
  874               $495.00
Barbie in Japan
  821               $500.00
Beautiful Bride
  1698 $2,100.00
Benefit Performance
  1667 $1,400.00
Black Magic Ensemble
  1609 $420.00
Bride's Dream
  947               $350.00
Busy Gal
  981               $450.00
Campus Sweetheart
  1616 $1,750.00
Cinderella
  872               $550.00
Commuter Set
  916               $1,400.00
Country Club Dance
  1627 $490.00
Dancing Doll
  1626 $525.00
Debutante Ball
  1666 $1,300.00
Dog 'n Duds
  1613 $350.00
Drum Majorette
  875               $265.00
Easter Parade
  971               $4,500.00
Evening Enchantment
  1695 $595.00
Fabulous Fashion
  1676 $595.00
Formal Occasion
  1697 $550.00
Fashion Editor
  1635 $850.00

Formal Luncheon			**On the Avenue**	
1656	$1,400.00		1644	$575.00
Garden Wedding			**Open Road**	
1658	$575.00		985	$385.00
Gay Parisienne			**Pajama Pow**	
964	$4,500.00		1806	$300.00
Glimmer Glamour			**Pan American Stewardess**	
1547	$5,000.00		1678	$5,000.00
Gold 'n Glamour			**Patio Party**	
1647	$1,750.00		1692	$375.00
Golden Glory			**Picnic Set**	
1645	$495.00		967	$365.00
Here Comes the Bride			**Plantation Belle**	
1665	$1,200.00		966	$600.00
Holiday Dance			**Poodle Parade**	
1639	$625.00		1643	$985.00
International Fair			**Rainbow Wraps**	
1653	$500.00		1798	$350.00
Intrigue			**Reception Line**	
1470	$425.00		1654	$600.00
Invitation to Tea			**Red Fantastic**, Sears	
1632	$600.00		1817	$850.00
Junior Prom			**Riding in the Park**	
1614	$695.00		1668	$625.00
Knitting Pretty, pink			**Roman Holiday**	
957	$450.00		968	$5,000.00
Let's Have a Ball			**Romantic Ruffles**	
1879	$325.00		1871	$250.00
Little Red Riding Hood			**Satin 'n Rose**	
880	$625.00		1611	$395.00
Magnificence			**Saturday Matinee**	
1646	$625.00		1615	$950.00
Make Mine Midi			**Sears Pink Formal**	
1861	$350.00		1681	$2,450.00
Masquerade			**Shimmering Magic**	
944	$250.00		1664	$1,750.00
Maxi 'n Midi			**Sleeping Pretty**	
1799	$375.00		1636	$375.00
Midnight Blue			**Smasheroo**	
1617	$850.00		1860	$275.00
Miss Astronaut			**Sorority Meeting**	
1641	$700.00		937	$300.00

Suburban Shopper	
969	$350.00
Sunday Visit	
1675	$595.00
Swirley-Cue	
1822	$300.00
Trailblazers	
1846	$250.00
Travel Togethers	
1688	$300.00
Tunic 'n Tights	
1859	$300.00
Under Fashions	
1655	$695.00
Velveteens, Sears	
1818	$850.00
Weekenders, Sears	
1815	$950.00
Wedding Wonder	
1849	$375.00
Wild 'n Wonderful	
1856	$300.00
Furniture, Suzy Goose	
Canopy Bed, display box	
1960s	$250.00
Chifferobe, cardboard box	
1960s	$250.00
Queen Size Bed, pink	
1960s	$600.00
Vanity, pink	$75.00
Vehicles	
Austin Healy, beige	
1964	$3,300.00
Beach Bus	
1974	$45.00
Mercedes, blue-green	
1968	$450.00
Speedboat, blue-green	
1964	$1,100.00
Sport Plane, blue	
1964	$3,000.00

Sun 'n Fun Buggy	
1971	$150.00
United Airlines	
1973	$75.00

E. BARROIS

1846 –1877, Paris, France. Assembled, sold, and distributed lady-type dolls with bisque heads, closed mouths, on kid and cloth bodies. The dolls' heads were made for Barrois by as yet undetermined French and German porcelain factories. Mark: EB

Poupée (Fashion-type)

Painted eyes

14" – 16"	$1,800.00 – 2,200.00
19" – 21"	$2,600.00 – 3,000.00

Glass eyes

14" – 16"	$2,800.00 – 3,200.00
19" – 21"	$3,600.00 – 4,000.00
23"	$4,500.00 – 4,700.00

13" Barrois poupée with painted eyes.
$1,600.00. *Courtesy of The Museum Doll Shop.*

BELTON-TYPE

1875 on, made by various German manufacturers including Bähr & Pröschild, Kestner, Simon & Halbig, and others. Solid dome bisque socket head doll with small holes in crown for stringing and/or wig application. Paperweight eyes, straight wristed wood and composition body, closed mouth, pierced ears. Belton-type is a name applied to this type of doll by modern doll collectors and is not a reference to a specific maker. Mark: none or mold numbers only.

20" Belton with a Bru-look. $3,500.00.
Courtesy of The Museum Doll Shop.

Bru-look face
12" – 14"	$2,500.00 – 3,000.00

French-Trade, dolls with a French look that were manufactured for the French market, some mold 137, 138
13" – 15"	$1,900.00 – 2,200.00
18" – 20"	$2,400.00 – 2,700.00
22" – 24"	$3,000.00 – 3,200.00

German look dolls
8"	$825.00 – 850.00
12"	$1,200.00 – 1,400.00
15"	$1,550.00 – 1,650.00
20"	$2,100.00 – 2,300.00

Mold 200: See Bähr & Pröschild listing.

14" Belton-style doll with closed mouth and a straight wristed body. $2,000.00.
Courtesy Richard W. Withington, Inc., Nashua, New Hampshire.

C.M. BERGMANN

1888 – 1931, Walterhausen, Thuringia, Germany. Doll factory that distributed in the United States through L. Wolf & Co. Bergmann had bisque doll heads made for them by Alt, Beck & Gottschalk, Armand Marseille, Simon & Halbig, and others. Registered trademarks: Cinderella 1897, Columbia 1904, My Gold Star 1926. Doll in good condition, appropriately dressed.

Character Babies, bisque socket head on bent-limb composition body

Open mouth

12" – 14"	$275.00 – 325.00
15" – 18"	$375.00 – 575.00

Mold 612, open/closed mouth

15"	$2,000.00 – 2,200.00

Mold 134 character toddler

12"	$950.00 – 1,000.00

Child, bisque socket head, open mouth, wigged, sleep or set eyes, ball-jointed composition body, mold 1916 or others

10"	$350.00 – 400.00
14" – 16"	$325.00 – 350.00
20" – 22"	$425.00 – 450.00
26" – 28"	$525.00 – 550.00
20" – 32"	$625.00 – 725.00
42"	$1,800.00 – 1,900.00

Flapper-type body

12"	$625.00 – 650.00
16"	$1,100.00 – 1,200.00

Marked with Simon & Halbig / Bergmann marks

10"	$575.00 – 625.00
14" – 16"	$450.00 – 500.00
18" – 20"	$525.00 – 550.00
24" – 28"	$600.00 – 725.00
36"	$1,500.00 – 1,600.00

Eleonore

18"	$550.00 – 600.00
25"	$700.00 – 800.00

BETSY MCCALL

Dolls based on *McCall's Magazine* paper doll Betsy McCall. Dolls listed are in excellent condition wearing original clothing, mint-in-box dolls can bring double the values listed.
Ideal Toy Corp., 1952 – 1953
Doll with vinyl head, on a hard plastic Toni body, saran wig

14"	$275.00 – 300.00

1958, vinyl, four hair colors, rooted hair, flat feet, slim body, round sleep eyes, may have swivel waist or one-piece torso, mark: "McCall 19©58 Corp." in circle

14"	$350.00 – 400.00

1959, vinyl, rooted hair, slender limbs, some with flirty eyes, one-piece torso, mark: "McCall 19©58 Corp." in a circle

19" – 20"	$300.00 – 350.00

1961, vinyl, five colors of rooted hair, jointed wrists, ankles, waist, blue or brown sleep eyes, four to six outfits available, mark: "McCall 19©61 Corp." in a circle

22"	$175.00 – 200.00
29"	$225.00 – 250.00

American Character Doll Co., 1957 to 1963
8" hard plastic doll with jointed knees, sleep eyes, molded eyelashes, metal barrettes in hair. First year these dolls had mesh cap saran wigs and plastic pin joints in knees. Second year they had vinyl skullcaps on their wigs and metal knee pins.

In undies	$225.00 – 250.00
In street dress	$225.00 – 275.00
In formalwear	$275.00 – 375.00

Betsy McCall by Robert Tonner. $30.00.
Courtesy of The Museum Doll Shop.

8" doll clothing

Dresses	$35.00 – 65.00
Shoes and socks	$35.00 – 40.00
Boxed outfit	$100.00 – 125.00

Vinyl doll, 1958 on, jointed at shoulder, neck and hip, sleep eyes

14"	$350.00 – 375.00
20"	$450.00 – 500.00
30"	$550.00 – 600.00
36"	$650.00 – 750.00

Additional joints at wrists, waist, knees, and ankles

22"	$350.00 – 400.00
29"	$500.00 – 575.00

Companion-size Betsy McCall, 1959, vinyl, rooted hair, mark: "McCall Corp//1959" on head

34"	$800.00 – 900.00

Linda McCall (Betsy's cousin), 1959, vinyl, Betsy face, rooted hair, mark: "McCall Corp//1959" on head

34"	$800.00 – 900.00

Sandy McCall (Betsy's brother), 1959, vinyl, molded hair, sleep eyes, red blazer, navy shorts, mark: "McCall 1959 Corp."; tag reads "I am Your Life Size Sandy McCall"

35"	$900.00 – 1,000.00

Uneeda

1964, vinyl, rooted hair, rigid vinyl body, brown or blue sleep eyes, slim pre-teen body, wore mod outfits, some mini-skirts, competitor of Ideal's Tammy

11½"	$95.00 – 125.00

Horsman

1974, vinyl with rigid plastic body, sleep eyes, came in Betsy McCall Beauty Box with extra hair piece, brush, bobby pins on card, eye pencil, blush, lipstick, two sponges, mirror, and other accessories, mark: "Horsman Doll Inc.//19©67" on head; "Horsman Dolls Inc." on torso

12½"	$50.00 – 60.00

1974, vinyl with rigid plastic teen type body, jointed wrists, sleep eyes, lashes, rooted hair with side part (some blond with ponytails), closed mouth, original clothing marked "BMc" in two-tone blue box marked "©1974//Betsy McCall — she WALKS with you," marks: "Horsman Dolls 1974"

29"	$250.00 – 275.00

Rothchild

1986, thirty-fifth anniversary Betsy, hard plastic, sleep eyes, painted lashes below eyes, single stroke eyebrows, tied ribbon emblem on back, marks: hang tag reads "35th Anniversary//BetsyMcCall// by Rothschild (number) 'Betsy Goes to a Tea Party,' or 'Betsy Goes to the Fair,'" box marked "Rothchild Doll Company// Southboro, MA 01722"

8"	$25.00 – 35.00

Robert Tonner

1996 to present, vinyl (some porcelain), rooted hair, rigid vinyl body, glass eyes, closed smiling mouth, mark: "Betsy McCall//by//Robert Tonner//©Gruner & Jahr USA PUB."

8"	$30.00 – 40.00 retail
14"	$69.00 – 100.00 retail
29"	$200.00 retail

BING ART DOLLS

Germany, 1921 – 1932. Gebrüder Bing was founded in 1882. In 1921 became a part of a conglomerate called the Bing Werke Corporation, this is when they began making their cloth "art dolls." Molded cloth face, sometimes with a heavy coating of gesso giving a composition appearance, cloth head and body, oil-painted features, wigged or painted hair, pin-jointed at neck, shoulders, and hips, seams down front of legs, mitt hands.

11¼" and 12" Bing art dolls. $700.00. pair *Courtesy of The Museum Doll Shop.*

Painted hair, cloth or felt, unmarked or "Bing" on bottom of foot

8"	$250.00 – 300.00
10" – 13"	$450.00 – 500.00
15"	$800.00 – 900.00

Wigged

10"	$375.00 – 425.00

BISQUE, UNKNOWN OR LITTLE KNOWN MAKERS

French

Various French manufacturers of bisque headed child dolls working from 1870 on. No separate listing for these makers. No damage, appropriately dressed.

Unknown Maker

Early desirable very French-style face, marks such as "J.D.," "J.M. Paris," and "H. G." (possibly Henri & Granfe-Guimonneau)

17"	$17,000.00 – 18,000.00
21"	$19,000.00 – 21,000.00
27"	$25,000.00 – 27,000.00

Jumeau or Bru style face, may be marked "W. D." or "R. R."

14"	$2,450.00 – 2,650.00
19"	$3,000.00 – 3,175.00
24"	$4,800.00 – 5,050.00
27"	$5,100.00 – 5,350.00

Closed mouth, marks: "F.1," "F.2," "J," "137," "136," or others

Excellent quality, unusual face

10" – 12"	$3,000.00 – 3,500.00
15" – 17"	$4,000.00 – 5,000.00
23" – 25"	$6,000.00 – 8,000.00

Standard quality, excellent bisque

13"	$2,200.00 – 2,450.00
18"	$3,200.00 – 3,450.00
23"	$4,300.00 – 4,500.00

Lesser quality, may have poor painting and/or blotches on cheeks

15"	$1,100.00 – 1,200.00
21"	$1,600.00 – 1,800.00
26"	$2,100.00 – 2,300.00

Open mouth

Excellent quality, ca. 1890 on, French body

15"	$1,300.00 – 1,500.00
18"	$2,100.00 – 2,300.00
21"	$2,300.00 – 2,400.00
24"	$3,000.00 – 3,100.00

High cheek color, ca. 1920s, may have five-piece papier-mâché body

15"	$575.00 – 625.00
19"	$750.00 – 800.00
23"	$900.00 – 950.00

Known Makers

Danel et Cie, 1889 – 1895, Paris, France,

bisque socket head on composition body, paperweight eyes, wigged, pierced ears

Paris Bébé
15"	$3,000.00 – 3,100.00
18"	$3,400.00 – 3,500.00
22"	$4,000.00 – 4,100.00

Bébé Francaise
14"	$3,500.00 – 3,600.00
20"	$4,300.00 – 4,400.00

Delcroix, Henri, 1887, Paris and Montreuil-sous-Bois, pressed bisque socket head, closed mouth, paperweight eyes, marks: "Pan Bébé"

12"	$6,000.00 – 7,000.00

Falck & Roussel, 1880s, socket head, closed mouth, paperweight eyes, wood and composition body, marks: "F.R."

15" – 16"	$12,000.00 – 14,000.00
18"	$16,000.00 – 17,000.00

Halopeau, A, 1881 – 1889, Paris, pressed bisque socket head, closed mouth, paperweight eyes, cork pate, French wood and composition body, marks: "H"

16" – 18"	$30,000.00 – 38,000.00
21" – 24"	$65,000.00 – 75,000.00

Maison Huret, 1878, pressed bisque socket head, closed mouth, paperweight eyes.

12" Paris Bébé by Danel. $2,500.00. *Courtesy of The Museum Doll Shop.*

15" Bébé Mascotte by May Freres Cie. $3,000.00. *Courtesy of The Museum Doll Shop.*

Composition body
13"	$7,000.00 – 11,000.00

Gutta-percha body
18"	$70,000.00 – 80,000.00

Wooden body
18"	$34,000.00 – 36,000.00

Lefebvre et Cie., Alexander, 1975, pressed bisque socket head, closed mouth, paperweight eyes, French wood and composition body, marks: "A.L."

22"	$35,000.00

Too few in database for a reliable range.

Joanny, Joseph Louis, 1888, pressed bisque socket head, closed mouth, paperweight eyes, French wood and composition body, marks: "J"

12" – 15"	$3,400.00 – 4,500.00
17" – 18"	$5,000.00 – 6,300.00
23"	$6,500.00 – 6,600.00

J.M. Bébé 0, 1880s, pressed bisque socket head, closed mouth, paperweight eyes, French wood and composition body, marks: "J.M."

19"	$3,222.00

Too few in database for a reliable range.

26"	$9,000.00

Too few in database for a reliable range.

M. Bebe, 1890s, pressed bisque socket head, closed mouth, paperweight eyes, pierced ears, French wood and composition body, marks: "M" with size number

14"	$1,350.00 – 1,400.00
19" – 23"	$2,600.00 – 3,000.00

May Freres Cie, 1890 – 1897, later Steiner (1898 on), closed mouth, paperweight eyes, pierced ears, composition body, marks: "Bébé Mascotte"

19" – 20"	$3,800.00 – 3,900.00

Mothereau, Alexandre, 1880 – 1895, pressed bisque socket head, closed mouth, paperweight eyes, French wood and composition body, marks: "B.M."

12" – 15"	$14,000.00 – 16,000.00
22" – 24"	$17,000.00 – 19,000.00
28" – 29"	$20,000.00 – 22,000.00

Pannier, 1875, pressed bisque socket head, closed mouth, paperweight eyes, French wood and composition body, marks: "C.P."

20"	$59,000.00

Too few in database for a reliable range.

Petite et Dumontier, 1878 – 1890, Paris, pressed bisque socket head, closed mouth, paperweight eyes, French wood and composition body, some with metal hands, marks: "P. D." with size number

16"	$10,000.00 – 11,000.00
18" – 19"	$12,000.00 – 14,000.00
23"	$15,000.00 – 16,000.00

Pintel et Godchaux, 1880 – 1889, Montreuil, France, pressed bisque socket head, closed mouth, paperweight eyes, French wood and composition body, trademark: "Bébé Charmant"

20" – 22"	$4,000.00 – 5,000.00

Open mouth

18" – 20"	$1,700.00 – 1,900.00

German

Various German manufacturers of bisque headed dolls working from 1870 on. No separate listing for these makers. Marks: May be unmarked, only a mold or size number, or Germany.

Baby

Character Baby, 1910 on, solid dome or wigged, open mouth, glass eyes, bent-limb composition body, marks: "G.B.", "S.& Q.", "P.M.", "F.B.", or unmarked

9" – 10"	$225.00 – 275.00
14" – 16"	$335.00 – 375.00
19" – 21"	$400.00 – 450.00

My Sweet Baby

23" toddler	$1,100.00 – 1,200.00

Newborn Baby, mold 110, 1924, maker A. Wislizenus, bisque head on cloth body, bisque or celluloid hands, marks: "Baby Weygh," "IV," others

10" – 12"	$225.00 – 275.00
14" – 17"	$400.00 – 425.00

Gerling Baby

17"	$575.00 – 625.00

Wolfe, Louis & Co, 1870 – 1930 on, Sonneberg, Germany, Boston, and New

6" German character baby with painted eyes. $175.00. *Courtesy of The Museum Doll Shop.*

15" bisque dolly face doll, marked "Germany." $425.00.
Courtesy of The Museum Doll Shop.

York City. They made and distributed dolls, also distributed dolls made for them by other companies such as Hertel Schwab & Co. and Armand Marseille. They made composition as well as bisque dolls and specialized in babies and Red Cross nurses before World War I. May be marked "L.W. & C."

Baby, open or closed mouth, sleep eyes

12"	$400.00 – 475.00

Sunshine Baby, solid dome, cloth body, glass eyes, closed mouth

15"	$1,000.00

Too few in database for a reliable range.

Child

Child, 1880 – 1890, closed mouth, wigged, glass eyes, kid or cloth body

17"	$600.00 – 625.00
23"	$850.00 – 875.00

Mold 50, shoulder head

14"	$800.00 – 825.00
22"	$1,200.00 – 1,275.00

Mold 120, 126, 132, Bru-look

13"	$2,500.00 – 2,600.00
19" – 21"	$3,800.00 – 4,000.00

Mold 51, swivel neck shoulder head

17"	$1,200.00 – 1,300.00

German-look doll, composition body

11" – 13"	$1,200.00 – 1,300.00
16" – 18"	$1,600.00 – 1,800.00

Mold 136, French-look

12" – 14"	$1,900.00 – 2,000.00
19" – 20"	$1,600.00 – 1,700.00

E.G., maker Ernst Grossman

16"	$2,500.00 – 2,600.00

Child, 1880 on, dolly face bisque head, wigged, glass eyes open mouth, ball-jointed composition body or kid body with bisque lower arms, marks: "G.B.," "K" inside "H," "L.H.K.," "P.Sch," "D.& K.," or unmarked

10" – 12"	$350.00 – 400.00
15"	$425.00 – 450.00
18" – 20"	$500.00 – 550.00
23" – 25"	$625.00 – 725.00

Mold 50, 51, square teeth

14" – 16"	$1,000.00 – 1,100.00

Mold 422, 444, 457, 478

17"	$600.00 – 650.00
23"	$800.00 – 825.00

9" baby, mold 210, probable maker Theodor Wendt. $225.00. *Courtesy of The Museum Doll Shop.*

18½" K&K Mama doll, c. 1924. $375.00. *Courtesy of The Museum Doll Shop.*

Princess, My Girlie, My Dearie, Pansy, Viola, G.&S., MOA, A.W.

13"	$350.00 – 375.00
18" – 20"	$275.00 – 325.00
22" – 24"	$350.00 – 400.00
26" – 28"	$425.00 – 475.00
32"	$550.00 – 600.00

Shoulder-head Child, 1880 on, molded hair American Schoolboy-type

12" – 14"	$475.00 – 550.00
18" – 20"	$650.00 – 750.00

Small Child, 1890 to mid 1910s, bisque socket head, open mouth, set or sleep eyes, five piece composition body

High quality bisque

5"	$325.00 – 350.00
8"	$375.00 – 400.00

Fully jointed body

7" – 8"	$600.00 – 650.00

Closed mouth

4" – 5"	$475.00 – 500.00
8"	$750.00 – 800.00

Character, 1910 on, glass eyes, open or open/closed mouth, solid dome or wigged, composition body

Mold 111

18" – 22"	$20,000.00 – 22,000.00

Too few in database for a reliable range.

Mold 125, smiling

13"	$6,000.00 – 6,500.00

Mold 159

23"	$1,100.00 – 1,200.00

Mold 163, painted eye, closed mouth

13" – 15"	$500.00 – 600.00

Mold 213, 214, maker Bawo & Dotter

13" – 14"	$4,900.00 – 5,200.00

Mold 221, toddler

16"	$2,500.00 – 2,600.00

Mold 411, shoulder-head lady

14"	$3,500.00

Too few in database for a reliable range.

Mold 838, P.M. Coquette

11"	$550.00 – 575.00

K&K Mama Doll, 1924, bisque shoulder head, American-made cloth Mama style body with composition limbs, glass eyes, made for George Borgfeldt

15" – 19"	$275.00 – 375.00

17" painted bisque toddler incised "KW" for Kohl & Wengeroth, c.1920s. $800.00. *Courtesy of Skinner In, Boston & Bolton, Massachusetts.*

Japanese, 1915 on, bisque head dolls often in imitation of the German bisque dolls. Distributed in the United States by companies such as Morimura Brothers, Yamato Importing Co., and others. Marks: 1915 to 1921 marked "Nippon," after 1921 marked "Japan."

Character Baby, bisque socket head, solid dome or wigged, open mouth with teeth, bent limb composition body

9"	$130.00 – 155.00
13"	$175.00 – 225.00
19"	$275.00 – 300.00
24"	$350.00 – 450.00

Hilda look-alike

19"	$900.00

Heubach pouty look-alike, 300 series

17"	$800.00 – 900.00

Child, bisque head, mohair wig, glass sleep eyes, open mouth, composition or kid body

14"	$200.00 – 225.00
16"	$250.00 – 275.00
26"	$450.00 – 475.00

8" pair of bisque headed dolls made by Morimura Brothers. $125.00. each. *Courtesy of The Museum Doll Shop.*

BLACK OR BROWN DOLLS

These dolls were homemade and made by various European and American manufacturers in shades ranging from black to tan. Sometimes a Caucasian mold was used in dark color, other times an ethnic sculpted mold was used. Prices are for dolls in good condition, appropriately dressed.

Wooden, eighteenth century English, carved

15"	$5,000.00*

All-bisque

Glass eyes, wigged

4" – 5"	$450.00 – 575.00

Hertwig, character

2½"	$85.00 – 100.00

Gerbruder Kunlenz

3½" – 5"	$500.00 – 600.00

Kestner, swivel neck

6"	$1,800.00 – 1,900.00

Simon & Halbig, 886

5" – 7"	$700.00 – 1,200.00

Bisque, 1880 on, French and German

7" bisque headed baby, marked "Nippon." $100.00. *Courtesy of The Museum Doll Shop.*

makers, bisque socket head, painted black or black color in slip, brown composition or kid body

French

Poupée (Fashion-type), kid body

   Unmarked

   14" – 15" $3,000.00 – 3,400.00

   FG

   14" $3,400.00 – 3,600.00

   Bru

   14" $19,000.00*

   17" $9,500.00 – 10,000.00

   Jumeau

   15" $8,500.00 – 9,000.00

Bébé

   B.M., closed mouth

   15" portrait $24,000.00*

   Bru

   Circle Dot

   17" – 19" $30,000.00 – 50,000.00

   Bru Jne

   23" $33,000.00 – 35,000.00

   Danel et Cie

   19" $6,250.00*

10" Tété Jumeau. $2,000.00. *Courtesy of The Museum Doll Shop.*

   E.D., open mouth

   16" $2,200.00 – 2,300.00

   22" $2,500.00 – 2,600.00

   Eden Bebe, open mouth

   15" $2,300.00 – 2,500.00

   Jumeau

   E.J., closed mouth

   15" – 17" $8,200.00 – 9,300.00

   Tété, open mouth

   10" $1,800.00 – 2,100.00

   15" $2,500.00 – 2,700.00

   20" $3,200.00 – 3,300.00

   Tété, closed mouth

   15" $4,500.00 – 4,700.00

   18" $4,900.00 – 5,100.00

   23" $5,900.00 – 6,100.00

   DEP, open mouth

   16" $2,400.00 – 2,600.00

   Lanternier

   18" – 20" $1,000.00 – 1,300.00

   Mothereau

   15" – 16" $16,500.00 – 18,000.00

   Paris Bebe, closed mouth

   13" $3,900.00 – 4,300.00

   16" $4,500.00 – 4,600.00

   19" $5,300.00 – 5,500.00

13" Indian doll with bisque head, made in Germany. $250.00. *Courtesy of The Museum Doll Shop.*

S.F.B.J.
Molds 226, 235
15" – 17"	$2,600.00 – 3,000.00
Mold 237	$16,500.00*

Molds 301, 60 (Unis France mark also), jointed composition body, open mouth
10" – 14"	$450.00 – 550.00
17"	$700.00 – 800.00

Steiner
Figure A series, closed mouth
10" – 11"	$3,300.00 – 4,000.00
18"	$5,500.00 – 5,900.00
22"	$6,300.00 – 6,500.00

Open mouth
13"	$4,100.00 – 4,300.00
16"	$4,500.00 – 4,800.00

Series C
18"	$5,800.00 – 6,000.00
21"	$6,000.00 – 6,200.00

German
Unmarked
Closed mouth
10" – 11"	$300.00 – 350.00
14"	$400.00 – 450.00
17"	$525.00 – 575.00
21"	$800.00 – 850.00

Open mouth
10"	$500.00 – 550.00
13"	$650.00 – 700.00
15"	$850.00 – 900.00

Painted bisque
Closed mouth
16"	$350.00 – 400.00
19"	$500.00 – 550.00

Open mouth
14"	$300.00 – 350.00
18"	$500.00 – 550.00

Ethnic features
15"	$3,000.00 – 3,200.00
18"	$3,800.00 – 4,000.00

Bähr & Pröschild, open mouth, mold 277, ca. 1891

10"	$750.00 – 800.00
12"	$1,050.00 – 1,150.00

Mold 244, Indian or native
14" – 16"	$2,100.00 – 2,300.00

Bye-Lo Baby
16"	$2,700.00 – 3,000.00

Handwerck, Heinrich, mold 79, 119
Open mouth
12"	$800.00 – 900.00
18" – 21"	$1,600.00 – 1,900.00
29"	$2,500.00 – 2,600.00

Heubach, Ernst (Koppelsdorf)
Mold 271, 1914, shoulder head, painted eyes, closed mouth
10"	$425.00 – 475.00

Mold 320, 339, 350
10"	$375.00 – 425.00
13"	$500.00 – 525.00
18"	$650.00 – 700.00

Mold 399, allow more for toddler
10" – 14"	$475.00 – 575.00
17"	$650.00 – 700.00

11½" Kestner 134. $600.00. *Courtesy of Alderfer Auction Co.*

20" poupée by Francois Gaultier. $11,000.00.
Courtesy of The Museum Doll Shop.

Mold 414

9"	$340.00 – 450.00
14"	$1,100.00*
17"	$715.00 – 950.00

Mold 418, grin

9"	$675.00 – 725.00
14"	$850.00 – 900.00

Mold 444, 451

9"	$250.00 – 300.00
14"	$550.00 – 600.00

Mold 452, brown

7½"	$425.00 – 500.00
10"	$550.00 – 625.00
15"	$675.00 – 725.00

Mold 458

10"	$465.00 – 495.00
15"	$700.00 – 775.00

Mold 463

12"	$650.00 – 750.00
16"	$950.00 – 1,050.00

Mold 1900

14"	$500.00 – 600.00
17"	$675.00 – 775.00

Heubach, Gebruder, Sunburst mark

Boy, eyes to side, open-closed mouth

12"	$2,300.00 – 2,500.00

Mold 7657, 7658, 7668, 7671

9"	$975.00 – 1,200.00
13"	$1,400.00 – 1,700.00

Mold 7661, 7686

10"	$900.00 – 1,100.00
14"	$2,300.00 – 2,500.00
17"	$3,000.00 – 3,500.00

Mold 8457, 9467, Indians

14"	$2,400.00 – 2,500.00

Kämmer & Reinhardt (K * R)

Child, no mold number

14" – 16"	$1,500.00 – 1,600.00
17" – 19"	$1,800.00 – 2,000.00

Mold 100

10" – 11"	$750.00 – 850.00
17" – 20"	$1,600.00 – 1,900.00

Mold 101, painted eyes

15" – 18"	$3,300.00 – 3,500.00

8½" black bisque doll by Ernst Heubach, all original. $425.00. *Courtesy of The Museum Doll Shop.*

Mold 101, glass eyes
15" – 17" $4,300.00 – 4,800.00
Mold 114
13" $5,000.00 – 5,500.00
Mold 116, 116a
15" $4,000.00 – 4,500.00
19" $5,900.00 – 6,200.00
Mold 122, 126, baby body
12" $700.00 – 750.00
18" $1,000.00 – 1,125.00
Mold 126, toddler
18" $1,400.00 – 1,600.00

Kestner, J. D.
    Baby, no mold number, open mouth, teeth
    10" $1,500.00
Too few in database for a reliable range.
    Hilda, mold 245
    12" – 14" $2,800.00 – 3,100.00
    18" $4,000.00 – 4,500.00
    Child, no mold number
    Closed mouth
    14" $800.00 – 1,000.00
    17" $1,500.00 – 1,700.00
    Open mouth
    12" $500.00 – 575.00
    16" $650.00 – 750.00
    Five-piece body
    9" $285.00 – 300.00
    12" $350.00 – 400.00

Koenig & Wernicke (KW/G)
    14" $900.00
Too few in database for a reliable range.
    18" $750.00 – 800.00
Too few in database for a reliable range.
    Ethnic features
    17" $1,000.00 – 1,100.00

Kuhnlenz, Gebruder
    Closed mouth
    15" $675.00 – 900.00
    18" $1,350.00 – 1,800.00
    Open mouth, mold 34.14, 34.16, 34.24, etc.
    7" – 9" $900.00 – 1,100.00

12" $1,300.00 – 1,400.00
Ethnic features
16" $3,800.00 – 4,000.00

Marseille, Armand
    No mold number, ebony
    11" $850.00
Too few in database for a reliable range.
    Mold 341, 351, 352, 362
    8" – 10" $550.00 – 650.00
    14" – 16" $725.00 – 825.00
    20" $1,100.00 – 1,200.00
    Mold 390, 390n
    16" $550.00 – 600.00
    19" $775.00 – 825.00
    23" $895.00 – 920.00
    28" $1,100.00 – 1,200.00
    Mold 966, 970, 971, 992, 995, some in composition
    9" $265.00 – 290.00
    14" $550.00 – 600.00
    18" $875.00 – 900.00

12" black bisque, marked "SFBJ 60." $500.00.
Courtesy of The Museum Doll Shop.

Mold 1894, 1897, 1902, 1912, 1914

12"	$525.00 – 575.00
14"	$750.00 – 800.00
18"	$850.00 – 900.00

Recknagel, marked "R.A.," mold 126, 138

16"	$800.00 – 950.00
22"	$1,275.00 – 1,430.00

Schoenau Hoffmeister (S PB H)

Hanna

7" – 8"	$400.00 – 450.00
10" – 12"	$550.00 – 600.00
15"	$700.00 – 750.00
18"	$850.00 – 900.00

Mold 1909

16"	$575.00 – 625.00
19"	$750.00 – 850.00

Simon & Halbig

Mold 639

14"	$6,400.00 – 6,800.00
18"	$9,000.00 – 10,000.00

Mold 739, open mouth

16"	$1,500.00 – 1,800.00
22"	$2,800.00 – 3,000.00

Closed mouth

13"	$1,500.00
17"	$2,400.00 – 2,600.00

Too few in database for reliable range.

5" black papier-mâché doll. $500.00. *Courtesy of George and Cynthia Orgeron.*

9" Golliwog made by Kathi Clarke. $125.00. *Courtesy of The Museum Doll Shop.*

Mold 939, closed mouth

18"	$3,000.00 – 3,300.00
21"	$4,300.00 – 4,500.00

Open mouth

13"	$2,300.00 original outfit

Too few in database for reliable range.

Mold 949, closed mouth

18"	$3,200.00 – 3,400.00
21"	$3,750.00 – 3,950.00

Open mouth

15"	$2,600.00 – 2,800.00

Mold 1009, 1039, 1079, open mouth

11" – 12"	$1,250.00 – 1,400.00
15" – 16"	$1,600.00 – 1,700.00
18"	$2,300.00 – 2,500.00

Pull-string sleep eyes

19"	$2,200.00 – 2,300.00

Mold 1248, open mouth

15"	$1,400.00 – 1,500.00
18"	$1,600.00 – 1,800.00

Mold 1272

20"	$1,800.00 – 2,000.00

Mold 1302, closed mouth, glass eyes, character face

18"	$9,000.00 – 10,000.00

Indian, sad expression, brown face
18"	$7,000.00 – 7,400.00

Mold 1303, Indian, thin face, man or woman
15" – 16"	$6,000.00 – 6,500.00
21"	$7,800.00 – 8,000.00

Mold 1339, 1368
16"	$5,700.00 – 5,900.00

Mold 1358
20" – 22"	$9,500.00 – 10,000.00

China

Frozen Charlie/Charlotte
3"	$100.00 – 135.00
6"	$225.00 – 250.00
8" – 9"	$300.00 – 350.00

Jointed at shoulder
3"	$150.00 – 200.00
6"	$300.00 – 350.00

Celluloid

All-celluloid
10"	$150.00 – 200.00
15"	$275.00 – 350.00
18"	$500.00 – 600.00

Celluloid shoulder head, kid body, add more for glass eyes
17"	$275.00 – 350.00
21"	$375.00 – 450.00

French-type, marked "SNF"
14"	$300.00 – 350.00
18"	$550.00 – 600.00

Kammer & Reinhardt, mold 775, 778
11"	$175.00 – 200.00
18"	$425.00 – 475.00

Cloth

Alabama Baby: See Alabama Baby section.
Babyland Rag Doll: See Babyland Rag Doll section.
Bruckner: See Bruckner section.

1930s Mammy-type
14"	$400.00 – 500.00
18"	$500.00 – 600.00

Chase: See Chase section.

20" black stockinette one-of-a-kind rag doll, late nineteenth – early twentieth century. $900.00. *Courtesy of Skinner Inc., Boston and Bolton, Massachusetts.*

Golliwog, 1895 to present, character from 1895 book *The Adventures of Two Dutch Dolls and a Golliwogg,* all-cloth, various English makers. See also Deans Rag.

1895 – 1920
13"	$750.00 – 800.00

1930 – 1950
11"	$300.00 – 375.00
15"	$400.00 – 475.00

1950 – 1970s
13" – 18"	$250.00 – 325.00

Stockinette Baby (often misidentified as Black Beecher), embroidered features, glass eyes
20" – 22"	$3,300.00 – 4,000.00

Composition, doll in good condition with original clothing

Effanbee

Baby Grumpy
16"	$525.00 – 600.00

Bubbles
17" – 22"	$650.00 – 750.00

Candy Kid, original shorts, robe, and gloves
12"	$300.00 – 350.00

Skippy, with original outfit
14"	$900.00

Too few in database for reliable range.

13½" Mindy, vinyl head on stuffed vinyl body. $250.00. *Courtesy of The Museum Doll Shop.*

Horsman
12"	$225.00 – 250.00

Ideal

Marama, Shirley Temple body, from the movie, *Hurricane*
13"	$900.00 – 1,000.00

Koenig & Wernicke, mold 134
14"	$450.00 – 500.00

One-of-a-Kind, homemade cloth, allow more for exceptionally well made or artful examples

1900 – 1920
15" – 18"	$250.00 – 500.00

1920 – 1940
15" – 18"	$175.00 – 250.00

Patsy-type
13" – 14"	$275.00 – 325.00

Tony Sarg Mammy with baby
18"	$900.00 – 1,100.00

Topsy-type, cotton pigtails
10" – 12"	$150.00 – 175.00

Rubber

Amosandra, from Amos & Andy radio show
10"	$100.00 – 125.00

Hard Plastic

Terri Lee

Benji, painted plastic, brown, 1946 – 1962, black lamb's wool wig
16"	$1,800.00 – 2,000.00

Patty Jo, 1947 – 1949
16"	$1,200.00 – 1,500.00

Bonnie Lou, black
16"	$1,200.00 – 1,800.00

Vinyl

FloJo, Florence Griffith Joyner, made by LJN
11½"	$15.00 – 20.00

Gotz

World of Children Series
23"	$150.00 – 180.00

Mindy, 1957, Earl Pullan Co., Canada, vinyl head with molded braids, stuffed vinyl body
15"	$200.00 – 250.00

Sara Lee, Ideal, 1950, vinyl head and limbs, cloth body, sleep eyes
17"	$325.00 – 375.00

BLEUETTE

1905 – 1960, France. This premium doll was first made in bisque and later in composition for a weekly children's periodical, *La Semanine de Suzette* (The Week of Suzette), that also produced patterns for Bleuette. Premiere Bleuette was a bisque socket head, Tété Jumeau, marked only with a "1" superimposed on a "2." She had set blue or brown glass eyes, open mouth with four teeth, wig, and pierced ears.

The composition jointed body was marked "2" on back and "1" on the sole of each foot. This mold was made only in 1905. S.F.B.J., a bisque socket head, began production in 1905, using a Fleischmann and Bloedel mold marked "6/0," with blue or brown glass eyes, wig, open mouth, and teeth. S.F.B.J. mold marked "SFBJ 60" or "SFBJ 301 1" was a bisque socket head, with an open mouth with teeth, wig, and blue or brown glass eyes. All Bleuettes were 10⅝" tall prior to 1933, after that all Bleuettes were 11⅜".

Bisque

Premiere, 1905

    10⅝" $3,800.00 – 4,000.00

SFJB 6/0, 1905 – 1915, head made in Germany

    10⅝" $2,000.00 – 2,200.00

SFBJ 60, 301, and 71 Unis/France 149//301, 1916 – 1933

    10⅝" $1,900.00 – 2,100.00

    11⅜" $2,000.00 – 2,200.00

Composition, 1930 – 1933

SFBJ or 71 Unis France 149 251

    10⅝" $2,000.00 – 2,200.00

SFBJ or 71 Unis France 149 251, 1933+

    11⅜" $1,500.00 – 1,900.00

BONNET HEAD

1860s – 1940s on, dolls made of a variety of materials by numerous manufacturers, all with molded bonnets or hats.

All bisque German immobiles, painted eyes

    5" $175.00 – 200.00

    7" – 8" $275.00 – 325.00

    10" $350.00 – 375.00

15" mid nineteenth century papier-mâché with molded bonnet. $3,525.00. *Courtesy of Skinner Inc., Boston and Bolton, Massachusetts.*

Bisque, socket or shoulder head, five-piece composition body, kid body, or cloth body

Painted eyes

    7" – 8" $125.00 – 200.00

    11" – 12" $300.00 – 375.00

    18" – 20" $500.00 – 600.00

Glass eyes

    7" – 9" $225.00 – 350.00

    12" – 15" $500.00 – 750.00

Alt, Beck & Gottschalk

Painted eyes

    18" $2,907.00*

Glass eyes

    18" $1,530.00

Too few in database for a reliable range.

China, blonde or black hair, painted eyes

    10" – 13" $120.00 – 160.00

Mid-nineteenth century, fine quality, molded painted bonnet

    11½" $8,225.00*

Handwerck, Max, WWI military figure, painted eyes, mark: "Elite"

Bisque socket head, glass eyes, molded helmet

    10" – 14" $1,700.00 – 1,800.00

Molded Military helmet, painted eyes

12"	$1,500.00*

Heubach, Gebruder

Mold 7975, "Baby Stuart," ca. 1912, glass eyes, removable molded bisque bonnet

13"	$1,900.00 – 2,100.00

Mold 7877, 7977, "Baby Stuart," ca. 1912, molded bonnet, closed mouth, painted eyes

8" – 9"	$775.00 – 825.00
11" – 13"	$1,200.00 – 1,300.00
15"	$1,400.00 – 1,500.00

Hertwig, molded bonnet, jointed shoulders

2½" – 4"	$75.00 – 100.00
18"	$425.00 – 475.00

Japan

8" – 9"	$85.00 – 95.00
12"	$125.00 – 145.00

Molded shirt or top

15"	$750.00 – 850.00
21"	$1,200.00 – 1,305.00

Recknagel, baby, painted eyes, open-closed mouth, teeth, molds 22, 28, 44,

11½" mid-nineteenth century china with molded bonnet. $8,225.00. *Courtesy of Skinner Inc., Boston and Bolton, Massachusetts.*

molded white boy's cap, bent-leg baby body

8" – 9"	$450.00 – 500.00
11" – 12"	$650.00 – 700.00

Stone bisque

8" – 9"	$150.00 – 175.00
12" – 15"	$250.00 – 350.00

Papier-mâché, mid-nineteenth century, painted eyes, molded painted bonnet

15"	$3,525.00*

Wax-over composition, cloth body with composition or wood lower limbs, glass eyes

13"	$400.00 – 500.00

7½" all-bisque with molded hat, c. 1870s. $300.00. *Courtesy of Skinner Inc., Boston and Bolton, Massachusetts.*

BUCHERER

1921 – 1930s, Armisil, Switzerland. Metal bodies with metal ball joints, composition head, hands, and feet, mark: "MADE IN SWITZERLAND PATENTS APPLIED FOR"

6½" – 7"	$200.00 – 225.00
Black man	$700.00*

Regional and characters such as baseball

player, fireman, military, Pinocchio
$300.00 – 350.00
Comic characters such as Becassine, Charlie Chaplin, Happy Hooligan, Katzenjammers, Maggie & Jiggs, Mutt & Jeff $400.00 – 450.00

BOUDOIR DOLLS

1915 – 1940s, made in France, Italy, and the United States. Long limbed dolls of a variety of materials, used primarily as decorative items, fancy costumes, usually 28" – 30".
Cloth mask face, 1920s
High quality with silk floss hair
$350.00 – 450.00
Average quality $200.00 – 250.00
Composition head, 1920 – 1940s
Smoker $250.00 – 300.00
High quality $150.00 – 200.00
Average quality $125.00 – 150.00
Hard plastic, 1940s $75.00 – 120.00

Composition boudoir smoker, Rudolph Valentino as "The Sheik." $350.00.
Courtesy of The Museum Doll Shop.

BRU

1866 – 1899, Bru Jne. & Cie, Paris and Montreuil-sous-Bois, France. Beautifully made pressed bisque headed dolls, metal spring in neck to attach head to shoulder plate. Bru eventually became one of the members of the S.F.B.J. syndicate (1899 – 1953). Bébés Bru with kid bodies are one of the most collectible dolls, highly sought after because of the fine quality of bisque, delicate coloring, and fine workmanship. Add more for original clothes and rare body styles.
Poupée (Fashion-type lady), 1866 – 1877, pressed bisque socket head attached to bisque shoulder plate with metal spring stringing, painted or glass eyes, pierced ears, cork pate, mohair wig, kid body,

American boudoir doll with cloth mask face, probable maker Blossom Doll Co. $400.00. *Courtesy of The Museum Doll Shop.*

15" Bru Smiler poupée on a kid body with bisque lower arms. $4,800.00. *Courtesy Richard W. Withington, Inc., Nashua, New Hampshire.*

mark: numbers only, some marked "B. Jne et Cie" on shoulder plate

12" – 13"	$3,900.00 – 4,200.00
15" – 17"	$3,200.00 – 3,500.00
20" – 21"	$4,200.00 – 4,800.00

Wooden lower arms

16" – 17"	$5,700.00 – 6,000.00

Wooden body

15" – 16"	$5,900.00 – 6,500.00

Smiler, 1873 on, closed smiling mouth, mark: size letters A through O

Kid body with kid or bisque lower arms

11"	$3,600.00 – 3,700.00
13" – 15"	$3,900.00 – 4,800.00
20" – 21"	$5,500.00 – 6,000.00

Wooden lower arms

16" – 19"	$4,500.00 – 5,000.00

Wooden body

15" – 16"	$6,100.00 – 6,500.00
18" – 21"	$8,500.00 – 9,000.00

Surprise Doll, poupée with two faces

13"	$1,100.00 – 14,000.00

Bru Breveté, 1879 – 1880, pressed bisque socket head on bisque shoulder plate, paperweight eyes, multi-stroked eyebrows, closed mouth with space between the lips, full cheeks, pierced ears, cork pate, skin wig, kid or wood articulated body, mark: size number only on head

11"	$15,000.00 – 17,000.00
14" – 16"	$15,000.00 – 17,000.00
19" – 22"	$22,000.00 – 26,000.00

Circle Dot or Crescent Mark Bru, 1879 – 1884, pressed bisque socket head on bisque shoulder plate, paperweight eyes, multi-stroked eyebrows, open/closed mouth with molded, painted teeth, full cheeks, pierced ears, cork pate, mohair or human hair wig, gusseted kid body with bisque lower arms

11"	$12,000.00 – 13,000.00
13" – 14"	$15,000.00 – 17,000.00
18" – 19"	$20,000.00 – 23,000.00
24"	$27,000.00 – 29,000.00
31"	$32,000.00 – 35,000.00

Bru Jne, 1880 – 1891, pressed bisque socket head on bisque shoulder plate with deeply molded shoulders, paperweight eyes, multi-stroked eyebrows, open/closed mouth with molded, painted teeth, pierced ears, cork pate, mohair or human

19" Bru Breveté with painted teeth. $22,000.00. *Courtesy of Skinner Inc., Boston and Bolton, Massachussetts.*

16" Circle Dot Bru. $18,500.00.
Courtesy of The Museum Doll Shop.

hair wig, gusseted kid body with wood upper arms, bisque lower arms and kid or wood lower legs

10"	$21,000.00
12" – 14"	$17,000.00 – 19,000.00
15" – 17"	$22,000.00 – 25,000.00
23" – 24"	$28,000.00 – 30,000.00
26" – 28"	$30,000.00 – 33,000.00

Bru Jne R, 1891 – 1899, pressed bisque socket head on bisque shoulder plate with deeply molded shoulders, paperweight eyes, multi-stroked eyebrows, open/closed mouth with 4 to 6 teeth, pierced ears, cork pate, mohair or human hair wig, articulated wood and composition body

Open mouth

12"	$1,500.00 – 1,600.00
18" – 21"	$2,900.00 – 3,200.00

Closed mouth

10½"	$4,000.00 – 4,500.00
12" – 13"	$2,200.00 – 2,600.00
19" – 21"	$3,000.00 – 3,500.00
27" – 29"	$6,000.00 – 9,000.00

Mechanical Specialty Dolls

Teteur (nursing), 1879 –1898. Open mouth for insertion of bottle, screw key at back of head allowed doll to drink

13"	$8,500.00 – 9,000.00
15" – 17"	$6,000.00 – 7,800.00
19" – 24"	$8,500.00 – 9,000.00

Bébé Gourmand (eating), 1880 on, doll has open mouth with tongue, bisque lower legs, food pellets went in through mouth and out through holes on the bottom of the feet, special shoes with a flap opening on the bottom allowed for food removal

16" – 18"	$22,000.00 – 26,000.00

Bébé Modele, 1880 on, Breveté face, carved wood body.

18" – 19"	$21,000.00 – 26,000.00

Bébé Automate (breathing, talking), 1892 on, key or lever in torso activates mechanism to simulate chest movement

19"	$4,600.00 – 4,800.00
24"	$15,000.00 – 17,000.00

16" Bru Jne, swivel neck bébé. $23,500.00.
Courtesy Richard W. Withington, Inc., Nashua, New Hampshire.

Bébé Baiser (kiss throwing), 1892 on, pull string mechanism raises dolls arm and simulates throwing a kiss

11"	$4,100.00 – 4,200.00
15"	$4,300.00 – 4,400.00
Bru shoes	$700.00 – 900.00

24" Bru Jne R Bébé Baiser (kiss throwing), c. 1892. $4,800.00. *Courtesy of The Museum Doll Shop.*

ALBERT BRUCKNER

1901 – 1930 on, Albert Bruckner, Jersey City, New Jersey. Made some dolls for the Horsman Babyland line. These dolls had molded cloth mask faces, cloth bodies and printed features. Later they made flat faced cloth dolls.

Molded cloth mask faces

12" – 14"	$220.00 – 250.00
Black	$450.00 – 500.00
Topsy-Turvy	$550.00 – 600.00

Flat faced, printed, 1925 on, such as Dollypop, Pancakes Baby, others

12" – 13"	$250.00 – 275.00

One end of a Bruckner Topsy Turvy doll. $575.00. *Courtesy of The Museum Doll Shop.*

Molded mask face boy by Bruckner. $250.00. *Courtesy of Louise Stevens.*

Bruckner Dollypop, flat faced rag doll, c. 1920s.
$275.00. *Courtesy of The Museum Doll Shop.*

BUDDY LEE

1920 – 1962, United States. Made by the H.D. Lee Co., Inc., as an advertising doll to spotlight their overalls and work gear. Doll with molded hair, painted side-glancing eyes, jointed shoulders, legs molded apart, all original clothing, mark: embossed "Buddy Lee"
Composition, 1920–1948
13"　　　$475.00 – 575.00
Hard Plastic, 1949 – 1962
13"　　　$375.00 – 400.00

BURGARELLA

1925 to WWII, Rome, Italy. Made by Gaspare Burgarella, designed by Ferdinando Stracuzzi. Mark: cloth label sewn into outfit "BURGARELLA Made in Italy"

Child, high quality composition, expressively painted eyes with heavy shading, high quality human hair or mohair wig, jointed at neck, shoulders, hips, and knees
16" – 18"　　　$900.00 – 1,200.00
22"　　　$1,300.00 – 1,400.00

BYE-LO BABY

1922 – 1952. Baby doll designed by Grace Storey Putnam to represent a three-day old infant. Distributed by George Borgfeldt & Co. Bisque heads made by German makers such as Hertel & Schwab, Kestner, and Kling. Cloth bodies made by K & K in the United States. Composition bodies made by Koenig & Wernicke in Germany. Composition head made by Cameo Doll Co.

All Bisque, 1925 on, made by Kestner, some with pink or blue booties, mark: "G. S. Putnam" on back, paper sticker on chest reads "Bye-Lo Baby"
Painted eyes
4"　　　$350.00 – 400.00
6"　　　$500.00 – 550.00
8"　　　$700.00 – 750.00
Glass eyes, wigged
5"　　　$700.00 – 800.00
8"　　　$1,400.00 – 1,500.00
Swivel neck, glass eyes
5"　　　$650.00 – 700.00
8"　　　$1,250.00 – 1,350.00
Bisque head, flange neck head on cloth body with "frog" style legs or straight legs, closed mouth, molded painted hair, blue sleep eyes, celluloid or composition hands, mark: head incised, some bodies stamped "Bye-Lo Baby"

15" Bye-Lo baby, bisque head, original clothing. $450.00.
Courtesy of The Museum Doll Shop.

Head circumference

8"	$500.00 – 525.00
10" – 12"	$450.00 – 500.00
16"	$750.00 – 800.00
18"	$1,000.00 – 1,100.00

Socket-head on composition body

13"	$2,000.00 – 2,400.00

Composition head, 1924 on, molded painted hair, sleep or painted eyes, closed mouth, cloth body

Head circumference

12"	$400.00 – 475.00
16"	$550.00 – 600.00

Celluloid, made by Karl Standfuss, Saxony, Germany

All celluloid

4"	$175.00 – 225.00
6"	$250.00 – 300.00

Celluloid head on cloth body

Head circumference

12"	$325.00 – 350.00
15"	$450.00 – 475.00

Wax, 1925, sold in New York boutiques

15"	$900.00 – 1,00.00

Wood, 1925, made by Schoenhut

	$1,700.00 – 2,000.00

Vinyl, cloth body, mark: "Grace Storey Putnam" on head

16"	$150.00 – 200.00

Other Putnam Dolls

Fly-Lo, 1926 –1930, bisque, ceramic, or composition head, glass or metal sleep eyes, molded painted hair, flange neck on cloth body, celluloid hands, satin wings in pink, green, or gold, mark: "Corp. by // Grace S. Putnam" on head

Bisque, less for ceramic

11"	$3,800.00 – 4,000.00
13"	$4,200.00 – 5,000.00

Composition

14"	$900.00 – 1,000.00

CABBAGE PATCH KIDS

1978 to present, initially designed by Xavier Roberts as an all-cloth needle-sculpted doll. Later licensing agreement led to vinyl headed dolls made by Coleco. Doll in perfect condition with original clothing and tags or paperwork.

1978 on, Babyland General Hospital, Cleveland, GA, cloth, needle sculpture

"A" blue edition

1978	$1,500.00 – 1,600.00

"B" red edition

1978	$1,200.00 – 1,300.00

"C" burgundy edition

1979	$900.00 – 1,000.00

"D" purple edition

1979	$800.00 – 900.00

"X" Christmas edition

1979	$1,200.00 – 1,300.00

"E" bronze edition

1980	$1,200.00 – 1,300.00

Preemie edition

1980	$650.00 – 750.00

Celebrity edition
| 1980 | $600.00 – 700.00 |

Christmas edition
| 1980 | $600.00 – 700.00 |

Grand edition
| 1980 | $750.00 – 800.00 |

New Ears edition
| 1981 | $125.00 – 150.00 |

Ears edition
| 1982 | $150.00 – 175.00 |

Green edition
| 1983 | $400.00 – 450.00 |

"KP" dark green edition
| 1983 | $550.00 – 600.00 |

"KPR" red edition
| 1983 | $550.00 – 600.00 |

"KPB" burgundy edition
| 1983 | $200.00 – 225.00 |

Oriental edition, pair
| 1983 | $260.00 – 285.00 |

Indian edition
| 1983 | $850.00 – $900.00 |

Hispanic edition
| 1983 | $750.00 – 800.00 |

"KPZ" edition
| 1983 – 1984 | $175.00 – 225.00 |

Champagne edition
| 1983 – 1984 | $900.00 – 950.00 |

"KPP" purple edition
| 1984 | $250.00 – 275.00 |

Sweetheart edition
| 1984 | $250.00 – 275.00 |

Bavarian edition
| 1984 | $250.00 – 275.00 |

World Class edition
| 1984 | $175.00 – 200.00 |

"KPF," "KPG," "KPH," "KPI," "KPJ" editions
| 1984 – 1985 | $100.00 - 200.00 |

Emerald edition
| 1985 | $200.00 – 250.00 |

Coleco Cabbage Patch Kids, 1983, have powder scent and black signature stamp

Cloth needle-sculpted Cabbage Patch boy Ohana, c. 1987. $500.00. pair *Courtesy of The Museum Doll Shop.*

Boys and girls	$75.00 – 95.00
Bald babies	$50.00 – 75.00
With freckles	$75.00 – 100.00
Black boys or girls	
With freckles	$150.00 – 175.00
Without freckles	$60.00 – 75.00
Red-Hair boys, fuzzy hair	
	$150.00 – 175.00
Tsukuda	$300.00

Too few in database for a reliable range.

1984 – 1985, green signature stamp in 1984, blue signature stamp in 1985. Most dolls are only worth retail price.

Single tooth, brunette with ponytail
$165.00 – 185.00

Popcorn hairdos, rare
$175.00 – 200.00

Gray-eyed girls $150.00 – 165.00

Freckled girl, gold hair
$75.00 – 95.00

Other

Baldies, popcorn curl with pacifier, red popcorn curls, single tooth, freckled girls, and gold braided hair are valued at retail to $65.00. Still easily obtainable for collectors are a host of other Cabbage Patch Kids, including ringmaster, clown, baseball player, astronaut, travelers, twins,

babies, Splash Kid, Cornsilk Kid, valued at
$30.00 – 50.00

1991 Convention Nurse Payne
$199.00

Too few in database for a reliable range.

Coleco Cabbage Patch Kid, c. 1987. $80.00. *Courtesy of The Museum Doll Shop.*

CAMEO DOLL CO.

1922 – 1930 on, New York City, Port Allegheny, Pennsylvania. Joseph L. Kallus's company made composition dolls, some with wood segmented bodies and cloth bodies. All in good condition with original clothing, allow less for crazed or undressed dolls.

Bisque

Baby Bo Kaye

Bisque head, made in Germany, molded hair, open mouth, glass eyes, cloth body, composition limbs, good condition, mark: "J.L. Kallus: Copr. Germany// 1394/30"

17" – 20" $2,500.00 – 2,800.00

All-bisque, molded hair, glass sleep eyes, open mouth, two teeth, swivel neck, jointed arms and legs, molded pink or blue shoes, socks, unmarked, some may retain original round sticker on body

5" – 6" $1,600.00 – 2,000.00

Celluloid

Baby Bo Kaye

Celluloid head, made in Germany, molded hair, open mouth, glass eyes, cloth body

12" – 16" $650.00 – 750.00

Composition

Annie Rooney, 1926, Jack Collins designer, all-composition, yarn wig, legs painted black, molded shoes

13" $475.00 – 500.00
17" $650.00 – 700.00

Baby Blossom, 1927, "DES, J.L.Kallus," composition upper torso, cloth lower body and legs, molded hair, open mouth

19" – 20" $550.00 – 650.00

Baby Bo Kaye

Composition head, molded hair, open

15" composition Scootles. $575.00. *Doll courtesy of Ruth Cayton.*

mouth, glass eyes, light crazing

14" $650.00 – 675.00

Bandy, 1929, composition head, wood segmented body, marked on hat "General Electric Radio," designed by J. Kallus

18½" $800.00 – 900.00

Betty Boop, 1932, composition head character, wood segmented body, molded hair, painted features, label on torso

11" $650.00 – 750.00

Champ, 1942, composition with freckles

16" $575.00 – 600.00

Giggles, 1946, "Giggles Doll, A Cameo Doll," composition, molded loop for ribbon

12" $375.00 – 425.00

14" $450.00 – 500.00

Ho-Ho, 1940, painted plaster, laughing mouth

5½" $175.00 – 200.00

Joy, 1932, composition head character, wood segmented body, molded hair, painted features, label on torso

10" $250.00 – 300.00

15" $375.00 – 425.00

Margie, 1929, composition head character, wood segmented body, molded hair, painted features, label on torso

10" $250.00 – 275.00

15" $425.00 – 475.00

17" $550.00 – 575.00

Pete the Pup, 1930 – 1935, composition head character, wood segmented body, molded hair, painted features, label on torso

9" $375.00 – 425.00

Pinkie, 1930 – 1935, composition head character, wood segmented body, molded hair, painted features, label on torso

10" $275.00 – 300.00

Popeye, 1935, composition head character, wood segmented body, molded

9" Margie, designed by Joseph Kallus. $250.00. *Doll courtesy of Ruth Cayton.*

hair, painted features, label on torso

14" $625.00 – 675.00

Pretty Bettsie, composition head, molded hair, painted side-glancing eyes, open/closed mouth, composition one-piece body and limbs, wooden neck joint, molded and painted dress with ruffles, shoes, and socks, triangular red tag on chest marked "Pretty Bettsie//Copyright J. Kallus"

18" $450.00 – 500.00

Scootles, 1925 on, Rose O'Neill design, all-composition, no marks, painted side-glancing eyes, paper wrist tag

7" – 8" $450.00 – 500.00

13" $425.00 – 475.00

15" $550.00 – 600.00

22" $1,100.00 – 1,200.00

Composition, sleep eyes

15" $700.00 – 800.00

Black composition

12" $650.00 – 750.00

Hard Plastic and Vinyl

Baby Mine, 1962 – 1964, vinyl and cloth, sleep eyes

16" $100.00 – 125.00

19" $150.00 – 200.00

Ho Ho, "Rose O'Neill," vinyl, laughing mouth, squeaker, tag

White, 7" $150.00 – 200.00
Black, 7" $225.00 – 275.00

Miss Peep, 1957 – 1970s, pin jointed shoulders and hips, vinyl

15"	$65.00 – 75.00
18"	$80.00 – 90.00

Black

18"	$110.00 – 125.00

Miss Peep, Newborn, 1962, vinyl head and rigid plastic body

14" – 18"	$30.00 – 40.00

Pinkie, 1950s

10" – 11"	$125.00 – 150.00

Scootles, 1964

14"	$175.00 – 195.00
20"	$350.00 – 375.00

1980s, Jesco

12"	$25.00 – 30.00
16"	$40.00 – 50.00

CATTERFELDER PUPPENFABRIK

1906 on, Catterfeld, Thuringia, Germany. Had heads made by Kestner. Trademark: "My Sunshine."

C.P. Child, 1902 on, dolly face, bisque socket head, glass sleep eyes, wigged, open mouth with teeth, ball-jointed composition body

Mold 264

14" – 16"	$600.00 – 700.00
25" – 28"	$900.00 – 1,000.00

C.P. Character child, 1910 on, bisque socket head, painted eyes, wigged, open mouth with teeth, ball-jointed composition body.

Mold: 207, 210, 215, 219, 217, others

15" – 16"	$8,500.00 – 9,000.00

18" Catterfelder Puppenfabrik baby, mold 201. $925.00. *Doll courtesy of Lucy DiTerlizzi.*

Mold 220, glass eyes

14"	$8,300.00 – 8,500.00

Character Baby, 1910 on, bisque socket head, molded hair or wig, painted or glass sleep eyes, composition baby body.

Mold: 200, 201, 207, 208, others

8" – 10"	$650.00 – 750.00
14" – 16"	$850.00 – 900.00
19" – 21"	$975.00 – 1,025.00

201, toddler

8" – 10"	$900.00 – 1,200.00

Mold 262, 263

15" – 17"	$50.00 – 500.00
20" – 22"	$650.00 – 700.00

262 toddler, five-piece composition body

18"	$800.00 – 825.00

CELLULOID

Early form of plastic made from nitrocellulose and a plasticizer such as camphor. Came into use in 1869 and an improved version became popular about 1905.

Made in numerous countries: England — Wilson Doll Co.,

Cascelliod Ltd. (Palitoy)

France — Petitcollin (profile of eagle head), Widow Chalory, Convert Cie, Parisienn Cellulosine, Neuman & Marx (dragon), Société Industrielle de Celluloid (SIC), Société Nobel Francaise (SNF in diamond), Sicoine

Germany — Bähr & Pröschild, Buschow & Beck (helmet Minerva), Catterfelder Puppenfibrik Co., Cuno & Otto Dressel, E. Maar & Sohn (3M), Emasco, Kämmer & Reinhardt, Kestner, Koenig & Wernicke, A. Hagendorn & Co., Hermsdorfer Celluloidwarenfabrik (lady bug), Dr. Paul Hunaeus, Kohn & Wengenroth, Rheinsche Gummi und Celluloid Fabrik Co. later known as Schildkröte (turtle mark), Max Rudolph, Bruno Schmidt, Franz Schmidt & Co., Schoberl & Becker (mermaid) who used Cellba as a tradename, Karl Standfuss, Albert Wacker

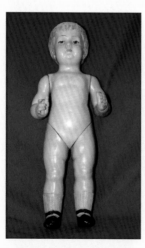

12½" all-celluloid doll bearing the "turtle" mark of Rheinische Gummi und Celluloid Fabrik Co. $135.00. *Doll courtesy of Ruth Cayton.*

USA — Averill, Bo-Peep (H.J. Brown), DuPont Viscaloid Co., Horsman, Irwin, Marks Bros., Parsons-Jackson (stork mark), Celluloid Novelty Co.

Baby, 1910 on, painted eyes, all celluloid

4" – 8"	$65.00 – 95.00
12" – 15"	$150.00 – 175.00
19" – 21"	$225.00 – 275.00

Marked France

16" – 18"	$250.00 – 300.00

Marked Japan

4" – 5"	$18.00 – 22.00
8" – 10"	$65.00 – 75.00
13" – 15"	$145.00 – 165.00

Occupied Japan

24"	$150.00 – 175.00

Child, painted eyes, jointed at shoulder and hips

5" – 7"	$50.00 – 75.00
11" – 14"	$125.00 – 150.00
18" – 20"	$190.00 – 220.00

Glass eyes

12" – 13"	$175.00 – 200.00
15" – 16"	$225.00 – 250.00

Marked France

7" – 9"	$150.00 – 175.00
15" – 18"	$300.00 – 350.00

Marked Japan

With molded clothing

3" – 4"	$50.00 – 60.00
8" – 9"	$125.00 – 150.00

Jointed shoulders only

3" – 4"	$18.00 – 22.00
8" – 10"	$30.00 – 40.00

Occupied Japan

6" – 8"	$90.00 – 100.00

In regional costume, tagged LeMinor, Poupée Magali, others

8"	$60.00 – 75.00
12" – 15"	$150.00 – 175.00
19"	$250.00 – 275.00

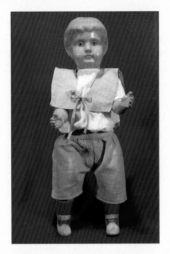

13½" all-celluloid boy with molded socks and shoes, marked KKK. $145.00. *Courtesy of The Museum Doll Shop.*

9" celluloid Kewpie-type Santa. $20.00. *Courtesy of The Museum Doll Shop.*

Carnival-type, may have feathers glued on head or body

    8" – 12" $35.00 – 45.00

Kewpie: See Kewpie listing.

Shoulder-head child, 1900 on, German, molded hair or wig, open or open/closed mouth, kid or cloth body, sometimes arms of other materials

Painted eyes

    16" – 18" $125.00 – 150.00

Glass eyes

    16" – 18" $200.00 – 225.00

Bye-Lo Baby: See Bye-Lo listing.

Socket head child, 1910 on, open mouth, glass sleep eyes, wig, composition body

Hermsdofer Celluloidwarenfabrik (lady bug mark), 1926

    17" $125.00 – 175.00

Heubach Köppelsdorf, mold 399

    11" $75.00 – 100.00

Jumeau

    13" $450.00 – 500.00

    16" $575.00 – 600.00

Kämmer & Reinhardt

Mold 700, character, painted eye, open/closed mouth

    14" – 15" $350.00 – 400.00

Mold 701, character, painted eye, closed mouth

    12" – 15" $900.00 – 1,200.00

12" celluloid dolly face shoulder-head doll. $100.00. *Doll courtesy of Ruth Cayton.*

18" celluloid Kestner 201 shoulder-head doll in original clothing. $425.00.
Doll courtesy of Ruth Cayton.

Mold 715, character, closed mouth
15" $650.00 – 700.00
Mold 717, character, closed mouth
15" – 17" $725.00 – 775.00
Kestner, mold 203 character baby
12" $425.00 – 450.00

7" Japanese celluloid crying baby. $65.00.
Courtesy of The Museum Doll Shop.

Koenig & Wernicke (K & W)
Toddler
15" – 19" $375.00 – 500.00
Max & Moritz
7" $300.00 – 350.00 each
Parsons-Jackson (stork mark)
Baby
12" $200.00 – 225.00
14" $250.00 – 275.00
Toddler
15" $375.00 – 400.00
Black
14" $475.00 – 500.00
Petitcolin
18" $375.00 – 400.00

7" celluloid baby, marked Made in USA. $75.00.
Courtesy of The Museum Doll Shop.

CENTURY DOLL CO.

1909 – 1930, New York City. Founded by Max Scheuer and sons; used bisque heads on many later dolls. In about 1929, Century merged with Domec to become the Doll Corporation of America. Some heads were made by Kestner, Herm Steiner, and other firms for Century.

Prices are for dolls in good condition, with original clothes or appropriately dressed. More for boxed, tagged, or labeled exceptional dolls.

Bisque

Baby, 1926, by Kestner, bisque head, molded and painted hair, sleep eyes, open-closed mouth, cloth body

13"	$575.00 – 625.00
16" – 18"	$650.00 – 750.00

Mold 275, solid dome, glass eyes, closed mouth, cloth body, composition limbs

14"	$900.00 – 950.00

Child

Molds 285, 287, by Kestner, bisque socket head, glass eyes, wig, ball-jointed body

14"	$625.00 – 675.00
19" – 24"	$600.00 – 650.00

Composition

Child, composition shoulder head, cloth body, composition arms and legs, molded hair, painted eyes

13" – 15"	$200.00 – 250.00

Century Baby, 1920s, composition flange head and hands, cloth baby body

13" – 15"	$125.00 – 175.00

18" Century baby, bisque head by Kestner. $750.00.
Courtesy of The Museum Doll Shop.

Chuckles, 1927 – 1929, composition shoulder head, arms, and legs, cloth body with crier, open mouth, molded short hair, painted or sleep eyes, two upper teeth, dimples in cheeks, came as a bent-leg baby or toddler

14" – 16"	$150.00 – 225.00
22"	$300.00 – 325.00

Mama Dolls, 1922 on, composition head, tin sleep eyes, cloth body, with crier, swing legs and arms of composition

16"	$225.00 – 250.00
23"	$350.00 – 375.00

Bisque shoulder head, mold 281

21"	$650.00 – 750.00

CHAD VALLEY

1917 – 1930s, Harbonne, England. Founded by Johnson Bros. in 1897, in 1917 began making all types of cloth dolls, early ones had stockinette faces, later felt, with velvet body, jointed neck, shoulders, hips, glass or painted eyes, mohair wig. Used designers such as Mabel Lucie Atwell and Norah Wellings.

Animals

Cat

12"	$215.00 – 230.00

Bonzo, cloth dog with painted eyes, almost closed mouth and smile

4"	$210.00 – 230.00
12"	$750.00 – 800.00

Bonzo, eyes open

5½"	$275.00 – 300.00
14"	$575.00 – 600.00

Dog, plush

12"	$260.00 – 280.00

Characters

Captain Blye, Fisherman, Long John Silver,

14" Chad Valley girl with glass eyes. $650.00.
Courtesy of The Museum Doll Shop.

Pirate, Policeman, Train Conductor, etc.
Glass eyes
10" – 12"	$225.00 – 250.00
18" – 20"	$1,200.00 – 1,800.00

Painted eyes
13" – 15"	$375.00 – 400.00
18" – 20"	$675.00 – 775.00

Ghandi/India
13"	$625.00 – 675.00

Rahmah-Jah
26"	$850.00 – 900.00

Child
Glass eyes
14"	$625.00 – 650.00
16"	$675.00 – 725.00
18"	$725.00 – 775.00

Painted eyes
9" – 10"	$175.00 – 200.00
12" – 15"	$375.00 – 425.00
18"	$575.00 – 625.00

Royal Family, all with glass eyes, 16" – 18"
Princess Alexandra
$1,400.00 – 1,500.00

Prince Edward, Duke of Windsor
$1,000.00 – 1,200.00
Princess Elizabeth
$1,400.00 – 1,600.00
Princess Margaret Rose
$1,000.00 – 1,200.00
Story Book Dolls
Dong Dell
14"	$400.00 – 475.00

My Elizabeth, My Friend
14"	$600.00 – 675.00

Snow White & Dwarfs
Dwarf, 6½"	$225.00 – 250.00
Set	$4,000.00 – 4,500.00

Red Riding Hood
14" – 19"	$450.00 – 600.00

Golliwog
14" – 16"	$100.00 – 125.00

22" Chad Valley Scotsman. $900.00. *Doll courtesy of Mimi Salzman.*

CHASE DOLL COMPANY

1889 to 1981, Pawtucket, Rhode Island. Founded by Martha Chase. Earlier dolls had heads of molded stockinette with heavily painted features including thick lashes, closed mouth, painted textured hair, jointed shoulder, elbows, knees, and hips; later dolls were jointed only at shoulders and hips. Later dolls had latex heads on vinyl coated bodies. All dolls listed are in good condition with original or appropriate clothing.

Baby or child, short hair with curls around face

13" – 16"	$650.00 – 700.00
17" – 20"	$700.00 – 775.00
24" – 26"	$850.00 – 900.00
30"	$1,000.00 – 1,300.00

Hospital-type, weighted doll with pierced nostrils and ear canals

20"	$500.00 – 550.00
29"	$450.00 – 550.00

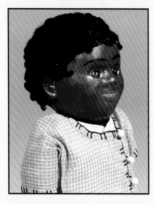

12¾" black Chase child. $16,450.00. *Courtesy of Skinner Inc., Boston and Bolton, Massachusetts.*

13" Chase child with basic hairstyle, original clothing. $650.00. *Courtesy of The Museum Doll Shop.*

Child
Molded bobbed hair

12" – 15"	$1,200.00 – 1,400.00
20" – 22"	$1,700.00 – 2,000.00

Side-parted painted hair

15" – 16"	$2,600.00 – 3,000.00

Characters, 1905 to 1920s, based on Alice in Wonderland, Dickens, Joel Chandler Harris books, and George Washington

Alice in Wonderland Characters

12"	$67,000.00 set of six

Dickens Characters, needle-sculpted hairstyles including buns, curls, etc., 15"

Lady	$1,100.00 – 1,500.00
Little Nell, braids	$1,400.00 – 1,600.00

George Washington

15"	$5,500.00 – 6,500.00

Black Child, ethnic features

13"	$16,450.00*

Mammy $6,000.00 – 6,500.00

Later Dolls, latex heads
Hospital Baby

14" – 15"	$200.00 – 250.00
19"	$300.00 – 400.00

Baby
12"	$175.00 – 225.00

Black
12"	$200.00 – 250.00

Child
15"	$250.00 – 275.00

Black
15"	$275.00 – 300.00

15" Chase lady. $1,400.00.
Courtesy of The Museum Doll Shop.

CHINA OR GLAZED PORCELAIN HEAD

1840 on. Most china shoulder head dolls were made in Germany by various firms. Prior to 1880, most china heads were pressed into the mold; later ones poured. Pre-1880, most china heads were sold separately with purchaser buying commercial body or making one at home. Original commercial costumes are rare; most clothing was homemade.

Early unusual features are glass eyes or eyes painted brown. After 1870, pierced ears and blond hair were found and, after 1880, more child china dolls, with shorter hair and shorter necks were popular. Most common in this period were flat tops and low brows and the latter were made until the mid-1900s. Later innovations were china arms and legs with molded boots. Most heads are unmarked or with size or mold number only, usually on the back shoulder plate.

Hair styles, color, complexion tint, and body help date the doll.

Dolls listed are in good condition with original or appropriate clothes. More for exceptional quality.

1840 Styles

China shoulder head with long neck, painted features, black or brown molded hair, may have exposed ears and pink complexion, with red-orange facial detail, may have bust modeling, cloth, leather, or wood body, nicely dressed, good condition

4" china doll on peg jointed wooden body. $250.00. *Courtesy of The Museum Doll Shop.*

18" pink china doll with covered wagon hairstyle. $950.00. *Courtesy of The Museum Doll Shop.*

Early marked china (Nuremberg, Rudolstadt)

14"	$2,275.00 – 2,400.00
17"	$2,835.00 – 3,000.00

Covered Wagon

Center part, combed back to form sausage curls, pink tint complexion

7" – 10"	$325.00 – 425.00
14" – 17"	$650.00 – 850.00
20" – 25"	$1,000.00 – 1,400.00
31"	$1,500.00 – 1,600.00

Pink complexion, bun or coronet

13" – 15"	$2,200.00 – 2,800.00
18" – 21"	$3,400.00 – 4,200.00

K.P.M. (Königliche Porzellanmanufaktur Berlin), 1840s – 1850s on, made china doll heads marked KPM inside shoulder plate

Pink tint lady

19"	$5,100.00 – 5,800.00

Brown haired man, marked

16" – 18"	$4,500.00 – 5,000.00
22" – 23"	$7,000.00 – 8,000.00

Brown haired lady with bun, marked

16" – 18"	$6,500.00 – 7,500.00

1850 Styles

China shoulder head, painted features, bald with black spot or molded black hair, may have pink complexion, cloth, leather, or wood body, china arms and legs, nicely dressed, good condition

Alice in Wonderland, snood, headband

12" – 14"	$675.00 – 775.00
16" – 18"	$875.00 – 975.00
20" – 22"	$1,150.00 – 1,300.00

Bald head, glazed china with black spot, human hair or mohair wig

12"	$750.00 – 800.00
14" – 16"	$1,100.00 – 1,300.00
21" – 24"	$1,700.00 – 2,000.00

Baderkinder (Frozen Charlies or Charlottes): See that section.

Greiner-type, painted black eyelashes, various hairdos

Painted eyes

14" – 15"	$1,100.00 – 1,300.00
18" – 22"	$1,800.00 – 2,100.00

Glass eyes

13" – 15"	$3,700.00 – 4,200.00
21" – 22"	$4,900.00 – 5,100.00

20" glass eyed china. $4,500.00. *Courtesy of The Museum Doll Shop.*

23" Merrie Marie by Art Fabric Mills.
$200.00. *Doll courtesy of the Morris Museum,
Morristown, New Jersey.*

14½" Peck Santa Claus patented in
1886. $275.00. *Doll courtesy of the Morris
Museum, Morristown, New Jersey.*

Improved Life Size Doll, with printed
underwear

16" – 18"	$125.00 – 150.00
20" – 24"	$175.00 – 225.00
30"	$300.00 – 325.00

Punch and Judy, pair

27"	$550.00 – 650.00

Brownies,1892 – 1907, produced by
Arnold Printworks. Printed cloth dolls
based on copyrighted figures of Palmer
Cox; 12 different figures, including
Canadian, Chinaman, Dude, German,
Highlander, Indian, Irishman, John Bull,
Policeman, Sailor, Soldier, and Uncle Sam

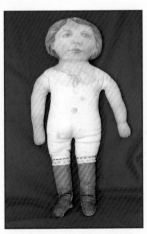

16" printed cloth doll made by the Art
Fabric Mills Co. $125.00. *Doll courtesy of
Ruth Cayton.*

Uncut sheet of printed cloth dolls made
by the Arnold Printworks. $400.00.
Courtesy of The Museum Doll Shop.

Single Doll

7½"	$75.00 – 100.00

Set of six, uncut

7½"	$250.00 – 300.00

Printed underwear, Dolly Dear, Flaked Rice, Merry Marie, etc.

7" – 9"	$85.00 – 95.00
16" – 18"	$125.00 – 150.00
20" – 24"	$175.00 – 225.00

Child with printed clothing, 1903

12" – 14"	$125.00 – 175.00
17" – 19"	$200.00 – 250.00

Cocheco Darkey

16"	$225.00 – 250.00

Foxy Grandpa

18"	$200.00 – 225.00
Our Soldier Boys	$125.00 – 150.00
Red Riding Hood	$150.00 – 175.00

Peck, 1886, Santa Claus/St. Nicholas

15"	$250.00 – 300.00

COLUMBIAN

1891 on, Oswego, New York. Emma E. Adams designed and made rag dolls, sold directly or through stores such as Marshall Field & Co. They won awards at the 1893 Chicago World Fair. She was succeeded by her sister, Marietta Adams Ruttan. Cloth dolls had hand-painted features, stitched fingers and toes.

14" – 15"	$5,000.00 – 5,800.00
19" – 23"	$6,200.00 – 7,200.00
28"	$9,000.00 – 11,000.00

COMPOSITION, UNKNOWN OR LITTLE KNOWN MAKER

Dolls listed are in good condition with original or appropriate dress. Allow more for exceptional dolls with elaborate costume or accessories.

American

Animal head doll, 1930s, all-composition on Patsy-type five-piece body, could be wolf, rabbit, cat, monkey

10"	$300.00 – 350.00

18" Columbian rag doll. $6,000.00. *Doll courtesy of the Morris Museum, Morristown, New Jersey.*

13" Jackie Robinson doll. $1,000.00. *Courtesy Otto & Ursula Mertz.*

Baby, 1910 on, wigged or molded hair, painted or sleep eyes, composition or cloth body with bent legs

12" – 14"	$175.00 – 225.00
18" – 20"	$250.00 – 300.00

Child, costumed in ethnic or theme outfit, all composition, sleep or painted eyes, mohair wig, closed mouth, original costume

Lesser quality

9" – 11"	$65.00 – 75.00

Better quality

9" – 11"	$125.00 – 145.00

Denny Dimwitt, Toycraft Inc, 1948, all-composition, nodder, painted clothing

11½"	$200.00 – 225.00

Early child, 1910 – 1920, all-composition, unmarked, painted features, may have molded hair

12"	$145.00 – 165.00
18" – 19"	$200.00 – 250.00

Character face, 1910 – 1920, unmarked, cork-stuffed cloth body, painted features, may have molded hair

12" – 15"	$150.00 – 200.00
18" – 20"	$250.00 – 300.00

13" American composition, unmarked, c, 1930s. $125.00. *Courtesy of The Museum Doll Shop.*

Jackie Robinson, complete in box

13"	$900.00 – 1,000.00

Kewty, 1930, made by Domec of Canada, all-composition, Patsy-type, molded bobbed hair, closed mouth, sleep eyes, bent left arm

13½"	$300.00 – 350.00

Lone Ranger, "TLR Co, Inc.//Doll Craft Novelty Co. NYC," cloth body, hat marked

20"	$800.00 – 900.00

Louis Vuitton, 1955, ceramic, composition, with labeled case and wardrobe

19"	$2,200.00

Too few in database for a reliable range.

Maiden America, "1915, Kate Silverman," all-composition, patriotic ribbon

8½"	$165.00 – 185.00

Mama doll, 1922 on, wigged or painted hair, sleep or painted eyes, cloth body, with crier and swing legs, lower composition legs and arms

16" – 18"	$225.00 – 250.00
20" – 22"	$325.00 – 350.00
24" – 26"	$400.00 – 450.00

Miss Curity, composition, eye shadow, nurse's uniform

18"	$475.00 – 500.00

Patsy-type girl, 1928 on, molded and painted bobbed hair, sleep or painted eyes, closed pouty mouth, composition or hard stuffed cloth body

9" – 10"	$125.00 – 150.00
14" – 16"	$225.00 – 275.00
19" – 20"	$275.00 – 300.00

With molded hair loop

12" – 15"	$150.00 – 200.00

Pinocchio, composition and wood character

16½"	$400.00 – 425.00

Puzzy, 1948, "H of P"

15"	$350.00 – 400.00

Quintuplets, 1934 on, all-composition, jointed five-piece baby or toddler body, molded hair or wig, with painted or sleep eyes, closed or open mouth

7" – 8"	$140.00 – 160.00
13"	$225.00 – 250.00

Refugee, Madame Louise Doll Co., 1945, represents victims of WWII

20"	$550.00 MIB

Santa Claus, composition molded head, composition body, original suit, sack

19"	$400.00 – 450.00

Shirley Temple-type girl, 1934 on, all-composition, five-piece jointed body, blond curly wig, sleep eyes, open mouth, teeth, dimples

16" – 19"	$400.00 – 450.00

Sizzy, 1948, "H of P"

14"	$250.00 – 300.00

Thumbs-Up, to raise money for ambulances during WWII, see photo first edition

8"	$150.00 – 175.00

Uncle Sam, various makers

All original, cloth body

13"	$900.00*

Ca. 1918, straw filled

30"	$450.00

Too few in database for a reliable range.

Whistler, composition head, cotton body, composition arms, open mouth

14½"	$200.00 – 225.00

German, composition head, composition or cloth body, wig or molded and painted hair, closed or open mouth with teeth, dressed, may be Amusco, Sonneberger Porzellanfabrik, or others.

Character Baby

Cloth body

18"	$275.00 – 325.00

Composition baby body, bent limbs

16"	$275.00 – 325.00

Child

Composition shoulder head, cloth body, composition arms

20"	$275.00 – 300.00

Socket head, all-composition body

12" – 14"	$175.00 – 200.00
19" – 21"	$325.00 – 350.00

Japanese

Quintuplets

7" – 9"	$175.00 – 250.00

COSMOPOLITAN DOLL & TOY CORP.

1950s on, Jackson Heights, New York. Dolls listed are in perfect condition with original clothing. Mint-in-box dolls can be double the values listed here, naked dolls bring ⅓ the values listed here.

Ginger, 1955 on, hard plastic, bent knees

7½"	$125.00 – 150.00

Vinyl Head

7½"	$100.00 – 125.00
Boxed Outfit	$50.00 – 60.00

Miss Ginger, 1957 on, vinyl, rooted hair, sleep eyes, teen doll, tagged clothes

10½"	$125.00 – 150.00

Cosmopolitan's Ginger, hard plastic. $125.00. *Courtesy of The Museum Doll Shop.*

Boxed Outfit $80.00 – 90.00
Little Miss Ginger, 1958 on, vinyl, rooted hair, sleep eyes, teen doll, tagged clothes
    8" $100.00 – 125.00

CRÈCHE

Figures of various materials made especially for religious scenes such as the Christmas manger scene. Usually not jointed, some with elaborate costumes. Some early created figures were gesso over wood head and limbs, fabric covered bodies with wire frames, later figures made of terracotta or other materials. Some with inset eyes.

Man, wood shoulder head, glass eyes, wire body
    8" $275.00 – 325.00
Too few in database for a reliable range.

Lady, carved shoulder head, glass eyes, wire body
    10½" $350.00 – 400.00
Too few in database for a reliable range.

Lady, gesso over wood, glass eyes, wire frame
    14½" $500.00 – 550.00
Too few in database for a reliable range.

Boy, gesso over wood, glass eyes
    7½" $550.00 – 600.00
Too few in database for a reliable range.

DEANS RAG BOOK CO.

1905 on, London. Subsidiary of Dean & Son, Ltd., a printing and publishing firm, used "A1" to signify quality, made Knockabout Toys, Tru-to-Life, Evripoze, and others. An early designer was Hilda Cowham.

Child
    10" $275.00 – 300.00
    16" – 17" $600.00 – 700.00
Printed cloth, cut and sew type
    9" – 10" $85.00 – 95.00
    15" – 16" $175.00 – 225.00
Mask face, velvet, with cloth body and limbs
    12" – 15" $125.00 – 175.00
    18" – 24" $275.00 – 350.00
    30" – 34" $475.00 – 550.00
    40" $625.00 – 700.00
Golliwogs
    11" – 13" $225.00 – 275.00
    15" $400.00 – 450.00

14" Dean's Tru-to-Life rag doll. $150.00.
Courtesy of Skinner Inc., Boston and Bolton, Massachusetts.

DELUXE READING

1955 – 1972, Elizabeth, New Jersey. Also used the names Deluxe Toy Creations, Deluxe Premium Corp., Deluxe Topper, Topper Toys, and Topper Corp. Dolls listed are complete, all original, in excellent-to-mint condition, hard plastic or vinyl.

Dawn. $30.00. *Courtesy of The Museum Doll Shop.*

Baby

Baby Boo, 1965, battery operated
    21" $100.00 – 150.00
Baby Catch A Ball, 1969 (Topper Toys), battery operated
    18" $128.00 MIB
Baby Magic, 1966, blue sleep eyes, rooted saran hair, magic wand has magnet that opens/closes eyes
    18" $125.00 – 175.00
Baby Peek 'N Play, 1969, battery operated
    18" $40.00 – 45.00
Baby Tickle Tears
    14" $30.00 – 35.00
Suzy Cute, move arm and face changes expressions
    7" $65.00 – 80.00

Child or Adult

Betty Bride, 1957, also called Sweet Rosemary, Sweet Judy, Sweet Amy, one-piece vinyl body and limbs, worth more if many accessories
    30" $75.00 – 85.00
Candy Fashion, 1958, made by Deluxe Premium, a division of Deluxe Reading, sold in grocery stores, came with three dress forms, extra outfits
    21" $125.00 – 175.00
Dawn Series, circa 1969 – 1970s, all-vinyl doll with additional friends, Angie, Daphne, Denise, Glori, Jessica, Kip, Long Locks, Majorette, Maureen, black versions of Van and Dale, accessories available, included Apartment, Fashion Show, outfits

Dawn and friends
    6" $25.00 – 35.00
Dawn & other outfits
    Loose, but complete $10.00+
    NRFP $35.00 – 45.00
  Fashion Show Stage in box
                   $65.00 – 75.00
Go Gos
Private Ida, 1965
    6" $40.00 – 45.00
Tom Boy, 1965
    6" $40.00 – 45.00
Little Miss Fussy, battery operated
    18" $25.00 – 35.00
Little Red Riding Hood, 1955, vinyl, synthetic hair, rubber body, book, basket
    23" $100.00 – 125.00
Penny Brite, 1963 on, all-vinyl, rooted blond hair, painted eyes, bendable and straight legs, extra outfits, case, furniture available, marks: "A - 9/B150 (or B65) DELUXE READING CORP.//c. 1963"
    8" $30.00 – 35.00

Outfit, NRFP $30.00 – 40.00
Kitchen set $50.00 – 60.00
Suzy Homemaker, 1964, hard plastic and vinyl, jointed knees, mark: "Deluxe Reading Co."
21" $45.00 – 55.00
Suzy Smart, ca. 1962, vinyl, sleep eyes, closed mouth, rooted blond ponytail, hard plastic body, The Talking School Doll, desk, chair, easel
25" $125.00 – 150.00
Sweet Rosemary, vinyl head, soft vinyl body, high-heel foot
28" $45.00 – 55.00

DEP

The "DEP" mark on the back of bisque heads stands for the French "Depose" or the German "Deponirt," which means registered. Some dolls made by Simon & Halbig have the "S&H" mark hidden above the "DEP" under the wig. Bisque head, swivel neck, appropriate wig, paperweight eyes, open or closed mouth, good condition, nicely dressed on French style wood and composition body. Dolls listed are in good condition with original or appropriate clothing.

Closed mouth
15" $2,050.00 – 2,150.00
18" – 20" $2,550.00 – 2,850.00
23" – 25" $3,150.00 – 3,800.00
Open mouth, including those marked Jumeau
13" – 15" $825.00 – 900.00
18" – 20" $1,000.00 – 1,200.00
23" – 25" $1,400.00 – 1,600.00
28" – 30" $1,900.00 – 2,200.00

DOLLHOUSE DOLLS

Small German dolls generally under 8" usually dressed as member of a family or in household-related occupations, often sold as a group. Made of any materials, but usually bisque head by 1880.

Dolls listed are in good condition with original clothes.

Bisque
Adult, man or woman, painted eyes, molded hair, wig
6" $200.00 – 225.00
Glass eyes
  Molded hair
  6" $350.00 – 400.00
  Wigged
  6" $500.00 – 550.00
Black man or woman, molded hair, original clothes
6" $400.00 – 475.00
Chauffeur, molded cap
6" $245.00 – 285.00

Pair of German bisque dollhouse grandparents. $500.00. pair *Courtesy of The Museum Doll Shop.*

Grandparents, or with molded on hats
  6" $235.00 – 265.00
Military man, mustache, original clothes
  6" $475.00 – 575.00
With molded-on helmet
  6" $700.00 – 775.00
Children, all-bisque
  4" $75.00 – 100.00
China
With early hairdo
  4" $300.00 – 400.00
With low brow or common hairdo, 1900 on
  4" $125.00 – 150.00
Composition, Papier-Mâche, Plaster, etc.
  5" $150.00 – 200.00

6½" Door of Hope Kindergartener. $1,500.00. *Courtesy of Skinner Inc., Boston and Bolton, Massachusetts.*

DOOR OF HOPE

1901 – 1950, Shanghai, China. Cornelia Bonnell started the Door of Hope Mission in Shanghai to help poor girls sold by families. As a means to learn sewing skills, the girls dressed carved pear wood heads from Ning-Po.

11" Door of Hope woman in cotton. $950.00. *Courtesy Richard W. Withington, Inc., Nashua, New Hampshire.*

The heads and hands were natural finish, stuffed cloth bodies were then dressed in correct representation for 26 different Chinese classes. Carved wooden head with cloth or wooden arms, original handmade costumes, in very good condition.

Dolls listed are in good condition with clean, bright clothing. Exceptional dolls could be higher. Values are lower for dolls in faded costumes.

Adult, man or woman
  11" – 13" $900.00 – 1,500.00
Bride $1,050.00 – 1,500.00
Elaborate Dress $1,100.00 – 1,200.00
Amah with Baby
  $1,100.00 – 1,200.00
Manchu Lady or Man
  $1,800.00 – 2,100.00
Policeman, "Made in China" hang tag
  11½" $2,025.00
Schoolchild
  7" – 8" $1,300.00 – 1,800.00

CUNO & OTTO DRESSEL

1857 – 1943, Sonneberg, Thüringia, Germany. The Dressel family began its business in the early 1700s and was dealing in toys from a very early date. Cuno and Otto became involved in the 1880s. The Dressels made wood, wax, wax-over-composition, papier-mâché, composition, china, and bisque heads for their dolls which they produced, distributed, and exported. Their bisque heads were made by Simon & Halbig, Armand Marseille, Ernst Heubach, Schoenau & Hoffmeister, and others. Dolls listed are in good condition with appropriate clothing.

8" Old Rip by Cuno & Otto Dressel, all original. $750.00. *Courtesy of The Museum Doll Shop.*

Holz-Masse, 1875 on. Composition shoulder head, wigged or molded hair, painted or glass eyes, cloth body, composition limbs, molded on boots

13" – 15"	$275.00 – 350.00
18" – 20"	$475.00 – 575.00

Glass eyes

12"	$400.00 – 500.00
16" – 18"	$550.00 – 650.00

Wigged

13"	$800.00 – 900.00

Bisque

Baby, 1910+, character face, marked "C.O.D.," more for toddler body

12" – 14"	$325.00 – 375.00
15" – 17"	$375.00 – 425.00
19" – 23"	$550.00 – 600.00

Child, mold 1912, open mouth, jointed composition body

14" – 16"	$300.00 – 350.00
18" – 22"	$400.00 – 450.00

Child, character face, closed mouth, jointed child or toddler body

Painted eyes

14" – 16"	$1,200.00 – 1,300.00
18" – 20"	$1,500.00 – 1,700.00

Glass eyes

15"	$2,200.00 – 2,500.00
18" – 20"	$3,200.00 – 3,500.00

Flapper, lady doll, closed mouth, five-piece composition body with thin legs and high heel feet, painted on hose up entire leg, mold 1469

12" – 15"	$3,300.00 – 3,800.00

Jutta

Baby, open mouth, bent-leg body

16" – 18"	$525.00 – 575.00
21" – 24"	950.00 – 1,100.00

Child, 1906 – 1921, open mouth, marked with "Jutta" or "S&H," mold 1914, 1348, 1349, etc.

14" – 16"	$450.00 – 525.00

17" – 19"	$600.00 – 675.00
21" – 24"	$825.00 – 875.00
25" – 29"	$1,050.00 – 1,200.00

Toddler

8"	$500.00 – 550.00
14" – 16"	$525.00 – 600.00
17" – 19"	$675.00 – 725.00

Portrait Dolls, 1896 on, bisque head, glass eyes, composition body

Admiral Dewey, Admiral Byrd

8"	$750.00 – 825.00
12" – 14"	$1,550.00 – 1,900.00

Buffalo Bill

10"	$700.00 – 750.00

Farmer, Old Rip, Witch

8"	$650.00 – 750.00
12"	$1,000.00 – 1,200.00

Father Christmas

12"	$1,500.00+

Uncle Sam

13" – 15½"	$1,400.00 – 1,700.00

E.D.

1857 – 1899, Paris. E.D. bébés, marked with "E.D." and a size number and the word "Depose," were made by Etienne Denamur. It is important to note that other dolls marked E.D. with no Depose mark were made when Emile Douillet was director of Jumeau and should be priced as Jumeau Tété face dolls. Denamur had no relationship with the Jumeau firm and his dolls do not have the spiral spring used to attach heads used by Jumeau. Denamur bébés have straighter eyebrows, slightly more recessed eyes, large lips, and lesser quality bisque. Smaller sizes of Denamure E.D. bébés may not have the Depose mark. Dolls listed are in good condition, appropriately dresssed. Allow more for exceptional clothing.

Closed mouth

11" – 15"	$3,200.00 – 3,800.00
18" – 22"	$3,900.00 – 4,300.00

Open mouth

14" – 16"	$1,300.00 – 1,600.00
18" – 21"	$1,800.00 – 2,000.00
25" – 27"	$2,300.00 – 2,400.00

13" closed mouth bébé marked "E 2 D." $3,600.00.
Doll courtesy of Turn of the Century Antiques, Denver, Colorado.

EDEN BÉBÉ

1890 – 1899, made by Fleischmann & Bloedel; 1899 – 1953, made by Société Francaise de Fabrication de Bébés & Jouet (S.F.B.J.). Dolls had bisque heads and jointed composition bodies.

Dolls listed are in good condition, appropriately dressed.

Closed mouth, pale bisque

14" – 16"	$1,900.00 – 2,100.00
18" – 22"	$2,200.00 – 2,500.00

24" open mouth bébé marked "Eden Bébé Paris 11." $2,000.00. *Courtesy Richard W. Withington Auction, Inc., Nashua, New Hampshire.*

EEGEE

1916 on, Brooklyn, New York. Owned by E. G. Goldberger, assembled and made dolls, some of their dolls had bisque heads imported from Armand Marseille. Eegee also made their own heads and complete dolls of composition, hard plastic, and vinyl. Dolls listed are in all original, good condition. Add more for exceptional doll, tagged, extra outfits, or accessories.

Composition

Baby, cloth body, bent limbs

16"	$100.00 – 125.00

Child, open mouth, sleep eyes

14"	$145.00 – 160.00
18"	$200.00 – 220.00

MaMa Doll, 1920s – 1930s, composition head, sleep or painted eyes, wigged or molded hair, cloth body with crier, swing legs, composition lower arms and legs

16"	$225.00 – 250.00
20"	$325.00 – 350.00

High color, five-piece body

13"	$900.00 – 1,200.00
19"	$1,600.00 – 1,800.00
22"	$2,100.00 – 2,300.00

Open mouth

15" – 18"	$1,500.00 – 1,700.00
20" – 26"	$1,900.00 – 2,100.00

21" Eden bébé with open/closed mouth, original chemise. $2,300.00. *Courtesy of Skinner Inc., Boston and Bolton, Massachusetts.*

22" Puppetrina by Eegee. $80.00. *Courtesy of The Museum Doll shop.*

Miss Charming, 1936, all-composition, Shirley Temple look-alike

19"	$400.00 – 450.00

Miss Charming, pin-back button $50.00

Hard Plastic and Vinyl

Andy, 1963, vinyl, teen-type, molded and painted hair, painted eyes, closed mouth

12"	$25.00 – 35.00

Annette, 1963, vinyl, teen-type fashion, rooted hair, painted eyes

11½"	$45.00 – 55.00

Child, 1966, marked "20/25 M/13"

19"	$40.00 – 50.00

Child, walker, all-vinyl, rooted long blond hair or short curly wig, blue sleep eyes, closed mouth

25"	$40.00 – 50.00
28"	$55.00 – 65.00
36"	$75.00 – 85.00

Babette, 1970, vinyl head, stuffed limbs, cloth body, painted or sleep eyes, rooted hair

15"	$30.00 – 40.00
25"	$55.00 – 65.00

Baby Care, 1969, vinyl, molded or rooted hair, sleep or set glassine eyes, drink and wet doll, with complete nursery set

18"	$35.00 – 45.00

Baby Carrie, 1970, rooted or molded hair, sleep or set glassine eyes with plastic carriage or carry seat

24"	$50.00 – 60.00

Baby Luv, 1973, vinyl head, rooted hair, painted eyes, open/closed mouth, marked "B.T. Eegee," cloth body, pants are part of body

14"	$30.00 – 40.00

Baby Susan, 1958, marked "Baby Susan" on head

8½"	$20.00 – 20.00

Baby Tandy Talks, 1963, pull string activates talking mechanism, vinyl head, rooted hair, sleep eyes, cotton and foam-stuffed body and limbs

14"	$25.00 – 35.00
20"	$55.00 – 65.00

Ballerina, 1964, vinyl head and hard plastic body

31"	$75.00 – 100.00

1967, vinyl head, foam-filled body

18"	$30.00 – 40.00

Barbara Cartland, painted features, adult

15"	$45.00 – 52.00

Beverly Hillbillies, Clampett family from 1960s TV sitcom

Car	$350.00

Granny Clampett, gray rooted hair

14"	$55.00 – 65.00

Fields, W. C., 1980, vinyl ventriloquist doll by Juro, division of Goldberger

30"	$150.00 – 200.00

Flowerkins, 1963, marked "F-2" on head, seven dolls in series

Boxed

16"	$50.00 – 60.00

Gemmette, 1963, rooted hair, sleep eyes, jointed vinyl, dressed in gem colored dress, includes child's jeweled ring, Misses Amethyst, Diamond, Emerald, Ruby, Sapphire, and Topaz

15½"	$50.00

Georgie, Georgette, 1971, vinyl head, cloth bodies, redheaded twins

22"	$40.00 – 50.00

Gigi Perreau, 1951, early vinyl head, hard plastic body, open/closed smiling mouth

17"	$550.00 – 700.00

Karena Ballerina, 1958, vinyl head, rooted hair, sleep eyes, closed mouth, hard plastic body, jointed knees, ankles, neck, shoulders, and hips, head turns when walks

21"	$45.00 – 55.00

Little Debutantes, 1958, vinyl head, rooted hair, sleep eyes, closed mouth, hard plastic

body, swivel waist, high-heeled feet

18"	$50.00 – 60.00
20"	$75.00 – 85.00

My Fair Lady, 1958, all-vinyl, fashion type, swivel waist, fully jointed

20"	$65.00 – 75.00

Parton, Dolly, 1978

11½"	$20.00 – 25.00
18"	$40.00 – 45.00

Posi Playmate, 1969, vinyl head, foam-filled vinyl body, bendable arms and legs, painted or rooted hair, sleep or painted eyes

12"	$15.00 – 20.00

Puppetrina, 1963 on, vinyl head, cloth body, rooted hair, sleep eyes, pocket in back for child to insert hand to manipulate doll's head and arms

22"	$75.00 – 85.00

Shelly, 1964, Tammy-type, grow hair

12"	$12.00 – 18.00

Sniffles, 1963, vinyl head, rooted hair, sleep eyes, open/closed mouth, marked "13/14 AA-EEGEE"

12"	$15.00 – 20.00

Susan Stroller, 1955, vinyl head, hard plastic walker body, rooted hair, closed mouth

20"	$65.00 – 75.00
23"	$80.00 – 90.00
26"	$90.00 – 100.00

Tandy Talks, 1961, vinyl head, hard plastic body, freckles, pull string talker

20"	$50.00 – 55.00

EFFANBEE

1910 to present, New York City. Founded by Bernard Fleischaker and Hugo Baum. This company began selling composition headed dolls.

16" composition baby marked Deco, c. 1915. $275.00. *Courtesy of The Museum Doll Shop.*

These heads were made for them by Otto Ernst Denivelle (marked Deco). Effanbee eventually did their own manufacturing. By the late 1920s they were one of the leading manufacturers of American composition dolls. They went on to make dolls of hard plastic and vinyl. The new management of the company is currently re-issuing many of the designs from the past. Values shown are for early dolls in good condition with original clothing, and for dolls from 1950 on in perfect condition with appropriate tags. More for exceptional dolls with wardrobe or accessories.

Bisque

Mary Jane, 1920, some with bisque heads, others all-composition, bisque heads manufactured by Lenox Potteries, New Jersey, for Effanbee, sleep eyes, composition body, wooden arms and legs, wears Bluebird pin

20"	$650.00 – 700.00

Early Composition
Babies
Baby Bud, 1918 on, all-composition, painted features, molded hair, open/closed mouth, jointed arms, legs molded to body. One finger goes into mouth.

6"	$175.00 – 195.00
Black	$200.00 – 225.00

Baby Dainty, 1912 on, name given to a variety of dolls, with composition heads, cloth bodies, some toddler types, some mama-types with crier

12" – 14"	$240.00 – 260.00
15"	$275.00 – 325.00
Vinyl	
10"	$30.00 – 40.00

Baby Effanbee, 1925, composition head, cloth body

12" – 13"	$165.00 – 185.00

Baby Evelyn, 1925, composition head, cloth body

17"	$250.00 – 275.00

Baby Grumpy, 1915 on, also later variations, composition character, heavily molded and painted hair, frowning eyebrows,

12" Effanbee Coquette, c. 1915. $400.00. *Courtesy of The Museum Doll Shop.*

25" mama doll, Rosemary. $450.00. *Courtesy of The Museum Doll Shop.*

painted intaglio eyes, pin-jointed limbs, cork-stuffed cloth body, gauntlet arms, pouty mouth

Mold #172, 174, 176

12" – 16"	$450.00 – 525.00
Black	$525.00 – 600.00

Baby Grumpy Gladys, 1923, composition shoulder head, cloth body, marked in oval "Effanbee//Baby Grumpy// copr. 1923"

15"	$300.00 – 350.00

Grumpy Aunt Dinah, black, cloth body, striped stocking legs

14½"	$400.00 – 425.00

Grumpykins, 1927, composition head, cloth body, composition arms, some with cloth legs, others with composition legs

12"	$275.00 – 300.00
Black	$325.00 – 375.00

Grumpykins, Pennsylvania Dutch Dolls, 1936, dressed by Marie Polack in Mennonite, River Brethren, and Amish costumes

12"	$225.00 – 250.00

Bubbles, 1924 on, composition shoulder head, open/closed mouth, painted teeth, molded and painted hair, sleep eyes, cloth body, bent cloth legs, some with composition toddler legs, composition arms, finger of left hand fits into mouth, wore heart necklace, various marks including "Effanbee//Bubbles//Copr. 1924//Made in U.S.A."

16" – 18"	$375.00 – 425.00
20" – 22"	$475.00 – 525.00
25" – 26"	$650.00 – 750.00

Lamkin, 1930 on, composition molded head, sleep eyes, open mouth, cloth body, crier, chubby composition legs, with feet turned in, fingers curled, molded gold ring on middle finger

16"	$450.00 – 475.00

Lovums, 1928 on, child doll, composition swivel head, shoulder plate, and limbs, cloth body, sleep eyes, molded and painted hair or wigged, can have bent baby legs or toddler legs

16" – 18"	$350.00 – 400.00
20" – 22"	$400.00 – 500.00

Pat-o-Pat, 1925 on, composition head, painted eyes, cloth body with mechanism that when pressed causes hands to clap

13"	$150.00 – 175.00
15"	$175.00 – 200.00

13" Babyette, c. 1943. $325.00. *Courtesy of The Museum Doll Shop.*

12" Candy Kid. $400.00. *Doll courtesy Marilyn and Mike Parsons.*

Character Children, 1912 on, composition, heavily molded hair, painted eyes, pin-jointed cloth body, composition arms, cloth or composition legs, some marked "Deco"

Cliquot Eskimo, 1920, painted eyes, molded hair, felt hands, mohair suit

18"	$525.00

Coquette, Naughty Marietta, 1915, composition girl, molded bow in hair, side-glancing eyes, cloth body

12"	$400.00 – 450.00

Harmonica Joe, 1923, cloth body, with rubber ball when squeezed, provides air to open mouth with harmonica

15"	$425.00 – 450.00

Irish Mail Kid, 1915, or Dixie Flyer, composition head, cloth body, arms sewn to steering handle of wooden wagon

10"	$325.00 – 350.00

Johnny Tu-face, 1912, composition head with face on front and back, painted features, open/closed crying mouth, closed smiling mouth, molded and painted hair, cloth body, red striped legs, cloth feet, dressed in knitted romper and hat

16"	$375.00 – 425.00

21" Historical Doll, The Monroe Doctrine. $2,500.00. *Doll courtesy of Maxine Evans.*

Pouting Bess, 1915, composition head with heavily molded curls, painted eyes, closed mouth, cloth cork stuffed body, pin jointed, mark: "162" or "166" on back of head

15"	$350.00 – 400.00

Whistling Jim, 1916, composition head, with heavily molded hair, painted intaglio eyes, perforated mouth, cork stuffed cloth body, black sewn-on cloth shoes, wears red striped shirt, blue overalls, mark, label: "Effanbee//Whistling Jim//Trade Mark"

15"	$350.00 – 375.00

MaMa Dolls, 1921 on, including Rosemary and Marilee, composition shoulder head, painted or sleep eyes, molded hair or wigged, cloth body, swing legs, crier, with composition arms and lower legs

14"	$275.00 – 300.00
17"	$350.00 – 400.00
25"	$450.00 – 500.00

Late Composition

American Children, 1936 – 1939 on, all-composition, designed by Dewees Cochran, open mouth, separated fingers can wear gloves, marks: heads may be unmarked, "Effanbee//Anne Shirley" on body

Babyette, 1943, eyes molded closed

13"	$325.00 – 400.00

Barbara Joan, Barbara Ann

17"	$700.00 – 750.00

Barbara Lou

21"	$900.00 – 925.00

Closed mouth, separated fingers, sleep or painted eyes, marks: "Effanbee// American//Children" on head; "Effanbee// Anne Shirley" on body

Painted eyes, Peggy Lou and others

19" – 21"	$2,000.00 – 2,200.00

Sleep eyes, Gloria Ann and others

17" – 21"	$1,800.00 – 2,000.00

Anne Shirley, 1936 – 1940, never advertised as such, same mold used for Little Lady, all-composition, more grown-up body style, mark: "EFFANBEE//ANNE SHIRLEY"

14" – 15"	$250.00 – 275.00
17" – 18"	$275.00 – 300.00
21"	$375.00 – 425.00
27"	$550.00 – 600.00

Movie Anne Shirley, 1935 – 1940, 1934 RKO movie character, Anne Shirley from *Anne of Green Gables* movie, all-composition, marked "Patsy" or other Effanbee doll, red braids, wearing Anne Shirley movie costume and gold paper hang tag stating "I am Anne Shirley." The Anne Shirley costume changes the identity of these dolls.

Mary Lee/Anne Shirley, open mouth, head marked "©Mary Lee," on marked "Patsy Joan" body

16"	$450.00 – 500.00

Patsyette/Anne Shirley, body marked "Effanbee// Patsyette// Doll"

9½"	$300.00 – 325.00

16" Effanbee Lil Sweetie. $45.00. *Doll courtesy of The Museum Doll Shop, Newport, Rhode Island.*

Patricia/Anne Shirley, body marked "Patricia"
15" $500.00 – 550.00
Patricia-kin/Anne Shirley, head marked "Patricia-kin," body marked "Effanbee// Patsy Jr.," hang tag reads "Anne Shirley"
11½" $325.00 – 375.00
Brother or Sister, 1943, composition head and hands, cloth body and legs, yarn hair, painted eyes
Brother
16" $250.00 – 300.00
Sister
12" $225.00 – 275.00
Candy Kid, 1946 on, all-composition, sleep eyes, toddler body, molded and painted hair, closed mouth
13" $375.00 – 425.00
Charlie McCarthy, 1937, composition head, hands, feet, painted features, mouth opens, cloth body, legs, marked: "Edgar Bergen's Charlie McCarthy//An Effanbee Product"
17" – 19" $675.00 – 775.00
19" $2,000.00* in box,
                       top hat, tails

Happy Birthday Doll, 1940, music box in body, heart bracelet
17" $1,050.00
Too few in database for a reliable range.
Historical Dolls, 1939 on, all-composition, jointed body, human hair wigs, painted eyes, made only three sets of 30 dolls depicting history of apparel, 1492 – 1939, very fancy original costumes, metal heart bracelet, head marked "Effanbee// American//Children," body "Effanbee// Anne Shirley"
21" $2,250.00 – 2,500.00
Historical Replicas, 1939 on, all-composition, jointed body, copies of sets above, but smaller, human hair wigs, painted eyes, original costumes
14" $500.00 – 600.00
Honey, 1947 – 1948, all-composition jointed body, human hair wig, sleep eyes, closed mouth
18" – 21" $300.00 – 400.00
Ice Queen, 1937 on, composition, open mouth, skater outfit
17" $850.00
Little Lady, 1939 on, used Anne Shirley mold, all-composition, wigged, sleep eyes, more grown-up body, separated fingers, gold paper hang tag, many in formals, as brides or fancy gowns with matching parasol, during war years yarn hair was used; may have gold hang tag with name, like Gaye or Carole
15" $275.00 – 350.00
18" $350.00 – 450.00
21" $400.00 – 425.00
27" $575.00 – 625.00
Mae Starr, 1928, talking doll, composition shoulder head, cloth body, open mouth, four teeth, with cylinder records, marked "Mae//Starr// Doll"
29" $700.00 – 750.00

Composition Charlie McCarthy doll.
$775.00. *Courtesy Otto and Ursula Mertz.*

Marionettes, 1937 on, puppets designed by Virginia Austin, composition, painted eyes

Clippo, clown

15"	$175.00 – 225.00

Emily Ann

14"	$175.00 – 225.00

Lucifer, black

15"	$525.00 MIB

Portrait Dolls, 1940 on, all-composition, Bo-Peep, Ballerina, Bride, Groom, Gibson Girl, Colonial Maid, etc.

12"	$275.00 – 350.00

Suzanne, 1940, all-composition, jointed body, sleep eyes, wigged, closed mouth, may have magnets in hands to hold accessories, more for additional accessories or wardrobe

14"	$350.00 – 375.00

Suzette, 1939, all-composition, fully jointed, painted side-glancing eyes, closed mouth, wigged

12"	$300.00 – 325.00

Sweetie Pie, 1939 on, also called Baby Bright Eyes, Tommy Tucker, Mickey, composition bent limbs, sleep eyes, caracul wig, cloth body, crier, issued again in 1952+ in hard plastic, cloth body, and vinyl limbs, painted hair or synthetic wigs, wore same pink rayon taffeta dress with black and white trim as Noma doll

16" – 18"	$375.00 – 425.00
20" – 24"	$450.00 – 550.00

W. C. Fields, 1929 on, composition shoulder head, painted features, hinged mouth, painted teeth. In 1980 made in vinyl. See Legend Series.
Marked: "W.C. Fields//An Effanbee Product"

17½"	$900.00 – 950.00

Patsy Family, 1928 on, composition through 1947, later issued in vinyl and porcelain, many had gold paper hang tag and metal bracelet that read "Effanbee Durable Dolls," more for black, special editions, costumes, or with added accessories

Babies

Patsy Baby, 1931, painted or sleep eyes, wigged or molded hair, composition baby body, advertised as Babykin, came also with cloth body, in pair, layettes, trunks, marks: on head "Effanbee//Patsy Baby"; on body "Effanbee //Patsy// Baby"

10" – 11"	$350.00 – 375.00

Patsy Babyette, 1932, sleep eyes, marked on head "Effanbee"; on body "Effanbee//Patsy //Babyette"

9"	$325.00 – 375.00

Patsy Baby Tinyette, 1934, painted eyes, bent-leg composition body, marked on head "Effanbee"; on body "Effan-bee//Baby//Tinyette"

7"	$300.00 – 375.00

Quints, 1935, set of five Patsy Baby

Tinyettes in original box, from FAO Schwarz, organdy christening gowns and milk glass bottles, excellent condition

Set of five

7"	$1,750.00 – 2,200.00

Children

Patsy, 1924, cloth body, composition legs, open mouth, upper teeth, sleep eyes, painted or human hair wig, with composition legs to hips, marked in half oval on back shoulder plate: "Effanbee//Patsy"

15"	$300.00 – 350.00

Patsy, 1928, all-composition jointed body, painted or sleep eyes, molded headband on red molded bobbed hair, or wigged, bent right arm, with gold paper hang tag, metal heart bracelet, marked on body: "Effanbee//Patsy//Pat. Pend.//Doll"

14"	$550.00 – 650.00

Patsy, Oriental with black painted hair, painted eyes, in fancy silk pajamas and matching shoes

14"	$750.00 – 800.00

Patsy, 1946, all-composition jointed body, bright facial coloring, painted or sleep eyes, wears pink or blue checked pinafore

14"	$450.00 – 500.00

Patsy Ann, 1929, all-composition, closed mouth, sleep eyes, molded hair, or wigged, marked on body: "Effanbee// 'Patsy-Ann'//©//Pat. #1283558"

19"	$650.00 – 700.00

Patsy Ann, 1959, limited edition, vinyl, sleep eyes, white organdy dress, with pink hair ribbon, marked "Effanbee//Patsy Ann//©1959" on head; "Effanbee" on body

15"	$245.00 – 285.00

Patsyette, 1931, composition

9"	$325.00 – 375.00

Black, Dutch, Hawaiian

9"	$650.00 – 700.00

Patsy Fluff, 1932, all-cloth, with painted features, pink checked rompers and bonnet

16"	$1,000.00

Too few in database for a reliable range.

Patsy Joan, 1931, composition

16"	$500.00 – 550.00

Patsy Joan, 1946, marked "Effanbee" on body, with extra "d" added

17"	$425.00 – 475.00

Patsy Jr., 1931, all-composition, advertised as Patsykins, marks: "Effanbee//Patsy Jr.//Doll"

11½"	$400.00 – 425.00

Patsy Lou, 1930, all-composition, molded red hair or wigged, marks: "Effanbee//Patsy Lou" on body

22"	$475.00 – 525.00

Patsy Mae, 1934, shoulder head, sleep eyes, cloth body, crier, swing legs, marks: "Effanbee//Patsy Mae" on head; "Effanbee// Lovums//c//Pat. No. 1283558" on shoulder plate

29"	$1,500.00 – 1,600.00

Patsy, all original. $600.00. *Courtesy of The Museum Doll Shop.*

Patsy Ruth, 1934, shoulder head, sleep eyes, cloth body, crier, swing legs, marks: "Effanbee//Patsy Ruth" on head; "Effanbee//Lovums//©//Pat. No. 1283558" on shoulder plate

 26" $1,600.00 – 1,700.00

Patsy Tinyette Toddler, 1935, painted eyes, marks: "Effanbee" on head; "Effanbee//Baby//Tinyette" on body

 7¾" $325.00 – 375.00

Tinyette Toddler, tagged "Kit & Kat"

 In Dutch costume $800.00 for pair

Wee Patsy, 1935, head molded to body, molded and painted shoes and socks, jointed arms and hips, advertised only as "Fairy Princess," pin back button, marks on body: "Effanbee//Wee Patsy"

 5¾" $425.00 – 475.00

 In trousseau box $650.00+

Patsy Family Related Items

Metal heart bracelet, reads "Effanbee Durable Dolls" (original bracelets can still be ordered from Shirley's Doll House)

    $25.00

Metal personalized name bracelet for Patsy family $65.00

Patsy Ann, Her Happy Times, ca. 1935, book by Mona Reed King $75.00

Patsy For Keeps, c 1932, book by Ester Marian Ames $125.00

Patricia Series, 1935, all sizes advertised in *Patsytown News*, all-composition slimmer bodies, sleep eyes, wigged, later WWII-era Patricia dolls had yarn hair and cloth bodies

Patricia, wig, sleep eyes, marked "Effanbee Patricia" on body

 15" $475.00 – 525.00

Patricia Ann, wig, marks unknown

 19" $700.00 – 750.00

Patricia Joan, wig, marks unknown, slimmer legs

 16" $600.00 – 650.00

Patricia-Kin, wig, mark: "Patricia-Kin" on head; "Effanbee//Patsy Jr." on body

 11½" $400.00 – 450.00

Patricia Lou, wig, marks unknown

 22" $550.00 – 600.00

Patricia Ruth, head marked: "Effanbee//Patsy Ruth," no marks on slimmer composition body

 27" $1,200.00 – 1,350.00

Patsy Related Dolls and Variants

Betty Bee, tousel head, 1932, all-composition, short tousel wig, sleep eyes, marked on body: "Effanbee//Patsy Lou"

 22" $375.00 – 400.00

Betty Bounce, tousel head, 1932 on, all-composition, sleep eyes, used Lovums head on body, marked: "Effanbee//'Patsy Ann'/ /©//Pat. #1283558"

 19" $350.00 – 400.00

15" composition Patricia/Anne Shirley with a 9" Patsyette. $500.00. and $350.00. *Courtesy of Richard Withington Inc., Nashua, New Hampshire.*

Betty Brite, 1932, all-composition, short tousel wig, sleep eyes, some marked: "Effanbee//Betty Brite" on body and others marked on head "© Mary-Lee"; on body, "Effanbee Patsy Joan," gold hang tag reads "This is Betty Brite, The lovable Imp with tiltable head and movable limb, an Effanbee doll"

16"	$300.00 – 350.00

Butin-nose, 1936 on, all-composition, molded and painted hair, features, distinct feature is small nose, usually has regional or special costume; name "button" misspelled to "Butin"

8"	$275.00 – 300.00
Cowboy	$325.00 – 350.00

Dutch pair, with gold paper hang tags reading: "Kit and Kat"

8"	$500.00 – 525.00

Oriental, with layette

8"	$525.00

Mary Ann, 1932 on, composition, sleep eyes, wigged, open mouth, marked: "Mary Ann" on head; "Effanbee/'Patsy Ann'//©// Pat. #1283558" on body

19"	$350.00 – 375.00

Mary Lee, 1932, composition, sleep eyes, wigged, open mouth, marked: "©//Mary Lee" on head; "Effanbee//Patsy Joan" on body

16½"	$325.00 – 350.00

Patsy/Patricia, 1940, used a marked Patsy head on a marked Patricia body, all-composition, painted eyes, molded hair, may have magnets in hands to hold accessories, marked on body: "Effanbee//'Patricia'"

15"	$500.00 – 550.00

Skippy, 1929, 14", advertised as Patsy's boyfriend, composition head, painted eyes, molded and painted blond hair, composition or cloth body, with composition molded shoes and legs, marked on head: "Effanbee//Skippy//©//P. L. Crosby"; on body "Effanbee//Patsy//Pat. Pend// Doll"

Military outfit	$425.00 – 450.00
Boy's outfit	$600.00 – 650.00
White Horse Inn, with pin	$1,400.00*

Rubber

Dy-Dee, 1934 on, hard rubber head, sleep eyes, jointed rubber bent-leg body, drink/wet mechanism, molded and painted hair, early dolls had molded ears, after 1940 had applied rubber ears, nostrils, and tear ducts, later made in hard plastic and vinyl, marked: "Effanbee//Dy-Dee Baby" with four patent numbers

Dy-Dee Wee

9"	$275.00 – 300.00
11"	$200.00 – 225.00
13"	$200.00 – 225.00
15"	$275.00 – 300.00
20"	$350.00 – 375.00

Dy-Dee in Layette Trunk, with accessories

15"	$575.00

Hard plastic head, soft rubber body, applied ears

11"	$175.00 – 200.00
15"	$250.00 – 275.00
20"	$375.00 – 425.00

Dy-Dee Accessories

Dy-Dee marked bottle	$15.00
Dy-Dee pattern pajamas	$25.00

Dy-Dee book, Dy-Dee Doll's Days, c 1937, by Peggy Vandegriff, with black and white pictures

5½" x 6¾"	$55.00

Hard Plastic and Vinyl

Alyssa, 1960 – 1961, vinyl head, hard plastic jointed body, walker, including elbows, rooted saran hair, sleep eyes

23"	$200.00 – 225.00

Armstrong, Louis, 1984 – 1985, vinyl
15½" $75.00 – 85.00
Baby Lisa, 1980, vinyl, designed by Astri Campbell, represents a three-month-old baby, in wicker basket with accessories
11" $75.00 – 100.00
Baby Lisa Grows Up, 1983, vinyl, toddler body, in trunk with wardrobe
$100.00 – 110.00
Button Nose, 1968 – 1971, vinyl head, cloth body
18" $25.00 – 35.00
Champagne Lady, 1959, vinyl head and arms, rooted hair, blue sleep eyes, lashes, hard plastic body, from Lawrence Welk's TV show, Miss Revlon-type
21" $225.00 – 275.00
23" $250.00 – 300.00
Churchill, Sir Winston, 1984, vinyl
$55.00 – 75.00
Currier & Ives, vinyl and hard plastic
12" $35.00 – 45.00

Effanbee Mickey, vinyl. $85.00. *Courtesy of The Museum Doll Shop.*

Disney dolls, 1977 – 1978, Snow White, Cinderella, Alice in Wonderland, and Sleeping Beauty
14" $145.00 – 185.00
16½" $300.00 – 325.00
Fluffy, 1954+, all-vinyl
10" $30.00 – 35.00
Black $40.00 – 45.00
Girl Scout $65.00 – 75.00
Gumdrop, 1962 on, vinyl, jointed toddler, sleep eyes, rooted hair
16" $30.00 – 35.00
Hagara, Jan, designer, all-vinyl, jointed, rooted hair, painted eyes
Christina, 1984
15" $100.00 – 110.00
Larry, 1985 $65.00 – 75.00
Laurel, 1984
15" $100.00 – 110.00
Lesley, 1985 $65.00 – 85.00
Half Pint, 1966 – 1983, all-vinyl, rooted hair, sleep eyes, lashes
11" $25.00 – 30.00
Happy Boy, 1960, vinyl, molded hair, tooth, freckles, painted eyes
11" $45.00 – 50.00
Hibel, Edna, designer, 1984 only, all-vinyl
Flower Girl $75.00 – 95.00
Contessa $75.00 – 95.00
Honey, 1949 – 1958, hard plastic (see also composition), saran wig, sleep eyes, closed mouth, marked on head and back: "Effanbee," had gold paper hang tag that read: "I am// Honey//An//Effanbee//Sweet/ /Child"
Honey,1949 – 1955, all-hard mouth, sleep eyes
14" $275.00 – 300.00
17" $350.00 – 400.00
24" $350.00 – 400.00
Honey Walker, 1952 on, all hard plastic with walking mechanism; Honey Walker Junior Miss, 1956 – 1957, hard plastic, extra joints

at knees and ankles permit her to wear flat or high-heeled shoes, add $50.00 for jointed knees, ankles

14"	$325.00 – 350.00
19"	$400.00 – 425.00

Humpty Dumpty, 1985 $55.00 – 75.00
Katie, 1957, molded hair

8½"	$40.00 – 50.00

Legend Series, vinyl

1980, W.C. Fields	$100.00 – 125.00
1981, John Wayne, cowboy	
	$125.00 – 150.00
1982, John Wayne, cavalry	
	$125.00 – 150.00
1982, Mae West	$75.00 – 100.00
1983, Groucho Marx	$50.00 – 70.00
1984, Judy Garland, Dorothy	
	$80.00 – 90.00
1985, Lucille Ball	$100.00 – 120.00
1986, Liberace	$95.00 – 120.00
1987, James Cagney	$45.00 – 65.00

Lil Sweetie, 1967, nurser with no lashes or brow

16"	$40.00 – 45.00

Limited Edition Club, vinyl

1975, Precious Baby	$150.00 – 175.00
1976, Patsy Ann	$160.00 – 180.00
1977, Dewees Cochran	$65.00 – 75.00
1978, Crowning Glory	$40.00 – 50.00
1979, Skippy	$150.00 – 175.00
1980, Susan B. Anthony	$40.00 – 50.00
1981, Girl with Watering Can	
	$60.00 – 70.00
1982, Princess Diana	$100.00 – 125.00
1983, Sherlock Holmes	$65.00 – 75.00
1984, Bubbles	$45.00 – 50.00
1985, Red Boy	$35.00 – 40.00
1986, China head	$25.00 – 30.00

1987 – 1988, Porcelain Grumpy, 2,500 made

	$100.00 – 125.00
Vinyl Grumpy	$40.00 – 50.00

Martha and George Washington, 1976 – 1977, all-vinyl, fully jointed, rooted hair, blue eyes, molded lashes

11" pair	$125.00 – 155.00

Mickey, 1956 – 1972, all-vinyl, fully jointed, some with molded hat, painted eyes

10"	$85.00 – 95.00

Miss Chips, 1966 – 1981, all-vinyl, fully jointed, side-glancing sleep eyes, rooted hair

17"	$35.00 – 45.00

Black

17"	$45.00 – 55.00

Noma, The Electronic Doll, 1950, hard plastic, cloth body, vinyl limbs, battery-operated talking doll wore pink rayon taffeta dress with black and white check trim

27"	$350.00 – 375.00

Polka Dottie, 1954, vinyl head, with molded pigtails on fabric body, or with hard plastic body

21"	$145.00 – 165.00

Latex body

11"	$100.00 – 120.00

Presidents, 1984 on

Abraham Lincoln

18"	$45.00 – 50.00

George Washington

16"	$45.00 – 50.00

Teddy Roosevelt

17"	$65.00 – 70.00

Franklin D. Roosevelt, 1985

	$50.00 – 55.00

Andrew Jackson, 1989

	$50.00 – 55.00

Pun'kin, 1966 – 1983, all-vinyl, fully jointed toddler, sleep eyes, rooted hair

11"	$20.00 – 25.00

Rootie Kazootie, 1954, vinyl head, cloth or hard plastic body, smaller size has latex body

11"	$100.00 – 120.00
21"	$145.00 – 165.00

Roosevelt, Eleanor, 1985, vinyl

14½"	$50.00 – 55.00

Santa Claus, 1982 on, designed by Faith Wick, "Old Fashioned Nast Santa," no. 7201, vinyl head, hands, stuffed cloth body, molded and painted features, marked "Effanbee//7201 c//Faith Wick"

18"	$65.00 – 75.00

Suzie Sunshine, 1961 – 1979, designed by Eugenia Dukas, all-vinyl, fully jointed, rooted hair, sleep eyes, lashes, freckles on nose, add $25.00 more for black

18"	$50.00 – 60.00

Sweetie Pie, 1952, hard plastic

27"	$300.00 – 325.00

Tintair, 1951, hard plastic, hair color set, to compete with Ideal's Toni

15"	$400.00 – 425.00

Twain, Mark, 1984, all-vinyl, molded features

16"	$55.00 – 65.00

Wicket Witch, 1981 – 1982, designed by Faith Wick, no. 7110, vinyl head, blond rooted hair, painted features, cloth stuffed body, dressed in black, with apple and basket, head marked: "Effanbee//Faith Wick//7110 19cc81"

18"	$65.00 – 75.00

FARNELL – ALPHA TOYS

1915 – 1930s, Acton, London. Cloth dolls with molded felt or velvet heads, cloth bodies, painted features, mohair wigs.

Baby

15"	$350.00 – 400.00
18"	$450.00 – 550.00

Child

10"	$250.00 – 275.00
14" – 15"	$400.00 – 425.00

Black

13"	$800.00 – 850.00

Too few in database for a reliable range.

Characters such as islanders, pirates etc.

15"	$400.00 – 450.00
Long Limbed Lady doll	
26"	$800.00 – 850.00

Too few in database for a reliable range.

King Edward VIII, in coronation robes

14"	$1,100.00*

King George VI, "H.M. The King"

15"	$650.00 – 700.00

Palace Guard, "Beefeater"

15"	$500.00 – 600.00

14" Farnell Alpha boy, velvet. $800.00. *Courtesy of The Museum Doll Shop.*

FRENCH POUPÉE

1869 on. Glass eyes, doll modeled as an adult lady, with bisque shoulder head, stationary or swivel neck, closed mouth, earrings, kid or kid and cloth body, nicely dressed, good condition. Add more for original clothing, jointed body, black, or exceptional doll.

Unmarked or with size number only

12" – 14"	$2,200.00 – 2,600.00
16" – 18"	$3,100.00 – 3,800.00
21"	$4,000.00 – 4,200.00
27"	$4,800.00 – 5,000.00

Wooden articulated body, glass eyes

13"	$5,100.00 – 5,600.00
15"	$6,500.00 – 6,900.00
18"	$7,000.00 – 7,500.00

Painted eyes, kid body

14" – 16"	$1,600.00 – 1,900.00

B.S., Blampoix

12" – 14"	$1,800.00 – 2,200.00
16" – 17"	$2,800.00 – 3,000.00
31"	$5,000.00*

Enamel eyes

24"	$4,200.00*

A. Dehors, 1860, swivel neck, bisque lower arms

Generic face, wooden body

14"	$2,400.00 – 2,500.00
17" – 20"	$5,000.00 – 9,000.00

Portrait face

17" – 18"	$17,000.00 – 20,000.00

L.D., Louis Doleac, kid body

17" – 20"	$3,000.00 – 5,300.00

Too few in database for a reliable range.

Simonne

Kid body

16" – 17"	$4,000.00 – 5,000.00

Wood body

18"	$6,700.00 – 7,200.00

Fortune Teller Dolls, fashion-type head with swivel neck, glass or painted eyes, kid body, skirt made to hold many paper "fortunes." Exceptional doll may be more.

Closed mouth

15"	$4,100.00+

Open mouth

18"	$3,100.00+

16½" French poupée with swivel neck, c. 1860s with wardrobe. $5,000.00. *Courtesy of Skinner Inc., Boston and Bolton, Massachusetts.*

18" smiling portrait type poupée by Alexandre Dehors. $20,000.00. *Courtesy of Skinner Inc., Boston and Bolton, Massachusetts.*

China, glazed finish, 1870 – 1880 hairstyle

15"	$1,700.00
Accessories	
Dress	$500.00+
Shoes, marked by maker	$500.00+
unmarked	$250.00
Trunk	$250.00+
Wig	$250.00+

15" poupée, unmarked. $3,000.00. *Courtesy of Skinner Inc., Boston and Bolton, Massachusetts.*

17" poupée by Simonne. $4,500.00. *Courtesy of The Museum Doll Shop.*

RALPH A. FREUNDLICH

1924 – 1945, New York City, later Clinton, Massachusetts. Ralph Freundlich worked for Jeanette Doll Co. then opened Silver Doll & Toy Manufacturing Co. in 1923. In 1924 it became Ralph Freundlich Inc. and made composition dolls. Dolls listed are in good condition wearing original clothing.

Trixbe (Patsy-type), all-composition girl, painted features, molded painted hair with bow pined into head

11"	$100.00 – 125.00

Baby Sandy, 1939 – 1942, all-composition, jointed toddler body, molded hair, painted or sleep eyes, smiling mouth

8"	$250.00 – 300.00
12"	$350.00 – 400.00

15"	$450.00 – 500.00
20"	$675.00 – 750.00

Dummy Dan, ventriloquist doll, Charlie McCarthy look-alike

15"	$100.00 – 125.00
21"	$150.00 – 200.00

General Douglas MacArthur, 1942, all-composition, jointed body, bent arm salutes, painted features, molded hat, jointed, in khaki uniform, with paper tag

18"	$300.00 – 400.00

Military dolls, 1942+, all-composition, molded hats, painted features, original clothes, with paper tag

Soldier, Sailor, WAAC, or WAVE

15"	$250.00 – 300.00

Orphan Annie and her dog, Sandy

12"	$525.00 – 625.00

Pinocchio, composition and cloth, with molded hair, painted features, brightly colored cheeks, large eyes, open/closed mouth, tagged: "Original as portrayed by C. Collodi"

16"	$425.00 – 500.00

8" composition Baby Sandy by Freundlich. $275.00. *Doll courtesy of Ruth Cayton.*

Little Orphan Annie and her dog Sandy. $625.00. *Courtesy of Otto and Ursula Mertz.*

Red Riding Hood, Wolf, Grandma, 1934, composition, set of three, in schoolhouse box, original clothes

9"	$775.00 – 875.00

Pig Baby, 1930s, composition pig head, with painted features on unmarked five-piece body, Freundlich presumed maker of similar composition cat, rabbit, and monkey dolls

9"	$350.00 – 400.00

FULPER POTTERY CO.

1918 – 1921, Flemington, New Jersey. Made dolls with bisque heads and all-bisque dolls. Sold dolls to Amberg, Colonial Toy Mfg. Co., and Horsman. "M.S." monogram stood for Martin Stangl, in charge of production. Dolls listed are in good condition with original or appropriate clothes.

Baby, bisque socket head, glass eyes, open mouth, teeth, mohair wig, bent-leg body

15" – 16"	$375.00 – 425.00
19" – 22"	$450.00 – 525.00

Toddler

16" – 17"	$625.00 – 700.00

Child, socket-head, glass eyes, open mouth

Kid body

18" – 22"	$300.00 – 350.00

Composition body

16" – 18"	$325.00 – 375.00
22" – 24"	$425.00 – 475.00

GABRIEL

The Lone Ranger Series, vinyl action figures with horses, separate accessory sets available. Dolls listed are in very good condition with original clothing and accessories. Mint-in-box dolls can bring double values listed.

Dan Reed on Banjo, blond hair, figure on palomino horse

9"	$40.00 – 50.00

Butch Cavendish on Smoke, black hair, mustache, on black horse

9"	$70.00 – 80.00

Lone Ranger on Silver, masked figure on white horse

9"	$75.00 – 100.00

Little Bear, Indian boy

6"	$80.00 – 100.00

Red Sleeves, vinyl Indian figure, black hair, wears shirt with red sleeves

9"	$80.00 – 100.00

Tonto on Scout, Indian on brown and white horse

9"	$75.00 – 100.00

GANS & SEYFARTH PUPPENBABRIK

1908 – 1922, Waltershausen, Thüringia, Germany. Made bisque dolls; had a patent for flirty and googly eyes. Partners separated in 1922, Otto Gans opened his own factory.

Baby, bent-leg, original clothes or appropriately dressed

16"	$450.00 – 500.00
20"	$575.00 – 625.00
25"	$700.00 – 775.00

Child, open mouth, composition body, original clothes, or appropriately dressed, no mold number or mold 6589

13" – 15"	$375.00 – 475.00
21" – 24"	$500.00 – 600.00
28"	$700.00 – 800.00

FRANCOIS GAULTIER

1860 – 1899. After 1899, became part of S.F.B.J., located near Paris. They made bisque doll heads and parts for lady dolls and for bébés and sold to many French makers including Gesland, Jullien, Petite et Dumontier, Rabery et Delphieu, and Thuillier. Also made all-bisque dolls marked "F.G." Dolls listed are in good condition, appropriately dressed.

Poupée (fashion-type), 1860 on, F.G., marked swivel head on bisque shoulder plate, kid body, may have bisque lower arms

Glass eyes

10" – 11"	$1,500.00 – 1,800.00
12" – 13"	$2,000.00 – 2,500.00

13" F.G. poupée. $2,500.00. *Courtesy of The Museum Doll Shop.*

15" – 17"	$2,500.00 – 3,100.00
18" – 20"	$2,800.00 – 3,000.00
23" – 24"	$3,000.00 – 3,200.00
Painted eyes	
16" – 17"	$1,800.00 – 2,000.00
Wood body	
16" – 18"	$4,750.00 – 5,200.00

Later one-piece shoulder head, kid body, often in regional dress

Painted eyes	
12" – 15"	$600.00 – 900.00
Glass eyes	
18"	$900.00 – 1,000.00

13" painted eye poupée marked "FG." $1,550.00. *Courtesy of The Museum Doll Shop.*

20" F.G. with incised block letters mark. $5,500.00. *Courtesy of The Museum Doll Shop.*

Bébé (child), "F.G." in block letters, 1879 – 1887, closed mouth, excellent quality bisque socket head, glass eyes, pierced ears, cork pate

Composition and wood body with straight wrists	
10" – 11"	$6,500.00 – 7,000.00
13" – 15"	$4,400.00 – 4,700.00
18" – 20"	$5,000.00 – 5,500.00
27" – 28"	$6,600.00 – 7,000.00
Kid body, may have bisque forearms	
10" – 12"	$4,700.00 – 4,900.00
13" – 15"	$4,600.00 – 5,100.00
17" – 19"	$5,000.00 – 6,000.00

Bébé (child), "F.G." inside scroll, 1887 – 1900, composition body, closed mouth

15" – 17"	$2,700.00 – 3,000.00
22" – 24"	$3,500.00 – 3,800.00
28"	$4,500.00 – 4,600.00
Composition body, open mouth	
14" – 16"	$1,600.00 – 1,800.00
20" – 24"	$2,000.00 – 2,600.00

GESLAND

1860 – 1928, Paris. Made, repaired, exported, and distributed dolls, patented a doll body, used heads from Francois Gaultier with "F.G." block or scroll mark. In 1926 became part of the Société Industrielle de France. Gesland's doll's body had metal articulated armature covered with padding and stockinette, with bisque or wood/composition hands and legs. Dolls listed are in good condition, appropriately dressed. Allow more for exceptional original clothing.

Poupée (fashion-type) Gesland, stockinette covered metal articulated fashion-type body, bisque lower arms and legs

14"	$5,000.00 – 6,000.00
16" – 17"	$4,000.00 – 5,000.00
23" – 24"	$5,000.00 – 5,500.00

Bébé (child) on marked Gesland body, closed mouth

12" – 14"	$4,400.00 – 4,800.00
17" – 20"	$5,300.00 – 5,700.00
22" – 24"	$5,800.00 – 6,300.00
28" – 30"	$5,000.00 – 6,000.00

RUTH GIBBS

1946 on, Flemington, New Jersey. Made dolls with china heads and limbs on cloth bodies. The dolls were designed by Herbert Johnson. Dolls listed are in good condition wearing original clothing, if in original box values can double.

Godey's Lady Book Dolls, pink-tint or white shoulder head, cloth body

7"	$100.00 – 115.00
12"	$150.00 – 175.00

Black

12"	$165.00 – 185.00

Caracul wig, original outfit

10"	$275.00 – 300.00

GILBERT TOYS

1909 – 1966, New Haven, Connecticut. Company founded on the invention of the Erector Set, went on to make dolls based on popular television characters. Dolls listed are in very good condition with all original clothing and accessories, mint-in-box dolls can bring double the value listed.

Honey West, 1965, vinyl, head and arms, hard plastic torso and legs, rooted blond hair, painted eyes, painted beauty spot near mouth, head marked "K73" with leopard

11½"	$140.00 – 160.00

The Man From U.N.C.L.E. characters from TV show of the 1960s

Other outfits available. (For photo, see Doll Values, third edition.)

Ilya Kuryakin (David McCallum)

12¼"	$140.00 – 175.00

Napoleon Solo (Robert Vaughn)

12¼"	$100.00 – 125.00

James Bond, Secret Agent 007, character from James Bond movies

12¼"	$100.00 – 125.00
Costume only	$180.00*

GIRL SCOUT DOLLS

1917 on, listed chronologically. Dolls listed are in good condition with original clothing.

1917, all-composition doll, painted features, mohair wig

    6½" $225.00 – 250.00

1920s Girl Scout doll in camp uniform, pictured in Girls Scout 1920 handbook, all-cloth, mask face, painted features, wigged, gray green uniform

    13" $600.00+

Grace Corry, Scout 1929, composition shoulder head, designed by Grace Cory, cloth body with crier, molded hair, painted features, original uniform, mark on shoulder plate: "by Grace Corry"; body stamped: "Madame Hendren Doll//Made in USA"

    13" $550.00 – 675.00

Averill Mfg. Co, 1936, all-cloth, printed and painted features

    16" $350.00 – 400.00

Georgene Novelties

1940 – 1946, all-cloth, flat-faced painted features, yellow yarn curls, wears original silver green uniform with red triangle tie, hang tag reads: "Genuine Georgene Doll//

13¾" Girl Scout by Georgene Novelties. $400.00. *Doll courtesy of Louise Stevens.*

8" Ginger, made by Cosmopolitan for Terri Lee, in original boxes. $225.00. *Courtesy of The Museum Doll Shop.*

A product of Georgene Novelties, Inc., NY//Made in U.S.A."

    15" $400.00 – 450.00

1946 – 1955, all-cloth, mask face, painted features and string hair

    13½" $225.00 – 250.00

1955 – 1957, same as previous listing, but now has a stuffed vinyl head

    13" $200.00 – 250.00

Terri Lee, 1949 – 1958, hard plastic, felt hats, oilcloth saddle shoes

    16" $700.00 – 900.00

    Outfit only $160.00*

Tiny Terri Lee, 1955 – 1958, hard plastic, walker, sleep eyes, wig, plastic shoes

    10" $175.00 – 200.00

Ginger, 1956 – 1958, made by Cosmopolitan for Terri Lee, hard plastic, straight-leg walker, synthetic wig

    7½" – 8" $175.00 – 225.00

Effanbee Honey, 1949 – 1957, hard plastic, mohair wig

    14" $125.00 – 150.00

    18" $250.00 – 300.00

Nancy Ann Storybook, 1957, Muffie, hard plastic

    8" $175.00 – 200.00

Vogue, 1956 – 1965, Ginny, hard plastic, straight-legged walker with sleep eyes and painted eyelashes, in 1957 had bending leg and felt hat

8" $250.00 – 300.00

Effanbee, Patsy Ann, 1959 on, all-vinyl jointed body, saran hair, with sleep eyes, freckles on nose, Brownie or Girl Scout

15" $300.00 – 350.00

Effanbee Suzette, 1960, jointed vinyl body, sleep eyes, saran hair, thin body, long legs

15" $350.00 – 400.00

Uneeda, 1961 – 1963, Ginny look-alike, vinyl head, hard plastic body, straight-leg walker, Dynel wig, marked "U" on head

8" $100.00 – 125.00

Effanbee Fluffy, 1964 – 1972, Vinyl dolls, sleep eyes, curly rooted hair, Brownie had blond wig, Junior was brunette, box had clear acetate lid, printed with Girl Scout trademark, and catalog number

8" $175.00 – 200.00

Effanbee Fluffy Cadette, 1965, vinyl, rooted hair, sleep eyes

11" $475.00 – 575.00

Effanbee Pun'kin Jr., 1974 – 1979, all-vinyl, sleep eyes, long straight rooted hair Brownie and Junior uniforms

11½" $75.00 – 100.00

Hallmark, 1979, all-cloth, Juliette Low, from 1916 handbook, wearing printed 1923 uniform

6½" $55.00 – 65.00

Jesco, 1985, Katie, all-vinyl, sleep eyes, long straight rooted hair, look-alike Girl Scout, dressed as Brownie and Junior

9" $65.00 – 75.00

Madame Alexander, 1992, vinyl, unofficial Girl Scout, sleep eyes

8" $110.00 – 130.00

GLADDIE

1928 – 1930 on. Tradename of doll designed by Helen Webster Jensen, made in Germany, body made by K&K for Borgfeldt. Flange heads made of bisque or biscaloid (a ceramic imitation of bisque), with molded hair, glass or painted eyes, open-closed mouth with two upper teeth and laughing expression, composition arms, lower legs, cloth torso, some with crier and upper legs. Mark "copyright" (misspelled). Dolls listed are in good condition, appropriately dressed.

Biscaloid ceramic head

18" – 20"	$1,300.00 – 1,500.00
23" – 24"	$1,600.00 – 1,800.00
29"	$1,900.00 – 2,000.00

Bisque head

14"	$2,800.00 – 3,000.00
18" – 20"	$4,000.00 – 5,000.00

20" Gladdie with Biscaloid (ceramic) head. $1,500.00. *Courtesy of The Museum Doll Shop.*

WM. AND F. & W. GOEBEL

1867 – 1930 on, Oeslau, Thüringia. Made porcelain and glazed china dolls, as well as bathing dolls, Kewpie-types, and others. Earlier mark was triangle with half moon. Supplied heads to other doll makers including Max Handwerck. Dolls listed are in good condition appropriately dressed. Exceptional dolls may be more.

5½" Goebel character child on five-piece composition body. $275.00. *Courtesy of The Museum Doll Shop.*

6" Goebel baby, open mouth. $175.00. *Courtesy of The Museum Doll Shop.*

Child, 1895

Socket head, open mouth, composition body, sleep or set eyes, no mold number or mold 120

10"	$100.00 – 135.00
12" – 16"	$275.00 – 350.00
17" – 23"	$375.00 – 425.00

Baby body

13"	$200.00 – 275.00

Shoulder head, open mouth, kid or cloth body, glass eyes

24"	$195.00 – 210.00

Character Child, after 1909

Molded hair, may have flowers or ribbons, painted features, with five-piece papier-mâché body

6"	$275.00 – 300.00
9"	$350.00 – 400.00

Molded on bonnet or hat, closed mouth, five-piece papier-mâché body, painted features

9"	$475.00 – 525.00

Character Baby, after 1909, open mouth, sleep eyes, five-piece bent-leg baby body

13" – 15"	$325.00 – 400.00
18" – 21"	$450.00 – 550.00

Toddler body

14"	$425.00 – 500.00

8" Goebel dolly face doll in factory outfit. $125.00. *Courtesy of The Museum Doll Shop.*

GOOGLY

Popular 1900 – 1925, various manufacturers. Doll with exaggerated side-glancing eyes. Round eyes were painted, glass, tin, or celluloid. When they move to side they are called flirty eyes. Most doll manufacturers of the period made dolls with googly eyes. With painted eyes, they could be painted looking to side or straight ahead; with inserted eyes, the same head can be found with and without flirty eyes. May have closed smiling mouth, composition or papier-mâché body, molded hair or wigged.

Dolls listed are in good condition appropriately dressed. Exceptional dolls can be more.

All-Bisque, jointed shoulders, hips, molded shoes, socks

Painted eyes, no maker's mark

3"	$150.00 – 200.00
5"	$300.00 – 350.00

Rigid neck, glass eyes, no maker's mark

3"	$225.00 – 275.00
5"	$425.00 – 465.00

7" Googly by Ernst Heubach, intaglio eyes. $450.00. *Courtesy of The Museum Doll Shop.*

Marked by maker, Molds 217, 330, 501

4" – 5"	$700.00 – 750.00
6" – 7"	$900.00 – 950.00

Swivel neck, glass eyes, no maker's mark

5"	$575.00 – 650.00
7"	$875.00 – 950.00

Marked by maker, Molds 189, 292

4" – 5"	$1,000.00 – 1,200.00
6" – 7"	$1,400.00 – 1,600.00

No mold number, jointed knees

7"	$2,500.00 – 2,800.00

Mold 111, jointed knees and elbows

7½"	$2,200.00 – 2,600.00

Kestner 211, with jointed elbows, knees, neck

5"	$2,800.00 – 3,000.00

Too few in database for a reliable range.

7"	$3,750.00 – 4,200.00

Too few in database for a reliable range.

Our Fairy, Mold 222, ca. 1914, wigged, glass eyes

7"	$1,100.00 – 1,200.00
11"	$1,600.00 – 1,800.00

Painted eyes, molded hair

5"	$450.00 – 550.00
8"	$750.00 – 850.00
12"	$950.00 – 1,500.00

Bisque head, painted or glass eye, composition body

Bähr & Pröschild, Marked "B.P.", Mold 686, ca. 1914, glass eyes

10"	$4,000.00 – 4,200.00

Demacol, made for Dennis Malley & Co., London, bisque socket head, glass eyes, closed watermelon mouth, mohair wig, five-piece composition toddler body

10" – 13"	$750.00 – 1,000.00

Goebel

Painted eyes

6" – 7"	$400.00 – 450.00
9" – 10"	$700.00 – 750.00
12"	$900.00 – 1,000.00

7" Gebruder Heubach Winker with intaglio eyes. $900.00. *Courtesy Richard W. Withington, Inc., Nashua, New Hampshire.*

Glass eyes

7" – 8"	$900.00 – 1,100.00
10" – 11"	$1,500.00 – 1,600.00
13"	$2,200.00 – 2,500.00

Handwerck, Max

Glass eyes, marked "Elite," bisque socket head, molded helmet

10" – 14"	$1,700.00 – 1,800.00

Painted eyes, molded Military helmet, painted eye

12"	$1,500.00*

Uncle Sam

12"	$2,900.00*

Two-faced with molded military caps

12"	$1,500.00*

Hertel Schwab & Co., 1914 on

Mold 163, solid dome, glass eyes, molded hair, closed smiling mouth, toddler body

12"	$4,000.00 – 4,500.00
16"	$6,700.00 – 7,200.00

Mold 165, socket head, glass eyes, closed smiling mouth

Baby

11" – 12"	$3,500.00 – 3,800.00
16"	$5,000.00 – 5,400.00

Toddler

11" – 12"	$4,400.00 – 4,600.00
15" – 16"	$6,500.00 – 7,000.00

Mold 172, solid dome, glass eyes, closed smiling mouth, baby body

15"	$6,500.00 – 7,000.00

Mold 173, solid dome, glass eyes, closed smiling mouth

Baby

10" – 11"	$3,500.00 – 3,800.00
16"	$5,800.00 – 6,200.00

Toddler

10" – 12"	$4,000.00 – 5,000.00
16"	$7,000.00 – 7,400.00

Heubach, Ernst

Mold 262, 264, ca. 1914, "EH," painted eyes, closed mouth

6" – 8"	$400.00 – 500.00
10" – 12"	$700.00 – 1,000.00

Mold 291, ca. 1915, "EH," glass eyes, closed mouth

7" – 9"	$1,200.00 – 1,400.00

Mold 318, ca. 1920, "EH," character, closed mouth

11"	$1,100.00 – 1,285.00
14"	$1,900.00 – 2,050.00

6¼" Googly made by Goebel, incised with "crown" mark. $425.00. *Doll courtesy of Ruth Cayton.*

7" glass-eyed Googly mold 10532 by Gebruder Heubach, c. 1920. $800.00. *Courtesy of The Museum Doll Shop.*

Mold 319, ca. 1920, "EH," character, painted eyes, tearful features

8"	$500.00 – 575.00
11"	$1,050.00 – 1,150.00

Mold 322, ca. 1915, character, glass eyes, closed smiling mouth

8" – 10"	$2,100.00 – 2,300.00

Heubach, Gebrüder

No mold number, painted eyes

6" – 7"	$575.00 – 650.00
9"	$700.00 – 800.00
13"	$1,500.00 – 1,700.00

7" Armand Marseille Mold 323, glass eyes. $900.00. *Courtesy of The Museum Doll Shop.*

Mold 8556, painted eyes

16"	$23,000.00*

Mold 8676, painted eyes

9"	$800.00 – 850.00
11"	$950.00 – 1,050.00

Mold 8678, glass eyes

6" – 7"	$900.00 – 1,000.00
9" – 11"	$1,400.00 – 1,600.00

Mold 8723, 8995, glass eyes

13"	$2,600.00 – 2,900.00

Mold 8764, Einco, shoulder head, glass eyes, closed mouth, for Eisenmann & Co.

11"	$3,500.00 – 3,800.00
18" – 20"	$11,500.00 – 13,500.00

Mold 9056, ca. 1914, square, painted eyes closed mouth

8"	$650.00 – 700.00

Mold 9573, glass eyes

6" – 7"	$800.00 – 900.00
9" – 11"	$1,300.00 – 1,500.00

Mold 9743, sitting, open-closed mouth, top-knot, star shaped hands

7"	$500.00 – 600.00

Winker, one eye painted closed

7"	$850.00 – 900.00
14"	$2,000.00 – 2,200.00

Mold 10542, glass eyes, wigged

7"	$750.00 – 900.00

Kämmer & Reinhardt

Mold 131, ca. 1914, "S&H//K*R," glass eyes, closed mouth

8½" toddler	$6,500.00 – 6,800.00
13"	$5,500.00 – 6,000.00
15" – 16"	$12,000.00 – 14,000.00

Kestner

Mold 221, ca. 1913, "JDK ges. gesch," character, glass eyes, smiling closed mouth

11" – 13"	$5,000.00 – 6,200.00
14" – 16"	$12,000.00 – 14,000.00

Kley & Hahn

Mold 180, ca. 1915, "K&H" by Hertel Schwab

13" Kestner 221 Googly. $6,200.00.
Courtesy of Skinner Inc., Boston & Bolton, Massachusetts.

& Co. for Kley & Hahn, character, glass eyes, laughing open-closed mouth

15"	$2,700.00 – 3,000.00
17"	$3,400.00 – 3,500.00

Lenci: See Lenci category.

Limbach, Marked with crown and cloverleaf, socket head, large round glass eyes, pug nose, closed smiling mouth

7" – 8"	$1,800.00 – 2,100.00

Armand Marseille

Mold 200, ca. 1911, glass eyes, closed mouth

8"	$1,250.00 – 1,500.00
11"	$2,000.00 – 2,500.00

Mold 210, ca. 1911, glass eyes, character, solid-dome head, painted eyes, closed mouth

6" - 8"	$600.00 – 1,500.00

Mold 223, ca. 1913, character, closed mouth

7"	$700.00 – 750.00
11"	$900.00 – 950.00

Mold 240, ca. 1914, "AM" dome, glass eyes, painted, closed mouth

10" – 11"	$3,000.00 – 3,100.00

Mold 252, "AM 248," ca. 1912, solid dome, painted eyes, molded tuft, painted eyes, closed mouth

9"	$1,300.00 – 1,500.00
12"	$2,100.00 – 2,400.00

Mold 253, "AM Nobbikid Reg. U.S. Pat. 066 Germany," ca. 1925

6" – 7"	$1,000.00 – 1,200.00
9" – 10"	$1,800.00 – 2,100.00

Mold 254, ca. 1912, "AM" dome, painted eyes, closed mouth

10"	$650.00 – 700.00

Mold 320, "AM 255," ca. 1913, dome, painted eyes

9"	$900.00 – 1,000.00
12"	$1,200.00 – 1,300.00

Mold 322, "AM," ca. 1914, dome, painted eyes

8"	$600.00 – 675.00
11"	$800.00 – 875.00

Mold 323, 1914 – 1925, glass eyes, also composition

7" – 8"	$900.00 – 1,100.00
10" – 11"	$1,500.00 – 1,600.00
13"	$2,200.00 – 2,500.00

6" Kestner all-bisque mold 189 in original box marked Tiny Tots. $1,500.00. *Courtesy Richard W. Withington, Inc, Nashua, New Hampshire.*

10¼" composition mask face Hug Me Kid.
$800.00. *Courtesy of The Museum Doll Shop.*

Mold 325, ca. 1915, character, closed mouth

9"	$675.00 – 725.00
14"	$900.00 – 1,000.00

P.M. Porzellanfabrik Mengersgereuth, ca. 1926, "PM" character, closed mouth, previously thought to be made by Otto Reinecke, Mold 950

11"	$3,100.00 – 3,200.00

Recknagel, no mold number

Glass eyes

7" – 8"	$900.00 – 1,100.00
10" – 11"	$1,500.00 – 1,600.00
13"	$2,200.00 – 2,500.00

Painted eyes

7" – 8"	$600.00 – 700.00

S.F.B.J.

Mold 245, glass eyes

7" – 8"	$2,900.00 – 3,200.00

Fully jointed body

10"	$3,800.00 – 4,100.00

Steiner, Herm, Mold 133, ca. 1920, "HS," closed mouth, papier-mâché body

8"	$650.00 – 700.00

Walter & Sohn, Mold 208, ca. 1920, "W&S," closed mouth, five-piece papier-mâché body, painted socks/shoes

8" – 9"	$700.00 – 1,000.00

Composition Face, 1911– 1914, all-composition head or composition mask face, cloth body, includes Hug Me Kids, Little Bright Eyes, and others

10" – 12"	$800.00 – 950.00

LUDWIG GREINER

1840 – 1874. Succeeded by sons, 1890 – 1900, Philadelphia, Pennsylvania. Papier-mâché shoulder-head dolls, with molded hair, painted or glass eyes, usually made up to be large dolls.

Dolls are listed in good condition appropriately dressed. Some wear is acceptable for these dolls but highly worn examples will bring half the value of good condition examples.

11½" Greiner, 1872 patent. $300.00.
Courtesy of The Museum Doll Shop.

With "1858" label

12"	$800.00 – 850.00
15" – 17"	$850.00 – 950.00
20" – 23"	$1,000.00 – 1,300.00
28" – 30"	$1,600.00 – 2,000.00
35" – 38"	$2,000.00 – 2,600.00

Glass eyes

21"	$2,000.00 – 2,100.00
26"	$2,400.00 – 2,600.00

With "1872" label

15"	$300.00 – 400.00
18" – 22"	$550.00 – 675.00
26" – 30"	$800.00 – 900.00
35"	$1,000.00 – 1,100.00

Gund's Christpher Robin, vinyl head, cloth body. $40.00. *Courtesy of The Museum Doll Shop.*

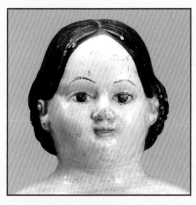

25" Greiner with open/closed mouth with teeth, c. 1850s. $1,800.00. *Courtesy of Skinner Inc., Boston and Bolton, Massachusetts.*

GUND

1898 on, Connecticut and New York. Adolph Gund founded the company making stuffed toys.

Character

Cloth mask face, painted features, cloth body

19"	$250.00 – 300.00

Plastic mask face, 1940s – 1950s, cloth body

16"	$35.00 – 45.00
21"	$45.00 – 55.00

Vinyl mask face, 1950s – 1960s, on plush body, included characters such as Popeye, Disney Pinocchio, Seven Dwarves, and others.

9" – 12"	$35.00 – 45.00

The Now Kids, 1970s, cloth dolls, yarn hair, hippies named Desmond and Rhoda.

Pair	$50.00 – 60.00

HALF DOLLS
(PINCUSHION DOLLS)

1900 – 1930s, Germany, Japan. Half dolls can be made of bisque, china, composition, or papier-mâché, and were used not only for pincushions but on top of jewelry or cosmetic boxes, brushes, lamps, and numerous other items of decor. The hardest to find have arms

Two Dressel and Kister china half-dolls. $450.00 each.
Courtesy of Skinner Inc., Boston and Bolton, Massachusetts.

molded away from the body as they were easier to break and thus fewer survived.

Dolls listed are in good condition, add more for extra attributes. Rare examples may bring more.

Arms Away

China or bisque figure, bald head with wig

4"	$125.00 – 140.00
6"	$185.00 – 210.00

Goebel mark, dome head, wig

5"	$175.00 – 195.00

Holding items, such as letter, flower

4"	$165.00 – 185.00
6"	$250.00 – 275.00

Marked by maker or mold number

4"	$185.00 – 200.00
6"	$275.00 – 300.00
8"	$375.00 – 400.00
12"	$850.00 – 900.00

Pincushion

6", flamenco dancer	$430.00

Arms In

Close to figure, bald head with wig

4"	$65.00 – 80.00
6"	$100.00 – 115.00

Hands attached

3"	$25.00 – 35.00
5"	$35.00 – 45.00
7"	$60.00 – 70.00

Decorated bodice, necklace, fancy hair, or holding article

3"	$100.00 – 125.00
4¾", holding tray, cups	$305.00

Marked by maker or mold number

5"	$125.00 – 135.00
6"	$145.00 – 155.00

With legs, dressed, fancy decorations

5"	$275.00 – 300.00
7"	$375.00 – 400.00

Papier mâché or composition

4"	$25.00 – 35.00
6"	$60.00 – 80.00

Jointed Shoulders

China or bisque, molded hair

5"	$125.00 – 145.00
7"	$175.00 – 200.00

Solid dome, mohair wig

4"	$200.00 – 220.00
6"	$350.00 – 400.00

Two deco-style china half-dolls with arms away, c. 1920s. $350.00 each. *Courtesy of Skinner Inc., Boston and Bolton, Massachusetts.*

Man or Child

4"	$100.00 – 120.00
6"	$130.00 – 160.00

Marked Germany

4"	$175.00 – 200.00
6"	$300.00 – 400.00

Marked Japan

3"	$15.00 – 25.00
6"	$40.00 – 50.00

Other Items

Brush, with porcelain figurine for handle, molded hair, may be holding something

9"	$65.00 – 75.00

Dresser box

Unmarked, with figurine on lid

7"	$325.00 – 350.00
9"	$425.00 – 450.00

Marked, with mold number, country, or manufacturer

5"	$265.00 – 285.00
6"	$325.00 – 350.00

HEINRICH HANDWERCK

1855 – 1932, Waltershausen, Thüringia, Germany. Made composition doll bodies, sent Handwerck molds to Simon & Halbig to make bisque heads. Trademarks included an eight-point star with French or German wording, a shield, and "Bébé Cosmopolite," "Bébé de Reclame," and "Bébé Superior." Sold dolls through Gimbels, Macy's, Montgomery Wards, and others. Bodies marked "Handwerk" in red on lower back torso. Patented a straight wrist body.

Dolls listed are in good condition appropriately dressed. Exceptional dolls may be more.

23" Heinrich Handwerck doll marked Simon Halbig. $650.00. *Courtesy of Skinner Inc., Boston and Bolton, Massachusetts.*

Socket-Head Child, 1885 on. Open mouth, sleep or set eyes, ball-jointed body, bisque socket head, pierced ears, appropriate wig, nicely dressed.

Molds 69, 79, 89, 99, 109, 119, or no number

10" – 12"	$500.00 – 600.00
14" – 16"	$625.00 – 675.00
18" – 22"	$575.00 – 625.00
22" – 24"	$600.00 – 700.00
26" – 28"	$725.00 – 800.00
30" – 33"	$850.00 – 1,000.00
36"	$1,700.00 – 1,900.00
40"	$3,000.00 – 3,100.00

Mold 79, 89, closed mouth

15"	$1,700.00 – 1,800.00
18" – 20"	$2,200.00 – 2,400.00
24"	$2,800.00 – 3,000.00

Mold 189, open mouth

15"	$800.00 – 850.00
18" – 22"	$950.00 – 1,100.00

Bébé Cosmopolite

19"	$1,000.00 boxed
28"	$1,500.00 boxed
33"	$2,2500.00

Shoulder-Head Child, 1885 on, open mouth, glass eyes, kid or cloth body.

Molds 139 or no numbers

12"	$200.00 – 225.00
15" – 16"	$300.00 – 325.00
18" – 22"	$350.00 – 400.00
24" – 25"	$425.00 – 500.00

16" Heinrich Handwerck, original clothing. $650.00. *Courtesy of The Museum Doll Shop.*

MAX HANDWERCK

1899 – 1928, Waltershausen, Thüringia, Germany. Made dolls and doll bodies, registered trademark, "Bébé Elite." Used heads made by Goebel.

Child, bisque socket head, open mouth, sleep or set eyes, jointed composition body

Size numbers only or molds 283, 286, 291, 297, 307, and others

16" – 18"	$300.00 – 325.00
22" – 24"	$400.00 – 450.00
31" – 32"	$650.00 – 700.00

Bébé Elite, 1900 on, bisque socket head, mohair wig, glass sleep eyes, mohair lashes, open mouth, pierced ears, jointed composition/wood body, marks: "Max Handwerck Bébé Elite 286 12 Germany" on back of head

15"	$400.00 – 450.00
19" – 21"	$500.00 – 575.00
27"	$650.00 – 725.00

Googly: See Googly category.

18" dolly face doll by Max Handwerck. $325.00. *Courtesy of The Museum Doll Shop.*

HARD PLASTIC

Hard plastic was developed during WWII and became a staple of the doll industry after the war ended. Numerous companies made hard plastic dolls from 1948 through the 1950s; dolls have all hard plastic jointed bodies, sleep eyes, lashes, synthetic wig, open or closed mouths.

Hard plastic doll, maker unknown, original cowgirl outfit, c. 1950s. $250.00.
Courtesy of The Museum Doll Shop.

Hard Plastic Child, 1950s, maker unknown, some marked U.S.A., original clothing and wig

14" – 16"	$250.00 – 275.00
18" – 20"	$300.00 – 350.00

Advance Doll & Toy Company, 1954 on, made heavy walking hard plastic dolls, metal rollers on molded shoes, named Winnie, and Wanda, later models had vinyl heads

18" – 24"	$200.00 – 225.00

Artisan Novelty Company, 1950s, hard plastic, wide crotch

Raving Beauty

20"	$100.00 – 125.00
Black	$225.00 – 275.00

Duchess Doll Corporation, 1948 – 1950s, made small hard plastic adult dolls, mohair wigs, painted or sleep eyes, jointed arms, stiff or jointed neck, molded and painted shoes, about 7" to 7½" tall, costumes stapled onto body, elaborately costumed or exceptional dolls may be more.

7"	$15.00 – 20.00

Fortune Doll Company

Pam (Ginny-type), hard plastic, sleep eyes, synthetic wig, closed mouth

8"	$55.00 – 65.00

Furga, Italy

Simonna outfit, MIB, 1967

	$300.00 – 330.00

Imperial Crown Toy Co. (Impco), 1950s, made hard plastic or vinyl dolls, rooted hair, synthetic wigs

Hard plastic walker

14"	$45.00 – 55.00
20"	$85.00 – 100.00

Vinyl

16"	$55.00 – 65.00

Kendall Company

Miss Curity, 1953, hard plastic, jointed only at shoulders, blond wig, blue sleep eyes, molded-on shoes, painted stockings, uniform sheet vinyl, "Miss Curity" marked in blue on hat

7½"	$40.00 – 50.00

19" Wanda Walker by Advance Doll Corp. $225.00. *Courtesy of The Museum Doll Shop.*

8" Pam, Fortune Doll Company. $60.00. *Courtesy of The Museum Doll Shop.*

Nun Doll, all hard plastic, sleep eyes, unmarked

12"	$45.00 – 65.00
17"	$100.00 – 125.00

Roddy of England, 1950 – 1960s, made by D.G. Todd & Co. Ltd., Southport, England, hard plastic walker, sleep or set eyes

12½"	$80.00 – 100.00

Walking Princess, tagged

11½"	$40.00 – 50.00

Rosebud of England, 1950s – 1960s, started in Raunds, Northamptonshire, England, by T. Eric Smith shortly after WWII.

Miss Rosebud, hard plastic, various shades of blue sleep eyes, glued-on mohair wig, jointed at the neck and hips, marked "Miss Rosebud" in script on her back and head and "MADE IN ENGLAND" on her upper back, more for rare examples or mint-in-box dolls

7½"	$75.00 – 85.00

Ross Products

Tina Cassini, designed by Oleg Cassini, hard plastic, marked on back torso, "TINA CASSINI"; clothes tagged "Made in British Crown Colony of Hong Kong"

12"	$175.00 – 200.00
Costume MIB	$100.00 – 125.00

HARTLAND PLASTICS

1954 – 1963, Hartland, Wisconsin. Made action figures and horses; many figures from Warner Brothers television productions. Purchased by Revlon Cosmetics in 1963 and stopped making toys. Others have bought the molds and make these products today. Dolls discussed here are the 1954 to 1963 dolls.

Television or Movie Characters, 8"

Annie Oakley, 1953 – 1956, played by Gail Davis in *Annie Oakley*

8"	$200.00 with horse

Bret Maverick, ca. 1958, played by James Garner in *Maverick*

8"	$750.00 MIB

Clint Bonner, 1957 – 1959, played by John Payne in *The Restless Gun*

8"	$135.00 – 160.00

Colonel Ronald MacKenzie, ca. 1950s, played by Richard Carlson, in *MacKenzies' Raiders*

8"	$810.00 with horse

Dale Evans, ca. 1958, #802, with horse, Buttermilk in *The Roy Rogers Show*

8"	$375.00 MIB

Gil Favor, ca. 1950s, *Rawhide*

8"	$685.00 with horse

Jim Hardie, 1958, played by Dale Roberson in *Tales of Wells Fargo*

8"	$275.00

Josh Randall, ca. 1950s, played by Steve McQueen in *Wanted Dead or Alive*

8"	$615.00 with horse

Major Seth Adams, 1957 – 1961, #824, played by Ward Bond in *Wagon Train*
8" $200.00 with horse
Marshall Johnny McKay, Lawman
8" $520.00
Paladin, 1957 – 1963, played by Richard Boone in *Have Gun, Will Travel*
8" $610.00 with horse
Roy Rogers, ca. 1955, and Trigger, *The Roy Rogers Show*
8" $485.00 MIB with Trigger
Sgt. William Preston, ca. 1958, #804, played by Richard Simmons in *Sgt. Preston of the Yukon*
8" $700.00 with horse
Will Barclay "Bat" Masterson, 1958 – 1960, played by Gene Barry in *Bat Masterson*
8" $310.00
Wyatt Earp, 1955 – 1961, played by Hugh O'Brien in *Life and Legend of Wyatt Earp*
8" $190.00 with horse
Other Figures
8" $380.00
Brave Eagle, #812, and his horse, White Cloud
Buffalo Bill, #819, Pony Express Rider
Chief Thunderbird, and horse, Northwind
Cochise, #815, with pinto horse from *Broken Arrow*
Jim Bowie, #817, with horse, Blaze
General George Custer, #814, and horse, Bugler
General George Washington, #815 and horse, Ajax
General Robert E. Lee, #808, and horse, Traveler
Lone Ranger, #801, and horse, Silver
Tonto, #805, and horse, Scout
All others, 8" $125.00 – 225.00
Baseball 8" Figures
Dick Groat with bat & hat $1,000.00*
Duke Snider $255.00*

Ernie Banks, #920 $430.00*
Hank Aaron, #912 $245.00*
Harvey Keunn $325.00*
Willie Mays $245.00*
Yogi Berra, boxed $280.00*
Ted Williams $135.00*

CARL HARTMANN

1889 – 1930s, Neustadt, Germany. Made and exported bisque and celluloid dolls, especially small dolls in regional costumes, called Globe Babies.
Child
Bisque socket head, open mouth, jointed composition and wood body
22" $500.00 – 700.00
Globe Baby
Bisque socket head, glass sleep eyes, open mouth, four teeth, mohair or human hair wig, five-piece papier-mâché or composition body with painted shoes and stockings
8" $225.00 – 275.00
12" $325.00 – 375.00

KARL HARTMANN

1911– 1926, Stockheim, Germany. Doll factory, made and exported dolls. Advertised ball-jointed dolls, characters, and papier-mâché dolls. Marked "KH."
Child, bisque socket head, open mouth, glass eyes, composition body
18" – 22" $250.00 – 325.00
26" $350.00 – 450.00
32" $675.00 – 725.00

HASBRO

1923, Pawtucket, Rhode Island. Founded by the Hassenfeld Brothers. Began making toys in 1943. One of their most popular toys was the G.I.Joe series which came out in 1964. Dolls listed are in good condition with original clothing and accessories, mint-in-package usually brings double the value listed. Dolls in played with condition bring ⅓ to ½ the value of complete examples.

Adam, 1971, boy for World of Love series, all-vinyl, molded painted brown hair, painted blue eyes, red knit shirt, blue denim jeans, mark: "Hasbro//U.S. Pat Pend//Made in//Hong Kong"

9" $14.00 – 18.00

Aimee, 1972, rooted hair, amber sleep eyes, jointed vinyl body, long dress, sandals, earrings

18" $25.00 – 35.00

4½" Hasbro's Dolly Darling, vinyl. $45.00. *Courtesy of The Museum Doll Shop.*

Adam & Peace from the World of Love series. $18.00 each. *Courtesy of The Museum Doll Shop.*

Bridal Sewing Set, 1950s, hard plastic dolls (6"), boxed with fabric and sewing supplies

Complete set $135.00 – 165.00

Charlie's Angels, 1977, vinyl, Jill, Sabrina, Kelly, Kris

8½" $30.00 – 40.00

Set of three $100.00 – 125.00

Dolly Darling, 1965

4½" $40.00 – 50.00

Flying Nun

4⅞" $60.00 – 70.00

12" $125.00 – 135.00

Jem: See Jem Section.

Leggie, 1972

10" $30.00 – 40.00

Black $50.00 – 60.00

Little Miss No Name, 1965

15" $100.00 – 125.00

Maxie, 1987, vinyl fashion doll

11½" $15.00 – 20.00

My Buddy, 1985, vinyl and cloth

24" $25.00 – 30.00

Peteena Poodle, 1966, vinyl fashion doll poodle

9½" $150.00 – 175.00

Sewing set, bridal party, hard plastic, made by Hasbro. $150.00. *Courtesy of The Museum Doll Shop.*

Pippi Longstocking, 1973, vinyl
    12" $20.00 – 30.00
Real Baby, 1984, designed by J. Turner
    18" $30.00 – 40.00
Show Biz Babies, 1967, 4"
Mamas and Papas
Mama Cass Elliott $150.00 – 180.00
Denny Doherty $100.00 – 125.00
Monkees
Individual $75.00 – 85.00
Set of four $325.00 – 350.00

9½" Peteena Poodle fashion doll. $175.00. *Courtesy of The Museum Doll Shop.*

Storykins, 1967, 3", includes Cinderella, Goldilocks, Prince Charming, Rumpelstiltskin, Sleeping Beauty, Snow White and Dwarfs
            $40.00 – 50.00 each
Sweet Cookie, 1972, vinyl, with cooking accessories
    18" $100.00 – 125.00
That Kid, 1967
    21" $85.00 – 95.00
World of Love Dolls, 1971
    9" $60.00 – 75.00
G.I. Joe Action Figures, 1964, hard plastic head with facial scar, painted hair and no beard. First price indicates doll lacking accessories or nude; second price indicates mint doll in package. Add more for pristine package.
G.I. Joe Action Soldier, flocked hair, Army fatigues, brown jump boots, green plastic cap, training manual, metal dog tag, two sheets of stickers
    11½" $400.00 – 450.00
Painted hair, red $300.00 – 350.00
Black, painted hair $1,200.00 – 1,300.00
Green Beret, teal green fatigue jacket, four pockets, pants, Green Beret cap with red unit flashing, M-16 rifle, 45 automatic

15" Little Miss No Name, c. 1965.
$125.00. *Courtesy of The Museum Doll Shop.*

pistol with holster, tall brown boots, four grenades, camouflage scarf, and field communication set

   11" $1,400.00 – 1,500.00

G.I. Joe Action Marine, camouflage shirt, pants, brown boots, green plastic cap, metal dog tag, insignia stickers, and training manual

   11" $275.00 – 300.00

G.I. Joe Action Sailor, blue chambray work shirt, blue denim work pants, black boots, white plastic sailor cap, dog tag, rank insignia stickers

          $225.00 – 250.00

G.I. Joe Action Pilot, orange flight suit, black boots, dog tag, stickers, blue cap, training manual

          $250.00 – 300.00

Dolls only, nude $85.00 – 95.00

G.I. Joe Action Soldier of the World, 1966, figures in this set may have any hair and eye color combination, no scar on face, hard plastic heads

Australian Jungle Fighter

          $1,000.00 – 1,050.00

British Commando, boxed

          $1,050.00 – 1,150.00

French Resistance Fighter

          $1,100.00 – 1,200.00

German Storm Trooper

          $1,100.00 – 1,200.00

Japanese Imperial Soldier

          $1,300.00 – 1,400.00

Russian Infantryman, boxed $1,100.00

Talking G.I. Joe, 1967 – 1969, talking mechanism added, semi-hard vinyl head, marks: "G.I. Joe®//Copyright 1964//By Hasbro®//Pat. No. 3,277,602//Made in U.S.A."

Talking G.I. Joe Action Soldier, green fatigues, dog tag, brown boots, insignia, stripes, green plastic fatigue cap, comic book, insert with examples of figure's speech

          $250.00 – 300.00

Talking G.I. Joe Action Sailor, denim pants, chambray sailor shirt, dog tag, black boots, white sailor cap, insignia stickers, Navy training manual, illustrated talking comic book, insert with examples of figure's speech

          $900.00 – 1,000.00

Talking G.I. Joe Action Marine, camouflage fatigues, metal dog tag, Marine training manual, insignia sheets, brown boots, green plastic cap, comic, and insert

          $700.00 – 800.00

Talking G.I. Joe Action Pilot, blue flight suit, black boots, dog tag, Air Force insignia, blue cap, training manual, comic book, insert

          $900.00 – 1,000.00

G.I. Joe Action Nurse, 1967, vinyl head, blond rooted hair, jointed hard plastic body, nurse's uniform, cap, red cross armband, white shoes, medical bag, stethoscope, plasma bottle, two crutches, bandages, splints, marks: "Patent Pending//©1967 Hasbro®//Made in Hong Kong"

Boxed $1,750.00 – 1,850.00

Dressed $900.00 – 1,000.00

Nude $125.00 – 150.00

G.I. Joe, Man of Action, 1970 – 1975, flocked hair, scar on face, dressed in fatigues with Adventure Team emblem on shirt, plastic cap, marks: "G. I. Joe®// Copyright 1964//By Hasbro®// Pat. No. 3, 277, 602//Made in U.S. A."
$65.00 – 75.00

Talking $150.00 – 175.00

G.I. Joe, Adventure Team, marks: "©1975 Hasbro ®//Pat. Pend. Pawt. R.I.," flocked hair and beard, six team members:

Air Adventurer, orange flight suit
$265.00 – 285.00

Astronaut, talking, white flight suit, molded scar, dog tag pull string
$400.00 – 450.00

Land Adventurer, black, tan fatigues, beard, flocked hair, scar
$300.00 – 350.00

Land Adventurer, talking, camouflage fatigues
$400.00 – 450.00

Sea Adventurer, light blue shirt, navy pants
$250.00 – 300.00

Talking Adventure Team Commander, flocked hair, beard, green jacket, and pants
$400.00 – 450.00

G.I. Joe Land Adventurer, flocked hair, beard, camouflage shirt, green pants
$100.00 – 150.00

G. I. Joe Negro Adventurer, flocked hair
$700.00 – 750.00

G. I. Joe, "Mike Powers, Atomic Man"
$45.00 – 55.00

G. I. Joe Eagle Eye Man of Action
$100.00 – 125.00

G.I. Joe Secret Agent, unusual face, mustache $400.00 – 450.00

Sea Adventurer w/Kung Fu Grip
$125.00 – 145.00

Bulletman, muscle body, silver arms, hands, helmet, red boots $100.00 – 125.00

Others

G.I. Joe Air Force Academy, Annapolis, or West Point Cadet $350.00 – 400.00

G.I. Joe Frogman, Underwater Demolition Set $250.00 – 300.00

G.I. Joe Secret Service Agent, limited edition of 200 $225.00 – 275.00

Accessory Sets, mint, no doll included

Adventures of G.I. Joe

Adventure of the Perilous Rescue	$250.00
Eight Ropes of Danger Adventure	$200.00
Fantastic Free Fall Adventure	$275.00
Hidden Missile Discovery Adventure	$150.00
Mouth of Doom Adventure	$150.00
Adventure of the Shark's Surprise	$200.00

Accessory Packs or Boxed Uniforms and Accessories

Air Force, Annapolis, West Point Cadet

	$200.00
Action Sailor	$350.00
Astronaut	$250.00
Crash Crew Fire Fighter	$275.00
Deep Freeze with Sled	$250.00
Deep Sea Diver	$250.00
Frogman Demolition Set	$375.00
Fighter Pilot, no package	$285.00*
Green Beret	$450.00
Landing Signal Officer	$250.00
Marine Jungle Fighter	$850.00
Marine Mine Detector	$275.00
Military Police	$325.00
Pilot Scramble Set	$275.00
Rescue Diver	$350.00
Secret Agent	$150.00
Shore Patrol	$300.00
Ski Patrol	$350.00

G.I. Joe Vehicles and Other Accessories, mint in package

Amphibious Duck, green plastic, Irwin
$600.00
Armored Car, green plastic, one figure
$150.00
Crash Crew Fire Truck, blue
$1,400.00
Desert Patrol Attack Jeep, tan, one figure
$1,400.00
Footlocker, with accessories
$400.00+
Iron Knight Tank, green plastic
$1,400.00
Jet Aeroplane, dark blue plastic
$550.00
Jet Helicopter, green, yellow blades
$350.00
Motorcycle and Side Car, by Irwin
$225.00
Personnel Carrier and Mine Sweeper
$700.00
Sea Sled and Frogman
$400.00
Space Capsule and Suit, gray plastic
$425.00
Staff Car, four figures, green plastic, Irwin
$900.00

Jem, 1986 – 1987
Jem dolls were patterned after characters in the animated Jem television series, 1985 – 1988, and include a line of 27 dolls. All-vinyl fashion type with realistically proportioned body, jointed elbows, wrists, and knees, swivel waist, rooted hair, painted eyes, open or closed mouth, and hole in bottom of each foot. All boxes say "Jem" and "Truly Outrageous!" Most came with cassette tape of music from Jem cartoon, plastic doll stand, poster, and hair pick. All 12½" tall, except Starlight Girls, 11". Dolls listed are in excellent condition, wearing complete original outfit.

Jem and Rio
Jem/Jerrica 1ˢᵗ issue
#4000 $25.00 – 30.00
Jem/Jerrica, star earrings
$30.00 – 40.00
Glitter 'n Gold Jem
#4001 $110.00 – 125.00
Rock 'n Curl Jem
#4002 $25.00 – 30.00
Flash 'n Sizzle Jem
#4003 $48.00 – 56.00
Rio, 1ˢᵗ issue
#4015 $25.00 – 30.00
Glitter 'n Gold Rio
#4016 $30.00 – 35.00
Glitter 'n Gold Rio, pale vinyl
#4016 $125.00 – 150.00
Holograms
Synergy
#4020 $50.00 – 60.00
Aja, 1ˢᵗ issue
#4201/4005 $50.00 – 60.00
Aja, 2ⁿᵈ issue
#4201/4005 $100.00 – 125.00
Kimber, 1ˢᵗ issue
#4202/4005 $40.00 – 50.00
Kimber, 2ⁿᵈ issue
#4202/4005 $80.00 – 90.00
Shana, 1ˢᵗ issue
#4203/4005 $250.00 – 275.00
Shana, 2ⁿᵈ issue
#4203/4005 $200.00 – 225.00
Danse
#4208 $35.00 – 45.00
Video
#4209 $20.00 – 25.00
Raya
#4210 $125.00 – 150.00
Starlight Girls, 11", no wrist or elbow joints
Ashley
#4211/4025 $30.00 – 40.00

Krissie
#4212/4025 $25.00 – 35.00
Banee
#4213/4025 $18.00 – 25.00
Misfits
Pizzazz, 1st issue
#4204/4010 $40.00 – 50.00
Pizzazz, 2nd issue
#4204/4010 $45.00 – 55.00
Stormer, 1st issue
#4205/4010 $40.00 – 50.00
Stormer, 2nd issue
#4205/4010 $50.00 – 60.00
Roxy, 1st issue
#4206/4010 $55.00 – 65.00
Roxy, 2nd issue
#4206/4010 $40.00 – 50.00
Clash
#4207/4010 $25.00 – 35.00
Jetta
#4214 $30.00 – 40.00
Accessories
Glitter 'n Gold Roadster
    $200.00 – 250.00
Rock 'n Roadster
    $75.00 – 90.00
JEM Guitar
    $30.00 – 40.00
New Wave Waterbed
    $40.00 – 50.00
Backstager
    $30.00 – 35.00
Star Stage
    $40.00 – 45.00
MTV jacket (promo)
    $100.00 – 125.00
Jem Fashions
Prices reflect NRFB (never removed from box or card), with excellent packaging. Damaged boxes or mint and complete, no packaging prices are approximately 25 percent less.

On Stage Fashions, 1st year, "artwork" on card
    Award Night
    #4216/4040 $30.00
    Music Is Magic
    #4217/4040 $30.00
    Dancin' the Night Away
    #4218/4040 $25.00
    Permanent Wave
    #4219/4040 $25.00
    Only the Beginning
    #4220/4040 $20.00
    Command Performance
    #4221/4040 $35.00
    Twilight in Paris
    #4222/4040 $25.00
    Encore
    #4223/4040 $35.00
On Stage Fashions, 2nd year, "photo" on card
    Award Night
    #4216/4040 $35.00
    Music Is Magic
    #4217/4040 $35.00

Maxie, c. 1987. $18.00. *Courtesy of The Museum Doll Shop.*

Permanent Wave			*Putting it All Together*	
#4219/4040	$30.00		#4240/4045	$75.00
Encore			*Running Like the Wind*	
#4223/4040	$30.00		#4241/4045	$125.00
Friend or Stranger			*We Can Change It*	
#4224/4040	$50.00		#4242/4045	$125.00
Come On In			*Broadway Magic*	
#4225/4040	$55.00		#4243/4045	$200.00
There's Melody Playing			*She Makes an Impression*	
#4226/4040	$280.00		#4244/4045	$90.00
How You Play Game			*Lightnin' Strikes*	
#4227/4040	$85.00*		#4245/4045	$45.00
Love's Not Easy			**Smashin' Fashions,** 1st year "artwork" on card	
#4228/4040	$100.00		(includes Rio fashions)	
Set Your Sails			*Rappin'*	
#4229/4040	$35.00		#4248/4051	$40.00

Flip Side Fashions, 1st year "artwork" on box

Up & Rockin'			*On the Road with Jem*	
#4232/4045	$20.00		#4249/4051	$25.00
Rock Country			*Truly Outrageous*	
#4233/4045	$35.00		#4250/4051	$125.00
Gettin' Down to Business			*Makin' Mischief*	
#4234/4045	$40.00		#4251/4050	$30.00
Let's Rock this Town			*Let the Music Play*	
#4235/4045	$30.00		#4252/4050	$30.00
Music in the Air			*Outta My Way*	
#4236/4045	$35.00		#4253/4050	$20.00*
Like a Dream			*Just Misbehavin'*	
#4237/4045	$30.00		#4254/4050	$65.00
Sophisticated Lady			*Winning Is Everything*	
#4238/4045	$30.00		#4255/4050	$31.00*
City Lights			**Smashin' Fashions,** 2nd year, "photo" on card	
#3129/4045	$20.00		(Misfits fashions only)	

Flip Side Fashions, 2nd year "photo" on box

			Let the Music Play	
Gettin' Down to Business			#4252/4050	$35.00
#4234/4045	$45.00		*Just Misbehavin'*	
Let's Rock this Town			#4254/4050	$75.00
#4235/4045	$35.00		*Gimme, Gimme, Gimme*	
Music in the Air			#4256/4050	$50.00*
#4236/4045	$40.00		*You Can't Catch Me*	
Sophisticated Lady			#4257/4050	$102.00*
#4238/4045	$35.00		*We're Off & Running*	
			#4258/4050	$35.00

You Gotta' Be Fast
#4259/4050 $45.00
There Ain't Nobody Better
#4260/4050 $50.00
Designing Woman
#4261/4050 $35.00
Rio Fashion, 2nd year only, "photo" on card
Rappin'
#4248/4051 $45.00
On the Road with Jem
#4249/4051 $30.00
Truly Outrageous
#4250/4051 $150.00
Time Is Running Out
#4271/4051 $25.00
Share a Little Bit
#4272/4051 $125.00
Congratulations
#4273/4051 $30.00
Universal Appeal
#4274/4051 $25.00
It Takes a Lot
#4275/4051 $25.00
It All Depends on Mood
#4276/4051 $15.00
Glitter 'n Gold Fashions, 2nd year only, "photo" on boxes
Fire and Ice
#4281/4055 $55.00
Purple Haze
#4282/4055 $30.00
Midnight Magic
#4283/4055 $30.00
Gold Rush
#4284/4055 $60.00
Moroccan Magic
#4285/4055 $75.00
Golden Days/Diamond Nights
#4286/4055 $50.00
Music Is Magic Fashion, 2nd year only, "photo" on boxes

Rock'n Roses
#4296/4060 $35.00
Splashes of Sound
#4297/4060 $25.00
24 Carat Sound
#4298/4060 $35.00
Star Struck Guitar
#4299/4060 $85.00
Electric Chords
#4300/4060 $25.00
Rhythm & Flash
#4301/4060 $35.00

HERTEL SCHWAB & CO.

1910 – 1930s, Stutzhaus, Germany. Porcelain factory founded by August Hertel and Heinrich Schwab, both designed doll heads used by Borgfeldt, Kley and Hahn, Koenig & Wernicke, Louis Wolf, and others. Made china and bisque heads as well as all-porcelain; most with character faces. Molded hair or wig, painted blue or glass eyes (often blue-gray), open mouth with tongue or closed mouth, socket or shoulder heads. Usually marked with mold number and "Made in Germany," or mark of company that owned the mold.

Baby, 1910 on, bisque head, molded hair or wig, open or open/closed mouth, teeth, sleep or painted eyes, bent-leg baby composition body

Mold 130, 142, 150, 151, 152

9" – 12"	$300.00 – 475.00
15" – 16"	$350.00 – 425.00
19" – 21"	$575.00 – 650.00
22" – 24"	$650.00 – 700.00

16" Hertel & Schwab baby, mold 151. $425.00. Courtesy of The Museum Doll Shop

Toddler body

14"	$550.00 – 600.00
20"	$700.00 – 800.00

Mold 1125 (so-called Patsy Baby)

12"	$975.00 – 1,025.00

Mold 126 (so-called Skippy)

9"	$825.00 – 875.00

Child

Mold 127, ca. 1915, character face, solid dome with molded hair, sleep eyes, open mouth, Patsy-type

15"	$1,350.00 – 1,450.00
17"	$2,000.00 – 2,400.00

Mold 131, ca. 1912, character face, solid dome, painted closed mouth

18"	$1,300.00

Too few in database for a reliable range.

Mold 134, ca. 1915, character face, sleep eyes, closed mouth

15"	$3,500.00 – 4,000.00

Mold 136, ca. 1912, "Made in Germany," character face, open mouth

7"	$325.00 – 375.00
18" – 20"	$500.00 – 550.00
24" – 25"	$600.00 – 700.00

Mold 140, ca. 1912, character, glass eyes, open/closed laughing mouth

12" – 15"	$3,400.00 – 4,200.00

Mold 141, ca. 1912, character, painted eyes, open/closed mouth

12" – 14"	$2,600.00 – 3,200.00
17" – 18"	$7,300.00 – 9,000.00

Mold 149, ca. 1912, character, glass eyes, closed mouth, ball-jointed body

17"	$8,500.00 – 9,500.00

Googly: See Googly category.

9" mold 126, so-called Skippy Baby. $875.00. *Courtesy of The Museum Doll Shop.*

HERTWIG & CO.

1864 – 1940s, Kutzhütte, Thüringia, Germany. Porcelain factory producing china and bisque dolls. Some distributed by Butler Brothers.

Half-Bisque Dolls, 1911 on, bisque head and torso, molded clothing, lower body cloth, lower arms and legs bisque

Child

4½"	$225.00 – 250.00

Adult

6½"	$325.00 – 350.00

4½" Hertwig half-bisque doll, molded blouse. $250.00. *Courtesy of The Museum Doll Shop.*

All Bisque: See All-Bisque section.
China Name Dolls: See China section.
Bisque Bonnet-Head: See Bonnet-Head section.

ERNST HEUBACH

1887 – 1930s, Köppelsdorf, Germany. In 1919, the son of Armand Marseille married the daughter of Ernst Heubach and merged the two factories. Mold numbers range from 250 to 452. They made porcelain heads for Dressel (Jutta), Revalo, and others. Dolls listed are in good condition, appropriately dressed.

Child, 1888 on
Mold 1900 with horseshoe mark, shoulder head, open mouth, glass eyes, kid or cloth body

10" – 12"	$125.00 – 150.00
18" – 22"	$225.00 – 300.00
26"	$500.00 – 550.00

Molds 250, 251, 275 (shoulder head), 302, open mouth, kid body

8" – 10"	$175.00 – 200.00
13" – 15"	$225.00 – 250.00
16" – 19"	$300.00 – 375.00
23" – 24"	$375.00 – 425.00
27" – 32"	$600.00 – 750.00
36"	$1,000.00

Painted bisque

8" – 12"	$140.00 – 160.00
16"	$200.00 – 225.00

Baby, 1910 on, open mouth, glass eyes, socket head, wig, five-piece bent-leg composition body, add more for toddler body, flirty eyes
Molds 250, 267, 300, 320, 321, 342

5" – 6½"	$250.00 – 275.00
8" – 11"	$300.00 – 350.00
14" – 17"	$400.00 – 450.00
19" – 21"	$500.00 – 550.00
25" – 27"	$725.00 – 950.00

Painted bisque, flirty eyes

24"	$375.00 – 425.00

7½" mold 342 on a bent-limb body, made by Ernst Heubach. $300.00. *Doll courtesy of Ruth Cayton.*

Character Child, 1910 on, painted eyes
Molds 261, 262, 271, and others, bisque shoulder head, cloth body

12"	$300.00 – 400.00

Mold 312 (for Seyfarth & Reinhard)

14"	$300.00 – 325.00
18"	$400.00 – 425.00
28"	$600.00 – 650.00

Baby, Newborn, 1925 on, solid dome, molded and painted hair, glass eyes, closed mouth, cloth body, composition or celluloid hands

Molds 338, 339, 340, 348, 349

10" – 12"	$375.00 – 425.00
14" – 16"	$475.00 – 575.00
17"	$600.00 – 650.00

Black, mold 444

12"	$375.00 – 425.00

8" Ernst Heubach babies, mold 250, in original chemises and paper tags which read "Little Sister." $600.00 pair. *Courtesy of The Museum Doll Shop.*

GEBRÜDER HEUBACH

1910 – 1938, Lichte, Thüringia, Germany. Porcelain factory founded in 1804 but did not make dolls until 1910. Made bisque heads and all-bisque dolls, characters, either socket or shoulder head, molded hair or wigs, sleeping or intaglio eyes, in heights from 4" to 26". Provided heads other to companies including Bauersachs, Cuno & Otto Dressel, Eisemann & Co., and Gebruder Ohlhaver. Mold numbers from 556 to 10633. Sunburst or square marks; more dolls with square marks. Dolls listed are in good condition, appropriately dressed.

Marked "Heubach," no mold number
Open/closed mouth, dimples

18"	$4,300.00 – 4,450.00
24"	$6,000.00 – 6,300.00

Adult, open mouth, glass eyes

14"	$4,400.00 – 4,500.00

Smile, painted eyes

15"	$3,400.00 – 3,500.00

Marked Heubach Googly: See Googly category.

18" Gebruder Heubach shoulder-head character boy with flocked hair. $1,600.00. *Courtesy of The Museum Doll Shop.*

Character Child
Shoulder Head
Mold 5777, Dolly Dimple, shoulder-head version

    17" – 19" $900.00 – 1,100.00

Mold 6688, ca. 1912, solid dome, molded hair, intaglio eyes, closed mouth

    10" $625.00

Mold 6692, ca. 1912, shoulder-head version, sunburst, intaglio eyes, closed mouth poutie

    14" – 16" $550.00 – 650.00

    20" $875.00 – 900.00

Mold 6736, ca. 1912, square, painted eyes, laughing mouth

    13" $1,000.00 – 1,100.00

    16" $1,700.00 – 1,900.00

Mold 7345, ca. 1912, sunburst, pink-tinted closed mouth

    17" $1,000.00 – 1,150.00

Mold 7644, ca. 1910, sunburst or square mark, painted eyes, open/closed laughing mouth

    14" $850.00 – 950.00

    17" $1,100.00 – 1,200.00

    20" $1,650.00 – 1,750.00

22" Dolly Dimples shoulder-head doll. $1,200.00. *Courtesy of The Museum Doll Shop.*

Mold 7847, solid dome shoulder head, intaglio eyes, closed smiling mouth, teeth

    20" $2,100.00

Too few in database for a reliable range.

Mold 7850, ca. 1912, "Coquette," open-closed mouth

    11" – 12" $650.00 – 750.00

    15" $950.00 – 1,000.00

Mold 7852, ca. 1912, molded hair in coiled braids

    16" $2,200.00

Too few in database for a reliable range.

Mold 7853, ca. 1912, downcast eyes

    14" $1,600.00 – 1,800.00

Mold 7925, ca. 1914, Mold 7926, ca. 1912, lady, glass eyes, smiling open mouth

    11" – 15" $1,400.00 – 2,000.00

Too few in database for a reliable range.

    18" – 20" $2,900.00 – 3,100.00

Too few in database for a reliable range.

Mold 7972, intaglio eyes, closed mouth

    20" $1,800.00 – 2,000.00

Mold 8221, square mark, dome, intaglio eyes, open/closed mouth

    14" $650.00 – 700.00

Too few in database for a reliable range.

Mold 9355, ca. 1914, square mark, glass eyes, open mouth

    13" $800.00 – 850.00

    19" $1,100.00 – 1,250.00

Socket Head
Mold 5636, ca. 1912, glass eyes, open/closed laughing mouth, teeth

    12" – 13" $1,700.00 – 1,800.00

    15" – 18" $2,300.00 – 2,600.00

Mold 5689, ca. 1912, sunburst mark, smiling open mouth

    14" $1,800.00 – 1,900.00

    17" $2,250.00 – 2,300.00

    22" $2,900.00 – 3,000.00

Mold 5730, "Santa," ca. 1912, sunburst mark, made for Hamburger & Co.

16"	$1,600.00 – 1,700.00
19" – 22"	$1,900.00 – 2,100.00
24" – 26"	$2,400.00 – 2,600.00

Mold 5777, "Dolly Dimple," ca. 1913, open mouth, for Hamburger & Co.

12" – 14"	$2,300.00 – 2,400.00
16" – 19"	$2,600.00 – 3,100.00
22" – 24"	$3,300.00 – 3,500.00

Mold 6969, ca. 1912, socket head, square mark, glass eyes, closed mouth

7" – 9"	$1,050.00 – 1,250.00
12" – 13"	$2,200.00 – 2,300.00
16" – 18"	$3,400.00 – 3,800.00
20" – 24"	$4,000.00 – 4,200.00

Mold 6970, ca. 1912, sunburst, glass eyes, closed mouth

7" – 9"	$850.00 – 950.00
12" – 13"	$2,100.00 – 2,400.00
16" – 18"	$3,200.00 – 3,600.00
20" – 24"	$4,100.00 – 4,900.00

14" Gebruder Heubach adult doll, c. 1890s. $4,400.00. *Courtesy of The Museum Doll Shop.*

Mold 6971, ca. 1912, intaglio eyes, closed smiling mouth in original costume box

11"	$1,200.00

Too few in database for a reliable range.

Molds 7246, 7247, 7248, ca. 1912, sunburst or square mark, closed mouth, glass eyes

7" – 9"	$850.00 – 950.00
12" – 13"	$2,100.00 – 2,400.00
16" – 18"	$3,200.00 – 3,600.00
20" – 24"	$4,100.00 – 4,400.00
26" – 28"	$4,500.00 – 6,000.00

Mold 7268, square, glass eyes, closed mouth

12"	$5,000.00

Too few in database for a reliable range.

Mold 7407, character, glass eyes, open-closed mouth

7" – 9"	$850.00 – 950.00
12" – 13"	$2,100.00 – 2,400.00
16" – 18"	$3,100.00 – 3,500.00
20" – 24"	$4,100.00 – 4,900.00

Mold 7602, 7603, ca. 1912, molded hair tufts, intaglio eyes

15" – 18"	$950.00 – 1,050.00

Mold 7604, ca. 1912, open/closed mouth, intaglio eyes

12" – 14"	$650.00 – 700.00
20"	$1,100.00 – 1,200.00

Mold 7622, 7623, ca. 1912, intaglio eyes, closed or open/closed mouth

16" – 18"	$1,100.00 – 1,300.00

Mold 7633, ca. 1912, laughing child, glass eyes

12" – 13"	$1,700.00 – 1,800.00
15" – 18"	$2,300.00 – 2,600.00

Mold 7681, dome, intaglio eyes, closed mouth

10" – 12"	$500.00 – 575.00

Mold 7711, ca. 1912, glass eyes, open mouth, flapper body

9" – 10"	$1,000.00 – 1,200.00
18"	$6,000.00 – 7,000.00

Mold 7746, ca. 1912, open/closed mouth with two teeth, ears sticking out from head

    14" $6,200.00

Too few in database for a reliable range.

Mold 7759, ca. 1912, dome, painted eyes, closed mouth

    12" $800.00 – 900.00

Molds 7788, 7850 (Coquette), ca. 1912, molded hair with bow

    11" $900.00 – 950.00

    14" – 15" $1,100.00 – 1,300.00

    20" $1,500.00 – 1,600.00

Mold 7911, ca. 1912, intaglio eyes, laughing open/closed mouth

    9" – 11" $625.00 – 700.00

    15" $850.00 – 950.00

Mold 7956, ca. 1912, intaglio eyes, molded hair

    15" – 19" $12,500.00 – 17,000.00

Mold 8191, "Crooked Smile," ca. 1912, square mark, intaglio eyes, laughing mouth

    11½" $1,200.00 – 1,300.00

    14" $1,500.00 – 1,600.00

    16" $2,800.00 – 3,000.00

Mold 8192, ca. 1914, sunburst or square mark, sleep eyes, open mouth

    11" – 13" $750.00 – 950.00

    18" – 20" $1,275.00 – 1,450.00

Mold 8316, "Grinning Boy," ca. 1914, wig, open/closed mouth, eight teeth, glass eyes

    16" $3,200.00 – 3,400.00

    19" $4,600.00 – 4,800.00

Mold 8381, "Princess Juliana," molded hair, ribbon, painted eyes, closed mouth

    14" – 16" $10,000.00 – 13,000.00

Mold 8413, ca. 1914, wig, sleep eyes, open/closed mouth, molded tongue, upper teeth

    8" $1,000.00 – 1,150.00

Too few in database for a reliable range.

    24" $7,000.00

Too few in database for a reliable range.

16" Gebruder Heubach mold # 8192. $1,100.00. *Courtesy Richard W. Withington, Inc., Nashua, New Hampshire.*

Mold 8429, square mark, closed mouth

    15" $2,500.00

Too few in database for a reliable range.

Mold 8686, glass eyes, open/closed mouth

    14" $3,200.00

Too few in database for a reliable range.

Mold 8774, "Whistling Jim," ca. 1914, smoker or whistler, square mark, flange neck, intaglio eyes, molded hair, cloth body, bellows

    14" $985.00

Too few in database for a reliable range.

Mold 8819, square mark, intaglio eyes, open/closed mouth

    9" $1,050.00

Too few in database for a reliable range.

Mold 8950, laughing girl, blue hair bow

    18" $6,900.00 – 7,200.00

Mold 9027, dome, intaglio eyes, closed mouth

    13" $1,200.00

Too few in database for a reliable range.

18" Gebrüder Heubach Coquette. $1,100.00.
Courtesy of The Museum Doll Shop.

Mold 9055, intaglio eyes, closed mouth
| 11" | $375.00 |

Too few in database for a reliable range.

Mold 9457, ca. 1914, square mark, dome, intaglio eyes, closed mouth, Eskimo
| 15" | $2,300.00 – 2,500.00 |
| 18" | $3,800.00 – 4,000.00 |

Mold 9746, square mark, painted eyes, closed mouth
| 7½" | $700.00 – 800.00 |

Mold 10532, ca. 1920, square mark, open mouth, five-piece toddler body
8½"	$1,000.00 – 1,100.00
13½"	$1,450.00 – 1,550.00
20" – 22"	$1,900.00 – 2,100.00
25"	$2,400.00 – 2,500.00

Mold 11173, "Tiss Me," socket head, wig
| 8" | $1,900.00 – 2,000.00 |

Too few in database for a reliable range.

Character Baby, socket head, 1911 on, bisque head, bent-limb body

Mold 6894, 6897, 7759, 7604, all ca. 1912, sunburst or square mark, intaglio eyes, closed mouth, molded hair
6" – 7"	$250.00 – 350.00
9" – 12"	$325.00 – 375.00
15"	$500.00 – 600.00
20"	$900.00 – 1,000.00

Toddler
| 14" | $850.00 – 950.00 |

Mold 7761, ca. 1912, squinted intaglio eyes, open/closed crying mouth
| 16" | $7,200.00 |

Too few in database for a reliable range.

Mold 7975, "Baby Stuart," ca. 1912, glass eyes, removable molded bisque bonnet
| 13" | $1,900.00 – 2,100.00 |

Molds 7877, 7977, "Baby Stuart," ca. 1912, molded bonnet, closed mouth, painted eyes
8" – 9"	$775.00 – 825.00
11" – 13"	$1,200.00 – 1,300.00
15"	$1,400.00 – 1,500.00

Mold 8420, ca. 1914, square mark, glass eyes, closed mouth
| 10" | $650.00 – 750.00 |
| 15" | $1,200.00 – 1,400.00 |

All Bisque: See All-Bisque section.

6" Gebruder Heubach baby, solid dome head, intaglio eyes. $250.00. *Courtesy of The Museum Doll Shop.*

E.I. HORSMAN

1878 – 1980s, New York City. Founded by Edward Imeson Horsman as company importing, assembling, wholesaling, and distributing various dolls and doll lines. From 1909 to 1919 they distributed Aetna Doll

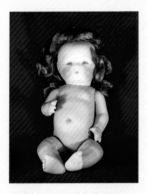

6" all-bisque Tynie Baby by Horsman. $1,785.00. *Courtesy of The Museum Doll Shop.*

& Toy Company's dolls, in 1919 the two companies merged. Eventually Horsman made their own dolls as well as distributing other lines. They took out their first patent for a complete doll in 1909 for a Bilikin doll. They made dolls of composition, rubber, hard plastic, and vinyl.

Dolls listed are in good condition with original clothing, add more for exceptional doll.

Early Composition on Cloth Body, composition head, sometimes lower arms, cloth body.

Baby Bumps, 1910 – 1917, composition head, cloth cork stuffed body, blue and white cloth label on romper, copy of K*R #100 Baby mold

11"	$250.00
Black	$300.00 – 350.00

Baby Butterfly, 1914 on, composition head, hands, cloth body, painted hair, features

13"	$250.00 – 300.00
15"	$350.00 – 400.00

Billiken, 1909, composition head, molded hair, slanted eyes, smiling closed mouth, on stuffed mohair or velvet body, marks: cloth label on body, "Billiken" on right foot

12"	$200.00 – 400.00

Campbell Kids, 1910 on, designed by Helen Trowbridge, based on Grace Drayton's drawings, composition head, painted and molded hair, side-glancing painted eyes, closed smiling mouth, composition arms, cloth body and feet, mark: "EIH a 1910," cloth label on sleeve "The Campbell Kids// Trademark by // Joseph Campbell// Mfg. by E.I. Horsman Co."

10" – 11"	$325.00 – 350.00
15" – 16"	$375.00 – 400.00

Can't Break "Em Characters, 1911on

Child, boy or girl

11" – 13"	$200.00 – 275.00

Cotton Joe, black

13"	$350.00 – 400.00

Little Mary Mix-up

15"	$350.00 – 375.00

13" composition Jackie Coogan Kid by Horsman. $475.00. *Courtesy of Turn of the Century Antiques, Denver, Colorado.*

16" Little Mary Mix Up by Horsman. $375.00. *Courtesy of The Museum Doll Shop.*

Master & Miss Sam, in patriotic outfits
    15" $350.00 – 375.00
Polly Pru
    13" $325.00 – 350.00
Gene Carr Kids, 1915 – 1916, 14" composition head, molded and painted hair, painted eyes, open/closed smiling mouth with teeth, big ears, cloth body, composition hands, original outfit, cloth tag reads "MADE GENE CARR KIDS U.S.A.//FROM NEW YORK WORLD'S// LADY BOUNTIFUL COMIC SERIES//By E.I. HORSMAN CO. NY."
Blink, Lizzie, Mike, Skinney
                      $350.00 – 400.00
Snowball, black $500.00 – 550.00
Gold Medal Baby, 1911 on, line of baby dolls with composition head and limbs, upper and lower teeth, included Baby

Suck-a-thumb, Baby Blossom, Baby Premier, and others
    10" $200.00 – 250.00
    12" $250.00 – 300.00
    19" $325.00 – 375.00
Early All-Composition Dolls
Peek-a-Boo, 1913, designed by Grace Drayton
    8" $100.00 – 125.00
Peterkin, 1914 – 1930
    11" $350.00 – 400.00
Puppy & Pussy Pippin, 1911, designed by Grace Drayton, composition head, plush body
                      $450.00 – 550.00
Composition Dolls on Cloth Body, 1920 on
Brother & Sister, 1937, marked: "Brother//1937//Horsman//©" and "Sister//1937//Horsman//©"Brother 21" and 23" Sister
             $300.00 – 350.00 each
Ella Cinders, 1928 – 1929, based on a cartoon character, composition head, black painted hair or wig, round painted eyes, freckles under eyes, open/closed

10" Baby Suck-A-Thumb by Horsman. $250.00. *Doll courtesy of Ruth Cayton.*

mouth, also came as all-cloth, mark: "1925//MNS"

14"	$400.00 – 450.00
18"	$650.00 – 700.00

Jackie Coogan, "The Kid," 1921 – 1922, composition head, hands, molded hair, painted eyes, turtleneck sweater, long gray pants, checked cap, button reads "HORSMAN DOLL// JACKIE// COOGAN// KID// PATENTED"

13½"	$450.00 – 475.00
15½"	$500.00 – 550.00

Jeanie Horsman, 1937, composition head and limbs, painted molded brown hair, sleep eyes, mark: "Jeanie© Horsman"

14"	$225.00 – 250.00

All-Composition Dolls, 1930 on

Body Twist, 1930, with jointed waist

11"	$200.00 – 250.00

Bright Star, 1937 – 1946

14"	$200.00 – 225.00
20"	$350.00 – 400.00

Child, including Gold Metal child

13" – 14"	$185.00 – 200.00
16" – 18"	$225.00 – 250.00
21"	$250.00 – 275.00

Campbell Kids, 1930 – 1940s, all composition

13"	$425.00 – 475.00

HEbee-SHEbees, 1925 – 1927, based on drawings by Charles Twelvetrees, painted features, molded undershirt and booties or various costumes

10½"	$500.00 – 575.00

All-bisque HEbee & SHEbee: See All-Bisque German section.

Jo Jo, 1937, blue sleep eyes, wig over molded hair, toddler body, mark: "HORSMAN JO JO//©1937"

13"	$325.00 – 375.00

Naughty Sue, 1937, jointed body

16"	$400.00 – 450.00

22" composition Baby Dimples. $400.00. *Courtesy of The Museum Doll Shop.*

Patsy-Type, names such as Sue, Babs, Joan were given to the various sizes

12"	$200.00 – 225.00
14"	$250.00 – 275.00

Roberta, 1937, all-composition

16"	$25.00 – 450.00

Composition Baby, 1920s – 1940s

Dimples, 1927 – 1937 on, composition head, arms, cloth body, bent-leg body, or bent-limb baby body, molded dimples, open mouth, sleep or painted eyes, marked "E.I. H."

13" – 14"	$225.00 – 250.00
16" – 18"	$275.00 – 325.00
20" – 22"	$350.00 – 400.00

Toddler

20"	$300.00 – 350.00
24"	$425.00 – 475.00

Tynie Baby, ca. 1924 – 1929, bisque or composition head, sleep or painted eyes, cloth body, some all-bisque, marks: "©1924//E.I. HORSMAN//CO. INC." or "E.I.H. Co. 1924" on composition or "©1924 by//E I Horsman Co. Inc//Germany// 37" incised on bisque head

All-bisque, with wardrobe, cradle

6"	$1,785.00
9"	$2,500.00

Bisque, head circumference

9"	$600.00
12"	$200.00
15"	$300.00

Composition heads and arms, cloth body

21"	$375.00 – 425.00

Vinyl, 1950s, boxed

15"	$90.00 – 110.00

Mama Dolls, 1920 on, composition head, arms, and lower legs, cloth body with crier and stitched hip joints so lower legs will swing, painted or sleep eyes, mohair or molded hair, models including Peggy Ann, Rosebud, and others

14" – 15"	$200.00 – 225.00
19" – 21"	$300.00 – 350.00

Hard Plastic and Vinyl. Dolls listed are in excellent condition with original clothing and tags. Allow more for mint-in-box doll. Add more for accessories or wardrobe.

Angelove, 1974, plastic/vinyl made for Hallmark

12"	$20.00 – 25.00

15" Horsman composition baby, all original. $200.00. *Courtesy of The Museum Doll Shop.*

12" Sue, Patsy-type doll, also came in a white version. $200.00. *Courtesy of The Museum Doll Shop.*

Answer Doll, 1966, button in back moves head

10"	$10.00 – 15.00

Baby First Tooth, 1966, vinyl head, limbs, cloth body, open/closed mouth with tongue and one tooth, molded tears on cheeks, rooted blond hair, painted blue eyes, mark: "©Horsman Dolls Inc. //10141"

16"	$30.00 – 40.00

Baby Sofskin, 1972 on, vinyl

12" – 15"	$35.00 – 40.00

Baby Tweaks, 1967, vinyl head, cloth body, inset eyes, rooted saran hair, mark: "54//HORSMAN DOLLS INC.//Copyright 1967/67191" on head

20"	$20.00 – 30.00

Ballerina, 1957, vinyl, one-piece body and legs, jointed elbows

18"	$50.00

Betty, 1951, all-vinyl, one-piece body and limbs

14"	$50.00 – 60.00

Vinyl head, hard plastic body
  16" $20.00 – 25.00
Betty Ann, vinyl head, hard plastic body
  19" $50.00 – 60.00
Betty Jane, vinyl head, hard plastic body
  25" $65.00 – 75.00
Betty Jo, vinyl head, hard plastic body
  16" $20.00 – 30.00
Bright Star, ca. 1952 on, all hard plastic
  15" $375.00 – 450.00
Bye-Lo Baby, 1972, reissue, molded vinyl head, limbs, cloth body, white nylon organdy bonnet dress, mark: "3 (in square)//HORSMAN DOLLS INC.//©1972"
  14" $30.00 – 35.00
1980 – 1990s
  14" $15.00 – 20.00
Celeste, portrait doll, in frame, eyes painted to side
  12" $30.00 – 35.00
Christopher Robin
  11" $30.00 – 35.00
Cinderella, 1965, vinyl head, hard plastic body, painted eyes to side
  11½" $25.00 – 30.00
Cindy, 1950s, all hard plastic child, "170"
  15" $125.00 – 175.00
  17" $175.00 – 200.00
  19" $200.00 – 225.00
Cindy Fashion-type doll, vinyl head, soft vinyl stuffed high-heel body
  15" $75.00 – 100.00
  18" $125.00 – 150.00
Vinyl head, solid vinyl body jointed at shoulders and hips, high-heel foot
  10" $25.00 – 30.00
Cindy Kay, 1950s+, all-vinyl child with long legs
  15" $70.00 – 80.00
  20" $110.00 – 125.00
  27" $200.00 – 225.00

15" Horsman Gold Medal boy, vinyl head, stuffed soft vinyl body. $70.00. *Courtesy of The Museum Doll Shop.*

Crawling Baby, 1967, vinyl, rooted hair
  14" $20.00 – 25.00
Disney Exclusives, 1981, Cinderella, Snow White, Mary Poppins, Alice in Wonderland
  8" $35.00 – 40.00
Elizabeth Taylor, 1976
  11½" $45.00 – 50.00
Floppy, 1958, vinyl head, foam body and legs
  18" $20.00 – 25.00
Flying Nun, 1965, TV character portrayed by Sally Field
  12" $100.00 – 125.00
Gold Medal Doll, 1953, vinyl head, soft vinyl foam stuffed body, molded hair
  26" $150.00 – 175.00
1954, vinyl, boy
  15" $65.00 – 75.00
Hansel & Gretel, 1963, vnyl head, hard plastic body, rooted synthetic hair, closed mouth, sleep eyes, marks: "MADE IN USA" on body, on tag "HORSMAN, Michael

Meyerberg, Inc.," "Reproduction of the famous Kinemins in Michael Myerberg's marvelous Technicolor production of Hansel and Gretel"

15"	$200.00 – 225.00

Jackie, 1961, vinyl doll, rooted hair, blue sleep eyes, long lashes, closed mouth, high-heeled feet, small waist, nicely dressed, designed by Irene Szor who says this doll named Jackie was not meant to portray Jackie Kennedy, mark: "HORSMAN//19©61//BC 18"

25"	$150.00 – 175.00

Lullabye Baby, 1967 – 1968, vinyl bent-leg body, rooted hair, inset blue eyes, drink and wet feature, musical mechanism, Sears 1968 catalog, came on suedette pillow, in terrycloth p.j.s, mark: "2580// B144 8 //HORSMAN DOLLS INC//19©67"

12"	$10.00 – 15.00

Mary Poppins, 1965, all in good condition with original clothing, mint-in-box can bring double the value listed

12"	$30.00 – 40.00
16"	$55.00 – 65.00
26", 1966	$75.00 – 100.00
36"	$150.00 – 175.00

In box with Michael and Jane, 1966

12" and 8"	$150.00 – 160.00

Police Woman, ca. 1976, vinyl, plastic fully articulated body, rooted hair

9"	$35.00 – 40.00

Poor Pitiful Pearl, 1963, from cartoon by William Steig, marked on neck: "Horsman 1963"

11"	$130.00 – 150.00
17"	$200.00 – 225.00

Ruthie, 1962

28"	$200.00 – 225.00

Tessie Talk, 1974, ventriloquist doll

16"	$15.00 – 20.00

MARY HOYER DOLL MFG. CO.

1937 – 1968, 1990 – present, Reading, Pennsylvania. Designed by Bernard Lipfert, all-composition, later hard plastic, then vinyl, swivel neck, jointed body, mohair or human hair wig, sleep eyes, closed mouth, original clothes, or knitted from Mary Hoyer patterns. Company re-opened by Hoyer's granddaughter in 1990. Dolls listed are in good condition with appropriate clothing.

Composition, less for painted eyes

14"	$375.00 – 425.00

Hard Plastic

In knit outfit

14"	$425.00 – 450.00

In tagged Hoyer outfit

14"	$450.00 – 625.00

Hard plastic Mary Hoyer. $425.00. *Courtesy of The Museum Doll Shop.*

Boy in original wig

    14" $525.00 – 550.00

Gigi, circa 1950, with round Mary Hoyer mark found on 14" dolls, only 2,000 made by the Frisch Doll Company

    18" $950.00 – 1,200.00

Vinyl, circa 1957 on

Vicky, all-vinyl, high-heeled doll, body bends at waist, rooted saran hair, two larger sizes 12" and 14" were discontinued

    10½" $90.00 – 100.00

Margie, circa 1958, toddler, rooted hair, made by Unique Doll Co.

    10" $70.00 – 75.00

Cathy, circa 1961, infant, made by Unique Doll Co.

    10" $20.00 – 25.00

Janie, circa 1962, baby

    8" $20.00 – 25.00

ADOLPH HÜLSS

1915 – 1930+, Waltershausen, Germany. Made dolls with bisque heads, jointed composition bodies. Trademark: "Nesthakchen," "h" in mold mark often resembles a "b." Heads made by Simon & Halbig.

Baby, bisque socket head, sleep eyes, open mouth, teeth, wig, bent-leg baby, composition body, add more for flirty eyes

Mold 156

14" – 15"	$550.00 – 575.00
17" – 19"	$625.00 – 675.00
23"	$800.00 – 825.00

Toddler

9" – 10"	$850.00 – 900.00
16"	$775.00 – 800.00
20"	$900.00 – 925.00

Painted bisque

22"	$200.00 – 225.00

9" pair of toddlers, mold 156, incised AW for Adolf Hulss. $850.00 each. *Courtesy of Skinner Inc., Boston and Bolton, Massachusetts.*

Child, bisque socket head, wig, sleep eyes, open mouth, teeth, tongue, jointed composition body

Mold 176

15"	$650.00 – 675.00
18"	$650.00 – 750.00
22"	$950.00 – 975.00

MAISON HURET

1812– 1930 on, France. May have pressed, molded bisque, or china heads, painted or glass eyes, closed mouths, bodies of cloth, composition, gutta-percha, kid, or wood, sometimes metal hands. Used fur or mohair for wigs, had fashion-type body with defined waist.

Look for dolls with beautiful painting on eyes and face; painted eyes are more common than glass, but the beauty of the painted features and/or wooden bodies increases the price.

16" Huret bébé. $12,000.00. *Courtesy of Skinner Inc., Boston and Bolton, Massachusetts.*

Bisque shoulder head, kid body with bisque lower arms, glass eyes

15"	$12,000.00 – 13,000.00
17" – 18"	$14,000.00 – 19,000.00

Gutta-percha body

17"	$12,000.00 – 13,000.00

Round face, painted blue eyes, cloth body

16" – 18"	$10,000.00 – 12,000.00

Wood body

17"	$21,000.00 – 24,000.00

Too few in database for a reliable range.

China shoulder head, kid body, china lower arms

17"	$15,000.00 – 20,000.00

Wood body

17"	$25,000.00 – 30,000.00

Gutta percha body

17"	$20,000.00 – 25,000.00

17" Huret poupée, c. 1860s. $14,000.00. *Courtesy of Skinner Inc., Boston and Bolton, Massachusetts.*

Huret Bébé, 1878, bisque head, articulated wooden body, glass eyes, closed mouth

13"	$10,000.00

Too few in database for a reliable range.

18"	$14,000.00

Too few in database for a reliable range.

19" on wooden body with metal hands
$48,875.00*

Prevost Era Lady or Gentleman, 1914 – 1918, elongated face on composition body

17" – 18"	$6,500.00 – 10,000.00

IDEAL NOVELTY AND TOY CO.

1906 – 1980s, Brooklyn, New York. Produced their own composition dolls in early years. Later made dolls of rubber, hard plastic, vinyl, and cloth. For the values listed, dolls made until

1950 must be in good condition with appropriate clothing, dolls made after 1950 must be in excellent condition with original clothing and tags.

Cloth

Dennis the Menace, 1976, all-cloth, printed doll, comic strip character by Hank Ketcham, blond hair, freckles, wearing overalls, striped shirt

7"	$10.00 – 15.00
14"	$15.00 – 20.00

Peanuts Gang, 1976 – 1978, all-cloth, stuffed printed dolls from Peanuts cartoon strip by Charles Schulz, Charlie Brown, Lucy, Linus, Peppermint Patty, and Snoopy

7"	$15.00 – 20.00
14"	$20.00 – 25.00

Snow White and the Seven Dwarves, 1939 on, cloth mask face dolls, cloth body

Snow White, black mohair wig, dress with dwarves printed on skirt

16"	$500.00 – 550.00

Dwarves

10"	$200.00 – 250.00 each

Strawman, 1939, all-cloth, scarecrow character played by Ray Bolger in *Wizard of Oz* movie, yarn hair, all original, wearing dark jacket and hat, tan pants, round paper hang tag

17"	$900.00 – 1,200.00
21"	$1,400.00 – 1,500.00

Composition

Early Character Children, composition heads, lower arms and sometimes shoes on cloth body, excelsior stuffed

Cracker Jack Boy, 1917, sailor suit, carries package of Cracker Jacks

14"	$350.00 – 375.00

Happy Hooligan, 1910

21"	$475.00 – 525.00

Liberty Boy, 1917, molded uniform

12"	$275.00 – 325.00

Naughty Marietta (Coquette-type), 1912

14"	$150.00

Snookums, 1910, plush body

14"	$500.00 – 600.00

10" cloth mask face dwarves by Ideal. $250.00 each. *Courtesy of The Museum Doll Shop.*

Uneeda Kid, 1914 – 1919, original clothing including rain slicker and biscuit box

16"	$475.00 – 500.00

Zu Zu Kid, 1916 – 1917

16"	$350.00 – 375.00

Child or Toddler, 1913 on, composition head, molded hair, or wigged, painted or sleep eyes, cloth or composition body, may have Ideal diamond mark or hang tag, original clothes

13"	$175.00 – 250.00
15" – 16"	$250.00 – 275.00
18"	$275.00 – 300.00

Baby Doll, 1913 on, composition head, molded hair or wigged, painted or sleep eyes, cloth or composition body, models such as Baby Mine, Our Pet, Prize baby, and others

15" – 16"	$175.00 – 250.00

Mama Doll, 1921 on, composition head and arms, molded hair or wigged, painted or sleep eyes, cloth body with crier and stitched swing leg, lower part composition

16"	$225.00 – 275.00
20"	$275.00 – 325.00
24"	$350.00 – 375.00

12" composition Dopey. $250.00. *Courtesy of The Museum Doll Shop.*

Flexy doll, Sunny Sam. $225.00. *Courtesy of The Museum Doll Shop.*

Babies, mid-1920s – 1940s, composition head, arms, and legs, cloth body

Flossie Flirt, 1924 – 1931, composition head, limbs, cloth body, crier, tin flirty eyes, open mouth, upper teeth, original outfit, dress, bonnet, socks, and shoes, mark: "IDEAL" in diamond with "U.S. of A."

14"	$225.00 – 250.00
18"	$250.00 – 275.00
20"	$300.00 – 350.00
22"	$350.00 – 375.00
24"	$375.00 – 400.00
28"	$400.00 – 425.00

Tickletoes, 1928 – 1939, composition head, rubber arms, legs, cloth body, squeaker in each leg, flirty sleep eyes, open mouth, two painted teeth, original organdy dress, bonnet, paper hang tag, marks: "IDEAL" in diamond with "U.S. of A." on head

14"	$275.00 – 300.00
17"	$300.00 – 325.00
20"	$325.00 – 350.00

Snoozie, 1933 on, composition head, painted hair, hard rubber hands and feet, cloth body, open yawning mouth, molded tongue, sleep eyes, designed by Bernard Lipfert, marks: "©B. Lipfert//Made for Ideal Doll & Toy Corp. 1933" or "©by B. Lipfert" or "IDEAL SNOOZIE//B. LIPFERT" on head

14"	$175.00 – 200.00
16"	$275.00 – 325.00
18"	$325.00 – 350.00
20"	$350.00 – 375.00

Princess Beatrix, 1938 – 1943, represents Princess Beatrix of the Netherlands, composition head, arms, legs, cloth body, flirty sleep eyes, fingers molded into fists, original organdy dress and bonnet

14"	$175.00 – 200.00
16"	$250.00 – 275.00
22"	$325.00 – 375.00
26"	$375.00 – 400.00

Soozie Smiles, 1923, two-headed composition doll with smiling face, sleep or painted eyes, and crying face with tears, molded and painted hair, cloth body and legs, composition arms, original clothes, tag, also in gingham check romper

15" – 17"	$375.00 – 425.00

Composition Child, 1920s – 1940s (including Celebrity and Characters)

Buster Brown, 1929, composition head, hands, legs, cloth body, tin eyes, red outfit, mark: "IDEAL" (in a diamond)

17"	$325.00 – 375.00

Charlie McCarthy, 1938 – 1939, hand puppet, composition head, felt hands, molded hat, molded features, wire monocle, cloth body, painted tuxedo, mark: "Edgar Bergen's//©CHARLIE MCCARTHY//MADE IN U.S.A."

8"	45.00 – 60.00

Cinderella, 1938 – 1939, all-composition, brown, blond, or red human hair wig, flirty

11" Pinocchio. $500.00. *Courtesy of Otto & Ursula Mertz.*

brown sleep eyes, open mouth, six teeth, same head mold as Ginger, Snow White, Mary Jane with dimple in chin, some wore formal evening gowns of organdy and taffeta, velvet cape, had rhinestone tiara, silver snap shoes, Sears catalog version has Celanese rayon gown, marks: none on head; "SHIRLEY TEMPLE//13" on body

13"	$300.00 – 325.00
16"	$325.00 – 350.00
20"	$350.00 – 375.00
22"	$375.00 – 400.00
25"	$400.00 – 425.00
27"	$425.00 – 450.00

Deanna Durbin, 1938 – 1941, all-composition, fully jointed, dark brown human hair wig, brown sleep eyes, open mouth, six teeth, felt tongue, original clothes, pin reads: "DEANNA DURBIN//A UNIVERSAL STAR," more for fancy outfits, marks: "DEANNA DURBIN//IDEAL DOLL" on head; "IDEAL DOLL//21" on body

15"	$500 .00 – 550.00
18"	$600.00 – 800.00
21"	$900.00 – 1,000.00
24"	$1,200.00 – 1,300.00

16" Betsy Wetsy with hard plastic head, vinyl body. $300.00. *Courtesy of The Museum Doll Shop.*

Flexy, 1938 – 1942, composition head, gauntlet hands, molded and painted hair, painted eyes, wooden torso and feet, flexible wire tubing for arms and legs, original clothes, paper tag, marks: "IDEAL DOLL//Made in U. S. A." or just "IDEAL DOLL" on head

Black Flexy, closed smiling mouth, tweed patched pants, felt suspenders

13½"	$300.00 – 325.00

Baby Snooks (Fannie Brice), open/closed mouth with teeth

13½"	$250.00 – 275.00

Clown Flexy, looks like Mortimer Snerd, painted white as clown

13½"	$200.00 – 225.00

Mortimer Snerd, Edgar Bergen's dummy, smiling closed mouth, showing two teeth

13½"	$250.00 – 275.00

Soldier, closed smiling mouth, in khaki uniform

13½"	$200.00 – 250.00

Sunny Sam and Sunny Sue, girl bobbed hair, pouty mouth, boy has smiling mouth

13½"	$200.00 – 250.00

Judy Garland
1939 – 1940, as Dorothy from *The Wizard of Oz,* all-composition, jointed, wig with braids, brown sleep eyes, open mouth, six teeth, designed by Bernard Lipfert, blue or red checked rayon jumper, white blouse, marks: "IDEAL" on head plus size number, and "USA" on body

13"	$1,000.00 – 1,100.00
15½"	$1,400.00 – 1,500.00
18"	$1,600.00 – 1,700.00

1940 – 1942, teen, all-composition, wig, sleep eyes, open mouth, four teeth, original long dress, hang tag reads "Judy Garland//A Metro Goldwyn Mayer//Star// in// 'Little Nellie//Kelly,'" original pin reads "JUDY GARLAND METRO GOLDWYN MAYER STAR," marks: "IN U.S.A." on head, "IDEAL DOLLS," a backwards "21" on body

15"	$700.00 – 800.00
21"	$1,000.00 – 1,100.00

Seven Dwarfs, 1938 on, composition head and cloth body, head turns, removable clothes, each dwarf has name on cap, pick, and lantern

12"	$250.00 – 300.00

Dopey, 1938, one of Seven Dwarfs, a ventriloquist doll, composition head and hands, cloth body, arms, and legs, hinged mouth with drawstring, molded tongue, painted eyes, large ears, long coat, cotton pants, felt shoes sewn to leg, felt cap with name, can stand alone, mark: "IDEAL DOLL" on neck

20"	$700.00 – 800.00

Snow White
1938 on, all-composition, jointed body, black mohair wig, flirty glass eyes, open mouth, four teeth, dimple in chin, used Shirley Temple body, red velvet bodice, rayon taffeta skirt pictures Seven Dwarfs, velvet cape, some unmarked, marks:

"Shirley Temple/18" or other size number on back

11½"	$475.00 – 500.00
13" – 14"	$500.00 – 550.00
19" – 21"	$650.00 – 750.00

1938 – 1939, with molded and painted bow and black hair, painted side-glancing eyes, add 50 percent more for black version, mark: "IDEAL DOLL" on head

14½"	$200.00 – 250.00
17½" – 19½"	$450.00 – 550.00

Shirley Temple: See Shirley Temple section.

Composition and Wood Dolls, 1940 on, segmented wooden body, strung with elastic

Jiminy Cricket

9"	$425.00 – 475.00

Ferdinand the Bull

9"	$400.00 – 450.00

Pinocchio, 1939

8"	$300.00 – 350.00
11"	$450.00 – 500.00
20"	$750.00 – 850.00

Magic Skin Dolls, 1940 on, latex body, stuffed, original clothing, these doll bodies are prone to disintegration

Baby Coos, 1948 – 1953, also Brother and Sister Coos, designed by Bernard Lipfert, hard plastic head, jointed arms, sleep eyes, molded and painted hair, closed mouth, squeeze box voice, later on cloth and vinyl body, marks on head "16 IDEAL DOLL// MADE IN U.S.A." or unmarked

14"	$90.00 – 100.00
16" – 18"	$125.00 – 135.00
20" – 22"	$145.00 – 165.00
27" – 30"	$195.00 – 215.00

Bonny Braids, 1951 – 1953, comic strip character, daughter of Dick Tracy and Tess Trueheart, vinyl head, jointed arms, one-piece body, open mouth, one tooth, painted

13" Bonnie Braids, vinyl head, latex body. $325.00.
Courtesy of The Museum Doll Shop.

yellow hair, two yellow saran pigtails, painted blue eyes, coos when squeezed, long white gown, bed jacket, toothbrush, Ipana toothpaste, mark: "©1951//Chi. Tribune//IDEAL DOLL//U.S.A." on neck

Baby

11½"	$250.00 – 275.00
14"	$325.00 – 350.00

Toddler, 1953, vinyl head, jointed hard plastic body, open/closed mouth with two painted teeth, walker

11½"	$125.00 – 150.00
13½"	$175.00 – 200.00

Magic Skin Baby, 1940, 1946 – 1949, hard plastic head, one-piece body and legs, jointed arms, sleep eyes, molded and painted hair, some with fancy layettes or trunks, latex usually darkened

13" – 14"	$50.00 – 75.00
15" – 16"	$75.00 – 100.00
17" – 18"	$100.00 – 125.00
20"	$125.00 – 135.00

Joan Palooka, 1953, daughter of comic strip character, Joe Palooka, vinyl head, "Magic Skin" body, jointed arms and legs, yellow molded hair, topknot of yellow saran, blue painted eyes, open/closed mouth, smells like baby powder, original pink dress with blue ribbons, came with Johnson's baby powder and soap, mark: "©1952//HAM FISHER//IDEAL DOLL" on head

14"	$175.00 – 200.00

Snoozie, 1951, open/closed mouth, vinyl head

11"	$100.00 – 125.00
16"	$125.00 – 150.00
20"	$150.00 – 175.00

Sparkle Plenty, 1947 – 1950, hard plastic head, "Magic Skin" body may be dark, yarn hair, character from Dick Tracy comics

14"	$175.00 – 200.00

Hard Plastic and Vinyl Dolls, all in good condition with original clothing, mint-in-box can bring double the value listed

Baby

11"	$35.00 – 45.00
14"	$55.00 – 65.00

Child

14"	$25.00 – 35.00

April Shower, 1969, vinyl, battery operated, splashes hands, head turns

14"	$35.00 – 40.00

Baby Pebbles, 1963 – 1964, character from the Flintstone cartoons, Hanna Barbera Productions, vinyl head, arms, legs, soft body, side-glancing blue painted eyes, rooted hair with topknot and bone, leopard print nightie and trim on flannel blanket, also as an all-vinyl toddler, jointed body, outfit with leopard print

14"	$165.00 – 170.00

Tiny Pebbles, 1964 – 1966, hard vinyl body, came with plastic log cradle in 1965.

8"	$65.00 – 75.00
12"	$90.00 – 100.00
16"	$110.00 – 130.00

Bamm-Bamm, 1964, character from Flintstone cartoon, Hanna Barbera Productions, all-vinyl head, jointed body, rooted blond saran hair, painted blue side-glancing eyes, leopard skin suit, cap, club

12"	$70.00 – 80.00
16"	$120.00 – 130.00

Belly Button Babies, 1971, Me So Glad, Me So Silly, Me So Happy, vinyl head, rooted hair, painted eyes, press button in belly to move arms, head, and bent legs, both boy and girl versions

White

9½"	$30.00 – 40.00

Black

9½"	$40.00 – 45.00

Betsy McCall: See Betsy McCall section.

Betsy Wetsy, 1937 – 1938, 1954 – 1956, 1959 – 1962, 1982 – 1985, open mouth for bottle, drinks, wets, came with bottle, some in layettes, marks: "IDEAL" on head, "IDEAL" on body

Hard rubber head, soft rubber body, sleep or painted eyes

11"	$100.00 – 125.00
13½"	$125.00 – 150.00
15"	$150.00 – 175.00
17"	$175.00 – 200.00
19"	$200.00 – 225.00

Hard plastic head, vinyl body

11½"	$250.00 – 300.00
13½"	$275.00 – 325.00
16"	$300.00 – 350.00
20"	$325.00 – 375.00

All-vinyl

11½"	$70.00 – 80.00
13½"	$90.00 – 100.00
16"	$110.00 – 120.00

Bizzie-Lizzie, 1971 – 1972, vinyl head, jointed body, rooted blond hair, sleep eyes, plugged into power pack, she irons, vacuums, uses feather duster, two D-cell batteries

White

18"	$50.00 – 60.00

Black

18"	$55.00 – 65.00

Butterick Sew Easy Designing Set, 1953, hard vinyl mannequin of adult woman, molded blond hair, came with Butterick patterns and sewing accessories

14"	$100.00 – 125.00

Captain Action® Superhero, 1966 – 1968, represents a fictional character who changes to become a new identity, vinyl articulated figure, dark hair and eyes

Captain Action

12"	$250.00 – 300.00
Batman disguise	$150.00
Silver Streak box only	$400.00

Too few in databases for a reliable range.

Capt. Flash Gordon accessories	$150.00
Phantom disguise only	$200.00
Steve Canyon disguise	$200.00
Superman set w/dog	$175.00
Lone Ranger outfit only	$150.00
Spiderman disguise only	$150.00
Tonto outfit only	$150.00

Action Boy

9"	$250.00
Robin accessories	$150.00
Special Edition	$300.00
Dr. Evil	$250.00
Dr. Evil Lab Set	$2,000.00

Super Girl

11½"	$300.00

Clarabelle, 1954, clown from Howdy Doody TV show, mask face, cloth body, dressed in satin Clarabelle outfit with noise box and horn, later vinyl face

16"	$200.00 – 225.00
20"	$225.00 – 250.00

Crissy® Family of Dolls, 1969 – 1974, 1982, vinyl grow-hair dolls. All dolls listed are in good condition with original clothing, mint-in-box dolls can bring double the value listed.

Baby Crissy, 1973 – 1976, all-vinyl, jointed body, legs and arms foam filled, rooted auburn grow hair, two painted teeth, brown sleep eyes, mark: "©1972//IDEAL TOY COPR.//2M 5511//B OR GHB-H-225" on back

White

24"	$75.00 – 85.00

Black

24"	$85.00 – 95.00

Beautiful Crissy, 1969 – 1974, all-vinyl, dark brown eyes, long hair, turn knob in back to make hair grow, some with swivel waist (1971), pull string to turn head (1972),

Ideal Velvet, grow-hair doll. $55.00. *Courtesy of The Museum Doll Shop.*

pull string to talk (1971), reissued ca. 1982 – 1983, first year the doll was sold the hair grew to floor length

White

18" $70.00 – 80.00

Black

17½" $80.00 – 90.00

1982 doll $35.00 – 40.00

Crissy's Friends, Brandi, 1972 – 1973; Kerry, 1971; Tressy, 1970 (Sears Exclusive); vinyl head, painted eyes, rooted growing hair, swivel waist

White

18" $65.00 – 75.00

Black

18" $70.00 – 80.00

Cinnamon, Velvet's Little Sister, 1972 – 1974, vinyl head, painted eyes, rooted auburn growing hair, orange polka dotted outfit, additional outfits sold separately, marks: "©1971//IDEAL TOY CORP.//G-H-12-H18// HONG KONG//IDEAL 1069-4 b" on head, "©1972//IDEAL TOY CORP.//U.S. PAT-3-162-976//OTHER PAT. PEND.//HONG KONG" on back

White

13½" $50.00 – 60.00

Black

13½" $60.00 – 70.00

Cricket, 1971 – 1972 (Sears Exclusive); **Dina**, 1972 – 1973; **Mia**, 1971; vinyl, members of the Crissy® family, growing hair dolls, painted teeth, swivel waist

15" $45.00 – 50.00

Tara, 1976, all-vinyl black doll, long black rooted hair that "grows," sleep eyes, marked "©1975//IDEAL TOY CORP//H-250//HONG KONG" on head and "©1970// IDEAL TOY CORP//GH-15//M5169-01// MADE IN HONG KONG" on buttock

15½" $75.00 – 85.00

Velvet

1971 – 1973, Crissy's younger cousin, talker

15" $40.00 – 45.00

1974, non-talker, other accessories, grow hair

White

15" $50.00 – 55.00

Black

15" $60.00 – 65.00

Daddy's Girl, 1961, vinyl head and arms, plastic body, swivel waist, jointed ankles, rooted saran hair, blue sleep eyes, closed smiling mouth, preteen girl, label on dress reads "Daddy's Girl," marks: "IDEAL TOY CORP.//g-42-1" on head, "IDEAL TOY CORP.//G-42" on body

38" $1,100.00 – 1,200.00

42" $1,300.00 – 1,400.00

Davy Crockett and his horse, 1955 – 1956, all-plastic, can be removed from horse, fur cap, buckskin clothes

4¾" $40.00 – 50.00

5" Flatsy doll, c. 1969. $30.00. *Courtesy of The Museum Doll Shop.*

22½" Kissy doll, original clothing. $100.00.
Courtesy of The Museum Doll Shop.

Diana Ross, 1969, from the Supremes (singing group), all-vinyl, rooted black bouffant hairdo, gold sheath, feathers, gold shoes, or chartreuse mini-dress, print scarf, and black shoes

17½"	$295.00 – 310.00

Dorothy Hamill, 1978, Olympic skating star, vinyl head, plastic posable body, rooted short brown hair, comes on ice rink stand with skates, also extra outfits available

11½"	$30.00 – 40.00

Evel Knievel, 1974 – 1977, all-plastic stunt figure, helmet, more with stunt cycle

7"	$20.00 – 25.00

Flatsy, 1969, flat vinyl doll with wire armature, rooted hair

6"	$20.00 – 40.00

Harmony, 1972, vinyl, battery operated, makes music with guitar

21"	$100.00 – 125.00

Harriet Hubbard Ayer, 1953, cosmetic doll, vinyl stuffed head, hard plastic (Toni) body, wigged or rooted hair, came with eight-piece H. H. Ayer cosmetic kit, beauty table, and booklet, marks: "MK 16//IDEAL DOLL" on head, "IDEAL DOLL//P-91" on body

14"	$150.00 – 175.00
16"	$175.00 – 200.00
19"	$200.00 – 225.00
21"	$225.00 – 250.00

Hopalong Cassidy, 1949 – 1950, vinyl stuffed head, vinyl hands, molded and painted gray hair, painted blue eyes, one-piece body, dressed in black cowboy outfit, leatherette boots, guns, holster, black felt hat, marks: "Hopalong Cassidy" on buckle

20"	$185.00 – 200.00
24"	$200.00 – 225.00

Plastic, with horse, Topper

4½"	$40.00 – 50.00

Howdy Doody, 1950 – 1953, television character, hard plastic head, red molded and painted hair, freckles, ventriloquist doll, mouth operated by pull string, cloth body and limbs, dressed in cowboy outfit, scarf reads "HOWDY DOODY," mark: "IDEAL" on head

18"	$500.00 – 525.00
20"	$525.00 – 550.00
24"	$550.00 – 575.00

1954, with vinyl hands, wears boots, jeans

20½"	$250.00 – 275.00
25"	$300.00 – 350.00

Jet Set Dolls, 1967, vinyl head, posable body, rooted straight hair, mod fashions, earrings, strap shoes, Chelsea, Stephanie, and Petula

24"	$45.00 – 55.00

Judy Splinters, 1949 – 1950, vinylite, TV character ventriloquist doll, open/closed mouth

18"	$200.00 – 225.00
22"	$250.00 – 275.00
36"	$325.00 – 350.00

Baby

15" $275.00 – 300.00

Kissy, 1961 – 1964, vinyl head, rigid vinyl toddler body, rooted saran hair, sleep eyes, jointed wrists, press hands together and mouth puckers, makes kissing sound, original dress, panties, t-strap sandals, marks: "©IDEAL CORP.//K-21-L" on head, "IDEAL TOY CORP.// K22//PAT. PEND." on body

White

22½" $100.00 – 125.00

Black

22½" $150.00 – 175.00

Kissy Baby, 1963 – 1964, all-vinyl, bent legs

22" $50.00 – 75.00

Tiny Kissy, 1963 – 1968, smaller toddler, red outfit, white pinafore with hearts, marks: "IDEAL CORP.//K-16-1" on head, "IDEAL TOY CORP./K-16-2" on body

White

16" $70.00 – 80.00

Black

16" $80.00 – 90.00

Lori Martin, 1961, character from *National Velvet* TV show, all-vinyl, swivel waist, jointed body including ankles, blue sleep eyes, rooted dark hair, individual fingers, dress shirt, jeans, black vinyl boots, felt hat, marks: "Metro Goldwyn Mayer Inc.// Mfg. by//IDEAL TOY CORP//38" on head, "©IDEAL TOY CORP.//38" on back

30" $725.00 – 750.00

38" $775.00 – 800.00

42" store display $2,000.00

Mary Hartline, 1952, from TV personality on *Super Circus* show, hard plastic, fully jointed, blond nylon wig, blue sleep eyes, lashes, black eye shadow over and under eye, red, white, or green drum majorette costume and baton, red heart paper hang

10½" Little Miss Revlon. $125.00. *Courtesy of The Museum Doll Shop.*

tag, with original box, marks: "P-91//IDEAL DOLL//MADE IN U.S.A." on head, "IDEAL DOLL//P-91 or IDEAL//16" on body

7½" $100.00 – 125.00

16" $350.00 – 400.00

22½" $1,100.00 – 1,300.00

Miss Clairol, Glamour Misty, 1965 – 1966, vinyl head and arms, rigid plastic legs, body, rooted platinum blond saran hair, side-glancing eyes, high-heeled feet, teen doll had cosmetics to change her hair, all original, marks: "©1965//IDEAL TOY CORP//W-12-3" on neck, "©1965 IDEAL" in oval on lower rear torso

12" $50.00 – 60.00

Miss Curity, 1953, hard plastic, saran wig, sleep eyes, black eye shadow, nurse's outfit, navy cape, white cap, Bauer & Black first aid kit and book, curlers, uses Toni body, mark: "P-90 IDEAL DOLL, MADE IN U.S.A." on head

14½" $300.00 – 350.00

Miss Ideal, 1961, all vinyl, rooted nylon hair, jointed ankles, wrists, waist, arms, legs, closed smiling mouth, sleep eyes, original dress, with beauty kit and comb, marks: "©IDEAL TOY CORP.//SP-30-S" head; "©IDEAL TOY CORP.//G-30-S" back

25"	$350.00 – 375.00
30"	$375.00 – 400.00

Miss Revlon, 1956 – 1959, vinyl, hard plastic teenage body, jointed shoulders, waist, hips, and knees, high-heeled feet, rooted saran hair, sleep eyes, lashes, pierced ears, hang tag, original dress, some came with trunks, mark: "VT 20// IDEAL DOLL." Dolls listed are in good condition with original clothing. Mint-in-box examples can bring double the values listed.

15"	$300.00 – 325.00
18"	$300.00 – 325.00
20"	$300.00 – 350.00
23"	$375.00 – 400.00
26", 1957 only	$300.00 – 350.00

Little Miss Revlon, 1958 – 1960, vinyl head and strung body, jointed head, arms, legs, swivel waist, high-heeled feet, rooted hair, sleep eyes, pierced ears with earrings, original clothes, with box, many extra boxed outfits available

10½"	$125.00 – 150.00

Mysterious Yokum, Li'l Honest Abe, 1953, son of comic strip character, Li'l Abner, hard plastic head, body, Magic Skin arms and legs, painted eyes, molded hair, forelock, wears overalls, one suspender, knit cap, and sock

	$125.00 – 150.00

Plassie, 1942, hard plastic head, molded and painted hair, composition shoulder plate, composition limbs, stuffed pink oilcloth body, blue sleep eyes, original dress, bonnet, mark: "IDEAL DOLL//MADE IN USA//PAT.NO. 225 2077" on head

16"	$100.00 – 125.00
19"	$125.00 – 135.00
22"	$135.00 – 150.00
24"	$160.00 – 170.00

Play Pal Family of Dolls, 1959 – 1962, all-vinyl, jointed wrists, sleep eyes, curly or straight saran hair, bangs, closed mouth, blue or red and white check dress with pinafore, three-year-old size, reissued in 1981 and 1982 from old molds, more for redheads, mark: "IDEAL TOY CORP.//G 35 OR B-19-1" on head

Patty

35"	$325.00 – 350.00

Bonnie Play Pal, 1959, Patti's three-month-old sister, made only one year, rooted blond hair, blue sleep eyes, blue and white check outfit, white shoes and socks

24"	$375.00 – 400.00

Johnny Play Pal, 1959, blue sleep eyes, molded hair, Patti's three-month-old brother

24"	$375.00 – 400.00

Peter, 38", and Patti, 35", Playpal. $850.00 and $350.00. *Courtesy of The Museum Doll Shop.*

Pattite, 1960, rooted saran hair, sleep eyes, red and white check dress, white pinafore with her name on it, looks like Patti Playpal

18"	$750.00 – 800.00
18"	$1,060.00 MIB

Penny Play Pal, 1959, rooted blond or brown curly hair, blue sleep eyes, wears organdy dress, vinyl shoes, socks, Patti's two-year-old sister, made only one year, marks: "IDEAL DOLL//32-E-L" or "B-32-B PAT. PEND." on head, "IDEAL" on back

32"	$275.00 – 325.00

Peter Play Pal, 1960 – 1961, gold sleep eyes, freckles, pug nose, rooted blond or brunette hair, original clothes, black plastic shoes, marks: "©IDEAL TOY CORP.// BE-35-38" on head, "©IDEAL TOY CORP.// W-38//PAT. PEND." on body

38"	$800.00 – 850.00

22" Saucy Walker. $250.00. *Courtesy of The Museum Doll Shop.*

Walker

38"	$850.00 – 875.00

Suzy Play Pal, 1959, rooted curly short blond saran hair, blue sleep eyes, wears purple dotted dress, Patti's one-year-old sister

28"	$375.00 – 400.00

Samantha, 1965 – 1966, from TV show *Bewitched,* vinyl head, body, rooted saran hair, posable arms and legs, wearing red witch's costume, with broom, painted side-glancing eyes, other costume included negligee, mark: "IDEAL DOLL//M-12-E-2" on head

12"	$175.00 – 225.00

All original, with broom

	$550.00 – 600.00

Mint-in-box $2,500.00 – 3,000.00

Tabitha, 1966, baby from TV show *Bewitched,* vinyl head, body, rooted platinum hair, painted blue side-glancing eyes, closed mouth, came in pajamas, mark: "©1965//Screen Gems, Inc.//Ideal Toy Corp.//T.A. 18-6//H-25" on head

12½"	$250.00 – 300.00

Mint-in-box $1,500.00

Saucy Walker, 1951 – 1955, all hard plastic, walks, turns head from side to side, flirty blue eyes, crier, open/closed mouth, teeth, holes in body for crier, saran wig, plastic curlers, came as toddler, boy, and "Big Sister"

14"	$175.00 – 200.00
16"	$200.00 – 225.00
22"	$250.00 – 275.00

Black

16"	$250.00 – 275.00

Big Sister, 1954

25"	$425.00 – 475.00

Smokey Bear, 1953 on, vinyl face and Bakelite paws, rayon plush stuffed body, vinyl forest ranger hat, badge, shovel, symbol of US National Forest Service, wears Smokey marked belt, twill trousers, came with Junior Forest Ranger kit, issued on 50th anniversary of Ideal's original teddy bear

18"	$185.00 – 200.00
25"	$225.00 – 250.00
1957, Talking	$100.00 – 125.00

Snoozie, 1958 – 1965, all-vinyl, rooted saran hair, blue sleep eyes, open/closed mouth, cry voice, knob makes doll wiggle, close eyes, crier, in flannel pajamas

14"	$175.00 – 200.00

1964 – 1965, vinyl head, arms, legs, soft body, rooted saran hair, sleep eyes, turn knob, she squirms, opens and closes eyes, and cries

20"	$70.00 – 80.00

Tammy Family Dolls, dolls listed are in good condition wearing original clothing, mint-in-box examples can bring double the values listed.

Ideal's Tammy. $60.00. *Courtesy of The Museum Doll Shop.*

Tammy's little sister Pepper. $40.00. *Courtesy of The Museum Doll Shop.*

Tammy, 1962+, vinyl head, arms, plastic legs and torso, head joined at neck base, marks: "©IDEAL TOY CORP.//BS12" on head, "©IDEAL TOY CORP.//BS-12//1" on back

White, 12"	$55.00 – 65.00
Black, 12"	$65.00 – 75.00
Pos'n, 12"	$55.00 – 65.00
Mom, 12½"	$40.00 – 45.00
Dad, 13"	$40.00 – 45.00
Ted, 12½"	$45.00 – 50.00
Pepper, 9"	$35.00 – 40.00
Clothing (MIP)	$70.00 – 80.00

Thumbelina, 1961 – 1962, vinyl head and limbs, soft cloth body, painted eyes, rooted saran hair, open/closed mouth, wind knob on back moves body, crier in 1962

16"	$225.00 – 275.00
20"	$275.00 – 300.00

1982 – 1983, all-vinyl one-piece body, rooted hair, non-moving, comes in quilted carrier, also black

7"	$20.00 – 30.00

14" Ideal's Toni, all original. $325.00. *Courtesy of The Museum Doll Shop.*

1982, 1985, reissue from 1960s mold, vinyl head, arms, legs, cloth body, painted eyes, crier, open mouth, molded or rooted hair, original with box

18"	$30.00 – 40.00

Thumbelina, Ltd. Production Collector's Doll, 1983 – 1985, porcelain, painted eyes, molded and painted hair, beige crocheted outfit with pillow booties, limited edition 1,000

18"	$65.00 – 75.00

Tiny Thumbelina, 1962 – 1968, vinyl head, limbs, cloth body, painted eyes, rooted saran hair, wind key in back makes body head move, original tagged clothes, marks: "IDEAL TOY CORP.//OTT 14" on head, "U.S. PAT. # 3029552" on body

14"	$75.00 – 85.00

Newborn Thumbelina, 1968, vinyl head and arms, foam stuffed body, rooted hair, painted eyes, pull-string to squirm

9"	$70.00 – 80.00

Toddler Thumbelina, 1969 – 1971, vinyl head and arms, cloth body, rooted hair, painted eyes

9"	$55.00 – 65.00

Tiffany Taylor, 1974 – 1976, all-vinyl, rooted hair, top of head turns to change color, painted eyes, teenage body, high-heeled, extra outfits available

19"	$60.00 – 70.00
Black, 19"	$80.00 – 90.00

Tuesday Taylor, 1976 – 1977, vinyl, posable body, turn head to change color of hair, clothing tagged "IDEAL Tuesday Taylor"

11½"	$40.00 – 50.00

Toni, 1949, designed by Bernard Lipfert, all hard plastic, jointed body, DuPont nylon wig, usually blue eyes, rosy cheeks, closed mouth, came with Toni wave set and curlers in original dress, with hang tag, marks: "IDEAL DOLL//MADE IN U.S.A." on head, "IDEAL DOLL" and P-series number on body

P-90, 14"	$275.00 – 325.00
P-91, 16"	$325.00 – 375.00
P-92, 19"	$425.00 – 475.00
P-93, 21"	$450.00 – 500.00
P-94, 22½"	$900.00 – 950.00

Whoopsie, 1978 – 1981, vinyl, reissued in 1981, marked: "22//©IDEAL TOY CORP// HONG KONG//1978//H298"

13"	$25.00 – 35.00

Wizard of Oz Series, 1984 – 1985, Tin Man, Lion, Scarecrow, Dorothy, and Toto, all-vinyl, six-piece posable bodies

9"	$30.00 – 35.00 each

Batgirl, Mera Queen of Atlantis, Wonder Woman, and Super Girl, 1967 – 1968, all-vinyl, posable body, rooted hair, painted side-glancing eyes, dressed in costume

11½"	$800.00 – 900.00
Mint-in-box	$1,200.00 – 1,500.00

JULLIEN

1827 – 1904, Paris, France. After 1904 became a part of S.F.B.J. Had a porcelain factory, won some awards, purchased bisque heads from Francois Gaultier. Dolls listed are in good condition, appropriately dressed.

Child, bisque socket head, wig, glass eyes, pierced ears, open mouth with teeth or closed mouth, on jointed composition body

Closed mouth

17" – 19"	$3,000.00 – 3,500.00
24" – 26"	$3,800.00 – 4,250.00

Open mouth

18" – 20"	$1,600.00 – 1,700.00
29" – 30"	$2,200.00 – 2,400.00

JUMEAU

1842 – 1899, Paris and Montreuil-sous-Bois; in 1899 joined in S.F.B.J. which continued to make dolls marked Jumeau through 1958. Founder Pierre Francois Jumeau made fashion dolls with kid or wood bodies, head marked with size number, bodies stamped "JUMEAU//MEDAILLE D'OR//PARIS." Early Jumeau heads were pressed pre-1890. By 1878, son Emile Jumeau was head of the company and made Bébé Jumeau, marked on back of head, on chemise, band on arm of dress. Tété Jumeaux have poured heads. Bébé Protige and Bébé Jumeau registered trademarks in 1886; bee mark in 1891; Bébé Marcheur in 1895; Bébé Francaise in 1896.

19" Jumeau Portrait Poupée on kid body. $6,600.00. *Courtesy Richard W. Withington, Inc., Nashua, New Hampshire.*

Mold numbers of marked EJs and Tétés approximate the following heights: 1 – 10", 2 – 11", 3 – 12", 4 – 13", 5 – 14", 6 – 16", 7 – 17", 8 – 18", 9 – 20", 10 – 21", 11 – 24", 12 – 26", 13 – 30".

Dolls listed are in good condition, nicely wigged, and with appropriate clothing. Exceptional doll may be much more.

Poupée Jumeau (so-called French fashion-type), 1860s on, marked with size number on swivel head, closed mouth, paperweight eyes, pierced ears, stamped kid body, add more for original clothes

Poupée Peau (kid body)

11" – 13"	$2,300.00 – 2,900.00
14" – 16"	$2,800.00 – 3,700.00
17" – 18"	$3,600.00 – 3,800.00
20"	$5,100.00 – 5,300.00

Poupée Bois (wood body), bisque lower arms

10" – 11"	$4,000.00 – 4,500.00
14" – 16"	$5,200.00 – 5,500.00

27" Jumeau Poupée with mature portrait face, on articulated wooden body. $22,325.00. *Courtesy of Skinner Inc., Boston and Bolton, Massachusetts.*

So-called Portrait face
19" – 21"	$6,600.00 – 7,200.00

Wood body
19" – 21"	$10,000.00 – 12,000.00

Mature face with wooden body
27"	$22,325.00*

Child Doll

Portrait, 1877 – 1883, closed mouth, paperweight eyes, pierced ears, wigged (sometimes skin wig), straight wristed composition body with separate balls at joints, head marked with size number only

Almond eye, First Series
12" – 14½"	$14,500.00 – 16,500.00
16" – 18½"	$18,500.00 – 22,500.00
20"	$25,000.00 – 30,000.00
23"	$33,000.00 – 37,000.00
25"	$54,000.00 – 64,000.00

Second Series
11" – 12"	$5,000.00 – 5,500.00
13" – 15"	$5,500.00 – 6,000.00
18" – 20"	$7,000.00 – 8,000.00
22"	$9,000.00 – 10,000.00
25"	$12,000.00 – 13,000.00

Long Face Triste Bébé, 1879 – 1886, head marked with number only, pierced applied ears, closed mouth, paperweight eyes, straight wrists on Jumeau marked body
21" – 23"	$22,000.00 – 24,000.00
26" - 27"	$25,000.00 – 27,000.00
31" – 33"	$28,000.00 – 30,000.00

Premiere, 1880, unmarked bébé
9" – 12"	$6,800.00 – 7,200.00
15" – 16"	$7,400.00 – 8,200.00

With exceptionally wonderful original Couturier outfit
12"	$15,000.00 – 19,500.00

Based on 3 examples sold at auction

E.J. Bébé, 1881 – 1886, earliest "EJ" mark above with number over initials, pressed bisque socket head, wig, paperweight eyes, pierced ears, closed mouth, jointed body with straight wrists
17" – 18"	$9,000.00 – 10,250.00
19" – 21"	$11,000.00 – 15,000.00
23" – 24"	$15,000.00 – 17,000.00

17½" Jumeau Poupée on wooden body with swivel waist. $6,000.00. *Courtesy of Skinner Inc., Boston and Bolton, Massachusetts.*

10¾" Portrait Jumeau, c. 1878. $14,000.00. *Courtesy of Skinner Inc., Boston and Bolton, Massachusetts.*

15" EJ, c. 1880s. $8,500.00. *Courtesy of Skinner Inc., Boston and Bolton, Massachusetts.*

EJ/A marked Bébé

25" $22,000.00 – 25,000.00

Mid "EJ," mark has size number centered between E and J (E 8 J), later with Déposé above

11"	$5,900.00 – 6,200.00
14" – 16"	$6,500.00 – 7,000.00
17"	$7,400.00 – 7,900.00
20"	$8,600.00 – 9,000.00
23"	$9,200.00 – 9,400.00
26"	$9,600.00 – 9,900.00

Déposé Jumeau, 1886 – 1889, poured bisque head marked, " Déposé Jumeau," and size number, pierced ears, closed mouth, paperweight eyes, composition and wood body with straight wrists, marked "Medaille d'Or Paris"

14" – 15"	$4,800.00 – 5,100.00
18" – 20"	$5,900.00 – 6,400.00
23" – 25"	$6,800.00 – 7,200.00

Tété Jumeau, 1885 on, poured bisque socket head, red stamp on head, stamp or sticker on body, wig, glass eyes, pierced ears, closed mouth, jointed composition body with straight wrists, may also be marked E.D. with size number when Douillet ran factory, uses tété face.

The following sizes were used for Tétés: 1 – 10", 2 – 11", 3 – 12", 4 – 13", 5 – 14½", 6 – 16", 7 – 17", 8 – 19", 10 – 21½", 11– 24", 12 – 26", 13 – 29", 14 – 31", 15 – 33", 16 – 34" – 35".

Bébé (Child), closed mouth

10"	$9,000.00 – 10,000.00
12" – 13"	$7,500.00 – 11,000.00
16" – 17"	$6,000.00 – 7,000.00
19" – 21½"	$7,200.00 – 10,000.00
24" – 26"	$10,000.00 – 10,200.00
29" – 31"	$10,300.00 – 10,500.00
33" – 35"	$10,700.00 – 11,000.00

21½" Jumeau Triste (long face), c. 1885. $22,000.00. *Courtesy of Skinner Inc., Boston and Bolton, Massachusetts.*

16" Jumeau Depose. $5,200.00. *Courtesy of The Museum Doll Shop.*

22" closed mouth Tété. $10,000.00. *Courtesy of Skinner Inc., Boston and Bolton, Massachusetts.*

Lady body

14" – 16"	$3,700.00 – 4,500.00
18" – 22"	$5,000.00 – 7,800.00

Open mouth, child

17"	$2,500.00 – 2,600.00
20" – 22"	$2,800.00 – 3,100.00
24" – 25"	$3,300.00 – 3,400.00
27" – 29"	$3,500.00 – 3,700.00
32"	$3,100.00 – 4,200.00

B. L. Bébé, 1892 on, marked "B. L." for the Louvre department store, socket head, wig, pierced ears, paperweight eyes, closed mouth, jointed composition body

18" – 20"	$4,200.00 – 4,500.00

Phonographe Jumeau, 1894 – 1899, bisque head, open mouth, phonograph in torso, working condition

24" – 25"	$7,000.00 – 8,000.00

R.R. Bébé, 1892 on, wig, pierced ears, paperweight eyes, closed mouth, jointed composition body with straight wrists

21" – 23"	$4,400.00 – 4,800.00

Mold 1907, child, some with Tété Jumeau stamp, sleep or set eyes, open mouth, jointed French body

14" – 16"	$1,900.00 – 2,100.00

19" – 20"	$2,600.00 – 2,900.00
23" – 26"	$3,200.00 – 3,900.00
29" – 32"	$3,900.00 – 4,100.00

Character Child

Mold 203, 208, and other 200 series, 1882 – 1899, glass eyes

20"	$70,000.00

Mold 217, crier

20"	$88,000.00

Too few in database for a reliable range.

21"	$110,000.00

Too few in database for a reliable range.

18" Tété Jumeau with original trousseau. $9,000.00. *Courtesy of The Museum Doll Shop.*

Jumeau Princess Elizabeth. $1,700.00. *Courtesy of The Museum Doll Shop.*

23" Jumeau Bébé Phonographe, key wind singing doll. $7,000.00. *Courtesy of Skinner Inc., Boston and Bolton, Massachusetts.*

Mold 230 child, 1910 on, open mouth socket head, glass eyes, wig, composition body

12"	$950.00 – 1,100.00
16"	$1,600.00 – 1,800.00
21" – 23"	$2,000.00 – 2,600.00

Mold 221, Great Ladies, 1940s – 1950s

10"	$550.00 – 650.00

Two-Faced Jumeau, crying and smiling

18"	$11,000.00 – 14,000.00

Too few in database for a reliable range.

Princess Elizabeth, made after Jumeau joined SFBJ and adopted Unis label, mark will be "71 Unis//France 149//306// Jumeau//1938//Paris," bisque socket head with high color, closed mouth, flirty eyes, jointed composition body

Mold 306

18" – 19"	$1,700.00 – 1,900.00
32" – 33"	$3,500.00 – 4,000.00

Accessories

Marked Jumeau shoes

5" – 6"	$300.00 – 400.00
7" – 10"	$600.00 – 700.00

KAMKINS

1919 – 1928, Philadelphia, Pennsylvania, and Atlantic City, New Jersey. Cloth doll made by Louise R. Kampes Studio. Clothes made by cottage industry workers at home. All-cloth, molded mask face, painted features, swivel head, jointed shoulders and hips, mohair wig. Dolls listed are in good, clean, unfaded condition, allow 50% less for soiled or faded examples.

18" – 20"	$1,800.00 – 2,300.00

Kamkins in original clothing. $2,000.00.
Courtesy of The Museum Doll Shop.

8½" open mouth dolly face by Kämmer & Reinhardt. $500.00. *Doll courtesy of Ruth Cayton.*

KÄMMER & REINHARDT

1885 – 1933, Waltershausen, Germany. Registered trademark K✡R, Majestic Doll, Mein Leibling, Die Kokette, Charakterpuppen (character dolls). Designed doll heads, most bisque were made by Simon & Halbig; in 1918, Schuetzmeister & Quendt also supplied heads; Rheinische Gummi und Celluloid Fabrik Co. made celluloid heads for Kämmer & Reinhardt. Kämmer & Reinhardt dolls were distributed by Bing, Borgfeldt, B. Illfelder, L. Rees & Co., Strobel & Wilken, and Louis Wolf & Co. Also made heads of wood and composition, later cloth and rubber dolls.

Mold numbers identify heads starting with 1) bisque socket heads; 2) shoulder heads, as well as socket heads of black or mulatto babies; 3) bisque socket heads or celluloid shoulder heads; 4) heads having eyelashes; 5) googlies, black heads, pincushion heads; 6) mulatto heads; 7) celluloid heads, bisque head walking dolls; 8) rubber heads; 9) composition heads, some rubber heads. Other letters refer to style or material of wig or clothing.

All dolls listed are in good condition with appropriate clothing.

Child

Bisque Socket-head child

Mold 192 (possibly as early as 1892), jointed composition body, sleep eyes.

Closed mouth

6" – 7"	$600.00 – 700.00
10" – 11"	$1,000.00 – 1,100.00
16" – 18"	$2,200.00 – 2,500.00
22" – 24"	$2,700.00 – 2,900.00

Open mouth

7" – 8"	$550.00 – 600.00
12" – 14"	$700.00 – 750.00
16" – 18"	$850.00 – 900.00
20" – 22"	$1,000.00 – 1,100.00
26" – 28"	$1,400.00 – 1,600.00

13" My Playmate, K*R 36 open mouth dolly face doll. $575.00. *Courtesy Richard W. Withington Auction, Inc., Nashua, New Hampshire.*

Child, Dolly Face, 1910 to 1930s, bisque head with open mouth, jointed composition body, sleep eyes.

No Mold Number or Molds 191, 401, 402, 403

On five-piece body

5" – 6"	$450.00 – 475.00
7" – 8"	$475.00 – 500.00
10"	$650.00 – 700.00

16" Kämmer and Reinhardt 101 Peter, painted eyes. $4,000.00. *Courtesy of Skinner Inc., Boston and Bolton, Massachusetts.*

Jointed composition body

8" – 10"	$550.00 – 650.00
12" – 14"	$475.00 – 575.00
16" – 18"	$650.00 – 700.00
19" – 21"	$725.00 – 775.00
28"	$1,100.00 – 1,200.00
30" – 32"	$1,300.00 – 1,400.00

Closed mouth, flapper body

14"	$2,400.00*

Child Shoulder-head Doll, kid body

14"	$350.00 – 400.00
19" – 22"	$450.00 – 475.00

Character Dolls, 1909 on

Mold 100, baby often referred to by collectors as "Kaiser Baby," solid dome head, intaglio eyes, open/closed mouth, composition bent-limb body

11" – 12"	$400.00 – 450.00
14" – 15"	$500.00 – 600.00
18" – 20"	$800.00 – 900.00

Mold 101, Peter or Marie, painted eyes, closed mouth, jointed body

7" – 8"	$1,700.00 – 2,200.00
10" – 12"	$2,400.00 – 2,700.00
14" – 15"	$3,500.00 – 3,600.00
17" – 18"	$4,100.00 – 4,500.00
19" – 20"	$5,000.00 – 5,200.00

13" K*R 114 Gretchen. $3,275.00. *Courtesy Richard W. Withington, Inc., Nashua, New Hampshire.*

Glass eyes

18" – 20" $9,000.00 – 12,500.00

Mold 102, Elsa or Walter, painted eyes, molded hair, closed mouth, very rare

14" $32,000.00

Too few in database for a reliable range.

22" $65,000.00

Too few in database for a reliable range.

Mold 103, painted eyes, closed mouth

19" $80,000.00+

Too few in database for a reliable range.

Mold 104, ca. 1909, painted eyes, laughing closed mouth, very rare

18" $80,000.00+

Too few in database for a reliable range.

Mold 105, painted eyes, open/closed mouth, very rare

21" $170,956.00

Too few in database for a reliable range.

Mold 106, painted intaglio eyes to side, closed mouth, very rare

22" $145,000.00

Too few in database for a reliable range.

Mold 107, Karl, painted intaglio eyes, closed mouth

12" $1,300.00

21" $46,000.00 – 56,000.00

Too few in database for a reliable range.

Mold 108, one example reported

$275,000.00+

Too few in database for a reliable range.

Mold 109, Elise, painted eyes, closed mouth

9" – 10" $3,000.00 – 3,500.00

12" – 14" $5,900.00 – 8,250.00

21" – 24" $19,000.00 – 21,000.00

Mold 112, painted open/closed mouth

13" – 14" $8,000.00 – 9,000.00

17" – 18" $10,000.00 – 12,000.00

Glass eyes

16" $10,500.00

Too few in database for a reliable range.

15" K*R 117, Mien Liebling. $4,000.00. *Courtesy Richard W. Withington, Inc., Nashua, New Hampshire.*

24" $14,000.00

Too few in database for a reliable range.

Mold 112X, flocked hair

17" $14,000.00 – 16,000.00

Mold 114, Hans or Gretchen, painted eyes, closed mouth

8" – 9" $2,000.00 – 2,200.00

12" – 13" $3,000.00 – 3,275.00

18" – 20" $7,000.00 – 7,400.00

25" $9,400.00 – 10,000.00

13½" Kämmer & Reinhardt mold 100 Kaiser baby. $475.00. *Doll courtesy of Ruth Cayton.*

10" mold 126 toddler with star-fish hands. $975.00. *Courtesy of Skinner Inc., Boston and Bolton, Massachusetts.*

Glass eyes

9"	$5,900.00 – 6,200.00
15"	$9,250.00 – 9,350.00

Mold 115, solid dome, painted hair, sleeping eyes, closed mouth, toddler

15"	$4,250.00 – 5,750.00

Mold 115A, sleep eyes, closed mouth, wig

Baby, bent-leg body

10" – 12"	$2,000.00 – 2,200.00
14" – 16"	$2,600.00 – 2,900.00
19" – 22"	$3,000.00 – 3,300.00

Toddler, composition, jointed body

15" – 16"	$3,750.00 – 4,300.00
18" – 20"	$4,900.00 – 5,300.00

Mold 116, dome head, sleep eyes, open-closed mouth

17"	$3,200.00 – 3,400.00

Mold 116A, sleep eyes, open/closed mouth or open mouth, wigged, bent-leg baby body

10" – 12"	$1,600.00 – 1,800.00
15" – 18"	$2,100.00 – 2,750.00
21" – 23"	$3,300.00 – 3,500.00

Toddler body

16" – 18"	$3,000.00 – 3,400.00

Mold 117, 117A Mein Liebling (My Darling), glass eyes, closed mouth

8" – 11"	$3,000.00 – 3,400.00
14" – 16"	$3,800.00 – 4,200.00
18" – 20"	$4,800.00 – 5,200.00
22" – 24"	$5,400.00 – 6,200.00
28" – 30"	$6,400.00 – 7,200.00

Flapper body

8"	$3,500.00

Too few in database for a reliable range.

Mold 117N, Mein Neuer Liebling (My New Darling), flirty eyes, open mouth

14" – 16"	$950.00 – 1,100.00
20" – 22"	$1,700.00 – 1,900.00
28" – 30"	$2,100.00 – 2,400.00

Mold 117X, socket head, sleep eyes, open mouth

14" – 16"	$850.00 – 950.00
22" – 24"	$1,300.00 – 1,400.00
30" – 32"	$1,600.00 – 1,800.00

Molds 118, 118A, sleep eyes, open mouth, baby body

11"	$1,100.00 – 1,200.00
15"	$1,300.00 – 1,500.00
18"	$1,900.00 – 2,200.00

14" Kämmer and Reinhardt 121, open mouth, bent limb body. $700.00. *Courtesy Richard W. Withington Auction, Inc., Nashua, New Hampshire.*

Mold 119, sleep eyes, open/closed mouth, marked "Baby," five-piece baby body

24" – 25"	$16,000.00

Too few in database for a reliable range.

Molds 121, 122, sleep eyes, open mouth, baby body

10" – 11"	$525.00 – 575.00
15" – 16"	$750.00 – 850.00
20"	$900.00 – 1,000.00
22" – 24"	$1,150.00 – 1,250.00

Toddler body

10"	$900.00 – 1,000.00
13" – 14"	$1,150.00 – 1,250.00
18" – 20"	$1,400.00 – 1,600.00

Mold 123 Max and Mold 124 Moritz, flirty sleep eyes, laughing/closed mouth, special body with molded shoes

16"	$12,000.00 – 15,000.00 each

Mold 126 Mein Liebling Baby (My Darling Baby), sleep or flirty eyes, bent-leg baby

10" – 12"	$475.00 – 550.00
14" – 16"	$550.00 – 600.00
18" – 20"	$600.00 – 650.00
22" – 24"	$675.00 – 725.00

15" baby, mold 126. $575.00. *Courtesy of The Museum Doll Shop.*

12½" Kämmer & Reinhardt cloth doll, c. 1927. $450.00. *Courtesy of The Museum Doll Shop.*

Toddler body

Five-piece body

6" – 7"	$750.00 – 850.00
9" – 10"	$925.00 – 975.00

Jointed composition body

15" – 17"	$850.00 – 950.00
22" – 24"	$1,100.00 – 1,400.00

Mold 127, 127N, domed head-like mold 126, bent-leg baby body, add more for flirty eyes

14" – 15"	$900.00 – 1,000.00
18" – 22"	$1,000.00 – 1,200.00

Toddler body

15" – 16"	$1,100.00 – 1,300.00
20" – 22"	$1,600.00 – 1,700.00
26"	$1,900.00 – 2,000.00

Mold 128, sleep eyes, open mouth, baby body

10"	$550.00 – 600.00
13" – 15"	$750.00 – 850.00
20" – 24"	$1,300.00 – 1,700.00

Original clothes, with layette in wicker basket

10"	$1,600.00

Too few in database for a reliable range.

Mold 131: See Googly section.

Mold 135, sleep eyes, open mouth, baby body

    13" – 16" $950.00 – 1,100.00

Mold 171 Klein Mammi (Little Mammi), dome, open mouth

    14" – 15" $3,000.00 – 3,500.00

Too few in database for a reliable range.

Mold 214, shoulder head, painted eyes, closed mouth, similar to mold 114, muslin body

    12" – 15" $2,300.00 – 2,600.00

Too few in database for a reliable range.

Mold 314, socket head, composition body, painted eyes, flocked hair

    14" $6,250.00*

Puz, composition head, cloth body

    16" – 17" $450.00 – 500.00

    25" $750.00 – 800.00

Cloth, 1927, wire armature body, needle-sculpted stockinette heads, painted features, wooden feet, all in good clean, un-faded condition

    12" – 13" $400.00 – 450.00

22" composition headed Kämmer & Reinhardt Puz with flirty eyes. $625.00. *Courtesy Richard W. Withington, Inc., Nashua, New Hampshire.*

KENNER

1947 to 2000, Cincinnati, Ohio. Purchased by Tonka Toys in 1987 and then by Hasbro in 1991, run as a separate division by both. Dolls listed are in very good condition with all original clothing and accessories.

Baby Bundles

White

    16" $10.00 – 15.00

Baby Yawnie, 1974, vinyl head, cloth body

    15" $15.00 – 20.00

Blythe, 1972, pull string to change color of eyes, "mod" clothes

    11½" $900.00 – 1,300.00

    11½" $2,920.00 MIB

Bob Scout, 1974

    9" $50.00 – 60.00

Butch Cassidy or Sundance Kid

    4" $10.00 – 15.00

Charlie Chaplin, 1973, all-cloth, walking mechanism

    14" $80.00 – 90.00

Cover Girls, 1978, posable elbows and knees, jointed hands

Dana, black

    12½" $40.00 – 50.00

Darci, 1979

    12½" $35.00 – 45.00

Erica, redhead

    12½" $90.00 – 100.00

Crumpet 1970, vinyl and plastic

    18" $90.00 – 100.00

Dusty, 1974, vinyl teenage doll

    11" $15.00 – 20.00

Skye, black, teenage friend of Dusty

    11" $20.00 – 25.00

Gabbigale, 1972

White

    18" $15.00 – 20.00

Kenner Hardy Boys, based on television show featuring Parker Stevenson and Shawn Cassidy. $45.00. each *Courtesy of The Museum Doll Shop.*

Black

18"	$30.00 – 35.00

Garden Gals, 1972, hand bent to hold watering can

6½"	$4.00 – 6.00

Hardy Boys, 1978, Shaun Cassidy, Parker Stevenson

12"	$35.00 – 45.00

Indiana Jones, 1981

12"	$130.00 – 150.00

International Velvet, 1976, Tatum O'Neill

11½"	$20.00 – 25.00

Jenny Jones and baby, 1973, all-vinyl, Jenny, 9", Baby, 2½"

set	$20.00 – 25.00

Rose Petal, 1984, scented

7"	$15.00 – 20.00

Six Million Dollar Man Figures, 1975 – 1977, TV show starring Lee Majors

Bionic Man, Big Foot

13"	$20.00 – 25.00

Bionic Man, Masketron Robot

13"	$25.00 – 30.00

Bionic Woman, Robot

13"	$75.00 – 85.00

Jaime Sommers, Bionic Woman

13"	$75.00 – 95.00

Oscar Goldman, 1975 – 1977, with exploding briefcase

13"	$40.00 – 50.00

Steve Austin, The Bionic Man

13"	$75.00 – 95.00

Steve Austin, Bionic Grip, 1977

13"	$75.00 – 95.00

Star Wars Figures, 1974 – 1978, large size action figures. First price indicates doll played with or missing accessories; second price is for mint-in-box/package doll. Complete doll in excellent condition would be somewhere in between. Never removed from box would bring greater prices.

Ben Obi-Wan Kenobi

12"	$75.00 – 95.00

Boba Fett

13"	$155.00 – 175.00

C-3PO

12"	$165.00 – 185.00

Chewbacca

12"	$125.00 – 145.00

Darth Vader

12"	$225.00 – 250.00

Han Solo

12"	$400.00 – 500.00

23" Kestner 257 baby. $1,150.00. *Courtesy of Skinner Inc., Boston and Bolton, Massachusetts.*

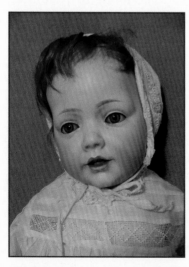

18" Kestner open mouthed, wigged, Hilda, mold #237. $3,000.00. *Courtesy Richard W. Withington, Inc., Nashua, New Hampshire.*

Head circumference

10½"	$1,100.00 – 1,300.00

Character Child, 1910 on, socket head, wig, glass eyes, composition and wood jointed body, add more for painted eyes.

Mold 143, 1897 on, precursor to character dolls, open mouth, glass eyes, jointed body

8"	$850.00 – 950.00
9" – 10"	$1,000.00 – 1,200.00
12" – 14"	$1,100.00 – 1,700.00
18" – 20"	$1,700.00 – 2,000.00

Mold 178, 179, 180, 181, 182, 184, 185, 186, 187, 189, 190, 191

Painted eyes

12"	$2,800.00 – 3,100.00
15"	$3,300.00 – 3,600.00
18"	$4,600.00 – 5,000.00

Glass eyes

12"	$3,200.00 – 3,500.00
15"	$4,800.00 – 5,200.00
18"	$6,000.00 – 6,500.00

Mold 206, fat cheeks, closed mouth, glass eyes child or toddler

12" – 15"	$9,000.00 – 10,000.00

Too few in database for a reliable range.

19"	$22,000.00 – 25,000.00

Too few in database for a reliable range.

Mold 208, for all-bisque, see that section.

Painted eyes

12"	$9,500.00 – 10,500.00

Glass eyes

16"	$6,750.00 – $9,000.00

Too few in database for a reliable range.

Mold 239, socket head, open mouth, sleep eyes

Toddler, also comes as baby

15" – 17"	$3,600.00 – 4,000.00

Mold 241, socket head, open mouth, sleep eyes

17" – 18"	$4,800.00 – 5,100.00
21" – 22"	$5,800.00 – 6,100.00

25"	$4,300.00 – 5,500.00
28" – 30"	$7,200.00 – 7,800.00

Lady Doll, 1898 on, bisque socket head, open mouth, glass eyes, composition body, slender waists and molded breasts

Mold 162

16" – 18"	$1,300.00 – 1,500.00

10" Kestner Gibson Girl. $850.00.
Courtesy of Skinner Inc., Boston and Bolton, Massachusetts.

"Gibson Girl" Mold 172, shoulder head, closed mouth, glass eyes, kid body, bisque forearms

10"	$850.00 – 950.00
15"	$1,500.00 – 1,600.00
18" – 21"	$2,400.00 – 3, 000.00

Wunderkind, set includes doll body with four interchangeable heads, some with extra apparel

With heads 174, 178, 184, and 185

11"	$9,000.00 – 9,500.00

With heads, 171, 179, 182, and 183

14½"	$12,650.00

Too few in database for a reliable range.

KEWPIE

1913 on, designed by Rose O'Neill. Manufactured by Borgfeldt, later Joseph Kallus, and then Jesco in 1984, and various companies with special license, as well as unlicensed companies. They were made of all-bisque, celluloid, cloth, composition, rubber, vinyl, zylonite, and other materials. Kewpie figurines (action Kewpies) have mold numbers 4843 through 4883. Kewpies were also marked with a round paper sticker on back, "KEWPIES DES. PAT. III, R. 1913; Germany; REG. US. PAT. OFF." On the front was a heart-shaped sticker marked "KEWPIE//REG. US.// PAT. OFF." May also be incised on the soles of the feet, "O'Neill." Dolls listed are in good condition, add more for label, accessories, original box, or exceptional doll.

All-Bisque

Immobiles, standing, legs together, immobile, no joints, blue wings, molded and painted hair, painted side-glancing eyes

2" – 2 ½"	$90.00 – 110.00
4"	$110.00 – 125.00
5"	$135.00 – 145.00
6"	$200.00 – 225.00

Jointed shoulders

2" – 2 ½"	$110.00 – 135.00
4"	$125.00 – 150.00
5"	$170.00 – 180.00
6"	$225.00 – 250.00
7"	$275.00 – 350.00
8"	$425.00 – 475.00
10"	$750.00 – 775.00
12"	$1,200.00 – 1,300.00

Jointed hips and shoulders

4"	$500.00 – 550.00

5" – 6"	$800.00 – 850.00
7" – 8"	$950.00 – 1,050.00
10"	$1,150.00 – 1,250.00
12½"	$1,300.00 – 1,350.00

Jointed shoulders with any article of molded clothing

2½"	$175.00 – 200.00
4½"	$2,600.00 pirate
6"	$295.00 – 330.00
8"	$300.00 – 375.00

With Mary Jane shoes

6½"	$500.00 – 575.00
6", MIB	$1,600.00*

Bisque Action Figures

Arms folded

6"	$525.00 – 600.00

Aviator

8½"	$775.00 – 850.00

Back, laying down, kicking one foot

4"	$150.00 – 200.00

Basket and ladybug, Kewpie seated

4"	$1,400.00 – 1,700.00

Bear holding Kewpie

3½"	$190.00 – 220.00

"Blunderboo," Kewpie falling down

1¾"	$400.00 – 465.00

Bottle, green beverage, Kewpie standing, kicking out

2½"	$525.00 – 575.00

Bottle stopper

2"	$100.00 – 150.00

Box, heart shaped, with Kewpie kicker atop

4"	$775.00 – 850.00

Bride and Groom

3½"	$300.00 – 350.00

Boutonnière

1½"	$85.00 – 110.00
2"	$115.00 – 135.00

Candy container

4"	$400.00 – 500.00

Card holder

2"	$400.00 – 500.00

With label

2¼"	$550.00 – 650.00

Carpenter, wearing tool apron

8½"	$975.00 – 1,100.00

Cat, black with Kewpie

2¼"	$250.00 – 300.00

Cat, on lap of seated Kewpie

2¼"	$625.00 – 675.00

Chick with seated Kewpie

2"	$525.00 – 575.00

Cowboy

10"	$700.00 – 800.00

Dog, with Kewpie on stomach

3"	$3,400.00*

Dog, with Red Cross Kewpie

4"	$250.00 – 300.00

Doodle Dog alone

1½"	$900.00 – 1,000.00
3"	$2,200.00 – 2,500.00

Doodle Dog with Kewpie

2½"	$1,000.00 – 1,500.00

Drum on brown stool, with Kewpie

3½"	$2,000.00 – 2,200.00

Farmer

6½"	$800.00 – 900.00

4" German all-bisque Kewpie Huggers. $250.00. *Courtesy of The Museum Doll Shop.*

Flowers, Kewpie with bouquet in right hand

5"	$825.00 – 925.00

Fly on foot of Kewpie

3"	$500.00 – 600.00

Gardener

4"	$475.00 – 525.00

Governor

2½"	$325.00 – 375.00
3¼"	$400.00 – 475.00

Hottentot, black Kewpie

3½"	$425.00 – 500.00
5"	$575.00 – 675.00
9"	$925.00 – 975.00

Huggers

2½"	$125.00 – 150.00
3½"	$175.00 – 225.00
4½"	$250.00 – 300.00

Inkwell, with writer Kewpie

4½"	$500.00 – 575.00

Jack-O-Lantern between legs of Kewpie

2"	$450.00 – 500.00

Jester, with white hat on head

4½"	$500.00 – 575.00

Kneeling

4"	$475.00 – 550.00

Vase, Kewpie holding teddy bear.
$600.00. *Courtesy of The Museum Doll Shop.*

Mandolin, green basket and seated Kewpie

2"	$275.00 – 325.00

Mandolin held by Kewpie in blue chair

4"	$800.00 – 900.00
	$1,900.00*

Mandolin, with Kewpie on moon swing

2½"	$4,400.00*

Mayor, seated Kewpie in green wicker chair

4½"	$775.00 – 875.00

Minister

5"	$200.00 – 250.00

Nursing bottle, with Kewpie

3½"	$500.00 – 600.00

Reader Kewpie seated with book

2"	$200.00 – 250.00
3½"	$275.00 – 325.00
4"	$450.00 – 500.00

Riding a Goat $5,750.00*

Sack held by Kewpie with both hands

4½"	$1,430.00*

Salt Shaker

2"	$150.00 – 175.00

Seated in fancy chair

4"	$325.00 – 400.00

Soldier bursting out of egg

4"	$6,900.00*

Soldier, Confederate

4"	$425.00 – 500.00

Soldier in egg

3½"	$6,600.00*

Soldier taking aim with rifle

3½"	$850.00 – 950.00

Soldier vase

6½"	$575.00 – 650.00

Soldier

2¾"	$450.00 – 500.00
4½"	$500.00 – 550.00

Stomach, Kewpie laying flat, arms and legs out

4"	$375.00 – 450.00

Tea Table, Kewpie seated at table pouring tea

4½"	$4,900.00*

Thinker

4" – 5"	$275.00 – 325.00

Traveler with dog and umbrella

3½"	$1,300.00 – 1,550.00

Traveler with umbrella and bag

4"	$350.00 – 400.00
5"	$500.00 – 550.00

Traveler with umbrella, riding in a hot air balloon

4"	$3,800.00*

Vase with card holder and Kewpie

2½"	$275.00 – 325.00

Vase with Doodle Dog and Kewpie

4½"	$2,600.00*

Vase with huggers

3¾"	$575.00 – 650.00

Writer, seated Kewpie with pen in hand

2"	$425.00 – 475.00
4"	$500.00 – 550.00

Carnival chalk Kewpie with jointed shoulders

13"	$75.00 – 125.00

Bisque Shoulder Head, on cloth body

Painted eyes

7"	$875.00 – 1,000.00

Glass eyes

12"	$2,500.00 – 2,800.00

Celluloid

Bride and Groom

4"	$15.00 – 40.00

Jointed arms, heart label on chest

5"	$80.00 – 100.00
8"	$165.00 – 185.00
12"	$275.00 – 325.00

China

Perfume holder, one piece with opening at back of head

4½"	$550.00 – 1,100.00

Salt Shaker

1¼"	$85.00 – 165.00

Dishes

Service for 4	$850.00 – 900.00
Service for 6	$1,000.00 – 1,200.00

Cloth

Richard Krueger "Kuddle Kewpie," silk screened face, stockinette or sateen body, tagged

10" – 13"	$325.00 – 400.00
18" – 23"	$725.00 – 800.00

Plush, with stockinette face, tagged

8"	$195.00 – 225.00

Composition, made by Cameo Doll Co., Mutual Doll Co., and Rex Doll Co.

Hottentot, all-composition, heart decal to chest, jointed arms, red winks, ca. 1946

11" – 13"	$400.00 – 450.00

All-composition, jointed body, blue wings

11"	$225.00 – 300.00
13"	$325.00 – 375.00

Composition head, cloth body, flange neck, composition forearms, tagged floral dress

11"	$250.00 – 300.00

Talcum container

One-piece composition talcum shaker with heart label on chest

7"	$175.00 – 25.00

A group of Kuddle Kewpies made by Richard Krueger. $325.00 – 725.00. *Courtesy of The Museum Doll Shop.*

Hard Plastic

Original box, 1950s, Kewpie design

8½" $275.00 – 300.00

Sleep eyes, five-piece body with starfish hands

14" $400.00 – 475.00

Metal

Figurine, cast steel on square base, excellent condition

5½" $40.00 – 55.00

Soap

Kewpie soap figure with cotton batting, colored label with rhyme, marked "R.O. Wilson, 1917"

4" $90.00 – 110.00

Vinyl, 1960s, Cameo Dolls, in very good condition with original clothing

12" $55.00 – 65.00

16" $70.00 – 80.00

27" $125.00 – 175.00

Jesco Dolls, 1980s, mint, all-original condition

8" $40.00 – 50.00

12" $50.00 – 60.00

18" $70.00 – 80.00

24" $140.00 – 160.00

R. John Wright, 1999 on, molded felt, jointed shoulders

Retail Price

6" $295.00 – 425.00

Secondary Market Price

6" $450.00 – 500.00

KLEY & HAHN

1902 – 1930s, Ohrdruf, Thüringia, Germany. Bisque heads, jointed composition or leather bodies, composition and celluloid head dolls. Was an assembler and exporter; bought heads from Bähr & Pröschild,

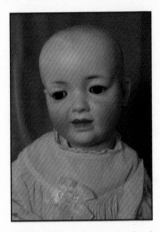

16" Kley & Hahn mold 525, open/closed mouth on bent limb body. $575.00. *Courtesy Richard W. Withington Auction, Inc., Nashua, New Hampshire.*

Kestner (Walkure), Hertel Schwab & Co, and Rheinische Gummi. Dolls listed in good condition, appropriately dressed.

Character Baby, bisque socket head, bent limb composition body, molds such as 133, 135, 138, 158, 160, 161, 167, 176, 525, 571, 680, and others

11" – 13" $425.00 – 550.00

16" – 18" $575.00 – 625.00

20" – 22" $575.00 – 625.00

24" – 26" $750.00 – 825.00

Toddler body

14" – 16" $1,500.00 – 1,700.00

18" – 21" $1,900.00 – 2,100.00

26" $2,300.00 – 2,500.00

Mold 567 (made by Bähr & Pröschild), character multi-face, laughing face, glass eyes, open mouth; crying face, painted eyes, open/closed mouth

11" $1,000.00 – 1,400.00

15" $1,950.00 – 2,100.00

17" $2,200.00 – 2,400.00

19" $2,400.00 – 2,600.00

Child, 1920, dolly face, sleep eyes, open mouth, molds 250, 282, or Walkure

12" – 13"	$450.00 – 475.00
16" – 18"	$450.00 – 550.00
22" – 24"	$525.00 – 600.00
28" – 30"	$725.00 – 825.00
33"	$1,000.00 – 1,100.00
40"	$2,600.00*

Mold 325, "Dollar Princess," open mouth

18" – 20"	$425.00 – 475.00
23" – 25"	$400.00 – 450.00

Character Child, 1912, bisque socket head, jointed composition body

Mold numbers 154, 166, 169

Closed mouth

14" – 16"	$1,700.00 – 2,100.00
19" – 20"	$2,400.00 – 2,700.00
27"	$3,000.00 – 3,300.00

Open mouth

17" – 20"	$1,000.00 – 1,200.00

Painted eye character, molds 520, 525, 526, 531

14" – 16"	$3,400.00 – 3,600.00
17" – 19"	$4,000.00 – 4,400.00
21"	$5,000.00 – 5,300.00
29"	$12,000.00 – 13,000.00

Mold 546, 549, ca. 1912, character face

15" – 16"	$4,100.00 – 4,700.00
18" – 21"	$5,000.00 – 5,500.00

Mold 554, 568, ca. 1912, character face

21"	$1,400.00

Too few in database for a reliable range.

C.F. KLING & CO.

1834 – 1940s, Ohrdruf, Thüringia, Germany. Porcelain factory that began making doll heads in 1879, made china, bisque, and all-bisque dolls, and snow babies. Often mold number marks are followed by size number. Dolls listed are in good condition, appropriately dressed, more for exceptional doll with elaborate molded hair or bodice.

Bisque Shoulder Head, 1880 on, molded hair, cloth or kid body

Painted eyes, molds such as 123, 124, 131, 167, 178, 182, 189, and others

7" – 8"	$275.00 – 325.00
12" – 13"	$350.00 – 475.00

28" Kley and Hahn, mold 282. $725.00. *Courtesy of The Museum Doll Shop.*

19" bisque shoulder head doll by Kling marked 190 with a K in a bell. $1,800.00. *Courtesy Richard W. Withington, Inc., Nashua, New Hampshire.*

15" – 16"	$700.00 – 1,000.00
18" – 20"	$900.00 – 1,000.00
23" – 25"	$1,000.00 – 1,200.00

Glass eyes, molds such as 190, 203, 214, 217, 247, 254, and others

| 15" – 16" | $1,200.00 – 1,500.00 |
| 22" – 23" | $2,000.00 – 2,500.00 |

Bisque Lady, molded bodices, fancy hair, molds such as 135,144, 170, and others

| 15" | $1,000.00 – 1,100.00 |
| 19" – 21" | $1,300.00 – 1,600.00 |

China Shoulder Head, 1880 on, molded hair, painted eyes, closed mouth, molds such as 131, 188, 189, 202, 220, 285, and others

13" – 15"	$275.00 – 325.00
18" – 20"	$575.00 – 700.00
24" – 25"	$650.00 – 750.00

Mold 188, glass eyes

| 18" – 20" | $450.00 – 500.00 |

Bisque socket head, 1900 on, open mouth, sleep eyes, jointed body, molds such as 370, 372, 373, 377

13"	$350.00 – 400.00
15"	$450.00 – 500.00
17"	$475.00 – 550.00
21"	$550.00 – 600.00

All-Bisque: See All-Bisque section.

24" bisque shoulder head incised 131, made by Kling. $1,100.00. *Doll courtesy of Ruth Cayton.*

KLUMPE

1952 – 1970s, Barcelona, Spain. Caricature figures made of felt over wire armature with painted mask faces. Figures represent professionals, hobbyists, Spanish dancers, historical characters, and contemporary males and females performing a wide variety of tasks. Of the 200 or more different figures, the most common are Spanish dancers, bull fighters, and doctors. Some Klumpes were imported by Effanbee in the early 1950s. Originally the figures had two sewn-on identifying cardboard tags. Dolls listed are in good condition.

Average figure

| 10½" | $95.00 – 125.00 |

Elaborate figure, MIB with accessories

| 10½" | $200.00 – 250.00+ |

11" Hunter, tagged Klumpe. $200.00. *Courtesy of The Museum Doll Shop.*

KNICKERBOCKER DOLL & TOY CO.

1927 – 1980s, New York, New York. Made dolls of cloth, composition, hard plastic, and vinyl.

Cloth

Clown

17"	$18.00 – 25.00

Disney Characters

Donald Duck, Mickey Mouse, etc., all-cloth

10½"	$475.00 – 525.00

Mickey Mouse, ca. 1930s, oilcloth eyes

15"	$3,100.00*

Pinocchio, cloth and plush

13"	$200.00 – 250.00

Seven Dwarfs, 1939 on, mask face, mohair beard, up-turned toes

14"	$225.00 – 260.00 each

Snow White, all-cloth, mask face

16"	$375.00 – 425.00

14" Knickerbocker Holly Hobbie, c. 1970s. $20.00. *Courtesy of The Museum Doll Shop.*

Holly Hobbie, 1970s, cloth, later vinyl

Cloth

7" – 9"	$8.00 – 20.00
14"	$20.00 – 25.00
26"	$65.00 – 80.00

Vinyl

16"	$25.00 – 35.00

Little Orphan Annie, 1977

16"	$20.00 – 30.00

Composition

"Blondie" comic strip characters, composition, painted features, hair

Alexander Bumsted, molded hair

9"	$375.00 – 425.00

Baby Dumpling

9"	$2,700.00*

Blondie Bumstead, mohair wig

11"	$725.00 – 800.00

Dagwood Bumsted, molded hair

14"	$950.00 – 1,050.00

Child, 1938 on, mohair wig, sleep eyes

15"	$220.00 – 265.00
18"	$275.00 – 300.00

11" cloth mask face Happy made by Knickerbocker. $250.00. *Courtesy of The Museum Doll Shop.*

Mickey Mouse, 1930s – 1940s, composition, cloth body

18"	$900.00 – 1,100.00

Jiminy Cricket, all-composition

10"	$500.00 – 550.00

Pinocchio, all-composition

14"	$500.00 – 550.00
14"	$1,500.00 original labeled box
17"	$775.00 – 825.00

Seven Dwarfs, 1939+

9"	$250.00 – 275.00 each

Sleeping Beauty, 1939+, bent right arm

15"	$375.00 – 425.00
18"	$450.00 – 495.00

Snow White, 1937+, all-composition, bent right arm, black wig

15"	$396.00 – 435.00
20"	$425.00 – 475.00

Molded hair and ribbon, mark: "WALT DISNEY//1937//KNICKERBOCKER"

13"	$250.00 – 275.00
15"	$250.00 – 300.00

Set of Snow White and Dwarves

	$3,600.00*

Plastic and Vinyl Mask Face Dolls, 1950s – 1960s

Plush Body

Pinocchio

13"	$40.00 – 60.00

Sleepy Head

23"	$30.00 – 35.00

Cloth Body

Lovely Lori

15"	$65.00 – 75.00

Hard Plastic and Vinyl

Bozo Clown

14"	$18.00 – 25.00
24"	$45.00 – 60.00

Cinderella, two faces, one sad; one with tiara

16"	$15.00 – 20.00

Flintstone characters

6"	$8.00 – 10.00
17"	$36.00 – 43.00

Kewpies: See Kewpie section.

Little House on the Prairie, 1978

12"	$25.00 – 35.00

"Little Orphan Annie" comic strip characters, 1982

Little Orphan Annie, vinyl

6"	$12.00 – 17.50

Daddy Warbucks

7"	$12.00 – 17.50

Punjab

7"	$12.00 – 17.50

Miss Hannigan

7"	$12.00 – 17.50

Molly

5½"	$8.00 – 12.00

Rattle Dolls

Hard plastic, jointed shoulders, painted side-glancing eyes

6"	$12.00 – 18.00

Soupy Sales, 1966, vinyl and cloth, non-removable clothes

13"	$110.00 – 135.00

16" Little Orphan Annie, c. 1977. $25.00.
Courtesy of The Museum Doll Shop.

Two-faced dolls, 1960s, vinyl face masks, one crying, one smiling

12"	$14.00 – 18.00

Dolly Pops, 1979 on, molded vinyl with synthetic hair, molded changeable vinyl clothing

½"	$10.00 – 15.00

GEBRUDER KNOCH

1887 – 1919, Neustadt, Thüringia, Germany. Porcelain factory that made bisque doll heads with cloth or kid body.

Shoulder Head

Mold 203, 205, ca. 1910

Mold 203, character face, painted eyes, closed mouth, stuffed cloth body

Mold 205, "GKN" character face, intaglio eyes, open-closed mouth, molded tongue

12" – 13"	$500.00 – 600.00

Too few in database for a reliable range.

14" – 15"	$675.00 – 725.00

Too few in database for a reliable range.

Socket Head

Mold 179, 181, 190, 192, 193, 201, ca. 1900, mold 201 also came as black, dolly face, glass eyes, open mouth

7" on five-piece body	
	$195.00 – 210.00
13"	$185.00 – 250.00
17"	$300.00 – 425.00

Mold 204, 205, ca. 1910, character face

15"	$865.00 – 1,150.00

Mold 206, ca. 1910, "DRGM" solid dome, intaglio eyes, open/closed mouth

11"	$750.00*

Mold 216, ca. 1912, "GKN" solid dome, intaglio eyes, laughing, open/closed mouth

12"	$315.00

Too few in database for reliable range.

229: See All-Bisque section.

230, 232, ca. 1912, molded bonnet, character shoulder head, painted eyes, open/closed laughing mouth

13"	$675.00 – 900.00
15"	$1,200.00 – 1,600.00

KÖNIG & WERNICKE GMBH

1912 – 1930s, Waltershausen, Germany. Had doll factory, made bisque or celluloid dolls with composition bodies, later dolls with hard rubber heads. Bought bisque heads from Bähr & Pröschild, Hertel & Schwab, and Armand Marseille. Made "My Playmate" for Borgfeldt. Dolls listed are in good condition, appropriately dressed.

Bisque Baby

Mold 98, 99, ca. 1910, *Mold 1070,* ca. 1915, "made in Germany" (made by Hertel Schwab & Co.), character, socket head, sleep eyes, open mouth, teeth, tremble tongue, wigged, composition bent-leg baby body

9" – 11"	$325.00 – 375.00
12"	$400.00 – 450.00
15" – 16"	$475.00 – 650.00
18" – 22"	$500.00 – 675.00
24" – 25"	$750.00 – 850.00

Toddler

11" – 13"	$825.00 – 875.00
15" – 17"	$750.00 – 850.00
19" – 20"	$1,000.00 – 1,200.00

Child, socket-head, composition body

Dolly face

15"	$475.00 – 525.00

Mold 1070, character child, sleep eyes

15"	$1,100.00 – 1,300.00

Character Child in Boy Scout uniform, open mouth

22"	$3,700.00*

Painted bisque child, regional dress

18"	$125.00 – 175.00

Composition Child, composition head on five-piece or fully-jointed body, open mouth, sleep eyes, add more for flirty eyes

14"	$225.00 – 300.00
16"	$350.00 – 450.00

RICHARD KRUEGER

1907 – 1950s, New York City. Made cloth mask faced dolls.

Child, 1930 on

Cloth body

10"	$85.00 – 100.00
12"	$115.00 – 135.00
16"	$155.00 – 185.00
20"	$225.00 – 250.00

Oilcloth body

10"	$65.00 – 80.00
14" – 16"	$85.00 – 100.00

Walt Disney and Other Characters

Donald Duck, angry

	$1,008.00*

Dwarf, plush beard

12½"	$200.00 – 250.00

Three Little Pigs

7"	$50.00 – 65.00 each

Pinocchio

16"	$425.00 – 475.00

Kuddle Kewpie: See Kewpie section.

Scootles, 1935, designed by Rose O'Neill, yarn hair

10"	$425.00 – 475.00
18"	$825.00 – 875.00

20" Little Bo Peep, cloth mask face. $250.00.
Courtesy of The Museum Doll Shop.

KÄTHE KRUSE

1910 to present, Prussia, after W.W.II, Bavaria. Made cloth dolls with molded stockinette heads and waterproof muslin bodies, heads, hair, and hands oil painted. Early dolls are stuffed with deer hair. Early thumbs are part of the hand; after 1914 they are attached separately, later again, they're part of the hand. Marked on the bottom of the left foot with number and name "Käthe Kruse," in black, red, or purple ink. After 1929, dolls had wigs, but some still had painted hair. Later dolls have plastic and vinyl heads. Original doll modeled after bust sculpture "Fiammingo" by Francois Duquesnois.

Dolls listed are in good condition, appropriately dressed, allow significantly less for dirty or faded examples.

16" Käthe Kruse Doll I with wide hips. $6,000.00. *Courtesy of the Morris Museum, Morristown, New Jersey.*

Cloth

Miniatures, dollhouse-size character dolls
6", set of three $6,100.00
Doll I Series, 1910 – 1929, all-cloth, jointed shoulders, wide hips, painted eyes and hair, three vertical seams in back of head, marked on left foot
16" $5,500.00 – 6,500.00
Ball-jointed knees, 1911, variant produced by Kämmer & Reinhardt
17" $6,000.00
Too few in database for reliable range.
Doll I Series, later model, 1929+, now with slim hips
17" $2,800.00 – 3,000.00
Doll IH Series, wigged version, 1930+
17" $3,200.00 – 3,500.00
Bambino, a doll for a doll, circa 1915 – 1925
8" $500.00
Too few in database for reliable range.
Doll II Series, "Schlenkerchen," ca. 1922 – 1936, smiling baby, open-closed mouth,

stockinette covered body and limbs, one seam head
13" $9,000.00 – 10,000.00
Doll V, VI, Sandbabies Series, 1920s+, "Traumerchen" (closed eyes) and "Du Mein" (open eyes) were cloth dolls with painted hair, weighted with sand or unweighted, with or without belly buttons, in 19⅝" and 23⅝" sizes. One- or three-seam heads, or cloth over cardboard. Later heads were made in the 1930s from a heavy composition called magnesit.
19⅝" – 23½" $5,000.00 – 5,500.00
Magnesit head, circa 1930s+
20" $1,500.00 – 1,600.00
Doll VII Series, circa 1927 – 1952
Two versions were offered
A smaller 14" Du Mein open eye baby, painted hair or wigged, three-seam head, wide hips, sewn on thumbs, 1927 – 1930
14" $2,200.00 – 2,400.00
Too few in database for reliable range.

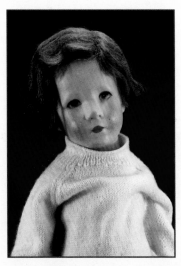

20" Doll VIII The German Child. $1,800.00. *Courtesy of The Museum Doll Shop.*

20" Käthe Kruse. $2,000.00.
Courtesy of Skinner Inc., Boston and Bolton, Massachusetts.

9" Käthe Kruse, synthetic head, foam padded stockinette body. $200.00.
Courtesy of The Museum Doll Shop.

A smaller Doll I version, with wide hips, separately sewn on thumbs, painted hair or wigged, after 1930 – 1950s slimmer hips and with thumbs formed with hand

    14" $2,000.00 – 2,500.00

Doll VIII Series, Deutsche Kind, the "German Child," 1929 on, modeled after Kruse's son, Friedebald, hollow head, swivels, one vertical seam in back of head, wigged, disk-jointed legs, later made in plastic during the 1950s

    20" $1,800.00 – 2,000.00

19" Käthe Kruse Traumerchen. $5,000.00. *Courtesy Richard W. Withington, Inc, Nashua, New Hampshire.*

Doll IX Series, "The Little German Child," 1929 on, wigged, one seam head, a smaller version of Doll VIII

    14" $1,600.00 – 1,800.00

Doll X Series, 1935 on, smaller doll I with one-seam head that turns

    14" $2,500.00 – 2,800.00

Doll XII Series, 1930s, Hempelchen with loose legs, three vertical seams on back of head, painted hair, button and band on back to make legs stand, the 14" variation has head of Doll I, the 16" variation also has the head of Doll I, and is known after 1940s as Hempelschatz, Doll XIIB.

    14" $1,300.00 – 1,500.00
    18" $2,100.00 – 2,500.00

Hard Plastic, 1948 – 1975, celluloid and other synthetics

US Zone mark

    14" $600.00 – 700.00

Turtle Mark Dolls, 1955 – 1961, synthetic bodies

    14" $275.00 – 325.00
    16" $350.00 – 400.00
    18" $450.00 – 500.00

1975 to date, marked with size number in centimeters, B for baby, H for hair, and G for painted hair

10"	$150.00 – 200.00
13"	$175.00 – 225.00

GEBRUDER KUHNLENZ

1884 – 1935, Kronach, Bavaria, Germany. Porcelain factory made dolls, doll heads, movable children, and swimmers. Butler Bros. and Marshall Field distributed their dolls.

Closed Mouth Child

Mold 28, 31, 32, 39, ca. 1890, bisque socket head, closed mouth, glass eyes, pierced ears, wig, wood and composition jointed body

8" – 10"	$850.00 – 1,100.00
15" – 16"	$1,600.00 – 1,700.00
21" – 23"	$2,400.00 – 2,700.00

Mold 34, Bru type, paperweight eyes, closed mouth, pierced ears, composition jointed body

12½" – 15"	$2,900.00 – 4,000.00
18" – 20"	$4,500.00 – 6,300.00

Mold 38, solid dome turned shoulder head, closed mouth, pierced ears, kid body

12" – 15"	$500.00 – 575.00
17" – 20"	$800.00 – 900.00

Mold 39, socket head

14"	$2,500.00*

Mold 46, socket head

17"	$1,000.00*

Open Mouth Child

Mold 41, 44, socket head, glass eyes, open mouth, composition body

9" – 10"	$525.00 – 575.00
15" – 19"	$650.00 – 750.00
24" – 26"	$950.00 – 1,000.00
30"	$1,400.00 – 1,600.00

Mold 165, ca. 1900, socket head, sleep eyes, open mouth, teeth

18"	$300.00 – 325.00
22" – 24"	$350.00 – 400.00
30" – 33"	$425.00 – 475.00

Mold 47, 61, shoulder head

14"	$350.00 – 400.00
18"	$400.00 – 425.00

Mold 44, small dolls marked "Gbr. K" in sunburst, socket head, glass eyes, open mouth, five-piece composition body

7" – 8"	$250.00 – 325.00

All-Bisque, swivel neck, molds 31, 41, 44, 56, others, glass eyes

5" – 7"	$650.00 – 1,000.00

A. & CIE. LANTERNIER

1915 – 1924, Limoges, France. Porcelain factory, made dolls and heads. Lady dolls were dressed in French provincial costumes, bodies by Ortyz; dolls were produced for Association to Aid War Widows.

Adult, ca. 1915

Marked "Caprice," "Lorraine," bisque socket head, open/closed mouth with teeth, composition adult body

13"	$750.00 – 800.00
16" – 18"	$8000.00 – 900.00
22"	$1,000.00 – 1,200.00

Painted eyes

12½"	$1,000.00 – 1,975.00

Child

"Cherie," "Favorite," "La Georgienne," or

20" Favorite by Lanternier. $725.00.
Courtesy of The Museum Doll Shop.

"*Toto,*" bisque socket head, open mouth with teeth, wig, composition jointed body

12" – 14"	$625.00 – 675.00
16" – 18"	$650.00 – 700.00
22" – 24"	$750.00 – 800.00
25" – 26"	$700.00 – 750.00

15" Cherie by Lanternier. $675.00.
Courtesy of The Museum Doll Shop.

LAWTON DOLL CO.

1979 to present, Turlock, California. Founded by Wendy Lawton. Dolls listed are mint-in-box dolls; dolls missing accessories or with flaws would be priced less.

Childhood Classics

Alice in Wonderland

1983	$3,000.00

Too few in database for a reliable range.

Anne of Green Gables, 1986

14"	$1,600.00

Too few in database for a reliable range.

Hans Brinker, 1985

14"	$700.00 – 750.00

The Blessing, 1990

13½"	$165.00 – 195.00

Heidi, 1984

14"	$300.00 – 400.00

June Amos & Mary Anne, 1996

16"	$1,305.00

Little Women, set of four, 1994 – 1995

15"	$1,525.00

Too few in database for a reliable range.

Li'l Princess, 1989

14"	$700.00 – 750.00

Pollyanna, 1986

14"	$650.00 – 700.00

Sarah's Sock Monkey, porcelain doll

12"	$55.00 – 65.00

Christmas Dolls

Christmas Joy

1988	$650.00 – 700.00

Noel

1989	$300.00 – 350.00

Christmas Angel

1990	$300.00 – 350.00

Yuletide Carole

1991	$300.00 – 350.00

Disney World Specials

1st Main Street	$200.00 – 300.00

9½" Katrena by Wendy Lawton for UFDC.
$225.00. *Courtesy of The Museum Doll Shop.*

2ⁿᵈ Liberty Square, 250 issued
$250.00 – 350.00
3ʳᵈ Tish $250.00 – 350.00
4ᵗʰ Karen, 50 issued $650.00 – 750.00
5ᵗʰ Goofy Kid, 100 issued
$650.00 – 750.00
6ᵗʰ Melissa & Her Mickey
$600.00 – 700.00
7ᵗʰ Christopher, Robin, Pooh
12" $600.00 – 700.00
Guild Dolls
Ba Ba Black Sheep, porcelain,1989
14" $200.00 – 300.00
Lavender Blue, 1990 $300.00 – 400.00
Uniquely Yours, 1995, porcelain
14" $120.00 – 170.00
Somebunny, 1997, porcelain
4½" $20.00 – 30.00
Special Editions
Marcella & Raggedy Ann, 1988
$645.00 – 695.00
Red Ridinghood, limited edition, 1992, porcelain
14" $150.00 – 175.00

Flora McFlimsey, 1993 $1,000.00
Too few in database for a reliable range.
Zudie's Coverlet, Fabric of America Collection, black, porcelain head, wooden body
16" $400.00 – 450.00
Other Specials
Beatrice Louise, UFDC, 1998 Luncheon
$890.00 – 975.00
Josephine, UFDC Regional
12" $700.00 – 750.00
Katrena, UFDC Convention, 2002
9½" $200.00 – 225.00
Little Colonel, Dolly Dears, Birmingham, AL $375.00 – 425.00
1ˢᵗ WL Convention, Lotta Crabtree
$1,300.00
Too few in database for a reliable range.
Lawton Gathering, 2003, one-of-a-kind porcelain doll
9" $200.00 – 225.00

LEATHER

Leather was an available resource for Native Americans to use for making doll heads, bodies, or entire dolls. It was also used by American doll makers such as Darrow and by French and Moroccan doll makers, as well as others. Some examples of Gussie Decker's dolls were advertised as "impossible for child to hurt itself" and leather was fine for teething babies.
Darrow, American, molded rawhide, These dolls are almost always found with very little original paint remaining, value listed reflects this condition
18" – 22" $550.00 – 650.00
French all-leather baby, molded head, jointed body, painted eyes
4" – 4½" $2,200.00 – 2,800.00

9" leather peddler doll, c. 1840s. $1,000.00. *Courtesy of Skinner Inc., Boston and Bolton, Massachusetts.*

20" rawhide doll by Darrow. $600.00. *Courtesy of The Museum Doll Shop.*

Native American Dolls
Apache, ca. 1900 11", buckskin doll with molded face $800.00
Eskimo, ca. 1940

10"	$110.00
12"	$125.00

Sioux,

ca. 1900, 11½", buckskin	$800.00
ca. 2005, 14" buckskin	$50.00

Moroccan leather dolls, 1900 – 1940s, souvenir type dolls depicting regional characters

9" – 11" $25.00 – 45.00

12" leather baby, made in Morocco. $200.00. *Courtesy of The Museum Doll Shop.*

LENCI

1919 to 2003, Turino, Italy. Lenci was the trademark and name of firm started by Enrico and Elena di Scavini, that made felt dolls with pressed faces, also made composition head dolls, wooden dolls, and porcelain figurines and dolls. Early Lenci dolls have tiny metal button, hang tags with "Lenci//Torino//Made in Italy."

9" Lenci Mascotte, Lombardi. $375.00.
Courtesy of The Museum Doll Shop.

Ribbon strips marked "Lenci//Made in Italy" were found in the clothes ca. 1925 – 1950. Some, but not all dolls have Lenci marked in purple or black ink on the sole of the foot. Some with original paper tags may be marked with a model number in pencil.

Dolls have felt swivel heads, oil-painted features, often side-glancing eyes, jointed shoulders and hips, lips, third and fourth fingers are often sewn together, sewn-on double felt ears, often dressed in felt and organdy original clothes, excellent condition. May have scalloped socks.

The most sought after are the well constructed early dolls from the 1920s and 1930s, when Madame Lenci had control of the design and they were more elaborate with fanciful, well made accessories. They carried animals of wood or felt, baskets, felt vegetables, purses, or bouquets of felt flowers. This era of dolls had eye shadow, dots in the corner of the eye, two-tone lips, with lower lip highlighted and, depending on condition, will command higher prices.

After WWII the company was purchased by the Garella Brothers. The later dolls of the 1940s and 1950s have hard cardboard-like felt faces, with less intricate details, like less elaborate appliqués, fewer accessories, and other types of fabrics such as taffeta, cotton, and rayon, all showing a decline in quality and should not be priced as earlier dolls. The later dolls may have fabric covered cardboard torsos. Model numbers changed over the years, so what was a certain model number early, later became another letter or number.

Dolls listed are in clean condition and wearing original clothing. Soiled, faded examples will bring significantly less. Add more for tags, boxes, or accessories. Exceptional dolls and rare examples may go much higher.

24" long limbed lady doll. $2,200.00.
Courtesy of The Museum Doll Shop.

Baby

13" – 15"	$1,700.00 – 1,900.00
18" – 22"	$2,700.00 – 3,000.00

Child

1920s – 1930s, softer face, more elaborate costume, face model numbers 300, 109, 149, 159, 111

13"	$1,300.00 – 1,500.00
17"	$1,900.00 – 2,100.00
21"	$2,200.00 – 2,350.00

Model 1500, scowling face

17" – 19"	$2,200.00 – 2,700.00

Model 500

21"	$1,600.00 – 1,800.00

1940s – 1950s+, hard face, less intricate costume

13"	$300.00 – 400.00
15"	$400.00 – 500.00
17"	$500.00 – 600.00

Small Dolls

Mascottes and Miniatures, 9"

Child	$300.00 – 375.00
Regional costume	$350.00 – 375.00

Long Limbed Lady Dolls

With adult face, flapper or boudoir body

12" Lenci girl. $1,300.00. *Doll courtesy of Carole Barboza.*

with long slim limbs

17"	$1,050.00 – 1,200.00
24" – 28"	$2,200.00 – 2,600.00
32"	$2,700.00 – 2,900.00
48"	$5,000.00

Too few in database for a reliable range.

Celebrities

Bach

17"	$2,500.00 – 2,850.00

Jack Dempsey

18"	$3,000.00 – 3,500.00

Marlene Dietrich

23" doll sitting on 30" stool	
	$10,500.00*

Tom Mix

18"	$3,000.00 – 3,500.00

Mendel

22"	$3,400.00 – 3,700.00

Mozart

11"	$2,100.00 – 2,200.00
14"	$2,900.00 – 3,100.00

Pastorelle

14"	$2,900.00 – 3,100.00

Characters

Aladdin

14"	$7,000.00 – 7,750.00

Athlete, Golfer, ca. 1930

17"	$2,700.00

a few moth holes

Aviator, girl with felt helmet

18"	$2,900.00 – 3,200.00

Becassine

11"	$925.00 – 975.00

Glass eyes

20"	$2,900.00 – 3,100.00

Benedetta

19"	$1,000.00 – 1,100.00

Black Child, in native garb

15"	$2,600.00 – 3,000.00

Court Gentleman

18"	$1,400.00 – 1,600.00

18" Lenci girl. $2,100.00.
Doll courtesy of Carole Barboza.

Cupid
17" $4,900.00 – 5,200.00
Devil
9" $1,500.00
Too few in database for a reliable range.
Fascist Boy, rare
14" $1,200.00 – 1,500.00
17", missing ear $1,250.00
Flower Girl, ca. 1930
20" $1,200.00 – 1,400.00
Henriette
26" $1,800.00 – 2,100.00
Indian
17" $3,200.00 – 3,600.00
Squaw with Papoose
17" $3,900.00 – 4,200.00
Laura
16" $950.00 – 1,100.00
Lucia 48, ca. 1930
14" $800.00 – 1,000.00
Pan, hoofed feet
8" $1,000.00
Too few in database for a reliable range.
Pierrot
21" $2,100.00 – 2,900.00

Pinocchio, MIB
11" $1,100.00
Salome, ca. 1920, brown felt, ball at waist allows doll to swivel
17" $3,000.00 – 3,500.00
Smoker
Painted eyes
28" $2,100.00 – 2,400.00
Glass eyes
24" $3,500.00 – 3,900.00
Sport Series
17" $3,000.00 – 4,000.00
Val Gardena
19" $800.00 – 900.00
Winking Boy
11" $950.00 – 1,050.00
Ethnic or Regional Costume
Bali dancer
15" $950.00 – 1,500.00
Eugenia
25" $900.00 – 1,100.00
Chinese Boy, ca. 1925
16" $1,700.00
Too few in database for a reliable range.

A pair of Lenci dolls, c. 1990s. $150.00 – 200.00 *Photo courtesy of The Museum Doll Shop.*

Madame Butterfly, ca. 1926

17"	$3,000.00 – 3,200.00
25"	$4,300.00 – 4,800.00

Marenka, Russian girl, ca. 1930

14"	$3,000.00 – 3,500.00

Scottish Girl, ca. 1930

14"	$600.00 – 700.00

Spanish Girl, ca. 1930

14"	$700.00 – 800.00
17"	$900.00 – 1,000.00

Tyrol Boy or Girl, ca. 1935

14"	$700.00 – 800.00

Eye Variations

Glass eyes

16"	$1,400.00 – 1,600.00
22"	$2,800.00 – 3,000.00

Flirty glass eyes

15"	$2,000.00 – 2,200.00
20"	$2,600.00 – 2,800.00

Surprise eye, Widow, "O" shaped eyes and mouth

19" – 20"	$3,200.00 – 3,400.00

Modern, 1979 on

13"	$95.00 – 125.00
21"	$150.00 – 200.00
26"	$175.00 – 225.00

Princess Di, 1985

14"	$325.00 – 375.00

Accessories

Lenci Dog	$100.00 – 150.00
Purse	$175.00 – 225.00

LENCI-TYPE

1920 – 1950. These were made by many English, French, or Italian firms like Anili, Gre-Poir, or Raynal from felt with painted features, mohair wig, original clothes. These must be in very good condition, tagged or unmarked.

Usually Lenci-types have single felt ears or no ears.

Child

Low quality

15" – 17"	$125.00 – 145.00

High Quality

15" – 17"	$350.00 – 450.00

Regional costume, makers such as Alma, Vecchiotti, and others

8" – 9"	$175.00 – 195.00
11" – 15"	$225.00 – 375.00

Smoker

16"	$350.00 – 400.00

Anili, founded by the daughter of Elena Di Scavini (Lenci), molded felt dolls

16" – 21"	$200.00 – 250.00

Gre Poir, France, New York City, 1927 – 1930s, Eugenie Poir made felt or cloth mask face dolls, unmarked on body, no ears, white socks with three stripes, hang tag, 16" – 18"

Cloth face	$375.00 – 425.00
Felt face	$500.00 – 550.00

Messina-Vat, 1923 on, Turin, Italy

20"	$375.00 – 450.00

Pressed felt doll by Messina-Vat. $400.00.
Photo courtesy of The Museum Doll Shop.

LIBERTY OF LONDON

1906 to 1950s, London, England. Liberty of London was founded in 1873. In 1920 they registered the name "Liberty" for their line of needle sculpted art dolls.

British Characters and Historical Figures, such as Shakespeare, John Bull, Queen Victoria, and others

9" – 10"	$175.00 – 225.00
Beefeater	$90.00 – 110.00

Coronation Dolls

9" – 10"	$225.00 – 250.00

Princess Elizabeth or Margaret

7"	$400.00 – 425.00

10" William Shakespeare doll by Liberty of London. $225.00. *Photo courtesy of The Museum Doll Shop.*

A.G. LIMBACH

1772 – 1927 on, Limbach, Thüringia, Germany. This porcelain factory made bisque head dolls, china dolls, bathing dolls, and all-bisque dolls beginning in 1872. Usually marked with three leaf clover.

All-Bisque

Child, small doll, molded hair or wigged, painted eyes, molded and painted shoes and socks, may have mark "8661," and cloverleaf, more for exceptional dolls

4" – 5"	$55.00 – 65.00
6" – 8"	$100.00 – 175.00
11" – 12"	$550.00 – 650.00

Paper sticker marked "Our Mary," all-bisque, glass sleep eyes, wigged

6" – 8"	$225.00 – 275.00

Baby, mold 8682, character face, bisque socket head, glass eyes, clover mark, bent-leg baby body, wig, open-closed mouth

8½"	$325.00 – 400.00

Child

May have name above mold mark, such as Norma, Rita, Wally, bisque socket head, glass eyes, clover mark, wig, open mouth

18" – 20"	$400.00 – 550.00

MAROTTES

1860 on and earlier. Bisque doll's head on wooden or ivory stick, sometimes with whistle, when twirled some play music, made by various French and German companies.

Bisque, open mouth

14"	$575.00 – 675.00

Gebruder Heubah head

11½"	$475.00 – 525.00

Marseille, Armand

Mold 3200, open mouth

13"	$1,000.00 – 1,300.00

Mold 600, closed mouth, squeaker mechanism

13"	$900.00 – 1,200.00

Schoenau & Hoffmeister, molds 4700,
4800, circa 1905

15"	$800.00 – 900.00
Celluloid	
11"	$200.00 – 250.00

German bisque headed Marottes.
$625.00 each. *Photo courtesy of Alderfer Auction Co.*

ARMAND MARSEILLE

1884 – 1950s, Sonneberg, Köppelsdorf, Thüringia, Germany. One of the largest suppliers of bisque doll heads, ca. 1900 – 1930, to such companies as Amberg, Arranbee, Bergmann, Borgfeldt, Butler Bros., Dressel, Montgomery Ward, Sears, Steiner, Wiegand, Louis Wolf, and others. Made some doll heads with no mold numbers, but names, such as Alma, Baby Betty, Baby Gloria, Baby Florence, Baby Phyllis, Beauty, Columbia, Duchess, Ellar, Florodora,

Mold 370 shoulder-head doll. $275.00. *Photo courtesy of The Museum Doll Shop.*

Jubilee, Mabel, Majestic, Melitta, My Playmate, Nobbi Kid, Our Pet, Princess, Queen Louise, Rosebud, Superb, Sunshine, and Tiny Tot. Some Indian dolls had no mold numbers. Often used Superb kid bodies, with bisque hands.

After WWII and into the 1950s the East German government continued to produce dolls marked AM.

Dolls listed are in good condition, appropriately dressed.

Child Doll, 1890 on, no mold number, or just marked "A.M.," and molds 390, Floradora, 1894, bisque socket head, open mouth, glass eyes, wig, composition fully jointed body. Dolls listed are in good condition, appropriately dressed, allow more for flirty eyes.

Composition Body

9" – 10"	$250.00 – 275.00
12" – 14"	$200.00 – 250.00
16" – 18"	$300.00 – 350.00
20" – 24"	$350.00 – 400.00
28" – 30"	$450.00 – 550.00
32" – 36"	$700.00 – 900.00
42"	$1,600.00 – 1,800.00

Five-piece body, high quality

6" – 7"	$225.00 – 250.00
10"	$250.00 – 275.00

Five-piece body, low quality

10" – 12"	$125.00 – 135.00
14" – 16"	$150.00 – 175.00

Molds Queen Louise, Rosebud

12" – 13"	$250.00 – 300.00
15" – 17"	$275.00 – 325.00
22" – 24"	$350.00 – 400.00
28"	$500.00 – 550.00
31"	$850.00 – 925.00

Mold Baby Betty

14" – 16"	$400.00 – 450.00
18" – 20"	$300.00 – 350.00

Kid Body

Shoulder head mold 370, 1894, 3200, Alma, Beauty, Floradora, Lily, Mabel, My Playmate, Princess, Rosebud

10" – 12"	$115.00 – 135.00
14" – 16"	$200.00 – 250.00
18" – 20"	$275.00 – 300.00
22" – 24"	$300.00 – 350.00

15" Armand Marseille mold 390, factory dressed. $275.00. *Photo courtesy of The Museum Doll Shop.*

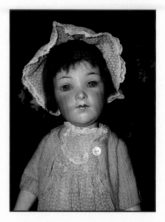

13" AM 400, closed mouth character doll. $1,600.00. *Doll courtesy of Turn of the Century Antiques, Denver, Colorado.*

Molds 1890, 1892, 1895, 1897, 1899, 1901, 1902, 1903, 1909

10" – 12"	$185.00 – 230.00
14" – 16"	$225.00 – 275.00
18" – 20"	$300.00 – 375.00
22" – 24"	$375.00 – 425.00

Character Baby

Baby Betty, usually found on child composition body, some on bent-leg baby body

16"	$500.00

Too few in database for reliable range.

Molds Kiddiejoy, 256, 259, 326, 327, 328, 329, 360a, 750, 790, 900, 927, 970, 971, 975, 980, 984, 985, 990, 991, 992 Our Pet, 995, 996, 1330, bisque solid-dome or wigged socket head, open mouth, glass eyes, composition bent-leg baby body, add more for toddler body or flirty eyes or exceptional doll

12"	$275.00 – 350.00
15"	$475.00 – 525.00
17"	$525.00 – 575.00
21"	$550.00 – 600.00
24"	$675.00 – 725.00

15" AM 985, open mouth doll on bent-limb baby body. $475.00. *Photo courtesy of The Museum Doll Shop.*

Mold 233

12" – 13"	$400.00 – 425.00
15"	$500.00 – 550.00

Mold 251/248

Open/closed mouth

10" – 12"	$500.00 – 600.00

Closed mouth

12"	$425.00 – 450.00

Mold 410, two rows of teeth

12"	$600.00 – 700.00

Mold 500, intaglio eye, bent-limb composition body

15"	$575.00 – 600.00

Mold 518

16" – 18"	$430.00 – 450.00

Mold 560A

15" – 16"	$475.00 – 500.00

Mold 580, 590

15" – 16"	$1,000.00 – 1,100.00
19"	$1,200.00 – 1,300.00

Mold 920

21"	$650.00

Too few in database for a reliable range.

Melitta, toddler

16"	$800.00 – 900.00

Character Child

Mold 225, ca. 1920, bisque socket head, glass eyes, open mouth, two rows of teeth, composition jointed body

14"	$3,000.00 – 3,600.00
19"	$4,000.00 – 4,650.00

Fany, ca. 1912, can be child, toddler, or baby

230, molded hair

15" – 16"	$6,000.00 – 7,000.00
18"	$8,500.00 – 9,500.00

231, wigged

13" – 14"	$4,500.00 – 5,000.00
16"	$5,800.00 – 6,100.00

Mold 250, ca. 1912, domed

9" – 13"	$575.00 – 600.00
15"	$600.00 – 650.00
18"	$750.00 – 875.00

Mold 251, ca. 1912, socket head, open-closed mouth

12" – 13"	$1,100.00 – 1,250.00
17" – 18"	$2,000.00 – 2,200.00

Mold 253: See Googly section.

Mold 310, Just Me, ca. 1929, bisque socket head, wig, flirty eyes, closed mouth, composition body

7½" – 8"	$1,300.00 – 1,500.00
9" – 10"	$1,600.00 – 1,900.00
11"	$2,000.00 – 2,200.00
13"	$2,900.00 – 3,000.00

Painted bisque, with Vogue labeled outfits

7" – 8"	$850.00 – 1,100.00
10"	$1,200.00 – 1,400.00

Mold 345, pouty

Painted intaglio eyes

10" – 11"	$2,400.00 – 2,800.00

Glass eyes

10"	$825.00 – 900.00

Mold 350, ca. 1926, glass eyes, closed mouth

16"	$1,950.00 – 2,250.00
20"	$2,500.00 – 2,850.00

Mold 360a, ca. 1913, open mouth
    12" $350.00 – 400.00
Mold 400, 401, ca. 1926, glass eyes, closed mouth
    13" $1,400.00 – 1,600.00
    26" $2,600.00*
Mold 449, ca. 1930, painted eyes, closed mouth
    13" $575.00 – 625.00
    18" $900.00 – 1,000.00

Painted bisque
    11" $250.00 – 350.00
    15" $575.00 – 765.00
Mold 450, glass eyes, closed mouth
    14" $575.00 – 700.00
Mold 500, 600, ca. 1910, domed shoulder head, molded/painted hair, painted intaglio eyes, closed mouth
    10" $500.00 – 650.00
    17" $700.00 – 750.00
Mold 520, ca. 1910, domed head, glass eyes, open mouth

Composition body
    12" $675.00 – 750.00
    19" $1,800.00 – 2,000.00

10½" painted bisque infant marked AM. $150.00. *Courtesy of The Museum Doll Shop.*

9" painted bisque *Just Me.* $1,100.00. *Photo courtesy of The Museum Doll Shop.*

Kid body
    16" $800.00 – 900.00
    20" $1,200.00 – 1,400.00
Mold 550, ca. 1926, domed, glass eyes, closed mouth
    14" – 15" $1,600.00 – 1,900.00
Mold 560, ca. 1910, character, domed, painted eyes, open/closed mouth or 560A, ca. 1926, wigged, glass eyes, open mouth
    14" $850.00 – 900.00
    22" $1,200.00 – 1,300.00
Mold 570, ca. 1910, domed, closed mouth
    12" $1,600.00 – 1,750.00
Mold 590, ca. 1926, sleep eyes, open/closed mouth
    9" $450.00 – 500.00
    16" $900.00 – 1,000.00
    18" – 20" $1,000.00 – 1,100.00
Mold 700, ca. 1920, closed mouth

Painted eyes
    12½" $1,800.00 – 2,000.00
Glass eyes
    14" $3,800.00 – 4,200.00
Mold 701, 711, ca. 1920, socket or shoulder head, sleep eyes, closed mouth
    16" $2,000.00 – 2,250.00

22" composition doll marked 2966, c. 1950. $175.00. *Photo courtesy of The Museum Doll Shop.*

Mold 800, ca. 1910, socket head, 840 shoulder head

18"	$2,000.00 – 2,200.00

Lady, 1910 on, bisque head, wigged, sleep eyes, open or closed mouth, composition lady body

Molds 400, 401, 14"

Open mouth	$1,200 .00 – 1,400.00
Closed mouth	$2,400.00 – 2,700.00
Painted bisque	$900.00 – 1,000.00

Newborn Baby, 1924 on, newborn, bisque solid-dome socket head or flange neck, may have wig, glass eyes, closed mouth, cloth body with celluloid or composition hands

Mold 341, My Dream Baby, 351, 345, Kiddiejoy, 352, Rock-A-Bye Baby, marked "AM"

11" – 13"	$200.00 – 225.00
14" – 16"	$250.00 – 300.00
22" – 24"	$375.00 – 425.00

On bent-limb composition body

11" – 12"	$275.00 – 325.00
16"	$350.00 – 375.00

With toddler body

28"	$900.00 – 1,200.00

Baby Gloria, solid dome, open mouth, painted hair, head circumference:

12"	$400.00 – 450.00
15"	$575.00 – 625.00

Baby Phyllis, head circumference:

9"	$375.00 – 450.00
13"	$425.00 – 500.00
15"	$575.00 – 600.00

Composition Child, 1940s – 1950s, mold 2966 and others, sleep eyes, synthetic wig, five-piece composition body (very thin cardboard like composition)

22"	$165.00 – 175.00

MARX TOY CORP.

1919 to present, Sebring, Ohio. Founded in 1919 as Louis Marx & Co. in New York City. Dolls listed are in perfect condition with original clothing.

Archie and Friends, characters from comics, vinyl, molded hair or wigged, painted eyes, in package

Archie, Betty, Jughead, Veronica

8½"	$18.00 – 25.00

Johnny Apollo Double Agent, vinyl, trench coat, circa 1970s

12"	$40.00 – 50.00

Miss Seventeen, 1961, hard plastic, high heeled, fashion-type doll, modeled like the German Bild Lilli (Barbie doll's predecessor), came in black swimsuit, black box, fashion brochure pictures 12 costumes, she was advertised as "A Beauty Queen"

18"	$125.00 – 175.00
Costume only, MIP	$36.00

Miss Marlene, hard plastic, high heeled, Barbie-type, ca. 1960s, blond rooted wig

11"	$100.00 – 120.00

Miss Toddler, also know as Miss Marx, vinyl, molded hair, ribbons, battery operated walker, molded clothing
  18" $125.00 – 155.00

Johnny West Family of Action Figures, 1965 – 1976

Adventure or Best of the West Series, rigid vinyl, articulated figures, molded clothes, came in box with vinyl accessories and extra clothes, had horses, dogs, and other accessories available. Dolls listed are complete with box and all accessories; allow more if never removed from box or special sets.

Bill Buck, brown molded-on clothing, 13 pieces, coonskin cap
  11½" $100.00 – 125.00

Captain Tom Maddox, blue molded-on clothing, brown hair, 23 pieces
  11½" $75.00 – 90.00

Chief Cherokee, tan or light color molded-on clothing, 37 pieces
  11½" $80.00 – 100.00

4½" Twinkie, vinyl doll with vinyl clothing and wigs. $55.00. *Courtesy of The Museum Doll Shop.*

Daniel Boone, tan molded-on clothing, coonskin cap
  11½" $95.00 – 115.00

Fighting Eagle, tan molded-on clothes, with Mohawk hair, 37 pieces
  11½" $115.00 – 135.00

General Custer, dark blue molded-on clothing, yellow hair, 23 pieces
  11½" $70.00 – 85.00

Geronimo, light color molded-on clothing
  11½" $55.00 – 75.00
  Orange body
  11½" $90.00 – 110.00

Jamie West, dark hair, molded-on tan clothing, 13 accessories
  9" $35.00 – 45.00

Jane West, blond hair, turquoise molded on clothing, 37 pieces
  11½" $60.00 – 75.00
  Orange body $35.00 – 45.00

Janice West, dark hair, turquoise molded-on clothing, 14 pieces
  9" $35.00 – 45.00

Jay West, blond hair, tan molded-on clothing, 13 accessories, later brighter body colors
  9" $80.00 – 100.00

Jed Gibson, c. 1973, black figure, molded-on green clothing
  12" $220.00 – 260.00

Johnny West, brown hair, molded-on brown clothing, 25 pieces
  12" $80.00 – 100.00

Johnny West, with quick draw arm, blue clothing
  12" $45.00 – 55.00

Josie West, blond, turquoise molded-on clothing, later with bright green body
  9" $35.00 – 45.00

Princess Wildflower, off-white molded-on clothing, with papoose in vinyl cradle, 22 pieces
  11½" $110.00 – 130.00

Sam Cobra, outlaw, with 26 accessories
    11½" $80.00 – 100.00

Sheriff Pat Garrett (Sheriff Goode in Canada), molded-on blue clothing, 25 pieces
    11½" $100.00 – 125.00

Zeb Zachary, dark hair, blue molded-on clothing, 23 pieces
    11½" $90.00 – 110.00

Knight and Viking Series, ca. 1960s, action figures with accessories

Gordon, the Gold Knight, molded-on gold clothing, brown hair, beard, mustache
    11½" $100.00 – 125.00

Sir Stuart, the Silver Knight, molded-on silver clothing, black hair, mustache, goatee
    11½" $100.00 – 125.00

Brave Erik, the Viking, with horse, ca. 1967, molded-on green clothing, blond hair, blue eyes
    11½" $100.00 – 125.00

Odin, the Viking, ca. 1967, brown molded-on clothing, brown eyes, brown hair, beard
    11½" $100.00 – 125.00

Sindy, ca. 1963+, in England by Pedigree, a fashion-type doll, rooted hair, painted eyes, wires in limbs allow her to pose, distributed in U.S. by Marx c. 1978 – 1982
    11" $45.00 – 65.00

Pedigree $90.00 – 110.00

Pedigree Sindy Majorette, box
        $480.00*

Gayle, Sindy's friend, black vinyl
    11" $100.00 – 115.00

Outfits $75.00 – 95.00

Soldiers, ca. 1960s, articulated action figures with accessories

Buddy Charlie, Montgomery Wards, exclusive, a buddy for GI Joe, molded-on military uniform, brown hair
    11½" $80.00 – 100.00

Stony "Stonewall" Smith, molded-on Army fatigues, blond hair, 36-piece accessories
    11½" $80.00 – 100.00

Others

Freddy Krueger, 1989, vinyl, pull string talker from horror movie *Nightmare on Elm Street*, character played by Robert England
    18" $40.00 – 50.00

PeeWee Herman, 1987 TV character, vinyl and cloth, ventriloquist doll in gray suit, red bow tie
    18" $20.00 – 30.00

Pull string talker
    18" $25.00 – 35.00

Twinkie, doll with vinyl clothing and wigs
    4½" $55.00 – 65.00

MATTEL

1959 to present, founded by Ruth and Elliot Handler. Many dolls of the 1960s and 1970s designed by Martha Armstrong Hand. Dolls listed are in excellent condition with all original clothing and accessories. Allow more for mint-in-box examples.

Baby Beans, 1971 – 1975, vinyl head, bean bag dolls, terry cloth or tricot bodies filled with plastic and foam
    12" $50.00 – 60.00

Talking
    12" $30.00 – 40.00

Baby First Step, 1965 – 1967, battery operated walker, rooted hair, sleep eyes, pink dress
    18" $75.00 – 120.00

Talking
    18" $120.00 – 150.00

Baby Go Bye-Bye and Her Bumpety Buggy, 1970, doll sits in car, battery

operated, 12 maneuvers

11"	$65.00 – 75.00

Baby's Hungry, 1967 – 1968, battery operated, eyes move and lips chew when magic bottle or spoon is put to mouth, wets, plastic bib

17"	$20.00 – 25.00

Baby Love Light, battery operated

16"	$14.00 – 18.00

Baby Pattaburp, 1964 – 1966, vinyl, drinks milk, burps when patted, pink jacket, lace trim

16"	$60.00 – 80.00

Baby Play-A-Lot, 1972 – 1973, posable arms, fingers can hold things, comes with 20 toys, moves arm to brush teeth, moves head, no batteries, has pull string and switch

16"	$18.00 – 22.00

Baby Say 'N See, 1967 – 1968, eyes and lips move while talking, white dress, pink yoke

17"	$95.00 – 125.00

16" Mrs. Beasley, glasses missing. $200.00. *Photo courtesy of The Museum Doll Shop.*

Baby Secret, 1966 – 1967, vinyl face and hands, stuffed body, limbs, red hair, blue eyes, whispers 11 phrases, moves lips

18"	$75.00 – 85.00

Baby Small Talk, 1968 – 1969, says eight phrases, infant voice, additional outfits available

10¾"	$40.00 – 50.00

Black

10¾"	$50.00 – 60.00

In Nursery Rhyme outfit

10¾"	$55.00 – 65.00

Baby Tender Love, 1970 – 1973, baby doll, realistic skin, wets, can be bathed

Newborn

13"	$50.00 – 60.00

Talking

16"	$25.00 – 35.00

Boxed

16"	$180.00*

Molded hairpiece, 1972

11½"	$9.00 – $30.00

Brother, sexed

11½"	$50.00 – 60.00

Baby First Step, 1965. $120.00. *Photo courtesy of The Museum Doll Shop.*

Baby Walk 'n Play, 1968
  11" $8.00 – 12.00
Baby Walk 'n See
  18" $12.00 – 18.00
Barbie: See that section.
Bozo, 1964
  18" $75.00 – 85.00
Big Jim Series, vinyl action figures, many boxed accessory sets available
Big Jim, black hair, muscular torso
  9½" $80.00 – 100.00
Big Josh, dark hair, beard
  9½" $25.00 – 35.00
Dr. Steele, bald head, silver tips on right hand
  9½" $40.00 – 50.00
Buffy and Mrs. Beasley, 1967 and 1974, characters from TV sitcom, *Family Affair*
Buffy, vinyl, rooted hair, painted features, holds small Mrs. Beasley, vinyl head, on cloth body
  6½" $175.00 – 200.00
Talking Buffy, vinyl, 1969 – 1971, holds tiny 6" rag Mrs. Beasley
  10¾" $340.00 – 360.00
Mrs. Beasley, 1965, vinyl head, cloth body
  16" $275.00 – 325.00
Mrs. Beasley, 1973, non-talker
  15½" $350.00 – 400.00
Captain Kangaroo, 1967, Sears only, talking character, host for TV kids program
  19" $40.00 – 50.00
Captain Laser, 1967, vinyl, painted features, blue uniform, silver accessories, batteries operate laser gun, light-up eyes
  12" $150.00 – 200.00
Casper, the Friendly Ghost, ca. 1964
  16" $80.00 – 100.00
1971
  5" $50.00 – 60.00
Chatty Cathy Series
Chatty Cathy, 1960 – 1963, vinyl head,

hard plastic body, pull string activates voice, dressed in pink and white checked or blue party dresses, 1963 – 1965, says 18 new phrases, red velvet and white lace dress, extra outfits available
Blond
  20" $250.00 – 300.00
Blond pigtail, boxed
  20" $610.00*
Black
  20" $1,000.00 – 1,400.00*
Charmin' Chatty, 1963 – 1964, talking doll, soft vinyl head, closed smiling mouth, hard vinyl body, long rooted hair, long legs, five records placed in left side slot, one-piece navy skirt, white middy blouse, with red sailor collar, red socks and saddle shoes, glasses, five disks, extra outfits and 14 more disks   available
  24" $150.00 – 200.00
Chatty Baby, 1962 – 1964, red pinafore over romper
  18" $80.00 – 110.00
Tiny Chatty Baby, 1963 – 1964, smaller version of Chatty Baby, blue romper, blue and white striped panties, bib with name, talks, other outfits available
  15½" $85.00 – 100.00
Black
  15½" $100.00 – 125.00
Tiny Chatty Brother, 1963 – 1964, boy version of Tiny Chatty Baby, blue and white suit and cap, hair parted on side
  15½" $85.00 – 95.00
Cheerful Tearful, 1966 – 1967, vinyl, blond hair, face changes from smile to pout as arm is lowered, feed her bottle, wets and cries real tears
  7" $65.00 – 75.00
  13" $40.00 – 50.00
Dancerina, 1969 – 1971, battery operated, posable arms, legs, turns, dances with

control knob on head, pink ballet outfit

24"	$145.00 – 165.00

Baby Dancerina, 1970, smaller version, no batteries, turn-knob on head, white ballet outfit

16"	$75.00 – 85.00

Black

16"	$125.00 – 150.00

Teeny Dancerina

12"	$25.00 – 35.00

Debbie Boone, 1978

11½"	$45.00 – 55.00

Dick Van Dyke, 1969, as Mr. Potts in movie, *Chitty Chitty Bang Bang,* all-cloth, flat features, talks in actor's voice, mark: "© Mattel 1969" on cloth tag

24"	$100.00 – 120.00

Drowsy, 1965 – 1974, vinyl head, stuffed body, sleepers, pull-string talker

15½"	$90.00 – 110.00
15½"	$200.00 MIB

Dr. Dolittle, 1968, character patterned after Rex Harrison in movie version, talker, vinyl with cloth body

24"	$40.00 – 50.00

All vinyl

6"	$15.00 – 20.00

Gramma Doll, 1970 – 1973, Sears only, cloth, painted face, gray yarn hair, says ten phrases, talker, foam-filled cotton

11"	$15.00 – 20.00

Grizzly Adams, 1971

10"	$40.00 – 50.00

Guardian Goddesses, 1979

11½"	$40.00 – 50.00

Herman Munster, 1965, cloth doll, talking TV character from *The Munsters*

21"	$150.00 – 175.00

Liddle Kiddles, 1966 on, small dolls of vinyl over wire frame, posable, painted features, rooted hair and came with bright costumes and accessories, packaged on

Liddle Kiddle, Goodnight Kiddle. $50.00.
Photo courtesy of The Museum Doll Shop.

8½" x 9½" cards, mark: "1965// Mattel Inc.// Japan" on back

Dolls listed are in excellent condition with all accessories. Add more for mint in package (or card) and never removed from package. Less for worn dolls with missing accessories.

1966, First Series

3501 Bunson Bernie

3"	$60.00 – 75.00

3502 Howard "Biff" Boodle

3½"	$85.00 – 115.00

3503 Liddle Diddle

2¾"	$125.00 – 150.00

3504 Lola Liddle

3½"	$90.00 – 115.00

3505 Babe Biddle

3½"	$200.00 – 225.00

3506 Calamity Jiddle

3"	$140.00 – 160.00

3507 Florence Niddle

2¾"	$85.00 – 100.00

3508 Greta Griddle

3"	$80.00 – 90.00

3509 Millie Middle
2¾" $45.00 – 55.00
3510 Beat A Diddle
3½" $155.00 – 180.00
1967, Second Series
3513 Sizzly Friddle
3" $100.00 – 120.00
3514 Windy Fiddle
2½" $200.00 – 225.00
3515 Trikey Triddle
2¾" $140.00 – 160.00
3516 Freezy Sliddle
3½" $120.00 – 130.00
3517 Surfy Skiddle
3" $60.00 – 70.00
3518 Soapy Siddle
3½" $55.00 – 75.00
3519 Rolly Twiddle
3½" $180.00 – 200.00
3548 Beddy Bye Biddle (with robe)
                             $60.00 – 70.00
3549 Pretty Priddle
3½" $50.00 – 65.00
1968, Third Series
3587 Baby Liddle
2¾" $175.00 – 200.00
3551 Telly Viddle
3½" $115.00 – 125.00
3552 Lemons Stiddle
3½" $60.00 – 75.00
3553 Kampy Kiddle
3½" $140.00 – 165.00
    Mint-in-Package $495.00
3554 Slipsy Sliddle
3½" $150.00 – 175.00
Storybook Kiddles, 1967 – 1968
                             $100.00 – 150.00
Skediddle Kiddles, 1968 – 1970
4" $90.00 – 150.00
Kiddles 'N Kars, 1969 – 1970
2¾" $177.50*

13" My Child doll, fabric over vinyl head.
$75.00. *Photo courtesy of The Museum Doll Shop.*

Tea Party Kiddles, 1970 – 1971
3½" $125.00 – 135.00
Lucky Locket Kiddles, 1967 – 1970
2" $45.00 – 55.00
Kiddle Kolognes, 1968 – 1970
2" $55.00 – 65.00
Kiddle Kones, 1968 – 1969
2" $65.00 – 85.00
Kola Kiddles, 1968 – 1969
2" $60.00 – 75.00
Kosmic Kiddle, 1968 – 1969
2½" $85.00 – 100.00

Mork and Mindy. $70.00 pair. *Photo courtesy of The Museum Doll Shop.*

Sweet Treat Kiddles, 1969 – 1970
    2" $80.00 – 100.00
Liddle Kiddle Playhouses, 1966 – 1968
                        $65.00 – 75.00
My Child, 1986, cloth over vinyl head, cloth body, synthetic wig
    13" $60.00 – 90.00
 Mork & Mindy, 1979
    9" $25.00 – 35.00
Osmond Family
Donny or Marie Osmond, 1978
    12" $25.00 – 35.00
Jimmy Osmond, 1979
    10" $40.00 – 50.00
Rock Flowers, 1970, vinyl mod dolls
    6" $30.00 – 35.00
Scooba Doo, 1964, vinyl head, rooted hair, cloth body, talks in Beatnik phrases, blond or black hair, striped dress
    23" $100.00 – 125.00
Shogun Warrior, all-plastic, battery operated
    23½" $100.00 – 225.00

6" Rock Flower doll, c. 1970. $35.00. *Photo courtesy of The Museum Doll Shop.*

Sunshine Family Dad. $35.00. *Photo courtesy of The Museum Doll Shop.*

Shrinkin' Violette, 1964 – 1965, cloth, yarn hair, pull-string talker, eyes close, mouth moves
    16" $175.00 – 200.00
Sister Belle, 1961 – 1963, vinyl, pull string talker, cloth body
    16" $65.00 – 75.00
Matty Mattel
    16" $65.00 – 75.00
Star Spangled dolls, uses Sunshine Family adults, marked "1973"
Pioneer Daughter $30.00 – 40.00
Sunshine Family, vinyl, posable, came with Idea Book, Father, Mother, Baby
Steve
    9" $30.00 – 40.00
Stephie
    7½" $30.00 – 40.00
Sweets
    3½" $30.00 – 40.00
Tatters, 1965 – 1967, talking cloth doll, wears rag clothes
    19" $95.00 – 110.00
Teachy Keen, 1966 – 1970, Sears only, vinyl head, cloth body, ponytail, talker, tells child to use accessories included, buttons, zippers, comb
    16" $20.00 – 30.00

Tippee Toes, c. 1968, battery drive riding/walking doll. $70.00. *Photo courtesy of The Museum Doll Shop.*

Tinkerbelle, 1969, talking, patter pillows
18" $18.00 – 22.00
Tippee Toes, 1968 – 1970, battery operated, legs move, rides accessory horse, tricycle, knit sweater, pants
17" $65.00 – 75.00
Tricycle/horse $10.00 – 40.00
Welcome Back Kotter, 1973, characters from TV sitcom
Freddie "Boom Boom" Washington, Arnold Horshack
9" $30.00 – 40.00
Vinnie Barbarino (John Travolta)
9" $70.00 – 80.00
Gabe Kotter
9" $15.00 – 25.00
Zython, 1977, has glow-in-the-dark head, enemy in Space 1999 series
                $80.00 – 90.00

MAWAPHIL

1920 – 1942, Atlanta Georgia. Dolls designed by Mary Waterman Philips, manufactured by the Rushton Co. Stockinette crib dolls and cloth mask face dolls.
Crib doll, all-cloth, stockinette or velveteen
8" – 12" $60.00 – 90.00
Cloth mask face doll, cloth body, appropriately dressed
15" $200.00 – 250.00

15" Little Miss Muffet cloth mask face doll for Mawaphil. $250.00. *Photo courtesy of The Museum Doll Shop.*

MEGO CORPORATION

1954 to 1982. Made many vinyl "action figure" dolls during the 1970s. Prices shown are for excellent

8" crib doll made for Mawaphil. $75.00.
Photo courtesy of The Museum Doll Shop.

condition dolls in original boxes, with all appropriate clothes and accessories

Action Jackson, 1971 – 1972, vinyl head, plastic body, molded hair, painted black eyes, action figure, many accessory outfits, mark: "©Mego Corp//Reg. U.S. Pat. Off.// Pat. Pend.//Hong Kong//MCMLXXI"

8"	$20.00 – 30.00

Black

8"	$45.00 – 55.00

Dinah-mite, Black

	$30.00 – 40.00

Batman, 1979

8"	$125.00 – 175.00

Arch enemies

8"	$65.00 – 75.00

Mobile Bat Lab, 1975

	$350.00 original box

Captain and Tennille, Daryl Dragon and Toni Tennille, 1977, recording and TV personalities, Toni Tennille doll has no molded ears

12½"	$40.00 – 55.00

Cher, 1976, TV and recording personality, husband Sonny Bono, all-vinyl, fully jointed, rooted long black hair, also as grow-hair doll

Cher

12"	$80.00 – 90.00

Growing Hair Cher, 1976

12"	$175.00 – 200.00

Sonny/Cher Theatre in the Round

	$225.00*

Star Brite costume $130.00*

Sonny Bono

12"	$35.00 – 45.00

CHiPs, 1977, California Highway Patrol TV show, Jon Baker (Larry Wilcox), Frank "Ponch" Poncherello (Erik Estrada)

8"	$30.00 – 40.00

Diana Ross, 1977, recording and movie personality, all-vinyl, fully jointed, rooted black hair, long lashes

12½"	$75.00 – 100.00

Farrah Fawcett, 1977, model, movie and television personality, starred as Jill in Charlie's Angels, vinyl head, rooted blond

Cher. $90.00. *Photo courtesy of The Museum Doll Shop.*

hair, painted green eyes
    12½" $40.00 – 50.00

Flash Gordon Series, ca. 1976, vinyl head, hard plastic articulated body

Dale Arden
    9" $100.00 – 125.00

Dr. Zarkov
    9½" $75.00 – 100.00

Flash Gordon
    9½" $75.00 – 100.00

Ming, the Merciless
    9½" $55.00 – 65.00

Happy Days Series, 1976, characters from *Happy Days* TV sitcom, Henry Winkler starred as Fonzie, Ron Howard as Richie, Anson Williams as Potsie, and Donny Most as Ralph Malph

Fonzie
    8" $65.00 – 75.00

Fonzie with motorcycle $125.00*

Richie, Potsie, Ralph, each
    8" $50.00 – 60.00

Jaclyn Smith, 1977, vinyl
    12½" $90.00 – 110.00

Joe Namath, 1970, football player, actor, soft vinyl head, rigid vinyl body, painted hair and features
    12" $75.00 – 100.00

Outfit, MIP $32.50

KISS, 1978, rock group, with Gene Simmons, Ace Frehley, Peter Cris, and Paul Stanley, all-vinyl, fully jointed, rooted hair, painted features and makeup
    12½" $110.00 – 130.00 each
                 $660.00 set of four

Kristy McNichol, 1978, actress, starred in TV show, *Family*, all-vinyl, rooted brown hair, painted eyes, marked on head: "©MEGO CORP.//MADE IN HONG KONG," marked on back: "©1977 MEGO CORP.// MADE IN HONG KONG"
    9" $25.00 – 35.00

Laverne and Shirley, 1977, TV sitcom, Penny Marshall played Laverne, Cindy Williams played Shirley, also, from the same show, David Lander as Squiggy, and Michael McKean as Lenny, all-vinyl, rooted hair, painted eyes
    11½" $50.00 – 60.00

Our Gang, 1975, from Our Gang movie shorts, that replayed on TV, included characters Alfalpha, Buckwheat, Darla, Mickey, Porky, and Spanky
    6" $15.00 – 25.00

Planet of the Apes

Planet of the Apes Movie Series, ca. 1970s

Astronaut
    8" $95.00 – 120.00

Ape Soldier
    8", Palitoy, MOC $800.00

Cornelius
    8" $80.00 – 100.00

Dr. Zaius
    8" $80.00 – 100.00

Zira
    8" $80.00 – 100.00

Star Trek figures, Lt. Uhura and Mr. Spock. $55.00 and $40.00 *Photo courtesy of The Museum Doll Shop.*

Planet of the Apes TV Series, ca. 1974

Alan Verdon

  8" $65.00 – 75.00

Galen

  8", Palitoy $140.00

General Urko

  8" $125.00 – 150.00

General Urko

  8", MOC $950.00

General Ursus

  8" $400.00 – 450.00

Peter Burke

  8" $125.00 – 150.00

Star Trek

Star Trek TV Series, ca. 1973 – 1975

Captain Kirk

  8" $55.00 – 65.00

Dr. McCoy

  8" $120.00 – 130.00

Klingon

  8" $35.00 – 45.00

Lt. Uhura

  8" $50.00 – 60.00

Mr. Scott

  8" $120.00 – 130.00

Mr. Spock

  8" $35.00 – 45.00

Star Trek Aliens, ca. 1975 – 1976

Andorian

  8" $275.00 – 325.00

Cheron

  8" $100.00 – 130.00

Mugato

  8" $250.00 – 300.00

Talos

  8" $200.00 – 250.00

The Gorn

  8" $100.00 – 125.00

The Romulan

  8" $500.00 – 600.00

Star Trek Movie Series, ca. 1979, 12½" dolls

Acturian $80.00 – 100.00

Captain Kirk $45.00 – 60.00

Commander Decker $45.00 – 60.00

Ilia $50.00 – 60.00

Klingon $75.00 – 85.00

Mr. Spock $80.00 – 100.00

Starsky and Hutch, 1976, police TV series, Paul Michael Glaser as Starsky, David Soul as Hutch, Bernie Hamilton as Captain Dobey, Antonio Fargas as Huggy Bear, also included a villain, Chopper, all-vinyl, jointed waists

  7½" $40.00 – 50.00

Suzanne Somers, 1978, actress, TV personality, starred as Chrissy in *Three's Company*, all-vinyl, fully jointed, rooted blond hair, painted blue eyes, long lashes

  12½" $45.00 – 55.00

Waltons, The, 1975, from TV drama series, set of two 8" dolls per package, all-vinyl

John Boy and Mary Ellen $25.00 – 35.00

Mom and Pop $25.00 – 35.00

Grandma and Grandpa $30.00 – 40.00

Wonder Woman Series, ca. 1976 – 1977, vinyl head, rooted black hair, painted eyes, plastic body

Lt. Diana Prince

  12½" $125.00 – 150.00

Nubia

  12½" $65.00 – 75.00

Nurse

  12½" $30.00 – 40.00

Queen Hippolyte

  12½" $75.00 – 100.00

Steve Trevor

  12½" $75.00 – 100.00

Wonder Woman

  12½" $125.00 – 150.00

Wizard of Oz, 1974
Dorothy, Glinda, Cowardly Lion,
Scarecrow, Tin Man $35.00 – 40.00
Munchkins $55.00 – 60.00

METAL HEADS

1850 – 1930 on. Made in Germany, Britain, and the United States, by various manufactures, including Buschow & Beck (Minerva), Alfred Heller (Diana), Karl Standfuss (Juno), and Art Metal Works. Various metals were used including aluminum, brass, and others, and they might be marked with just a size and country of origin or unmarked. Dolls listed are in good condition with original or appropriate dolls. Dolls with chipped paint will bring significantly less.

15" metal head doll with glass eyes and wig. $160.00. *Courtesy of The Museum Doll Shop.*

13" metal shoulder-head doll, painted features. $130.00. *Photo courtesy of The Museum Doll Shop.*

Metal shoulder head, cloth or kid body, molded and painted hair, glass eyes, more for wigged

12" – 14"	$150.00 – 175.00
16" – 18"	$200.00 – 250.00
20" – 22"	$250.00 – 275.00

Painted eyes

12" –14"	$125.00 – 150.00
20" – 22"	$200.00 – 225.00

All-metal or with composition body, metal limbs

Baby

11" – 15"	$100.00 – 150.00

Child

15"	$250.00 – 300.00
20"	$350.00 – 400.00

Mama doll, metal shoulder head, cloth body

18"	$200.00 – 250.00

Swiss: See Bucherer section.

15" metal socket-head child on composition body. $250.00. *Courtesy of The Museum Doll Shop.*

22" Beecher Missionary Ragbaby. $3,000.00. *Courtesy of The Museum Doll Shop.*

doll often erroneously referred to as "a black Beecher," which is quite different in construction from a true Black Beecher

21" – 23" $5,000.00 – 5,600.00

MISSIONARY RAGBABIES

1893 – 1910, Elmira, New York. Julia Jones Beecher, wife of Congregational Church pastor Thomas K. and sister-in-law of Harriet Beecher Stowe, made Missionary Ragbabies with the help of the sewing circle of her church. The dolls were made from old silk or cotton jersey underwear, with hand-painted and needle sculpted features. All proceeds were used for missionary work. Sizes 16" to 23" and larger.

Dolls listed are in good condition, appropriately dressed.

16" $2,500.00 – 2,800.00
21" – 23" $3,900.00 – 4,500.00

Black Beecher, same construction and appearance as the white babies but from brown fabric with black yarn hair. Please note, this is not the black stockinette

MOLLY-'ES

1920 to 1970s, Philadelphia, Pennsylvania. International Doll Co. was founded by Mollye Goldman.

Molly-'es made cloth mask faced dolls, doll clothing, briefly Raggedy Ann, as well as composition and vinyl dolls. Her mask faced dolls had yarn or mohair hair, painted features, sewn joints at the shoulders and hips.

Cloth, fine line painted lashes, pouty mouth

Child

15"	$110.00 – 135.00
18"	$140.00 – 150.00
24"	$175.00 – 200.00
29"	$250.00 – 300.00

Internationals

13"	$95.00 – 110.00
15"	$150.00 – 175.00
27"	$200.00 – 275.00

Lady

16"	$150.00 – 175.00
21"	$200.00 – 275.00

Princess, Thief of Baghdad

Prince, cloth

23"	$700.00 – 750.00

Princess

Composition 15"	$575.00 – 625.00
Cloth, 18"	$600.00 – 650.00

Sabu, composition

15"	$550.00 – 650.00

Sultan, cloth

19"	$650.00 – 750.00

Composition

Baby

15"	$150.00 – 200.00
21"	$225.00 – 275.00

Cloth body

18"	$100.00 – 125.00

Toddler

15"	$250.00 – 300.00
21"	$275.00 – 325.00

Child

15"	$175.00 – 200.00
18"	$225.00 – 275.00

Lady, add more for ball gown

16"	$275.00 – 325.00
21"	$400.00 – 500.00

Hard Plastic

Baby

14"	$65.00 – 85.00
20"	$100.00 – 135.00

Cloth body

17"	$55.00 – 75.00
25"	$100.00 – 125.00

Child

14"	$150.00 – 175.00
18"	$325.00 – 375.00
25"	$400.00 – 425.00

Lady

17"	$250.00 – 300.00
20"	$325.00 – 375.00
25"	$375.00 – 425.00

Vinyl

Baby

8½"	$12.00 – 20.00
12"	$18.00 – 25.00
15"	$28.00 – 40.00

Child

8"	$12.00 – 20.00
10"	$18.00 – 25.00
15"	$28.00 – 40.00

Little Women

9"	$45.00 – 55.00

15" Molly-'es International doll, cloth mask face. $125.00. *Courtesy of The Museum Doll Shop.*

MONICA DOLLS

1941 – 1951. Monica Dolls from Hollywood, designed by Hansi Share, made composition and later hard plastic dolls with long faces and painted or sleep eyes, and eye shadow. A unique feature of the dolls is very durable rooted human hair. Unmarked, but wore paper wrist tag reading "Monica Doll, Hollywood."

20" Monica Doll, composition with inset hair. $600.00. *Courtesy of The Museum Doll Shop.*

Composition dolls had pronounced widow's peak in center of forehead.

Composition, 1941 – 1949, painted eyes, Veronica, Jean, and Rosalind were names of 17" dolls produced in 1942.

15"	$350.00 – 450.00
17"	$500.00 - 600.00
20"	$600.00 – 700.00

Hard plastic, 1949 – 1951, sleep eyes, Elizabeth, Marion, or Linda

14"	$400.00 – 500.00
18"	$500.00 – 600.00

MORAVIAN

1872 – present, Bethlehem, Pennsylvania. Cloth dolls made by the Ladies Sewing Society of the Moravian Church Guild. Fund rasier to support church work. Flat faced rag doll with sewn joints at shoulders, elbows, hips, and knees, hand-painted faces,

dressed in pink or blue gingham with apron and double bonnet, 18".

19th – early 20th century
$2,500.00 – 3,800.00

1920s – 1940s
$1,500.00 – 2,000.00

1950s to present
$150.00 – 250.00

18" Moravian doll, c. 1990s. $250.00. *Courtesy of The Museum Doll Shop.*

MULTI-FACE, MULTI-HEAD DOLLS

1866 – 1930 on. Various firms made dolls with two or more faces, or more than one head.

Bisque

French

Bru, Surprise poupée, awake/asleep faces

12" $9,500.00

Too few in database for a reliable range.

Jumeau, crying, laughing faces, cap hides knob

18"	$15,950.00

Too few in database for a reliable range.

SFBJ, mold 200 character faces, laughing, crying

18"	$4,200.00*

German

Bergner, Carl, bisque socket head, two or three faces, sleeping, laughing, crying, molded tears, glass eyes, on composition jointed body may have molded bonnet or hood, marked "C.B." or "Designed by Carl Bergner"

12"	$1,600.00 – 1,800.00
15"	$1,900.00 – 2,100.00

Kammer and Reinhardt, set of four bisque character heads, composition body

12"	$13,000.00*

Kestner, J. D., ca. 1900+, Wunderkind, bisque doll with set of several different mold number heads that could be attached to body, set of one doll and body with additional three heads and wardrobe, with heads 174, 178, 184, and 185

11"	$9,000.00 – 9,500.00

15" double-face bisque headed doll. $2,000.00. *Courtesy Richard W. Withington, Inc., Nashua, New Hampshire.*

15" Trudy by Three In One Doll Corporation, composition head. $275.00. *Courtesy of The Museum Doll Shop.*

With heads, 171, 179, 182, and 183

14½"	$12,650.00

Too few in database for a reliable range.

Kley & Hahn, solid-dome bisque socket head, painted hair, smiling baby and frowning baby, closed mouth, tongue, glass eyes, baby body

13"	$1,500.00 – 1,700.00

Simon & Halbig, smiling, sleeping, crying, turn ring at top of head to change faces, glass/painted eyes, closed mouth

14½"	$3,000.00 – 3,200.00

Awake, asleep faces

11"	$3,000.00*

Hermann Steiner topsy turvy baby

8"	$500.00 – 600.00

Cloth

Topsy-Turvy, one black, one white head

Babyland

Painted face

13"	$800.00 – 900.00

Lithographed face

13"	$650.00 – 750.00

Bruckner

13"	$600.00 – 700.00

Composition

Berwick Doll Co., Famlee Dolls, 1926 on,

Famlee doll with inter-changeable composition heads, in original box. $750.00. *Courtesy of The Museum Doll Shop.*

composition head and limbs, cloth body with crier, neck with screw joint, allowing different heads to be screwed into the body, painted features, mohair wigs and/or molded and painted hair, came in sets of two to 12 heads, with different costumes for each head

Seven-head set including baby, girl in fancy dress, girl in sports dress, Indian, and clown

16" $900.00 – 1,100.00

Effanbee, Johnny Tu Face

16" $375.00 – 425.00

Too few in database for a reliable range.

Ideal, 1923, Soozie Smiles, composition, sleep or painted eyes on happy face, two faces, smiling, crying, cloth body, composition hands, cloth legs, original romper and hat

15½" $300.00 – 400.00

Three-in-One Doll Corp., 1946 on, Trudy, composition head with turning knob on top, cloth body and limbs, three faces, "Sleepy, Weepy, Smiley," dressed in felt or fleece snowsuit or sheer dresses, more for exceptional doll

15½" $250.00 – 300.00

Papier-mâché

Smiling/crying faces, glass eyes, cloth body, composition lower limbs

19" $650.00 – 700.00

Wax

Bartenstein, glass eyes, carton body, crier

Black face/white face

12" $1,100.00 – 1,200.00

Smiling/crying faces

15" $550.00 – 600.00

MUNICH ART DOLLS

1908 – 1920s. Marion Kaulitz hand painted heads designed by Marc-Schnur, Vogelsanger, and Wackerle, dressed in German or French regional costumes. Usually composition heads and bodies distributed by Cuno &

Otto Dressell and Arnoldt Doll Co.
Composition, painted features, wig, composition body, unmarked

17" – 18"	$8,000.00 – 10,000.00
19" girl	$24,000.00*

NANCY ANN STORYBOOK

1936 on, San Francisco, California. Started by Nancy Ann Abbott. Made small painted bisque and hard plastic dolls with elaborate costumes. Also made an 8" toddler doll to compete with Vogue's Ginny, 10" fashion dolls and larger size "style show" dolls.

Painted bisque, mohair wig, painted eyes, head molded to torso, jointed limbs, either sticker on outfit or hang tag, in box, later made in hard plastic.

Dolls listed are in good condition with original clothing and wrist tags. Allow more for mint-in-box, add

6" Pretty Maid, painted bisque, stiff legs. $225.00.
Courtesy of The Museum Doll Shop.

30 percent or more for black dolls. Selected auction prices reflect once-only extreme high prices and should be noted accordingly. Painted bisque baby prices vary with outfits.

Painted Bisque

1936 – 1937, pink/blue mottled or sunburst box with gold label, gold foil sticker on clothes "Nancy Ann Dressed Dolls," marked "87," "88," or "93," "Made in Japan," no brochure

Baby

3½" – 4½"	$375.00 – 475.00
With cradle	
3¾"	$1,525.00*

Child

5"	$1,300.00 – 1,400.00

1938, early, marked "America" (baby marked "87," "88," or "93" "Made in Japan"), colored box, sunburst pattern with gold label, gold foil sticker on clothes: "Judy Ann," no brochure

Baby

3½" – 4½"	$375.00 – 425.00

Child

5"	$550.00 – 600.00

1938, late

Marked "Judy Ann USA" and "Story Book USA" (baby marked "Made in USA" and "88," "89," and "93" "Made in Japan"), colored box, sunburst pattern with gold or silver label, gold foil sticker on clothes: "Storybook Dolls," no brochure

3½" – 4½"	$375.00 – 425.00
5"	$350.00 – 400.00

Complete with teddy bear, dress tagged "Judy Ann," blue box, silver dots, marked "Japan 1146"

5"	$650.00 – 750.00
Judy Ann mold	$400.00 – 500.00
Storybook mold	$275.00 – 350.00

Jointed Bisque

Pussy Cat, Pussy Cat, complete with pet

5"	$250.00 – 300.00

1939, child, Story Book Doll USA, molded socks and molded bangs, baby has star-shaped hands, colored box with small silver dots, silver label, gold foil sticker on clothes, "Storybook Dolls," no brochure

Baby

3½" – 4½"	$125.00 – 175.00

Child

5"	$200.00 – 250.00

Spring, molded sock, molded bang

5"	$2,645.00*

1940, child has molded socks only, baby has star-shaped bisque hands, colored box with white polka dots, silver label, gold foil sticker on clothes, "Storybook Dolls," has brochure

Baby

3½" – 4½"	$100.00 – 135.00

Child

5"	$175.00 – 225.00

1941 – 1942, child has pudgy tummy, or slim tummy; baby has star-shaped hands or fist, white box with colored polka dots,

Nancy Ann Storybook baby, hard plastic. $60.00. *Courtesy of The Museum Doll Shop.*

with silver label, gold foil bracelet with name of doll and brochure

Baby

3½" – 4½"	$100.00 – 125.00

Child

5"	$225.00 – 275.00

1943 – 1947, child has one-piece head, body, and legs, baby has fist hands, white box with colored polka dots, silver label, ribbon tie or pin fastener, gold foil bracelet with name of doll and brochure

Baby

3½" – 4½"	$100.00 – 125.00

Child

5"	$65.00 – 85.00

Hard Plastic

1947 – 1949, child has hard plastic body, painted eyes, baby has bisque body, plastic arms and legs, white box with colored polka dots with "Nancy Ann Storybook Dolls" between dots, silver label, brass snap, gold foil bracelet with name of doll and brochure, more for special outfit

Baby

3½" – 4½"	$75.00 – 90.00

Child

5½"	$55.00 – 75.00

1949 on, both have black sleep eyes, white box with colored polka dots and "Nancy Ann Storybook Dolls" between dots, silver label, brass or painted snaps, gold foil bracelet with name of doll and brochure

Baby

3½" – 4 ½"	$60.00 – 75.00

Child

5"	$40.00 – 50.00

Special Dolls

Mammy and Baby, marked "Japan 1146" or America mold

5"	$1,000.00 – 1,200.00

Storybook USA
5" $1400.00 – 500.00
Topsy, bisque black doll, jointed leg
All-bisque $450.00 – 500.00
Plastic arms $150.00 – 200.00
All-plastic, painted or sleep eye
$125.00 – 150.00
White boots, bisque jointed leg dolls
5" Add $50.00
Series Dolls, depending on mold mark
American Girl Series, all-bisque
Western Miss $850.00 – 900.00
Around the World Series, all-bisque
Chinese $1,000.00 – 1,200.00
English Flower Girl $350.00 – 400.00
Portuguese $425.00 – 475.00
Poland $375.00 – 450.00
Russia $1,100.00 – 1,200.00
Other Countries $300.00 – 400.00
Masquerade Series, all-bisque
Ballet Dancer, Cowboy, Pirate
$700.00 – 800.00
Sports Series, all-bisque
$1,200.00 – 1,500.00
Flower Series, bisque $300.00 – 400.00

Muffy, hard plastic. $200.00. *Courtesy of The Museum Doll Shop.*

Margie Ann Series, all-bisque
Margie Ann $125.00 – 175.00
  Other outfits $250.00 – 350.00
Powder & Crinoline Series
$125.00 – 175.00
Operetta or Hit Parade Series, bisque or plastic $140.00 – 175.00
Big and Little Sister Series, or Commencement Series (except baby), hard plastic $75.00 – 100.00
Bridal, Dolls of the Day, Dolls of the Month, Fairytale, Mother Goose, Nursery Rhyme, Religious, and Seasons Series, painted or sleep eye $60.00 – $75.00
Other Dolls
Audrey Ann, toddler, marked "Nancy Ann Storybook 12"
6" $900.00 – 975.00
Baby Sue Sue, 1960s, vinyl
Doll only $125.00 – 150.00
Outfit $50.00 – 65.00
Debbie, hard plastic in school dress, name on wrist tag/box
10" $200.00 – 250.00
Vinyl head, hard plastic body
10" $75.00 – 100.00
Hard plastic walker
10½" $125.00 – 150.00
Vinyl head, hard plastic walker
10½" $65.00 – 75.00
Lori Ann, vinyl
7½" $100.00 – 140.00
Little Miss Nancy Ann, 1959, high-heel fashion doll
8½" $125.00 – 175.00
Miss Nancy Ann, 1959, marked "Nancy Ann," vinyl head, rooted hair, rigid vinyl body, high-heeled feet, in undergarments or in day dress
10½" $100.00 – 150.00
Boxed outfit only $55.00 – 75.00

Muffie, 1953 – 1956

1953, hard plastic, wig, sleep eyes, strung straight leg, non-walker, painted lashes

8"	$300.00 – 350.00
8"	$870.00 MIB with extra outfit

1954, hard plastic walker, molded eyelashes, brows

In undies only

8"	$95.00 – 135.00

Dressed

8"	$175.00 – 225.00

1955 – 1956, vinyl head, molded or painted upper lashes, rooted saran wig, walker or bent-knee walker

8"	$150.00 – 175.00

1968+, reissued, hard plastic

8"	$90.00 – 105.00

Nancy Ann Style Show, ca. 1954, hard plastic, sleep eyes, long dress, unmarked

18"	$700.00 – 900.00

Long pink floral organdy costume

18"	$1,100.00*

Vinyl head, plastic body, all original, complete

18"	$400.00 – 500.00

NELKE

1917 to 1930, Philadelphia, Pennsylvania. Harry Nelke founded the Elke Knitting Mills Co. in 1901 and began making stockinette crib dolls in 1917. The dolls were made of a silky stockinette fabric with painted features. Clothing integral to body, added band of stockinette around neck, and/or added collars, hats, etc. Dolls listed are in clean, un-faded condition.

8" – 10"	$75.00 – 95.00
13" – 15"	$125.00 – 150.00

Nelke stockinette crib dolls. $75.00 – $100.00. *Courtesy of The Museum Doll Shop.*

GEBRUDER OHLHAVER

1913 – 1930, Sonneberg, Germany. Had Revalo (Ohlhaver spelled backwards omitting the two H's) line; made bisque socket and shoulder head and composition dolls. Bought heads from Ernst Heubach, Gebrüder Heubach and others. Dolls listed are in good condition with original or appropriate clothing.

Baby or Toddler, character face, bisque socket head, glass eyes, open mouth, teeth, wig, composition and wood ball-jointed body, bent-leg for baby

Baby

15" – 17"	$375.00 – 425.00
21"	$600.00 – 650.00

Toddler

14"	$650.00 – 750.00
22"	$850.00 – 950.00

Child, Mold 150, or no mold number, bisque socket head, open mouth, sleep

eyes, composition body

14" – 16"	$375.00 – 475.00
18" – 20"	$675.00 – 725.00
24" – 28"	$750.00 – 850.00

Character, bisque solid dome with molded and painted hair, intaglio eyes, composition body

Molded curl with bow, on five-piece body

9"	$300.00 – 350.00

Coquette-type, molded hair ribbon with bows

High quality bisque

11" – 12"	$650.00 – 750.00

Low quality bisque

11" – 12"	$375.00 – 450.00

18" baby for Gebrüder Ohlhaver, marked Revalo. $500.00. *Courtesy of The Museum Doll Shop.*

OLD COTTAGE DOLLS

Late 1948 on, England. Dolls were designed by Greta and Susi Fleischmann. Made with hard rubber or plastic heads, felt body, some with wire armature, oval hang tag has trademark "Old Cottage Dolls," special characters may be more.

8" – 9"	$145.00 – 160.00
12" – 13"	$275.00 – 325.00

Tweedle Dee or Tweedle Dum, circa 1968

10"	$400.00 – 425.00
	pair $1,000.00*

ORIENTAL DOLLS

1850 to present. Dolls depicting Asian peoples. Made by companies in Germany, America, Japan, and others.

All-Bisque

Heubach, Gebrüder, Chin-Chin

4"	$300.00 – 350.00

Kestner

6"	$1,400.00 – 1,700.00
8"	$1,600.00 – 1,900.00

Simon & Halbig, mold 852, ca. 1880, all-bisque, Oriental, swivel head, yellow tint bisque, glass eyes, closed mouth, wig, painted socks and curled pointed toe shoes

4½"	$650.00 – 700.00
5½"	$875.00 – 950.00
7"	$975.00 – 1,025.00

5" German all-bisque Oriental baby, glass eyes. $500.00. *Courtesy of The Museum Doll Shop.*

Unmarked or unknown maker, presumed German or French

6"	$450.00 – 550.00

European Bisque

Bisque head, jointed body

Barrois Poupee, swivel neck, glass eyes, kid body

15"	$10,000.00

Too few in database for reliable range.

Belton-type, mold 193, 206

10"	$1,900.00 – 2,075.00
14"	$2,500.00 – 2,700.00

Bru, pressed bisque swivel head, glass eyes, closed mouth

17"	$20,000.00
20"	$26,000,00

Kestner, J. D., 1899 – 1930+, mold 243, bisque socket head, open mouth, wig, bent-leg baby body, add more for original clothing

13" – 14"	$4,500.00 – 5,000.00
16" – 18"	$5,800.00 – 6,300.00

Solid dome, painted hair

15"	$4,500.00 – 5,000.00

Armand Marseille, 1925, mold 353, solid-dome bisque socket head, glass eyes, closed mouth

Baby body

7½"	$1,000.00 – 1,200.00
9" – 12"	$850.00 – 950.00
14" – 16"	$1,200.00 – 1,500.00

Toddler

16"	$1,200.00 – 1,500.00

Painted bisque

7"	$350.00

Too few in database for a reliable range.

Schmidt, Bruno, marked "BSW," mold 500, ca. 1905, glass eyes, open mouth

14"	$1,900.00 – 2,100.00

Too few in database for a reliable range.

18"	$2,200.00

Too few in database for a reliable range.

18" Kestner 243 Oriental baby. $6,300.00. *Courtesy of Skinner Inc., Boston and Bolton, Massachusetts.*

Schoenau & Hoffmeister, mold 4900, bisque socket head, glass eyes, open mouth, tinted composition wood jointed body

10"	$500.00 – 600.00

Simon & Halbig, mold 1079, 1129, 1159, 1199,1329, bisque socket head, glass eyes, open mouth, pierced ears, composition wood jointed body

10"	$1,300.00 – 1,400.00
12" – 13"	$1,500.00 – 2,000.00
16" – 18"	$2,100.00 – 2,600.00
20" – 24"	$2,900.00 – 3,900.00

Unknown maker, socket head, jointed body, closed mouth, glass eyes

4½"	$400.00 – 500.00
8" – 10"	$450.00 – 550.00
12" – 14"	$900.00 – 1,100.00
20"	$2,600.00 – 2,800.00

Composition

Amusco, 1925

17"	$1,000.00 – 1,200.00

Effanbee

Butin-nose, in basket with wardrobe, painted Oriental features including black bobbed hair, bangs, side-glancing eyes, excellent color and condition

8" $400.00 – 500.00

Patsy, painted Oriental features, including black bangs, straight across the forehead, brown side-glancing eyes, dressed in silk Chinese pajamas and matching shoes, excellent condition

14" $700.00 – 800.00

Horsman

Molded turban head child, 1910 on, composition head and lower arms, cloth body, molded turban on head, painted eyes

11" $375.00 – 425.00

Jap Rose Kids, 1911 on, composition head, arms, cloth body, molded painted hair, painted eyes, made as an advertising tie-in to Jap Rose soap

13" boy or 14" girl $350.00 – 375.00

Baby Butterfly, 1914+, composition head, hands, cloth body, painted hair, features

13" $250.00 – 300.00

15" $350.00 – 400.00

Quan-Quan Co., California, Ming Ming Baby, all-composition jointed baby, painted features, original costume, yarn queue, painted shoes

9" $125.00 – 150.00

11" $175.00 – 200.00

Traditional Chinese

Man or woman, composition type head, cloth-wound bodies, may have carved arms and feet, in traditional costume

11" $200.00 – 275.00

14" $400.00 – 475.00

Traditional Japanese

Ichimatsu, 1870s on, a play doll made of papier-mâché-type material with gofun finish of crushed oyster shells, swivel head, shoulder plate, cloth midsection, upper arms, and legs, limbs and torso are

11" composition Ming Ming baby made by Quan-Quan Co. of California. $200.00.
Courtesy of The Museum Doll Shop.

papier-mâché, glass eyes, pierced nostrils. Early dolls may have jointed wrists and ankles, in original dress, later 1950s+ dolls imported by Kimport.

Meiji era, ca. 1870s – 1912

10" – 12"	$450.00 – 600.00
16" – 18"	$750.00 – 900.00
22" – 24"	$1,500.00 – 1,800.00

Child

Painted hair

1920s

12" – 15"	$375.00 – 450.00
17" – 18"	$575.00 – 625.00
24"	$825.00 – 875.00

1930s

12" – 15"	$350.00 – 425.00
17" – 18"	$550.00 – 600.00

1940s on

10" – 12"	$90.00 – 100.00
14" – 16"	$125.00 – 150.00

Lady

1920s – 1930s

12" – 14"	$200.00 – 250.00
16"	$250.00 – 275.00

1940s – 1950s

12" – 14"	$70.00 – 95.00
16"	$100.00 – 135.00

Hina Matsuri, Emperor or Empress, seated

Ca. 1890s

8"	$500.00 – 575.00

Ca. 1920s

4" – 6"	$150.00 – 175.00
10" – 12"	$250.00 – 300.00

Warrior

1880 – 1890s

16"	$750.00 – 850.00

Too few in database for a reliable range.

On horse

15"	$1,000.00 – 1,100.00

Too few in database for a reliable range.

1920s

15"	$350.00 – 400.00

Too few in database for a reliable range.

On horse

13"	$800.00 – 850.00

Japanese baby, ca. 1920s, bisque head, sleep eyes, closed mouth, papier-mâché body

8"	$50.00 – 70.00
14"	$65.00 – 90.00

14" traditional Japanese doll. $400.00.
Courtesy of The Museum Doll Shop.

Glass eyes

8"	$95.00 – 125.00
14"	$200.00 – 265.00

Gofun finish of crushed oyster-shell head, painted flesh color, papier-mâché body, glass eyes, and original clothes

8" – 10"	$55.00 – 75.00
14" –18"	$95.00 – 185.00

Wooden dolls

Door of Hope: See Door of Hope section.

PAPIER-MÂCHÉ

Pre-1600 on. Papier-mâché is an elastic substance made of paper pulp and a variety of additives. Dolls of papier-mâché were being made in France as early as the sixteenth century. In Germany and France papier-mâché dolls were being mass produced in molds for heads after 1810. It reached heights of popularity by mid-1850s and was also used for bodies. Papier-mâché shoulder head, glass or painted eyes, molded and painted hair, sometimes in fancy hairdos. Usually no marks.

Dolls listed are in good condition, nicely dressed. More for exceptional examples, considerably less for dolls which have been repainted.

Molded Hair Papier-mâché, so-called Milliner's Models, 1820 – 1860s, molded hair, a shapely waist, kid body, and wooden limbs

Apollo top knot (beehive), side curls

10" – 12"	$950.00 – 1,300.00
16" – 18"	$1,900.00 – 2,125.00

Braided bun, side curls

9" – 11"	$950.00 – 1,100.00
15"	$1,400.00 – 1,600.00

Center part, molded bun

9" – 10"	$750.00 – 950.00
13"	$1,100.00 – 1,200.00

Center part, sausage curls

14"	$575.00 – 675.00
21"	$950.00 – 1,050.00

Coiled braids over ears, braided bun

9" – 11"	$1,000.00 – 1,100.00
20" – 21"	$2,100.00 – 2,300.00

Covered Wagon or Flat Top hair style

8" – 10"	$350.00 – 450.00
14" – 16"	$650.00 – 750.00

Molded bonnet, kid body, wood limbs, bonnet painted to tie under chin, very rare

15"	$1,700.00

Too few in database for a reliable range.

Molded comb, side curls, braided coronet

16"	$3,000.00 – 3,300.00

Too few in database for a reliable range.

9" papier-mâché with Apollo's Knot hairstyle. $900.00. *Courtesy of The Museum Doll Shop.*

Early Type Shoulder Head, 1840s – 1860s cloth body, wooden limbs, with topknots, buns, puff curls, or braids, dressed in original clothing or excellent copy, may have some wear, more for painted pate

Painted eyes

9" – 12"	$350.00 – 675.00
16" – 18"	$950.00 – 1,050.00
21" – 24"	$1,000.00 – 1,300.00
26" – 30"	$1,600.00 – 1,950.00

German papier-mâché (so-called Milliner's Models), 10" with side curls and beehive hairstyle, 9" with long curls. $950.00 and 750.00 each. *Courtesy of Alderfer Auction Co.*

Glass eyes

18" – 20"	$1,700.00 – 1,900.00
24"	$2,200.00 – 2,400.00

Long curls

14"	$850.00 – 950.00
16"	$1,350.00 – 1,550.00

Pre-Greiner-Type, 1850s, German or American made shoulder-head, molded painted black hair, black glass eyes, cloth body

18" – 22"	$1,600.00 – 1,900.00
28" – 32"	$2,300.00 – 2,800.00

French Type, 1835 – 1850, made by German companies for the French trade, painted black hair, brush marks, solid dome, shoulder head, some have nailed on wigs, open mouth, bamboo teeth, kid or leather body, appropriately dressed

Glass eyes

13" – 14"	$1,200.00 – 1,700.00
18" – 20"	$2,000.00 – 2,550.00
28"	$4,200.00*

Painted eyes

8" – 12"	$600.00 – 800.00
14" – 16"	$1,100.00 – 1,500.00

Wooden jointed body

6" – 8"	$700.00 – 775.00

Papier-mâché, American, Greiner, 1858 – 1883: See Greiner section.

Sonneberg Taufling: See Sonneberg Taufling section.

Patent Washable, 1879 – 1910s, shoulder head with mohair wig, open or closed mouth, glass eyes, cloth body, composition limbs, made by companies such as F. M. Schilling and others

Better quality

12" – 15"	$575.00 – 650.00
18"	$675.00 – 700.00
22" – 24"	$825.00 – 925.00

10¼" papier-mâché (so-called Milliner's Model), c.1850s. $475.00.
Courtesy of Skinner Inc., Boston and Bolton, Massachusetts.

13" French style papier-mâché doll. $1,200.00.
Courtesy of The Museum Doll Shop.

Lesser quality

10" – 12"	$125.00 – 175.00
14" – 16"	$225.00 – 250.00

Sonneberg –Type, 1880 – 1910, "M & S Superior," Muller & Strasburger, Cunno & Otto Dressel and others, shoulder-head, with blond or molded hair, painted blue or brown eyes, cloth body, with kid or leather arms and boots

13" – 15"	$275.00 – 350.00
18" – 20"	$475.00 – 575.00

Glass eyes

12"	$400.00 – 500.00
16" – 18"	$550.00 – 650.00

Wigged

13"	$800.00 – 900.00

Papier-mâché Child, 1920 on, head has brighter coloring, wigged, child often in ethnic costume, stuffed cloth body and limbs, or papier-mâché arms

French

9" – 13"	$100.00 – 125.00
13" – 15"	$200.00 – 275.00

23" shoulder head marked "M & S Superior 2015." $625.00. *Courtesy Richard W. Withington, Inc., Nashua, New Hampshire.*

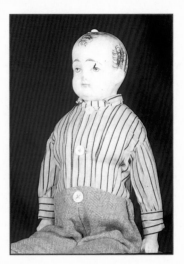

15" papier-mâché Sonneberg-type child. $400.00. *Courtesy of The Museum Doll Shop.*

German

10"	$70.00 – 80.00
15"	$150.00 – 165.00

Unknown maker

8"	$50.00 – 60.00
12"	$90.00 – 115.00
16"	$9150.00 – 175.00

Clowns, papier mâché head, with painted clown features, open or closed mouth, molded hair or wigged, cloth body, composition or papier-mâché arms, or five-piece jointed body

8"	$200.00 – 235.00
14"	$450.00 – 485.00
20"	$755.00 – 785.00
26"	$875.00 – 925.00

Eden Clown, socket head, open mouth, blue glass eyes, blond mohair wig, five-piece jointed body, all original with labeled box

16"	$4,000.00*

PARIAN-TYPE, UNTINTED BISQUE

1850 – 1900 on, Germany. The term "parian" as used in doll collecting refers to dolls of untinted bisque, in other words, the doll's skin tone is white rather than tinted. These dolls were at the height of their popularity from 1860 through the 1870s. They are often found with molded blond hair, some with fancy hair arrangements and ornaments or bonnets, can have glass or painted eyes, pierced ears, may have molded jewelry or clothing. Occasionally solid dome with wig. Cloth body, nicely dressed in good condition. Dolls listed are in good condition, appropriately dressed. Exceptional examples may be much higher.

13" parian-type bisque doll with glass eyes, original clothes. $1,200.00. *Courtesy of The Museum Doll Shop.*

Lady
Common hair style
Undecorated, simple molded hair

8" – 10"	$145.00 – 185.00
15"	$275.00 – 325.00
21" – 25"	$425.00 – 525.00

Molded bodice, fancy trim

17"	$600.00 – 800.00

Fancy hair style, with molded combs, ribbons, flowers, bands, or snoods, cloth body, untinted bisque limbs, more for very elaborate hairstyle

Painted eyes, pierced ears

14" – 16"	$675.00 – 900.00
18" – 22"	$900.00 – 1,400.00
24"	$1,500.00 – 1,600.00

Painted eyes, ears not pierced

13"	$625.00 – 700.00

Decorated shoulder plate

14" – 16"	$1,400.00 – 1,700.00
17" – 21"	$1,800.00 – 2,500.00

Glass eyes, pierced ears

15"	$1,400.00 – 1,600.00
20"	$2,500.00 – 2,700.00

Swivel neck, glass eyes

15"	$2,400.00 – 2,700.00

Alice in Wonderland, molded headband or comb

8" – 10"	$1,000.00 – 1,300.00
14" – 16"	$500.00 – 625.00
19" – 21"	$650.00 – 750.00

Countess Dagmar, no mark, head band, cluster curls on forehead

19" – 21"	$1,050.00 – 1,300.00

22" parian-type with swivel neck and glass eyes, c. 1860s. $3,200.00. *Courtesy of Skinner Inc., Boston and Bolton, Massachusetts.*

16" parian-type Empress Eugenie. $1,100.00. *Courtesy of Alderfer Auction Co.*

Dolly Madison

18" – 22"	$850.00 – 1,400.00

Empress Eugenie, headpiece snood

15"	$1,000.00 – 1,100.00
25"	$1,100.00 – 1,300.00

Irish Queen, Limbach, clover mark, #8552

14" – 16"	$575.00 – 700.00

Molded hat, blond or black painted hair

Painted eyes

16"	$2,000.00 – 2,300.00
19"	$2,500.00 – 2,900.00

Glass eyes

14"	$2,100.00 – 2,400.00
17"	$2,800.00 – 3,000.00

Necklace, jewels, or standing ruffles

17"	$9,700.00

Too few in database for a reliable range.

Princess Augusta Victoria, molded shoulder plate with cross necklace, glass eyes

13"	$2,200.00 – 2,500.00

Men or Boys, center or side-part hair style, cloth body, decorated shirt and tie

20" untinted bisque with a molded blouse. $1,000.00. *Courtesy Richard W. Withington Auction, Inc., Nashua, New Hampshire.*

Painted eyes

13"	$675.00 – 775.00
17"	$925.00 – 1,000.00

Glass eyes

16"	$2,400.00 – 2,825.00

RONNAUG PETTERSEN

1901 – 1980, Norway. Made cloth dolls, pressed felt head, usually painted side-glancing eyes, cloth bodies, intricate costumes, paper tags.

7" – 8"	$100.00 – 150.00
14½"	$400.00 – 500.00

7½" cloth dolls made by Ronnaug Pettersen of Norway. $100.00 each. *Courtesy of The Museum Doll Shop.*

DORA PETZOLD

Germany, 1919 – 1930+. Made and dressed dolls, molded composition head, painted features, wig, stockinette body, sawdust filled, short torso, free-formed thumbs, stitched fingers, shaped legs

18"	$950.00 – 1,100.00
20" – 22"	$1,200.00 – 1,500.00

PHILADELPHIA BABY (SHEPPARD BABY)

1900, Philadelphia, Pennsylvania. Rag baby sold by the J.B. Sheppard & Co. store. Molded stockinette, painted features, sewn joints at shoulders, hips, and knees.

Dolls listed are in good condition, appropriately dressed

18" – 22"	$4,100.00 – 4,500.00

Dolls listed are in somewhat worn condition

18" – 22"	$1,500.00 – 2,000.00

Good condition doll with music box in torso $4,500.00 – 5,000.00

21" Philadelphia baby, molded stockinette. $3,500.00. *Courtesy of The Museum Doll Shop.*

PLEASANT COMPANY

1985 – present. Middleton, Wisconsin, founded by Pleasant T. Rowland. In 1998 the company was purchased by Mattel, Inc.

American Girl®, vinyl doll with wig

18"	$87.00 – 110.00 retail
	$50.00 – 75.00 secondary market

18" Addy made by Pleasant Company. $65.00. *Courtesy of The Museum Doll Shop.*

POLISH RELIEF DOLLS

1914 on, Paris, France. Polish Relief dolls were created in the workshop of Madame Lazarski during and shortly after WWI. This project provided work for war refugees and the money raised from the sale of the dolls aided Polish widows and orphans. Cloth dolls with embroidered features and floss hair.

16 " child	$300.00 – 375.00

11" Polish Relief doll. $250.00. *Courtesy of The Museum Doll Shop.*

PRESBYTERIAN RAG DOLL

1885 on, Bucyrus, Ohio. The First Presbyterian Church made cloth dolls as a fund raiser. Cloth doll with "pie-shaped gussetted" piece across top of head, flat face, painted hair and features, mitten hands, 17".

1880s – 1930s	$2,500.00 – 3,800.00
1950s – 1980s	$250.00 – 350.00

17" Presbyterian rag doll, c. 1960s. $350.00 each. *Courtesy of The Museum Doll Shop.*

RABERY & DELPHIEU

1856 – 1930 and later, Paris. Became part of S.F.B.J. in 1899. Some heads pressed (pre-1890) and some poured, purchased some heads from Francois Gaultier.

Dolls listed are in good condition, appropriately dressed. Exceptional dolls may be more.

Child

Closed mouth, bisque socket head, paperweight eyes, pierced ears, mohair wig, cork pate, French composition and wood jointed body

13" – 15"	$4,000.00 – 5,600.00
22" – 24"	$4,000.00 – 4,600.00

Open mouth, row of upper teeth

18" – 21"	$1,400.00 – 1,600.00
24" – 26"	$1,650.00 – 2,100.00

14½" bébé by Rabery et Delphieu, closed mouth. $5,100.00. *Courtesy of The Museum Doll Shop.*

RAGGEDY ANN & ANDY

1915 to present. Rag doll designed by Johnny Gruelle in 1915, made by various companies. Ann wears dress with apron; Andy, shirt and pants with matching hat.

P.J. Volland, 1918 – 1934, early dolls marked "Patented Sept. 7, 1915," all-cloth, tin or wooden button eyes, painted features, some have sewn knee or arm joints, sparse brown or auburn yarn hair, oversize hands, feet turned outward, dolls listed are in clean un-faded condition, appropriately dressed

16" Volland Raggedy Ann. $2,300.00.
Courtesy of McMasters-Harris Auctions.

Raggedy Ann and Andy, 15" – 16"

Painted face	$2,200.00 – 2,300.00
Printed face	$1,300.00 – 1,500.00

Beloved Belindy, 1926 – 1930, painted face, 1931 – 1934, print face

15"	$3,000.00 – 3,500.00

Pirate Chieftain and other characters

18"	$2,200.00 – 2,400.00

Exposition, 1935

Raggedy Ann, no eyelashes, no eyebrows, outline nose, no heart, satin label on hem of dress

18"	$5,000.00 – 6,000.00

Too few in database for a reliable range.

Mollye Goldman, 1935 – 1937, marked on chest "Raggedy Ann and Andy Dolls Manufactured by Molly'es Doll Outfitters," nose outlined in black, red heart on chest, reddish-orange hair, multicolored legs, blue feet, some have oilcloth faces

15"	$850.00 – 900.00
17" – 21"	$1,000.00 – 1,350.00

Georgene Novelties, 1938 – 1962, Ann has orange hair and a top knot, six different mouth styles; early ones had tin eyes, later ones had plastic, six different noses, seams in middle of legs and arms to represent knees and elbows, feet turn forward, red and white striped legs, all have hearts that say "I love you" printed on chest, tag sewn to left side seam, several variations, all say "Georgene Novelties, Inc."

Raggedy Ann or Andy, 1930s – 1960s, nose outlined with black, 1938 – 1944

15" – 17"	$850.00 – 1,000.00
19" – 21"	$1,200.00 – 1,500.00

Awake/Asleep 1940s, nose outlined black, pair

14"	$1,400.00 – 1,800.00

Plain nose, pair

14"	$900.00 – 1,000.00

Long Nose face, 1944 – 1946

19"	$1,000.00 – 1,200.00

Curved nose edges, 1946 on

15"	$275.00 – 325.00
20" – 22"	$600.00 – 750.00

Beloved Belindy, 1940 – 1944

18"	$1,000.00 – 1,200.00

Knickerbocker, 1962 – 1982, printed features, hair color change from orange to red, there were five mouth and five

19" Georgene Raggedy Ann with outlined nose and 18" Beloved Belindy. $1,200.00 each. *Courtesy of The Museum Doll Shop.*

eyelash variations, tags were located on clothing back or pants seam

Raggedy Ann or Andy
1964, cloud box

15"	$300.00 – 350.00

Later examples

15"	$100.00 – 150.00
19"	$175.00 – 225.00
30" – 36"	$300.00 – 400.00

Musical Ann

15"	$100.00 – 150.00

Raggedy Ann Talking

19"	$125.00 – 200.00

18" Knickerbocker Raggedy Ann. $175.00. *Doll courtesy of Yakety Yak Dolls.*

Beloved Belindy, ca. 1965

15"	$900.00 – 1,000.00

Camel with Wrinkled Knees

15"	$275.00 – 350.00

Nasco/Bobbs-Merrill, 1972, cloth head, hard plastic doll body, printed features, apron marked "Raggedy Ann"

24"	$125.00 – 150.00

Bobbs-Merrill Co., 1974, ventriloquist dummy, hard plastic head, hands, foam body, printed face

30"	$125.00 – 175.00

Applause Toy Company, 1981 – present, owned by Hasbro which also markets Raggedy Ann through its Playskool line

8"	$10.00 – 15.00
17"	$40.00 – 50.00
48"	$125.00 – 175.00

Raggedy Anns and Andy, by Applause. $15.00 to $40.00. *Courtesy of The Museum Doll Shop.*

Limited Editions
75ᵗʰ anniversary Ann or Andy, 1992

19"	$75.00 – 85.00

Molly-E Baby Ann, 1993

13"	$80.00 – 90.00

Ann or Andy, 1994

13"	$80.00 – 90.00

US Patent Ann, 1995

17"	$100.00 – 125.00

Stamp Ann, 1997

17" $55.00 – 65.00

R. John Wright, present, molded felt doll

The Magical Hour Ann

9" $350.00 – 450.00

Ann or Andy

17" $600.00 – 900.00

JESSIE MCCUTCHEON RALEIGH

1916 – 1920, Chicago, Illinois. McCutcheon was a businesswoman who developed a line of dolls. These were distributed by Butler Brothers and perhaps others. She produced dolls of cloth and composition.

Shoebutton Sue, flat face, painted spit curls, mitten hands, sewn on red shoes, shown in 1921 Sears catalog

15" $1,900.00*

Baby, composition head on composition body

12" $300.00 – 400.00

18" $450.00 – 500.00

Child

Composition head on composition body

11" $400.00 – 475.00

13" $500.00 – 550.00

18" $750.00 – 950.00

Composition head on cloth body with composition lower arms and legs

22" – 24" $300.00 – 350.00

RAYNAL

1922 – 1930 on, Paris. Edouard Raynal made dolls of felt, cloth, or

16" Raynal baby, cloth head, celluloid hands. $500.00. *Courtesy Richard W. Withington, Inc., Nashua, New Hampshire.*

with celluloid heads with widely spaced eyebrows. Dressed, some resemble Lenci, except fingers were together or their hands were of celluloid, marked "Raynal" on soles of shoes and/or pendant.

Cloth, 1922, molded head, cloth body, sometimes celluloid hands

14" – 16" $800.00 – 900.00

17" – 18" $1,800.00 – 2,200.00+

Celluloid, 1936, then Rhodoid

Baby

18" – 24" $575.00 – 675.00

Vinyl, 1960s – 1970s

Margareth

14" $50.00 – 60.00

THEODOR RECKNAGEL

1886 – 1930, Alexandrienthal, Coburg, Germany. Made bisque and composition doll heads of varying quality, incised or raised mark, wigged or molded hair, glass or painted eyes, open or closed mouth, flange neck or socket head. Dolls listed are in good condition, appropriately dressed.

Baby

Mold 23, 121, 126, 1924, bent-limb baby body, painted or glass eyes

6" – 7"	$250.00 – 300.00
8" – 9"	$325.00 – 350.00

Bonnet head baby, painted eyes, open-closed mouth, teeth, mold 22, 28, 44, molded white boy's cap, bent-leg baby body

8" – 9"	$450.00 – 500.00
11" – 12"	$650.00 – 700.00

Oriental baby, solid-dome bisque socket head, sleep eyes, closed mouth five-piece yellow tinted body

11"	$2,300.00*

Mold 137, Newborn, ca. 1925, flange neck, sleep eyes, closed mouth, cloth body, boxed

13"	$545.00*

8½" Recknagel bonnet baby in original chemise stamped Baby Bunting. $475.00.
Courtesy of The Museum Doll Shop.

Child

Dolly face, 1890s – 1914

Mold 1907, 1909, 1914, open mouth, glass eyes

7" – 9"	$125.00 – 150.00
12"	$175.00 – 200.00
15" – 18"	$225.00 – 300.00
22" – 24"	$325.00 – 400.00
29", mold 1909	$650.00

Character face, ca. 1910+, may have crossed hammer mark

7" – 8"	$300.00 – 350.00
12" – 14"	$675.00 – 750.00

Mold 57, open/closed mouth with teeth, molded hair

9" – 10"	$500.00 – 575.00

Mold 31, 32, Max and Moritz

8"	$625.00 – 675.00 each

Googly: See googly section.

REGIONAL DRESS DOLLS

This category describes dolls costumed in regional dress to show different nationalities, facial characteristics, or cultural background. Examples are dolls in regional costumes that are commonly sold as souvenirs to tourists. These dolls became popular about 1875 and continue to be made today. A well-made beautiful doll with accessories or wardrobe may be more.

Bisque, German

10"	$175.00 – 225.00

Painted bisque

4"	$45.00 – 65.00
10"	$85.00 – 110.00

Celluloid

8"	$40.00 – 50.00
15"	$100.00 – 125.00

9" German bisque doll in Indian costume. $200.00. *Courtesy of The Museum Doll Shop.*

9" pair of Turkish cloth dolls. $200.00 pair. *Courtesy of The Museum Doll Shop.*

Cloth

8"	$100.00 – 155.00
13"	$125.00 – 175.00

Composition Child

8"	$150.00 – 185.00
13"	$200.00 – 250.00

Native American Indian, cloth, leather, natural fibers, etc.

8"	$175.00 – 225.00
13"	$225.00 – 300.00
23"	$300.00 – 350.00

Skookum, 1913 on, designed by Mary McAboy, painted features, with side-glancing eyes, mohair wigs, cloth figure wrapped in Indian blanket, with folds representing arms, wooden feet, later plastic, label on bottom of foot, box marked "Skookum Bully Good"

6"	$45.00 – 65.00
10" – 12"	$150.00 – 200.00
14" – 16"	$475.00 – 550.00
18" – 20"	$650.00 – 800.00
27" – 33"	$1,200.00 – 1,550.00

8" celluloid head, cloth body. $40.00. *Courtesy of The Museum Doll Shop.*

Hard Plastic, regional dress, unmarked or unknown maker

7"	$8.00 – 15.00
12"	$20.00 – 30.00

4" hard plastic in British costume. $8.00 each. *Courtesy of The Museum Doll Shop.*

A group of Skookum Indian dolls. $45.00 – 200.00. *Courtesy of The Museum Doll Shop.*

Baitz, Austria, 1970s, painted hard plastic, painted side-glancing eyes, open "o" mouth, excellent quality, tagged and dressed in regional dress

8"	$55.00 – 75.00

Vinyl

6"	$20.00 – 30.00
12"	$45.00 – 55.00

Russian, 1920 on, all-cloth, molded and painted stockinette head, hands, in regional costumes

7"	$55.00 – 70.00
15"	$125.00 – 150.00
18"	$160.00 – 180.00

RELIABLE TOY CO.

1920 on, Toronto, Canada. Made composition, hard plastic, and vinyl dolls.

Composition, all-composition, or composition shoulder head and arms on cloth body, some with composition legs. Dolls listed are in good condition, appropriately dressed.

Barbara Scott Ice Skating Doll

15"	$500.00 – 575.00

Her Highness

15"	$350.00 – 375.00

18" Native American doll, cloth and fur. $300.00. *Courtesy of The Museum Doll Shop.*

Hiawatha or Indian child

10½"	$40.00 – 50.00
13"	$85.00 – 110.00
16"	$145.00 – 175.00

Military Man

| 14" | $225.00 – 275.00 |

Mountie

| 17" | $300.00 – 350.00 |

Scottish Child

| 14" | $85.00 – 110.00 |
| 17" | $160.00 – 185.00 |

Shirley Temple

| 18" - 22" | $1,000.00 – 1,200.00 |

Toddler

| 13" | $150.00 – 200.00 |

Baby, 1930s

| 20" | $200.00 – 250.00 |

Hard Plastic

Baby, 1958, sleep eyes, open mouth

| 8" | $40.00 – 50.00 |

Indian child, all-hard plastic

| 8" | $20.00 – 30.00 |

Toni, P-90

| 14" | $300.00 – 350.00 |

Vinyl

Margaret, 1955, vinyl head, vinyl-flex body, rooted hair

| 19" | $30.00 – 40.00 |

Suzie, walker

| 9" | $15.00 – 20.00 |

REMCO INDUSTRIES

1959 – 1974, Harrison, New Jersey. One of the first companies to market with television ads.

Dolls listed are in good condition with original clothing and accessories, allow more for mint in box.

Addams Family, 1964

Lurch

| 5½" | $45.00 – 55.00 |

Morticia

| 4¾" | $100.00 – 128.00 |

Uncle Fester

| 4½" | $40.00 – 50.00 |

Baby Crawl-Along, 1967

| 20" | $15.00 – 20.00 |

Baby Glad 'N Sad, 1967, vinyl and hard plastic, rooted blond hair, painted blue eyes

| 14" | $10.00 – 15.00 |

Baby Grow a Tooth, 1968, vinyl and hard plastic, rooted hair, blue sleep eyes, open/closed mouth, one tooth, grows her own tooth, battery operated

| 15" | $15.00 – 20.00 |

Black

| 14" | $20.00 – 25.00 |

Baby Know It All, 1969

| 17" | $15.00 – 20.00 |

Baby Laugh A Lot, 1970, rooted long hair, painted eyes, open/closed mouth,

4½" Paul McCartney doll by Remco. $85.00.
Courtesy of The Museum Doll Shop.

teeth, vinyl head, hands, plush body, push button and she laughs, battery operated

16" $15.00 – 20.00

Baby Stroll A Long, 1966

15" $10.00 – 15.00

Beatles, 1964, vinyl and plastic, Paul McCartney, Ringo Starr, George Harrison, and John Lennon, Paul 4⅞", all others 4½" with guitars bearing their names

Set of 4 $750.00 – 900.00

Individual Beatles $75.00 – 95.00

Dave Clark Five, 1964, set of five musical group, vinyl heads, rigid plastic bodies

Set $60.00 – 65.00

Dave Clark

5" $10.00 – 15.00

Other band members have name attached to leg

3" $6.00 – 10.00

Heidi and friends, 1967, in plastic case, rooted hair, painted side-glancing eyes, open/closed mouth, all-vinyl, press button and dolls wave

Heidi

5½" $45.00 – 55.00

Herby

4½" $30.00 – 40.00

Jan, Oriental

5½" $40.00 – 50.00

Pip

5½" $40.00 – 50.00

Winking Heidi, 1968

5½" $25.00 – 35.00

Hildy

4½" $35.00 – 45.00

Jeannie, I Dream of

6" $45.00 – 55.00

Plastic Bottle Playset, 6" Jeannie doll and accessories $115.00 – 130.00

Jumpsy, 1970, vinyl and hard plastic, jumps rope, rooted blond hair, painted

Dr. John Littlechap. $70.00. *Courtesy of The Museum Doll Shop.*

blue eyes, closed mouth, molded-on shoes and socks

14" $15.00 – 20.00

Black

14" $20.00 – 25.00

Laurie Partridge, 1973

19" $95.00 – 125.00

L.B.J., 1964

5½" $20.00 – 25.00

Littlechap Family, 1963+, vinyl head, arms, jointed hips, shoulders, neck, black molded and painted hair, black eyes, box

Set of four boxed together

                        $400.00 – 480.00

Dr. John Littlechap

14½" $60.00 – 75.00

Judy Littlechap

12" $50.00 – 65.00

Libby Littlechap

10½" $60.00 – 70.00

Lisa Littlechap

13½" $40.00 – 50.00

Littlechap Accessories

Dr. John's Office $275.00 – 325.00

Bedroom $75.00 – 110.00

Family room $75.00 – 110.00

12" Polly Puff, c. 1970. $35.00. *Doll courtesy of Joan Allen.*

Dr. John Littlechap's outfits

Golf outfit	$30.00 MIP
Medical	$65.00 MIP
Suit	$50.00 MIP
Tuxedo	$70.00 MIP
Lisa's outfits	
Evening dress	$90.00 MIP
Coat, fur trim	$50.00 MIP
Libby's, Judy's outfits	
Jeans/sweater	$30.00 MIP
Dance dress	$45.00 MIP

Mimi, 1973, vinyl and hard plastic, battery operated singer, rooted long blond hair, painted blue eyes, open/closed mouth, record player in body, sings "I'd Like to Teach the World to Sing," song used for Coca-Cola® commercial; sings in different languages

19"	$50.00 – 60.00

Black

19"	$75.00 – 85.00

Lily Munster, #1822, 1964, vinyl, one-piece body, played by Yvonne DeCarlo

4¾"	$90.00 – 105.00

Grandpa Munster, #1821, 1964, vinyl head, one-piece plastic body

4¾"	$95.00 – 110.00

Orphan Annie, 1967

15"	$95.00 – 120.00

Polly Puff, 1970, vinyl, came with inflatable furniture

12"	$30.00 – 35.00

Sweet April, 1971, vinyl

5½"	$25.00 – 35.00

Black

5½"	$35.00 – 40.00

6" I Dream of Jeannie Playset by Remco. $120.00. *Courtesy of The Museum Doll Shop.*

Tippy Tumbles, 1968, vinyl, rooted red hair, stationary blue eyes, does somersaults, batteries in pocketbook

16"　　　$45.00 – 55.00

Tumbling Tomboy, 1969, rooted blond braids, closed smiling mouth, vinyl and hard plastic, battery operated

17"　　　$10.00 – 15.00

RICHWOOD TOYS INC.

1950s – 1960s, Annapolis, Maryland. Produced hard plastic dolls.

Sandra Sue, 8", 1940s, 1950s, hard plastic, walker, head does not turn, slim body, saran wigs, sleep eyes. Some with high-heeled feet, only marks are number under arm or leg. All prices reflect outfits with original socks, shoes, panties, and accessories.

Dolls listed are in good condition with appropriate clothing and tags, naked, played with dolls will bring a quarter to a third the value listed.

8", Flat feet, in camisole, slip, panties, shoes, and socks　　$150.00 – 200.00

In school dress　　$150.00 – 200.00

In party/Sunday dress　　$175.00 – 225.00

Special coat, hat, and dress, limited editions, Brides, Heidi, Little Women, Majorette

$200.00 – 250.00

Sport or play clothes　　$100.00 – 150.00

Twin Sandra Sues, MIB　　$395.00

Too few in database for a reliable range.

High-heeled feet, camisole, slip, panties, shoes, socks　　$95.00 – 125.00

In school dress　　$100.00 – 150.00

In party/Sunday dress　　$125.00 – 175.00

Special coat, hat and dress, limited editions, Brides, Heidi, Little Women, Majorette

$125.00 – 175.00

Sport or play clothes　　$95.00 – 125.00

MIB Twin Sandra Sues　　$350.00

Too few in database for a reliable range.

Sandra Sue Outfits, mint, including all accessories

School dress　　$10.00 – 15.00

Party dress　　$20.00 – 25.00

Specials　　$35.00 – 50.00

Sport sets　　$20.00 – 25.00

Cindy Lou, 14", hard plastic, jointed dolls were purchased in bulk from New York distributor, fitted with double-stitched wigs by Richwood

In camisole, slip, panties, shoes, and socks

$200.00 – 250.00

In school dress　　$200.00 – 250.00

In party dress　　$225.00 – 250.00

In special outfits　　$225.00 – 275.00

In sports outfits　　$200.00 – 250.00

Cindy Lou Outfits, mint, including all accessories

School dress　　$35.00 – 45.00

Party dress　　$45.00 – 50.00

Special outfit　　$50.00 – 60.00

Sports clothes　　$35.00 – 45.00

GRACE CORRY ROCKWELL

1926 – 1928, United States. Artist who designed dolls. Her bisque doll heads were made in Germany and were distributed by Borgfeldt. Her composition headed dolls were made by Averill.

Pretty Peggy, bisque socket head, open mouth.

12" – 14"　　$3,000.00 – 5,000.00

16" – 19"　　$4,500.00 – 6,600.00

Little Sister & Brother, composition, smiling mouth, molded hair

14"　　　$450.00 – 550.00

ROHMER

1857 – 1880, Paris, France. Mme. Rohmer held patents for doll bodies, made dolls of various materials. Dolls listed are in good condition, appropriately dressed; may be much more for exceptional dolls.

Poupée (so-called Fashion-type), bisque or china glazed shoulder or swivel head on shoulder plate, closed mouth, kid body with green oval stamp, bisque or wood lower arms

Glass eyes

13" – 16"	$4,000.00 – 5,000.00
17" – 19"	$7,200.00 – 9,500.00

Painted eyes

13" – 16"	$3,500.00 – 4,200.00
18"	$5,400.00 pink tint

ROLDAN

1960s – 1970s, Barcelona, Spain. Roldan characters are similar to Klumpe figures in many respects. They are made of felt over a wire armature with painted mask faces. Like Klumpe, Roldan figures represent professionals, hobbyists, dancers, historical characters, and contemporary males and females performing a wide variety of tasks. Some, but not all Roldans, were imported by Rosenfeld Imports and Leora Dolores of Hollywood. Figures originally came with two sewn-on identifying cardboard tags. Roldan characters most commonly found are doctors, Spanish dancers, and bull fighters. Roldan characters tend to have somewhat smaller heads, longer necks, and more defined facial features than Klumpe. Dolls listed are all in good, clean, un-faded condition, allow more for elaborate figure with many accessories.

Common figures	$95.00 – 150.00

GERTRUDE F. ROLLINSON

1916 – 1929, Holyoke, Massachusetts. Designed and made cloth dolls with molded faces, painted over the cloth on head and limbs, treated to be washable. Painted hair or wigged, some closed mouth, others had open/closed mouths with painted teeth. Some dolls closely resemble the dolls of the Chase Company while others are heavily sanded between coats of paint giving them a look of composition. Rollinson had her dolls made by the Utley Co. (later called

23" Rollinson wigged cloth doll. $1,600.00.
Courtesy of The Museum Doll Shop.

273

New England Doll Company), and distributed by G. Borgfeldt, L. Wolf, and Strobel & Wilken.

Painted hair

13" – 15"	$800.00 – 1,200.00

Wigged

23"	$1,400.00 – 1,600.00

RUBBER

1860s on, various European and American makers produced rubber dolls.

Goodyear Doll, molded shoulder-head doll in the style of the china and papier-mache dolls of the era

16" – 18"	$550.00 – 750.00

American rubber doll, 1920s on

Baby

12" – 15"	$65.00 – 75.00

16" Goodyear rubber doll with molded flower in hair. $550.00. *Courtesy of The Museum Doll Shop.*

SASHA

1945 – 2001. Sasha dolls were created by Swiss artist, Sasha Morgenthaler, who handcrafted 20" children and 13" babies in Zurich, Switzerland, from the 1940s until her death in 1975. Her handmade studio dolls had cloth or molded bodies, five

13" rubber baby, c. 1920s. $70.00. *Courtesy of The Museum Doll Shop.*

different head molds, and were hand painted by Sasha Morgenthaler. To make her dolls affordable as children's playthings, she licensed Götz Puppenfabric (1964 – 1970 & 1995 – 2001) in Germany and Frido Trendon Ltd. (1965 – 1986) in England to manufacture 16" Sasha dolls in series. The manufactured dolls were made of rigid vinyl with painted features.

Price range reflects rarity, condition, and completeness of doll, outfit, and packaging, and varies with geographic location. Dolls listed are in good condition, with original clothing. Allow more for mint in box.

Original Studio Sasha Doll, ca. 1940s – 1974, made by Sasha Morgenthaler in Switzerland, some are signed on soles of feet, have wrist tags or wear labeled clothing

20" $5,000.00 – 9,000.00 up

Götz Sasha Doll, 1964 – 1970, Germany, girls or boys, two face molds, marked "Sasha Series" in circle on neck and in three-circle logo on back, three different boxes were used, identified by wrist tag and/or booklet

16" $1,200.00 – 1,500.00

Frido-Trendon Ltd., 1965 – 1986, England, unmarked on body, wore wrist tags and current catalogs were packed with doll

Child, 1965 – 1968, packaged in wide box

16" $500.00 – 600.00

Child, 1969 – 1972, packaged in crayon tubes

16" $450.00 – 500.00

Sasha Pintucks. $400.00. *Courtesy of The Museum Doll Shop.*

Sexed Baby, 1970 – 1978, cradle, styrofoam cradles package or straw box and box

White or black $100.00 – 300.00

Unsexed Baby, 1978 – 1986, packaged in styrofoam wide or narrow cradles or straw basket and box $125.00 – 175.00

Child, 1973 – 1975, packaged in shoe box style box

16" $250.00 – 300.00

Black child $275.00 – 325.00

Child, 1975 – 1980, white, shoe box style box

16" $175.00 – 225.00

Black child $175.00 – 225.00

1980 – 1986, white, packaged in photo box with flaps $150.00 – 200.00

#1 Sasha Anniversary doll

16" $175.00 – 300.00

117S, Sasha "Sari," 1986, black hair, estimated only 400 produced before English factory closed January 1986

16" $700.00 – 800.00

130E Sasha "Wintersport," 1986, blond hair

16" $400.00 – 600.00

330E Gregor Sandy (hair) "Hiker"

16" $1,225.00*

Limited Editions, made by Trendon Sasha Ltd. in England, packaged in box with outer sleeve picturing individual doll, limited edition Sasha dolls marked on neck with date and number, number on certificate matches number on doll's neck.

1981 "Velvet," girl, light brown wig, 5,000 production planned

$400.00 – 450.00

1982 "Pintucks" girl, blond wig, 6,000 production planned

$350.00 – 400.00

1983 "Kiltie" girl, red wig, 4,000 production planned

$400.00 – 500.00

1984 "Harlequin" girl, rooted blond hair, 4,000 production planned

$250.00 – 350.00

1985 "Prince Gregor" boy, light brown wig, 4,000 production planned

$275.00 – 350.00

1986 "Princess Sasha" girl, blond wig, 3,500 production planned, but only 350 were made

$1,000.00 – 1,500.00

Götz Dolls Inc., 1995 +, Germany, they received the license in September 1994; dolls introduced in 1995.

Child, 1995 – 1996, marked "Götz Sasha" on neck and "Sasha Series" in three circle logo on back, about 1,500 of the dolls produced in 1995 did not have mold mark on back, earliest dolls packaged in generic Götz box, currently in tube, wear wrist tag, Götz tag, and have mini-catalog

16½" $150.00 – 250.00

Baby, 1996, unmarked on neck, marked "Sasha Series" in three circle logo on back, first babies were packaged in generic Götz box or large tube, currently packaged in small "Baby" tube, wears Sasha wrist tag, Götz booklet and current catalog

12" $125.00 – 150.00

BRUNO SCHMIDT

1898 – 1930, Waltershausen, Germany. Made bisque, composition, and wooden head dolls, after 1913 also celluloid. Acquired Bähr & Pröschild in 1918. Often used a heart-shaped tag. Dolls listed are in good condition, appropriately dressed.

Character Baby, bisque socket head, glass eyes, composition bent leg body

Mold 2092, ca. 1920, Mold 2097, ca. 1911

13" – 15"	$375.00 – 450.00
18" – 20"	$550.00 – 750.00

Mold 2097, toddler

15"	$850.00 – 900.00
21"	$1,200.00 – 1,400.00
34"	$1,700.00 – 1,800.00

Child, BSW, no mold numbers, bisque socket head, jointed body, sleep eyes, open mouth, add $50.00 more for flirty eyes

14"	$350.00 – 450.00
18" – 20"	$450.00 – 500.00
22" – 24"	$525.00 – 625.00

Character, Oriental, mold 500, ca. 1905, yellow tint bisque socket head, glass eyes, open mouth, teeth, pierced ears, wig, yellow tint composition jointed body

11"	$1,300.00 – 1,450.00
18"	$1,650.00 – 1,900.00

Mold 529, "2052," ca. 1912, painted eyes, closed mouth

20"	$2,800.00 – 4,000.00

Mold 539, "2023," ca. 1912, solid dome or with wig, painted eyes, closed mouth

24"	$3,000.00 – 3,200.00

Mold 537, "2033" (Wendy), ca. 1912, sleep eyes, closed mouth

12" – 13"	$16,500.00 – 18,000.00
15" – 17"	$23,000.00 – 25,000.00
20"	$32,000.00 – 34,000.00

Mold 2048, ca. 1912, Tommy Tucker, 2094, 2096, ca. 1920, solid dome, molded and painted hair or wig, sleep eyes, open or closed mouth, composition jointed body

Open mouth

12" – 14"	$950.00 – 1,150.00
18" – 20"	$1,200.00 – 1,350.00
26" – 28"	$1,800.00 – 2,000.00

Mold 2072, ca. 1920, sleep eyes, closed mouth

16"	$2,300.00 – 2,550.00
19"	$2,800.00 – 3,000.00

FRANZ SCHMIDT

1890 – 1937, Georgenthal, Thüringia, Germany. Made, produced, and exported dolls with bisque, composition, wood, and celluloid heads. Used bisque heads made by Simon & Halbig.

Heads marked "S & C": mold 269, 293, 927, 1180, 1310.

Heads marked "F.S. & C": mold 1250, 1253, 1259, 1262, 1263, 1266, 1267, 1270, 1271, 1272, 1274, 1293, 1295, 1296, 1297, 1298, 1310.

Walkers: mold 1071, 1310.

Dolls listed are in good condition, appropriately dressed.

Baby, bisque head, solid dome or cut out for wig, bent-leg body, sleep or set eyes, open mouth, some pierced nostrils, add more for flirty eyes

Mold 1271, 1272, 1295, 1296, 1297, 1310

10" – 12"	$350.00 – 400.00
13" – 14"	$425.00 – 450.00
18" – 20"	$500.00 – 550.00
22" – 24"	$750.00 – 825.00

Toddler

10" – 12"	$750.00 – 850.00
18" – 20"	$900.00 – 1,000.00
22" – 25"	$1,275.00 – 1,375.00
25"	$1,450.00 – 1,600.00

Character Face

Mold 1266, 1267, ca. 1912, marked "F.S. & Co.," solid dome, painted eyes, closed mouth

14"	$2,750.00 – 2,850.00
19"	$3,700.00 – 3,900.00

Mold 1270, ca. 1910, solid dome, painted eyes, open/closed mouth

9"	$575.00 – 650.00
13"	$1,500.00 – 1,800.00

With two faces

16"	$1,275.00 – 1,450.00

Child

Dolly face, Mold 269, ca. 1890s, Mold 293, ca. 1900, marked "S & C," open mouth, glass eyes

5" – 7" on five-piece body	
	$300.00 – 375.00
10" – 12"	$450.00 – 525.00
19" – 23"	$450.00 – 550.00
27" – 29"	$700.00 – 900.00

Mold 1259, ca. 1912, marked "F.S. & Co." character, sleep eyes, pierced nostrils, open mouth

15"	$400.00 – 500.00

Mold 1262, 1263, ca. 1910, marked "F.S. & Co.," painted eyes, closed mouth

14"	$5,400.00 – 5,800.00

Too few in database for a reliable range.

Mold 1272, ca. 1910, marked "F.S. & Co.," solid dome or wig, sleep eyes, pierced nostrils, open mouth

9½"	$850.00 – 950.00

SCHMITT & FILS

1854 – 1891, Noget-sur-Marne and Paris, France. Made bisque and wax-over-bisque or wax-over-composition dolls. Heads were pressed. Used neck socket like on later composition Patsy dolls.

Dolls listed are in good condition, appropriately dressed; more for exceptional doll with wardrobe or other attributes.

Child, pressed bisque head, closed mouth, glass eyes, pierced ears, mohair or human hair wig, French composition and wood eight ball-jointed body with straight wrists

Early round face

12" – 14"	$9,500.00 – 10,500.00
13", trousseau, box	$12,000.00
18" – 24"	$15,500.00 – 18,000.00

Long face modeling

16" – 18"	$13,000.00 – 15,000.00
24" – 26"	$19,500.00 – 21,000.00

Wax over papier mâché, swivel head, cup and saucer type neck, glass eyes, closed mouth, eight ball-jointed body

16" – 17"	$3,000.00 – 3,500.00

SCHOENAU & HOFFMEISTER

1901 – 1939, Burggrub, Bavaria. Had a porcelain factory, produced bisque heads for dolls, also supplied other manufacturers, including Bruckner, Dressel, Eckhardt, E. Knoch, and others.

Dolls listed are in good condition, appropriately dressed. More for exceptional dolls.

Baby, bisque solid-dome or wigged socket head, sleep eyes, teeth, composition bent-leg body, closed mouth, newborn, solid dome, painted hair, cloth body, may have celluloid hands, add more for original outfit

Solid dome infant

10" – 12"	$600.00 – 700.00
13" – 15"	$800.00 – 900.00

Mold 169, 170 (Porzellanfabrik Burggrub), bent-limb body

13" – 15"	$275.00 – 325.00
18" – 20"	$400.00 – 475.00
23" – 25"	$500.00 – 575.00

Hanna, sleep eyes, open/closed mouth,

bent-leg baby body, $100.00 more for toddler

13" – 15"	$400.00 – 500.00
18" – 20"	$625.00 – 725.00
22" – 24"	$850.00 – 1,150.00

Princess Elizabeth, 1929, socket head, sleep eyes, smiling open mouth, chubby leg toddler body

16" – 17"	$1,750.00 – 1,950.00
20" – 22"	$2,100.00 – 2,350.00

Child, dolly face, bisque socket head, open mouth with teeth, sleep eyes, composition ball-jointed body

Mold 1906, 1909, 2500, 4000, 4600, 4700, 5500, 5700, 5800

14" – 16"	$300.00 – 400.00
18" – 21"	$400.00 – 450.00
26" – 27"	$500.00 – 650.00

Mold 914, ca. 1925, character

30"	$625.00*

Mold 4900, ca. 1905, Oriental, dolly face

10"	$400.00 – 475.00

A. SCHOENHUT & CO.

1872 – 1930 on, Philadelphia, Pennsylvania. Made all-wood dolls, using spring joints, had holes in bottoms of feet to fit into stands. Later made elastic strung with cloth bodies. Carved or molded and painted hair or wigged, intaglio or sleep eyes, open or closed mouth. Later made composition dolls.

Dolls listed are in good condition, appropriately dressed; more for exceptional doll.

Infant

Graziano Infants, circa May 1911– 1912

Schnickel – Fritz, carved hair, open/closed

grinning mouth, four teeth, large ears, toddler

    15" $3,000.00 – 3,600.00*

Tootsie Wootsie, carved hair, open/closed mouth, two upper teeth, large ears on child body

    15" $3,800.00 – 4.200.00

Too few in database for a reliable range.

Model 107, 107W (walker), 108, 108W (walker)

Baby, nature (bent) limb, 1913 – 1926

    13" $475.00 – 550.00

Toddler, 1917 – 1926

    11" $675.00 – 750.00

Toddler, 1913 – 1926

    14" $675.00 – 750.00

Toddler, elastic strung, 1924 – 1926

    14" $675.00 – 750.00

Toddler, cloth body with crier

    14" $750.00 – 825.00

Model 109W, 110W, 1921 – 1923

Baby, nature (bent) limb, sleep eye, open mouth

    13" $450.00 – 500.00

Toddler, sleep eye

    14" $700.00 – 800.00

Bye-Lo Baby, "Grace S. Putnam" stamp, cloth body, closed mouth, sleep eyes

    13" $2,400.00*

Child

Salesman's cut-away sample child

                    $3,400.00*

Graziano Period, 1911– 1912, dolls may have heavily carved hair or wigs, painted intaglio eyes, outlined iris, all with wooden spring-jointed bodies and are 16" tall, designated with 16 before the model number, like "16/100"

Model 100, girl, carved hair, solemn face

Model 101, girl, carved hair, grinning, squinting eyes

Model 102, girl, carved hair, bun on top

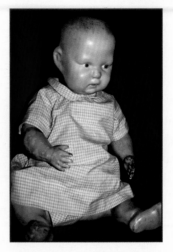

15" Schoenhut baby. $550.00. *Doll courtesy of Ruth Cayton.*

Model 103, girl, carved hair, loose ringlets

Model 200, boy, carved hair, short curls

Model 201, boy, carved hair, based on K*R 114

Model 202, boy, carved hair, forelock

Model 203, boy, carved hair, grinning, some with comb marks

Carved hair dolls of this early period; add more if excellent condition, original clothes

    16" $3,000.00 – 3,600.00

Too few in database for a reliable range.

Model 300, girl, long curl wig, face of 102

Model 301, girl, bobbed wig with bangs, face of 300

Model 302, girl, wig, based on K*R 101

Model 303, girl, short bob, no bangs, grinning, squinting eyes

Model 304, girl, wig in braids, ears stick out

Model 305, girl, snail braids, grinning, face of 303

Model 306, girl, wig, long curls, face of 304

Model 307, girl, short bob, no bangs, "dolly-type" smooth eye

Model 400, boy, short bob, K*R 101 face

Group of Schoenhut circus figures. $1,300.00 group. *Courtesy of Skinner Inc., Boston and Bolton, Massachusetts.*

Model 401, boy, side-part bob, face of 300/301

Model 402, boy, side-part bob, grin of 303

Model 403, boy, dimple in chin

Wigged dolls, with intaglio eyes, outlined iris of this period, more if original costume and paint

    16" $1,200.00 – 1,500.00

Transition Period, 1911– 1912, designs by Graziano and Leslie, dolls may no longer have outlined iris, some models have changed, dolls measure 16" – 17", now have a groove above knee for stockings

Model 100, girl, same, no iris outline

Model 101, girl, short carved hair, bob/bow, round eyes, smile

Model 102, girl, braids carved around head

Model 103, girl, heavy carved hair in front/fine braids in back

Model 104, girl, fine carved hair in front/fine braids in back

Model 200, boy, carved hair, same, no iris outline

Model 201, boy, carved hair, same, iris outline, stocking groove

Model 202, boy, carved hair, same, smoother

Model 203, boy, smiling boy, round eyes, no iris outline

Model 204, boy, carved hair brushed forward, serious face

Carved hair is smoother, may no longer have outlined iris, some with stocking groove, more for excellent condition and original costume

    16" $1,800.00 – 2,200.00

Model 300, girl, long curl wig, dimple in chin

Model 301, girl, bob wig, face of 102

Model 302, girl, wig, same like K*R 101

Model 303, girl, wig, similar to 303G, smiling, short bob, no bangs

Model 304, girl, wig, braids, based on K*R

Model 305, girl, wig, braids, face of 303

Model 306, girl, long curl wig, same face as 304

Model 307, girl, smooth eyeball

Model 400, boy, same (like K*R 101)

Model 401, boy, like K*R 114 (304)

Model 402, boy, smiling, round eyes

Model 403, boy, same as 300 with side part bob

Model 404, boy, same as 301, side part bob Wigged boy or girl, similar to earlier models with some refinements, more for excellent condition, original costume

16" $1,000.00 – 1,400.00

Classic Period, 1912– 1923, some models discontinued, some sizes added, those marked with † were reissued in 1930

Model 101, girl, short carved hair bob, no iris outline

1912 – 1923†
14" $1,900.00 – 2,200.00
1911 – 1916
16" $2,200.00 – 2,400.00

Model 102, girl, heavy carved hair in front, fine braids in back

1912 – 1923
14" $1,700.00 – 1,900.00
1911 – 1923
16" $1,800.00 – 2,000.00
1912 – 1916
19" – 21" $1,900.00 – 2,100.00

14½" Schoenhut character child in original union suit. $2,200.00. *Courtesy of Skinner Inc., Boston and Bolton, Massachusetts.*

Model 105, girl, short carved hair bob, carved ribbon around head

1912 – 1923
14" – 16" $1,600.00 – 1,900.00
1912 – 1916
19" – 21" $1,900.00 – 2,100.00

Model 106, girl, carved molded bonnet on short hair, 1912 – 1916

14" $2,000.00 – 2,200.00
16" $2,400.00 – 2,600.00
19" $2,600.00 – 2,800.00

Model 203, 16" boy, same as transition
Model 204, 16" boy, same as transition†
Model 205, carved hair boy, covered ears

1912 – 1923
14" – 16" $2,200.00 – 2,400.00
1912 – 1916
19" – 21" $2,400.00 – 2,600.00

Model 206, carved hair boy, covered ears, 1912 – 1916

19" $2,400.00 – 2,600.00

Model 207, carved short curly hair boy, 1912 – 1916

14" $2,200.00 – 2,400.00

Model 300, 16" wigged girl, same as transition period, 1911 – 1923

Model 301, 16" wigged girl, same as transition, 1911 – 1924

Model 303, 16" wigged girl, same as transition 305, 1911 – 1916

Model 307, long curl wigged girl, smooth eye, 1911 – 1916

16" $825.00 – 850.00

Model 308, girl, braided wig, 1912 – 1916

14" $750.00 – 800.00
Bobbed hair, 1912 – 1924
19" $850.00 – 900.00
Bob or curls, 1917 – 1924
19" – 21" $850.00 – 900.00

Model 309, wigged girl, two teeth, long curls, bobbed hair, 1912 – 1913

16" $775.00 – 825.00

1912 – 1916

19" – 21"	$800.00 – 875.00

Model 310, wigged girl, same as 105 face, long curls, 1912 – 1916

14" – 16"	$700.00 – 775.00
19" – 21"	$775.00 – 825.00

Model 311, wigged girl, heart shape 106 face, bobbed wig, no bangs

1912 – 1916

14" – 16"	$750.00 – 825.00

1912 – 1913

19"	$775.00 – 850.00

Model 312, wigged girl, bobbed, 1912 – 1924; bobbed wig or curls, 1917 – 1924

14"	$700.00 – 775.00

Model 313, wigged girl, long curls, smooth eyeball, receding chin, 1912 – 1916

14" – 16"	$750.00 – 800.00
19" – 21"	$775.00 – 825.00

Model 314, wigged girl, long curls, wide face, smooth eyeball, 1912 – 1916

19"	$565.00 – 725.00

Model 315, wigged girl, long curls, four teeth, triangular mouth, 1912 – 1916

21"	$775.00 – 825.00

Model 403, 16" wigged boy, same as

22" Schoenhut Miss Dolly. $875.00. *Courtesy of Skinner Inc., Boston and Bolton, Massachusetts.*

transition, bobbed hair, bangs, 1911 – 1924

Model 404, 16" wigged boy, same as transition, 1911 – 1916

Model 405, boy, face of 308, bobbed wig, 1912 – 1924

14"	$550.00 – 650.00
19"	$850.00*

Model 407, wigged boy, face of 310 girl, 1912 – 1916

19" – 21"	$725.00 – 825.00

Miss Dolly, model 316, open mouth, teeth, wigged girl, curls or bobbed wig, painted or decal eyes, all four sizes, circa 1915 – 1925

15" – 21"	$775.00 – 875.00

Model 317, sleep eyes, open mouth, teeth, wigged girl, long curls or bob, sleep eyes, four sizes, 1921 – 1928

15" – 21"	$900.00 – 1,100.00

Composition doll, 1924, molded curly hair, painted eyes, closed mouth

13"	$800.00 – 900.00

Manikin

Model 175, man with slim body, ball-jointed waist, circa 1914 – 1918

19"	$2,400.00*

Small doll such as circus figures, storybook and comic characters

Circus performers, rare figures may be much higher, bisque head

Bareback Lady Rider or Ringmaster

9", all original	$650.00

Clowns

8"	$250.00 – 300.00
32", store display	$4,500.00

Lion Tamer

8½"	$350.00 – 450.00

Ringmaster

8"	$250.00 – 325.00

Animals, some rare animals may be much higher

A group of Schoenhut Pinn family dolls, made from clothes pins. $100.00 each. *Courtesy of The Museum Doll Shop.*

Gorilla	
8"	$2,185.00
Kangaroo	$1,250.00
Quacky Doodles, Daddy and children	
	$1,239.00
Bandwagon	$7,000.00
Seven Bandsmen	$14,000.00

Cartoon Characters
Maggie and Jiggs, from cartoon strip "Bringing up Father"

7" – 9"	$525.00 – 600.00 each

Max and Moritz, carved figures, painted hair, carved shoes

8"	$600.00 – 650.00 each
14"	$8,500.00*
Mary and her lamb	$1,500.00*

Pinn Family, all wood, egg-shaped head, original costumes

Mother, and four children	$667.00
Individual Pinn dolls	
5" – 9"	$75.00 – 150.00
Rolly-Dolly figures	
9" – 12"	$350.00 – 850.00
Teddy Roosevelt	
8"	$800.00 – 1,600.00
Safari set w/animals	$8,000.00*

SCHUETZMEISTER & QUENDT

1889 – 1930 on, Boilstadt, Gotha, Thüringia, Germany. A porcelain factory that made and exported bisque doll heads, all-bisque dolls, and Nankeen dolls. Used initials "S & Q," mold 301 was sometimes incised "Jeannette." Dolls listed are in good condition, appropriately dressed.

Baby, character face, bisque socket head, sleep eyes, open mouth, bent-leg body
Mold 201, 204, 300, 301, ca. 1920

10" – 12"	$300.00 – 350.00
14"	$350.00 – 400.00
19"	$425.00 – 500.00

Mold 252, ca. 1920, character face, black baby

15"	$500.00 – 575.00

Child
Mold 101, 102, ca. 1900, dolly face

17"	$350.00 – 400.00
22"	$400.00 – 475.00

Mold 1376, ca. 1900, character face

19"	$475.00 – 550.00

S.F.B.J.

Société Francaise de Fabrication de Bebes & Jouets, 1899 – 1930+, Paris and Montreuil-sous-Bois. Competition with German manufacturers forced many French companies to join together including Bouchet, Fleischmann & Bloedel, Gaultier, Rabery & Delphieu, Bru, Jumeau, Pintel & Godchaux, Remignard and Wertheimer, and others. This alliance lasted until the 1950s. Fleischman owned controlling interest. See also Unis France. Dolls listed are in good condition, appropriately dressed; more for exceptional dolls.

Child, bisque head, glass eyes, open mouth, pierced ears, wig, composition jointed French body

Jumeau type, no mold number, open mouth

13" – 15"	$950.00 – 1,000.00
20" – 22"	$1,550.00 – 1,650.00
24" – 26"	$1,950.00 – 2,050.00
28"	$2,200.00 – 2,300.00

Mold 301

6" – 8" on five-piece body	
	$175.00 – 200.00
8" – 10"	$675.00 – 775.00
12" – 14"	$625.00 – 700.00
18" – 20"	$850.00 – 900.00
22" – 24"	$950.00 – 1,000.00
26" – 28"	$975.00 – 1,100.00

Kiss Thrower

24"	$1,650.00 – 1,750.00

Bleuette: See Bleuette section.

Mold 60

6" – 8"	$425.00 – 450.00
12" – 14"	$495.00 – 525.00
18" – 21"	$550.00 – 650.00
28"	$700.00 – 800.00

Papier-mâché head

8" – 10"	$150.00 – 200.00
16" – 18"	$300.00 – 350.00

Character Faces, bisque socket head, wigged or molded hair, set or sleep eyes, composition body, some with bent baby limb, toddler or child body, mold number 227, 235, and 236 may have flocked hair, add $100.00 for toddler body

Mold 226, glass eyes, closed mouth

18" – 20"	$1,900.00 – 2,200.00

Mold 227, open mouth, teeth, glass eyes

14"	$1,700.00 – 1,900.00
17"	$2,000.00 – 2,200.00
19" – 21"	$2,900.00 – 3,300.00

Mold 230, glass eyes, open mouth, teeth

12" – 14"	$650.00 – 700.00
20" – 22"	$1,000.00 – 1,200.00

Mold 233, ca. 1912, crying mouth, glass eyes

14" – 16"	$3,600.00 – 4,000.00

Mold 234

18"	$2,800.00 – 3,050.00

14" open/closed mouth character marked "SFBJ 235 Paris." $1,400.00. *Courtesy Richard W. Withington, Inc., Nashua, New Hampshire.*

11" S.F.B.J mold 236, open/closed mouth character. $1,500.00. *Courtesy of The Museum Doll Shop.*

Mold 235, glass eyes, open/closed mouth
14"	$1,300.00 – 1,400.00
18"	$1,700.00 – 1,800.00
21"	$2,300.00*

Mold 236, glass eyes, laughing open/closed mouth
Baby
12" – 13"	$700.00 – 800.00
15" – 17"	$850.00 – 950.00
20" – 22"	$1,400.00 – 1,500.00

Toddler
13"	$1,900.00 – 2,000.00
15"	$2,200.00 – 2,300.00

Mold 237, glass eyes, open/closed mouth
13" – 14"	$2,900.00 – 3,000.00
16" – 17"	$3,800.00 – 4,000.00

Mold 238, small open mouth
18"	$2,200.00 – 2,400.00

Mold 239, ca. 1913, designed by Poulbot
13"	$7,500.00 – 8,000.00

Mold 242, ca. 1910, nursing baby
13" – 15"	$2,900.00 – 3,000.00

Mold 247, glass eyes, open/closed mouth
13"	$1,900.00 – 2,100.00
16"	$2,000.00 – 2,200.00

Mold 248, ca. 1912, glass eyes, lowered eyebrows, very pouty closed mouth
10" – 12"	$7,500.00 – 8,000.00*

Mold 250, open mouth with teeth
12", trousseau box	$3,300.00
18" – 20"	$3,250.00 – 3,400.00

Mold 251, open/closed mouth, teeth, tongue
15"	$1,400.00 – 1,500.00

Mold 252, baby, closed pouty mouth, glass eyes
8"	$2,000.00 – 2,200.00
10"	$3,200.00 – 3,500.00
15"	$3,800.00 – 4,000.00
26"	$10,750.00*

22" S.F.B.J. mold 301. $950.00. *Courtesy of The Museum Doll Shop.*

SHIRLEY TEMPLE

1934 on, Ideal Novelty Toy Corp., New York. Designed by Bernard Lipfert,

Dolls listed are in very good condition, all original. Add more for exceptional dolls or special outfits like Ranger or Wee Willie Winkie.

Composition, 1934 – 1940s. Composition head and jointed body, dimples in cheeks, green sleep eyes, open mouth, teeth, mohair wig, tagged original dress, center-snap shoes. Prototype dolls may have paper sticker inside head and bias trimmed wig.

27" composition Shirley Temple. $1,600.00. *Courtesy of Skinner Inc., Boston and Bolton, Massachusetts.*

Shirley Temple

11"	$850.00 – 950.00
13"	$650.00 – 700.00
16"	$725.00 – 775.00
17"	$800.00 – 850.00
18"	$900.00 – 950.00
20"	$1,000.00 – 1,050.00
22"	$1,100.00 – 1,150.00
27"	$1,600.00 – 1,650.00

Baby Shirley

18"	$1,000.00 – 1,100.00
21"	$1,200.00 – 1,300.00

Hawaiian, "Marama," Ideal used the composition Shirley Temple mold for this doll representing a character from the movie *Hurricane*, black yarn hair, wears grass skirt, Hawaiian costume

18"	$875.00 – 950.00

Shirley at the Organ, special display stand with composition Shirley Temple at non-functioning organ, music provided by record — $4,400.00*

Accessories:

Button, three types	$125.00
Buggy, wicker or wood	$500.00 – 575.00
Dress, tagged	$125.00 – 575.00
Satin pajama, tagged	$670.00
Trunk	$175.00 – 225.00

Reliable Shirley Temple, composition, made in Canada

18" – 22"	$1,000.00 – 1,200.00

Japanese, unlicensed Shirley dolls

All-bisque

6"	$195.00 – 225.00

Celluloid

5"	$125.00 – 175.00
8"	$200.00 – 225.00

Celluloid, Dutch Shirley Temple, ca. 1937+, all-celluloid, open crown, metal pate, sleep eyes, dimples in cheeks, marked: "Shirley Temple" on head, may have additional marks, dressed in Dutch costume

13"	$295.00 – 320.00
15"	$295.00 – 320.00

Composition, Japanese, heavily molded brown curls, painted eyes, open/closed mouth with teeth, body stamped "Japan"

7½"	$250.00 – 275.00

Vinyl, dolls listed are in excellent condition, original clothes, accessories. The newer the doll the more perfect it must be to command higher prices.

1957, all-vinyl, sleep eyes, synthetic rooted wig, open/closed mouth, teeth, came in two-piece slip and undies, tagged Shirley Temple, came with gold plastic script pin reading "Shirley Temple," marked on back of head "ST//12"

12"	$350.00 – 375.00

1958 – 1961, marked on back of head "S.T.//15," "S.T.//17," or "S.T.//19," some had flirty ("Twinkle") eyes; add more for flirty eyes or 1961 Cinderella, Bo Peep, Heidi, and Red Riding Hood

15"	$325.00 – 375.00
17"	$400.00 – 450.00
19"	$450.00 – 500.00

1960, jointed wrists, marked "ST-35-38-2"

35" – 36"	$1,800.00 – 2,100.00

1972, Montgomery Wards reissue, plain box

17"	$175.00 – 200.00

7½" all-composition Shirley, made in Japan. $250.00. *Courtesy of The Museum Doll Shop.*

12" vinyl 1957 Shirley Temple doll. $375.00. *Courtesy Richard W. Withington, Inc., Nashua, New Hampshire.*

1973, red dot "Stand Up and Cheer" outfit, box with Shirley pictures, extra outfits available

16"	$125.00 – 150.00

1982 – 1983

8"	$25.00 – 30.00
12"	$30.00 – 35.00

1984, by Hank Garfinkle, marked "Doll Dreams & Love"

36"	$200.00 – 225.00

1994 on, Shirley Temple Dress-Up Doll, Danbury Mint, similar to 1987 doll; no charge for doll, get two outfits bimonthly

16"	$40.00 – 60.00

1996 Danbury Mint, Little Colonel, Rebecca/Sunnybrook Farm, and Heidi

16"	$20.00 – 25.00

Porcelain

1987 on, Danbury Mint

16"	$65.00 – 85.00

1990 on, Danbury Mint, designed by Elke Hutchens, in costumes from *The Little Princess, Bright Eyes, Curly Top, Dimples,*

36" companion-size Shirley Temple, all original. $2,000.00. *Doll courtesy of Susan Mitchell.*

and others, marked on neck: "Shirley Temple//1990."

20" $150.00 – 175.00

1997 Toddler, Danbury Mint, designed by Elke Hutchens, porcelain head, arms, legs, cloth body, pink dress, more dolls in the toddler series include Flower Girl and others

20" $95.00 – 100.00

SIMON & HALBIG

1869 – 1930 on, Hildburghausen and Grafenhain, Germany. Porcelain factory, made heads for Jumeau (200 series), bathing dolls (300 series), porcelain figures (400 series), perhaps doll house or small dolls (500 – 600 series), bisque head dolls (700 series), bathing and small dolls (800 series), more bisque head dolls (900 – 1000 series). The earliest models of a series

had the last digit of their model number ending with an 8, socket heads ended with 9, shoulder heads ended with 0, and models using a shoulder plate for swivel heads ended in 1.

Dolls listed are in good condition, appropriately dressed. All original or exceptional dolls may be more.

Shoulder-head child, 1870s, molded hair, painted or glass eyes, closed mouth, cloth body with bisque lower arms, appropriately dressed, marked "S&H," no mold number

13" – 15"	$1,100.00 – 1,200.00
17" – 19"	$1,375.00 – 1,700.00
21" – 23"	$2,200.00 – 2,400.00

Swivel neck

9" – 10"	$1,250.00
12"	$1,500.00

Poupée (fashion–type doll), 1870s, bisque socket head with bisque shoulder-plate on kid or twill over wood body, closed mouth, glass eyes, wigged

Kid body

15" – 18"	$2,200.00 – 2,700.00

13½" Simon Halbig lady on twill body. $4,000.00. *Doll courtesy of Turn of the Century Antiques, Denver, Colorado.*

Twill covered body

10" – 11"	$3,000.00 – 3,500.00
15" – 16"	$4,500.00 – 5,500.00

Closed-mouth child, 1879, socket head, most on composition and wood body, glass eyes, wigged, pierced ears, appropriately dressed

Mold 719

18" – 22"	$5,000.00 – 6,000.00

Mold 739

15"	$1,575.00 – 2,100.00

Mold 749

21"	$2,800.00 – 3,400.00

Mold 905, 908

15" – 17"	$3,300.00 – 4,300.00

Mold 919

15"	$5,300.00 – 7,200.00
19"	$6,000.00 – 8,150.00

Mold 929

14"	$1,725.00 – 2,300.00
23"	$2,450.00 – 3,400.00
25"	$6,600.00*

25" Simon and Halbig 979, open mouth, c. 1880s. $2,900.00. *Courtesy of Skinner Inc., Boston and Bolton, Massachusetts.*

18" Baby Blanche, dolly face doll. $400.00. *Courtesy of The Museum Doll Shop.*

Mold 939

14" –16"	$2,300.00 – 2,500.00
18" – 20"	$2,600.00 – 3,000.00

Mold 949

10"	$2,000.00 – 2,200.00
14" – 16"	$1,950.00 – 2,550.00
21" – 23"	$3,000.00 – 3,400.00
31"	$4,250.00 – 4,500.00

Mold 720, 740, 940, 950, dome shoulder head, kid body

8" – 10"	$500.00 – 600.00
14" –18"	$850.00 – 1,200.00
20" – 22"	$1,200.00 – 1,500.00

All-bisque child, 1880 on, swivel neck, peg jointed shoulders and hips, glass eyes, open or closed mouth, wigged

Mold 886

7", in presentation box	$1,600.00
8"	$600.00 – 800.00

Open-mouth socket-head child, 1889 – 1930s, composition body (sometimes French), wigged, glass eyes may be stationary or sleep, appropriately dressed

Mold 530, 540, 550, 570, Baby Blanche

19"	$425.00 – 475.00
22"	$500.00 – 575.00

15" Simon & Halbig on bent-limb body, mold 126. $850.00. *Courtesy of The Museum Doll Shop.*

Mold 719, 739, 749, 759, 769, 939, 979
Mold 749

5½"	$375.00 – 550.00
9" – 13"	$950.00 – 1,100.00
15" – 17"	$1,375.00 – 1,800.00
20" – 22"	$2,200.00 – 2,700.00
23" with Edison phonograph mechanism in torso	$4,900.00 – 5,400.00

Mold 905, 908

18"	$1,750.00 – 2,200.00
22"	$1,425.00 – 2,600.00

Mold 949

15" – 17"	$1,150.00 – 1,450.00
22" – 24"	$1,550.00 – 1,700.00
29"	$2,350.00 – 2,500.00

Mold 1009

15" – 16"	$675.00 – 775.00
19" – 21"	$825.00 – 925.00
24" – 25"	$1,125.00 – 1,400.00

Mold 1029

16" – 18"	$475.00 – 575.00
24" – 25"	$700.00 – 800.00
28"	$825.00 – 900.00

Mold 1039, 1049, 1059, 1069, 1078, 1079

8" – 9" on five-piece body
$500.00 – 550.00

9" on flapper body
$500.00 – 600.00

12" – 13"	$875.00 – 975.00

13" on walker body
$1,100.00 – 1,400.00

16" – 18"	$675.00 – 750.00
20" flirty eye	$750.00 – 800.00
23" – 25"	$850.00 – 925.00
34"	$1,400.00 – 1,600.00
44"	$4,200.00*

Mold 1109

13"	$750.00 – 800.00
18"	$1,000.00 – 1,000.00

Mold 1248, 1249, Santa

6"	$500.00 – 650.00
10" – 12"	$650.00 – 825.00
15"	$775.00 – 825.00
18" – 20"	$900.00 – 1,000.00
24"	$1,200.00 – 1,600.00
26" – 28"	$1,700.00 – 1,900.00
38"	$3,800.00 – 4,000.00

15" Simon & Halbig 1079 on Jumeau body. $650.00. *Courtesy of The Museum Doll Shop.*

18" Simon & Halbig 1079, c. 1920s, all original. $800.00. *Courtesy of The Museum Doll Shop.*

Open-mouth shoulder-head child, 1889 – 1930s, kid body
Mold 1009, 1039

12" – 13"	$950.00 – 1,100.00
19"	$350.00 – 525.00
23"	$750.00 – 1,000.00

Mold 1010, 1040, 1170, 1080

18"	$425.00 – 575.00
25"	$600.00 – 800.00
28"	$675.00 – 900.00

Mold 1250, 1260, open mouth

16"	$500.00 – 625.00
19"	$600.00 – 800.00
23"	$800.00 – 1,075.00

Character Face, 1909 on, bisque socket-head, composition body, wig or molded hair, glass or painted eyes, open or closed mouth, appropriately dressed
Mold 150, ca. 1912, intaglio eyes, closed mouth

21"	$15,500.00

Too few in database for a reliable range.

Mold 151, ca. 1912, painted eyes, closed laughing mouth

15"	$3,750.00 – 5,000.00

Too few in database for a reliable range.

Mold 153, ca. 1912, molded hair, painted eyes, closed mouth

17"	$27,000.00

Too few in database for a reliable range.

Mold 600, ca. 1912, sleep eyes, open mouth

17"	$900.00

Too few in database for a reliable range.

Mold 729, ca. 1888, laughing face, glass eyes, open/closed mouth

16"	$1,900.00 – 2,550.00

Mold 969, ca. 1887, open smiling mouth

19"	$5,700.00 – 7,600.00

Too few in database for a reliable range.

Mold 1019, ca. 1890, laughing, open mouth

14"	$4,275.00 – 5,700.00

Too few in database for a reliable range.

Mold 1269, 1279, sleep eyes, open mouth

14"	$1,100.00 – 1,500.00
16"	$3,500.00 MIB
25"	$2,550.00

Mold 1299, ca. 1912, marked "S&H"

13"	$1,200.00 – 1,600.00

Mold 1448, ca. 1914, bisque socket head, sleep eyes, closed mouth, pierced ears, composition/wood ball-jointed body

16"	$17,500.00

Too few in database for a reliable range.

Portrait, Mary Pickford

40"	$34,000.00*

Little Women, 1909, mold 1160 shoulder-head lady, fancy hairdo wig, closed mouth, glass eyes, cloth body with bisque lower limbs, appropriately dressed

6" – 7"	$325.00 – 375.00
10" – 11"	$425.00 – 475.00
14"	$625.00 – 675.00

7" Simon & Halbig lady, mold 1159. $900.00.
Courtesy of The Museum Doll Shop.

Baby, character face, 1910 on, molded hair or wig, painted or glass eyes, open or closed mouth, bent-leg baby body, appropriately dressed, add more for flirty eyes or toddler body

Mold 1294, ca. 1912, glass eyes, open mouth

16"	$550.00 – 750.00
19"	$800.00 – 1,100.00

Mold 1294, clockwork mechanism moves eyes

26"	$1,575.00*

Mold 1428, ca. 1914, glass eyes, open-closed mouth

13"	$1,200.00 – 1,600.00

Toddler

12"	$2,600.00 – 2,700.00
16"	$2,100.00 – 2,300.00

Mold 1488, ca. 1920, glass eyes, open-closed or open mouth

20"	$3,375.00 – 4,500.00+

Mold 1489, "Baby Erika," ca. 1925, glass eyes, open mouth, tongue

20"	$4,200.00*

Mold 1498, ca. 1920, solid dome, painted or sleep eyes, open/closed mouth

24"	$3,700.00*

Lady doll, 1910 on, bisque socket head, composition lady body, sleep eyes, wigged, appropriately dressed

Mold 1079, open mouth, glass eyes

24"	$1,500.00 – 2,000.00

Mold 1159, ca. 1894, glass eyes, open mouth, Gibson Girl

15" on flapper body	
	$2,400.00 – 2,600.00
20"	$2,000.00 – 2,200.00

Mold 1303, ca. 1902, lady face, glass eyes, closed mouth

14"	$5,815.00

Too few in database for a reliable range.

Mold 1305, ca. 1902, old woman, glass eyes, open/closed laughing mouth

18"	$10,035.00

Too few in database for a reliable range.

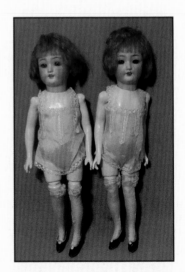

A pair of 15" Simon Halbig 1159 dolls on flapper bodies. $5,000.00 pair. *Courtesy Richard W. Withington, Inc., Nashua, New Hampshire.*

Mold 1308, ca. 1902, old man, molded mustache/dirty face, may be solid dome

    18" $4,200.00 – 5,600.00

Too few in database for a reliable range.

Mold 1388, ca. 1910, glass eyes, closed smiling mouth, teeth, wig

    20" $24,000.00*

Mold 1469, ca. 1920, flapper, glass eyes, closed mouth

    15" $2,625.00 – 3,500.00

SNOW BABIES

1901 – 1930 on. All-bisque dolls covered with ground porcelain slip to resemble snow, made by Bähr & Pröschild, Hertwig, C.F. Kling, Kley & Hahn, and others, Germany. Mostly unjointed, some jointed at shoulders and hips. The Eskimos named Peary's daughter Marie, born in 1893, Snow Baby, and her mother published a book in which she called her daughter Snow Baby and showed a picture of a little girl in white snowsuit. These little figures have painted features, various poses.

Figures listed are in good condition, allow more for exceptional figures.

New Snow Babies are being made today. Department 56 makes a line of larger scale figures (see below) and reproductions of earlier Snow Babies are being produced in Germany and by individual artisans.

Single Snow Baby, standing or sitting

    1½" $50.00 – 60.00

    3" – 4" $300.00 – 400.00

Riding on bear

                    $300.00 – 350.00

Riding on sled

    2" $150.00 – 200.00

Pulled by dogs

    3" $275.00 – 375.00

Riding on reindeer

    2½" $300.00 – 325.00

With Broom

    4½" $500.00 – 550.00

Snow Babies, made in Germany. $50.00 to $125.00. *Courtesy of The Museum Doll Shop.*

Two Snow Babies, molded together
1½"	$100.00 – 125.00
3"	$200.00 – 250.00

Two on sled
2½"	$200.00 – 275.00

Mold 3200, Armand Marseille, candy container, two Snow Babies on sled
11"	$3,100.00*

Three Snow Babies, molded together
3"	$300.00 – 350.00

Three on sled
2½"	$300.00 – 350.00

Snow Baby doll, jointed hips, shoulders
4"	$300.00 – 400.00
5"	$400.00 – 500.00

New Snow Babies

Today's commercial reproductions are by Dept. 56 and are larger and the coloring is more like cream. Dept. 56 Snow Babies and their Village Collections are collectible on the secondary market. As with all newer collectibles, items must be mint to command higher prices. Current pieces range from about $18.00 – 30.00, more for limited edition and special pieces

1986

Snow Baby winged clip ornament
$45.00 – 60.00

Climbing on Snowball, w/candle
$95.00 – 118.00

Snow Baby on Brass Ribbon $153.00*

1987

Snow Baby Adrift $90.00 – 125.00

1988

Snow Baby on Votive $45.00 – 65.00

Pony Express $70.00 – 90.00

1989

All Fall Down, set 4 $65.00 – 85.00

Finding Falling Star $125.00 – 200.00

Penguin Parade $50.00 – 70.00

1990 on, various $15.00 – 30.00

SONNEBERG TAUFLING (MOTCHMANN TYPE)

1851 – 1900 on, Sonneberg, Germany. Various companies made an infant doll with special separated body with bellows and voice mechanism. Motchmann is erroneously credited with the body style; but he did patent the voice mechanism. Some bodies stamped "Motchmann" refer to the voice mechanism. The Sonneberg Taufling was made with head, shoulder plate, pelvis, lower arms and lower legs of papier-mâché/composition, wax over papier-mâché, china, and bisque. Body parts put together

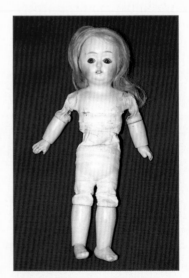

7" wax over composition Sonneberg Taufling (Motschmann type). $650.00. *Courtesy of The Museum Doll Shop.*

with twill cloth in what are called "floating" joints. These dolls have glass eyes, closed mouth or open mouth, painted hair, or wigged. Dolls listed are in good condition.

Bisque: See also Steiner, Jules.

French-type

19"	$2,700.00 – 3,000.00

China

6" – 7"	$4,500.00 – 5,500.00
9" – 10"	$3,500.00 – 4,000.00
16"	$5,600.00 – 6,600.00

Papier-mâché/composition or wax over papier-mâché

10" – 12"	$750.00 – 1,000.00
18" – 20"	$1,500.00 – 2,000.00
22" – 24"	$2,200.00 – 2,400.00

Wood, carved wooden socket head, closed mouth, twill and wood torso, nude

17"	$1,000.00*

MARGARETE STEIFF

1877 to present, Giengen, Wurtemburg, Germany. Known today for their plush stuffed animals, Steiff made clothes for children, dolls with mask faces in 1889, clown dolls by 1898. Most Steiff dolls of felt, velvet, or plush have seam down the center of the face, but not all. Registered trademark button in ear in 1905. Button type eyes, painted features, sewn-on ears, big feet/shoes enable them to stand alone.

Prices are for older dolls, newer dolls are much less. Dolls listed are in good condition, for soiled, ragged, or worn dolls, use 25% or less of this price.

Adults

14½" – 18"	$2,000.00 – 2,500.00

Characters

Man with pipe, some moth holes, some soil

17"	$1,300.00*

Military Men in uniform and conductors, firemen, etc.

10½"	$1,275.00 – 1,700.00
18"	$3,200.00 – 4,275.00

Children

12" – 14"	$1,300.00 – 1,500.00
16" – 18"	$1,650.00 – 1,850.00

Made in U.S. Zone Germany, 1947 – 1953, glass eyes

12"	$550.00 – 650.00

Rubber head doll, cloth body

13"	$200.00 – 250.00

Vinyl characters, wire armature in body

Max or Moritz

4"	$125.00 – 175.00

17" Steiff character man with center seam face, glass eyes. $1,300.00. *Courtesy of The Museum Doll Shop.*

Limited Edition Dolls, 1986 – 1987, felt, characters such as tennis lady, Gentleman in morning coat, Peasant lady, Peasant Jorg $100.00 – 150.00

16" Steiff boy. $1,500.00. *Courtesy of The Museum Doll Shop.*

HERMANN STEINER

1909 – 1930 on, near Coburg, Germany. Porcelain and doll factory. First made plush animals, then made bisque, composition, and celluloid head dolls. Patented the Steiner eye with moving pupils.

Baby

Mold 240, circa 1925, newborn, solid dome, closed mouth, sleep eyes

16" $300.00 – 350.00

Mold 246, circa 1926, character, solid dome, glass eyes, open/closed mouth, laughing baby, teeth, cloth or composition body

15" $475.00 – 600.00

Topsy Turvy baby doll

8" $500.00 – 600.00

Child

Dolly face, no mold number, open mouth, glass eyes, jointed composition body

8" – 10" $150.00 – 225.00

18" – 20" $300.00 – 325.00

Living Steiner-eye doll, character with molded hair and Steiner patented eye

10" $575.00 – 650.00

Mold 128, character bisque socket head, sleep eyes, open mouth, teeth, wig, composition/wood jointed body

9" $650.00 – 700.00*

Mold 401, shoulder head, solid dome, painted eyes, open/closed laughing mouth, teeth, molded tongue

15" $350.00 – 475.00

JULES STEINER

1855 – 1891 on, Paris. Made dolls with pressed heads, wigs, glass eyes, pierced ears on jointed composition bodies. Advertised talking, mechanical jointed dolls and bébés. Some sleep eyes were operated by a wire behind the ear, marked "J. Steiner." May also carry the Bourgoin mark.

Dolls listed are in good condition, appropriately dressed. Add more for original clothes, rare mold numbers.

Bébé with Taufling (Motchmann type) body, solid dome bisque head, shoulders, hips, lower arms and legs, with twill body in-between, closed mouth, glass eyes, wig

13" – 14" $5,300.00 – 6,500.00

20" – 22" $4,300.00 – 6,000.00

Gigoteur, crying, kicking child, key-wound mechanism, solid dome head, glass eyes, open mouth, two rows tiny teeth, pierced ears, mohair wig, papier-mâché torso

    18" – 20" $1,800.00 – 2,200.00

Round face Bébé, 1870s, early unmarked, pale pressed bisque socket head, rounded face, pierced ears, bulgy paperweight eyes, open mouth, two rows teeth, pierced ears, wig, composition/wood jointed body

    16" – 18" $5,500.00 – 6,800.00

21" bébé, marked "J. Steiner Paris Fre. A 13." $5,200.00. *Courtesy Richard W. Withington, Inc., Nashua, New Hampshire.*

Closed mouth, round face, dimples in chin

    16" – 18" $10,000.00 – 11,500.00

Bébé with Series marks, 1880 on, Bourgoin red ink, Caduceus stamp on body, pressed bisque socket head, cardboard pate, wig, pierced ears, closed mouth, glass paperweight eyes, French composition/papier-mâché (purple) body with straight wrists or bisque hands, Series C and A more common, marked with series mark: Sie and letter and number; rare Series B, E, F, and G models may be valued much higher

Series A or C

8" – 10"	$6,500.00 – 8,000.00
14" – 16"	$6,500.00 – 7,000.00
21" – 23"	$8,500.00 – 11,000.00
27"	$11,500.00 – 12,500.00
34" – 38"	$16,000.00 – 20,000.00

Series E

24"	$22,000.00*

Series F

24"	$48,000.00*

Series G

19"	$26,000.00 – 29,000.00

Bébé with Figure marks, 1887 on, bisque socket head, pierced ears, closed mouth, glass eyes, wig, composition/wood jointed French body, may use body marked "Le Parisien" or "Le Petit Parisien," head marked figure: "Fire" and letter and number, and "J. Steiner," figure marks including A, B, C, D, and E, A and C are the most often found

Closed mouth

A or C

8" – 10"	$4,400.00 – 4,600.00
14" – 16"	$4,400.00 – 4,900.00
20" – 24"	$5,000.00 – 5,900.00
34"	$8,000.00 – 10,000.00

17" Steiner Gigoteur (crying, kicking). $1,700.00. *Courtesy Richard W. Withington, Inc., Nashua, New Hampshire.*

Open mouth
Figure A
18" – 22"	$2,600.00 – 3,000.00

Figure D
18"	$14,500.00*

Figure E
30"	$21,000.00*

8" Steiner Le Petite Parisien, lever eyes. $4,600.00. *Doll courtesy of George and Cynthia Orgeron.*

SUN RUBBER

1919 – 1950s, Barberton, Ohio. Made rubber and later vinyl dolls. Dolls listed are in excellent condition, allow less for faded, cracked dolls or missing paint.

Psyllium, 1937, molded painted hard rubber, moving head, blue pants, white suspenders, black shoes and hat
10"	$10.00 – 15.00

One-piece Squeeze dolls, 1940s, designed by Ruth E. Newton, molded clothes, squeaker, names such as Bonnie Bear, Happy Kappy, Rompy, and others
8"	$30.00 – 45.00

So-Wee, 1941, molded hair, painted or sleep eyes
10" – 12"	$35.00 – 60.00

Sunbabe, 1950, drink and wet baby, painted eyes, molded hair
11" – 13"	$75.00 – 100.00

Betty Bows, 1953, molded hair with loop for ribbon, drink and wet baby, jointed body
11"	$75.00 – 100.00

Tod L Dee, 1950s, all-vinyl soft stuffed one-piece body, molded underclothes and shoes, molded painted hair, sleep eyes, open mouth, also a Tod L Tee and Tod L Tim.
10"	$45.00 – 65.00

Amosandra: See Black Dolls.
Gerber Baby: See Advertising Dolls.

12" Sun Rubber girl with molded loop for ponytail ribbon. $70.00. *Courtesy of The Museum Doll Shop.*

14" Swaine toddler marked "D.I.,"
open/closed mouth and intaglio eyes.
$900.00. *Doll courtesy of Ruth Cayton.*

SWAINE & CO.

1910 – 1927, Huttensteinach,
Thüringia, Germany. Made porcelain
doll heads. Marked "S & Co.," with
green stamp. May also be incised
"DIP" or "Lori."

Baby

Baby Lori, marked "Lori," solid dome,
open/closed mouth molded hair, sleep
eyes

18"	$1,400.00 – 1,600.00
23"	$2,000.00 – 2,500.00

Mold 232, Lori variation, open mouth

12" – 14"	$750.00 – 1,000.00
20" – 23"	$1,300.00 – 1,600.00

DI, solid dome, intaglio eyes, closed
mouth

11" – 13"	$600.00 – 800.00
16", toddler	$2,100.00

DV, solid dome, sleep eyes, closed mouth

13"	$1,000.00 – 1,200.00
15"	$1,300.00 – 1,450.00

FP, S&C, socket head, sleep eyes, closed
mouth

8"	$750.00 – 850.00

Too few in database for a reliable range.

Child

AP, socket head, intaglio eyes, closed
mouth

15"	$5,200.00*

BP, socket head, open/closed smiling
mouth, teeth, painted eyes

14½"	$4,500.00 – 5,500.00

Too few in database for reliable range.

DIP, S&C, socket head, sleep eyes, closed
mouth

8" – 9"	$595.00 – 795.00
13" – 14"	$1,300.00 – 1,600.00

TEBBETTS SISTERS

1922 on, Pittsburg, Pennsylvania.
Mary, Elizabeth, Marion, and Ruth
Tebbetts patented and made cloth
dolls.

Petiekins, cloth mask face, crepe or
flannel body

6½"	$375.00 – 475.00

6½" Sweet Petiekins, cloth mask face. $475.00.
Courtesy of The Museum Doll Shop.

Baby Sister, needle-sculpted stockinette doll with painted features, wigged

    18" $1,500.00 – 2,000.00

TERRI LEE

1946 – 1962, Lincoln, Nebraska, and Apple Valley, California. Company was founded by Violet Lee Gradwohl, the company went out of business in 1962. In 1997, Fritz Duda, Violet's nephew, was instrumental in founding Terri Lee Associates which is making Terri Lee dolls now. First dolls composition, then hard plastic and vinyl, the modern dolls are now being produced of a newer type of hard plastic. Closed pouty mouth, hand-painted features, wigged, jointed body. Values listed are for dolls in good condition and wearing original clothing. Allow significantly less for undressed, played-with dolls. Dolls in mint condition, or with fancy

Linda Baby. $145.00. *Courtesy of The Museum Doll Shop.*

costume or additional wardrobe will bring more.

Terri Lee

Composition, 1946 – 1947

    16" $300.00 – 400.00

Painted hard plastic, 1947 – 1949

    16" $1,200.00 – 1,600.00

Flesh colored hard plastic, 1949 – 1952

    16" $600.00 – 700.00

Hard plastic, 1952 – 1962

    16" $350.00 – 450.00

    16", MIB $650.00 – 750.00

Vinyl, less if sticky, 1950 – 1951

    16" $550.00 – 650.00

Talking

    16" $500.00 – 600.00

Hard plastic, 1997 – 2005

    16" $200.00 – 250.00 retail

Benji, painted plastic, brown, 1946 – 1962, black lamb's wool wig

    16" $1,800.00 – 2,000.00

Connie Lynn, 1955, hard plastic, sleep eyes, fur wig, bent-limb baby body

    19" $350.00 – 450.00

Gene Autry, 1949 – 1950, painted plastic

    16" $1,600.00 – 1,800.00

Jerri Lee, hard plastic, caracul wig

    16" $400.00 – 500.00

16" Terri Lee, hard plastic. $350.00.
Courtesy of The Museum Doll Shop.

Vinyl
16" $1,200.00 – 1,500.00
Linda Lee, 1950 – 1951, vinyl
12" $60.00 – 75.00
1952 – 1958, vinyl baby
10" $120.00 – 145.00
Mary Jane, Terri Lee look-alike, hard plastic walker
16" $200.00 – 265.00
Patty Jo, 1947 – 1949
16" $1,200.00 – 1,500.00
Bonnie Lou, black
16" $1,200.00 – 1,800.00
Tiny Terri Lee, 1955 – 1958
10" $150.00 – 195.00
Accessories
Terri Lee Outfits:

Girl Scout/Brownie uniform	$50.00
Heart Fund	$325.00
Plaid skirt, coat, hat	$660.00*
School dress	$150.00
Shoes	$35.00
Winter outfit, fur trim	$660.00*
Jerri Lee Outfits:	
Gene Autrey	$865.00*

A. THUILLIER

1875 – 1893, Paris. Made bisque head dolls with composition, kid, or wooden bodies. Some of the heads were reported made by Francoise Gaultier. Bisque socket head or swivel on shoulder plate, glass eyes, closed mouth with white space, pierced ears, cork pate, wig, nicely dressed, in good condition. Doll in good condition, appropriately dressed. Exceptionally beautiful dolls may run more.
Child, closed mouth
12" – 13" $33,000.00 – 36,000.00

16" – 18" $42,000.00 – 47,000.00
21" – 24" $55,000.00 – 65,000.00

ROBERT TONNER

1991 to present, Hurley, New York. Robert Tonner is a fashion designer and sculptor who has created numerous dolls in porcelain and vinyl. Tonner Company also owns Effanbee Dolls.
Ann Estelle, 1999, a Mary Engelbreit character, hard plastic, blond wig, glasses
10" $69.00 retail
Betsy McCall: See Betsy McCall section.
Kripplebush Kids, 1997, hard plastic, Marni, Eliza, Hannah
8" $55.00 retail
Tyler Wentworth, 1999, fashion-type, long, straight brunette, blond, or red hair
16" $79.99 retail
Kitty Collier, 2000, blond, brunette, or red head
18" $89.00 retail

Tiny Kitty Collier, c. 2005. $90.00.
Courtesy of The Museum Doll Shop.

TROLLS

Trolls portray supernatural beings from Scandinavian folklore. They have been manufactured by various companies including Helena and Martii Kuuslkoski who made Fauni Trolls, ca. 1952+ (sawdust filled cloth dolls); Thomas Dam, 1960+; Scandia House, later Norfin®; Uneeda Doll and Toy Wishniks®; Russ Berrie; Ace Novelty; Treasure Trolls; Applause Toys; Magical Trolls; and many other companies who made lesser quality vinyl look-alikes, mostly unmarked, to take advantage of the fad. Most are all-vinyl or vinyl with stuffed cloth bodies.

Troll Figures

2½"	$8.00 – 10.00
5"	$15.00 – 20.00
7"	$25.00 – 30.00
10"	$35.00 – 40.00
12"	$40.00 – 45.00
15"	$55.00 – 65.00

Troll Animals
Cow, unmarked

6"	$95.00 – 125.00

Donkey, Dam, 1964

9"	$110.00 – 150.00

Monkey, Thomas Dam

7"	$230.00*

Mouse, Thomas Dam

5"	$170.00*

Tailed Troll, Thomas Dam

6½"	$190.00*

UNEEDA

1917 on, New York City. Made composition head dolls, including Mama dolls and made the transition to plastics and vinyl.

Composition
Rita Hayworth as "Carmen," 1939, from *The Loves of Carmen* movie, all-composition, red mohair wig, unmarked, cardboard tag

14"	$425.00 – 500.00

Hard Plastic and Vinyl
Baby Dollikins, 1960, vinyl head, hard plastic jointed body with jointed elbows, wrists, and knees, drink and wet

21"	$150.00 – 200.00

Baby Trix, 1965

19"	$18.00 – 25.00

Bareskin Baby, 1968

12½"	$15.00 – $20.00

Blabby, 1962+

14"	$18.00 – 25.00

Coquette, 1963+

16"	$15.00 – 20.00

Black

16"	$25.00 – 35.00

21" Fairy Princess by Uneeda. $90.00. *Courtesy of The Museum Doll Shop.*

Dollikin, 1957 on, multi-joints, marked "Uneeda//2S"

19"	$175.00 – 225.00
21", Ballerina	$405.00

Fairy Princess, 1961

32"	$75.00 – 100.00

Freckles, 1960, vinyl head, rigid plastic body, marked "22" on head

32"	$65.00 – 75.00

1973, ventriloquist doll, vinyl head, hands, rooted hair, cotton stuffed cloth body

30"	$45.00 – 60.00

Jennifer, 1973, rooted side-parted hair, painted features, teen body, mod clothing

18"	$15.00 – 20.00

Magic Meg w/Hair That Grows, vinyl and plastic, rooted hair, sleep eyes

16"	$30.00 – 45.00

Pir-thilla, 1958, blows up balloons, vinyl, rooted hair, sleep eyes

12½"	$8.00 – 12.00

Purty, 1973, long rooted hair, vinyl, plastic, painted features

11"	$20.00 – 25.00

Pollyanna, 1960, for Disney

11"	$25.00 – 35.00
17"	$50.00 – 70.00
31"	$100.00 – 125.00

Saranade, 1962, vinyl head, hard plastic body, rooted blond hair, blue sleep eyes, red and white dress, speaker in tummy, phonograph and records came with doll, used battery

21"	$75.00 – 100.00

Suzette (Carol Brent)

12"	$100.00 – 125.00

Tiny Teen, 1957 – 1959, vinyl head, rooted hair, pierced ears, six-piece hard plastic body, high-heeled feet to compete with Little Miss Revlon, wrist tag

10½"	$75.00 – 90.00

UNIS FRANCE

1922 – 1930 on. Mark used by S.F.B.J. (Société Francaise de Fabrication de Bebes & Jouets) after 1922 is Union Nationale Inter-Syndicale.

Child

Mold 60, 301, bisque head, fully jointed composition/wood body, wig, sleep eyes, open mouth

8" – 10"	$375.00 – 475.00
13" – 16"	$500.00 – 600.00
21" – 23"	$625.00 – 775.00

Five-piece composition body, glass eyes

5" – 8"	$250.00 – 300.00
10" – 14"	$300.00 – 350.00

Mold 247, 251, toddler body

15"	$1,100.00 – 1,450.00
27"	$1,700.00 – 2,300.00

6" Unis France mold 60, painted eyes. $275.00. *Courtesy of The Museum Doll Shop.*

VINYL

1950s on. By the mid-1950s, vinyl (polyvinylchloride) was being used for dolls. Material that was soft to the touch and processing that allowed hair to be rooted were positive attractions. Vinyl became a desirable material and the market was soon deluged with dolls manufactured from this product. Many dolls of this period are of little known manufacturers, unmarked, or marked only with a number. With little history behind them, these dolls need to be mint in box and complete to warrant top prices. With special accessories or wardrobe values may be more.

Unknown Maker

Baby, vinyl head, painted or sleep eyes, molded hair or wig, bent legs, cloth or vinyl body

12"	$8.00 – 10.00
16"	$10.00 – 12.00
20"	$16.00 – 20.00

20" Sayco vinyl Miss America. $50.00. *Courtesy of The Museum Doll Shop.*

Ballerina Belle by the Belle Doll & Toy Co. of Brooklyn, 1950s. $60.00. *Courtesy of The Museum Doll Shop.*

Child, vinyl head, jointed body, painted or sleep eyes, molded hair or wig, straight legs

14"	$10.00 – 14.00
22"	$18.00 – 25.00

Adult, vinyl head, painted or sleep eyes, jointed body, molded hair or wig, smaller waist with male or female modeling for torso

8"	$20.00 – 25.00
18"	$55.00 – 75.00

Known Maker

Baby Barry

Alfred E. Newman

20"	$135.00 – 175.00

Captain Kangaroo

19"	$95.00 – 125.00
24"	$185.00 – 215.00

Christopher Robin

18"	$100.00 – 135.00

Daisy Mae

14"	$125.00 – 175.00

Emmett Kelly (Willie the Clown)

15"	$135.00 – 160.00
21"	$200.00 – 275.00

Li'l Abner

14"	$100.00 – 150.00
21"	$150.00 – 200.00

13" Poor Pitiful Pearl, c. 1955. $400.00. *Courtesy of The Museum Doll Shop.*

Mammy Yokum, 1957
Molded hair
14"	$90.00 – 125.00
21"	$195.00 – 225.00

Yarn hair
14"	$125.00 – 150.00
21"	$200.00 – 250.00

Nose lights up
23"	$275.00 – 325.00

Pappy Yokum, 1957
14"	$85.00 – 100.00
21"	$195.00 – 225.00

Nose lights up
23"	$275.00 – 325.00

Belle Doll & Toy Co, Brooklyn, New York, 1950s
Ballerina
18"	$50.00 – 60.00

Dee & Cee, Canada
Calypso Bill, 1961, black, vinyl, marked "DEE CEE"
16"	$50.00*

Glad Toy/BrookGlad
Poor Pitiful Pearl, 1955, vinyl, some with stuffed one-piece vinyl bodies, others

jointed
13"	$225.00 – 550.00
17"	$250.00 – 300.00

Playmates, 1985 on, made animated talking dolls using a tape player in torso powered by batteries, extra costumes, tapes, and accessories available, more for black versions
Amazing Amy, Maddy, ca.1998, vinyl, cloth body, interactive
20"	$50.00 – 65.00

Cricket, 1986 on
25"	$95.00 – 125.00

Corky, 1987 on
25"	$95.00 – 125.00

Jill, 1987, hard plastic, jointed body
33"	$225.00 – 300.00

Sayco, 1907 – 1950s, New York City, USA, first made composition dolls, then hard plastic and vinyl dolls
Miss America Pageant, 1950s
11"	$20.00 – 45.00
20"	$40.00 – 60.00

Shindana, 1968 – 1983, Operation Bootstrap, Los Angeles, ethnic features
14"	$50.00 – 65.00

Julie by Worlds of Wonder. $125.00. *Courtesy of The Museum Doll Shop.*

Talking Tamu, black, ethnic features
    16" $145.00 – 180.00
Tomy
Kimberly, 1981 – 1985, closed mouth, more for black
    17" $35.00 – 55.00
Getting Fancy Kimberly, 1984, open mouth with teeth
    17" $45.00 – 65.00
Tristar
Poor Pitiful Pearl, ca. 1955+, vinyl jointed doll came with extra party dress
    11" $90.00 – 125.00
Worlds of Wonder, ca. 1985 – 1987+, Fremont, California, made talking dolls and Teddy Ruxpin powered by batteries, had extra accessories, voice cards
Pamela, The Living Doll, 1986+
    21" $75.00 – 100.00
Julie, 1987 on
    24" $100.00 – 125.00
    Extra costume $20.00 – 30.00
Teddy Ruxpin, 1985+, animated talking bear
    20" $65.00 – 80.00

VOGUE DOLL CO.

1930s on, Medford, Massachusetts. Jennie Graves started the company and dressed "Just Me" and Arranbee dolls in the early years, before Bernard Lipfert designed Ginny. After several changes of ownership, Vogue dolls was purchased in 1995 by Linda and Jim Smith.

Ginny Family

Toddles, 1937 – 1948, composition, name stamped in ink on bottom of shoe, some early dolls which have been identified as "Toodles" (spelled with two o's) are blank dolls from various companies used by Vogue, painted eyes, mohair wig, jointed body; some had gold foil labels reading "Vogue."

Dolls listed are in good condition with original clothes. More for fancy outfits such as Red Riding Hood or Cowboy/Cowgirl or with accessories.
    8" $450.00 – 625.00
Ginny, 1948 – 1950, painted eye, hard plastic, strung joints, marked "Vogue" on head, "Vogue Doll" on body, painted eyes, molded hair with mohair wig, clothing tagged "Vogue Dolls" or "Vogue Dolls, Inc. Medford Mass.," inkspot tag on white with blue letters.
    8" $375.00 – 425.00
Ginny, 1953, hard plastic, sleep eyes, strung joints
    8" $450.00 – 550.00
Outfit only $65.00 – 90.00+
Ginny, 1950 – 1954, 8", hard plastic walkers, sleep eyes, painted lashes, strung, dynel wigs, new mark on back torso: "GINNY//VOGUE DOLLS//INC. //PAT PEND.// MADE IN U.S.A."

Toddles, composition. $575.00.
Courtesy of The Museum Doll Shop.

Strung Ginny. $500.00. *Courtesy of The Museum Doll Shop.*

Common dress	$250.00 – 350.00
1950 Julie #8	$695.00*
1951 Glad #42	$995.00*
1952 Beryl	$2,025.00*
1952 Carol Kindergarten	$925.00*
1953 Pamela #60	$510.00*
Black Ginny, 1953 – 1954	
8"	$500.00 – 600.00
8"	$2,000.00 MIB

Ginny, 1954 – 1956, hard plastic, seven-piece body, molded lash walkers, sleep eyes, Dynel or saran wigs, marked: "VOGUE" on head, "GINNY//VOGUE DOLLS//INC.//PAT. NO. 2687594//MADE IN U.S.A." on back of torso

8"	$195.00 – 225.00
Outfit only	$40.00+

Davy Crockett, coonskin cap, brown jacket, pants, toy rifle, in box

8"	$935.00*

Crib Crowd, 1950, baby with curved legs, sleep eyes, poodle cut (caracul) wig

8"	$550.00 – 650.00
Easter Bunny	
8"	$1,000.00 – 1,400.00

Ginny, 1957 – 1962, hard plastic, bent-knee (jointed) walker, molded lashes, sleep eyes, dynel or saran wigs, marked "VOGUE" on head, "GINNY//VOGUE DOLLS//INC.// PAT.NO.2687594//MADE IN U.S.A."

8"	$125.00 – 175.00
Outfit only	$40.00+

Ginny, 1960, unmarked, big walker carried 8" doll dressed just like her

36"	$350.00

Too few in database for a reliable range.

Ginny, 1963 – 1965, soft vinyl head, hard plastic walker body, sleep eyes, molded lashes, rooted hair, marked: "GINNY," on head, "GINNY//VOGUE DOLLS, Inc.//PAT. NO.2687594//MADE IN U.S.A." on back

8"	$35.00 – 50.00

Ginny, 1965 – 1972, all-vinyl, straight legs, non-walker, rooted hair, sleep eyes, molded lashes, marked "Ginny" on head, "Ginny//VOGUE DOLLS, INC." on back

8"	$35.00 – 50.00

Ginny, 1972 – 1977, all-vinyl, non-walker, sleep eyes, molded lashes, rooted hair, some with painted lashes, marked "GINNY" on head, "VOGUE DOLLS©1972/ /MADE IN HONG KONG//3" on back, made in Hong Kong by Tonka

8"	$30.00 – 50.00

Ginny, 1977 – 1982, 1977 – 1979, "Ginny From Far-Away Lands," made in Hong Kong by Lesney, all-vinyl, sleep eyes, jointed, non-walker, rooted hair, chubby body, same as Tonka doll overall, marked "GINNY" on head, "VOGUE DOLLS 1972// MADE IN HONG KONG//3"; painted eyes, 1980 – 1981, marked "VOGUE DOLLS// ©GINNYTIM//1977" on head, "VOGUE DOLLS©1977//MADE IN HONG KONG" on back

8"	$25.00 – 35.00

Sasson Ginny, 1981 – 1982, made in Hong Kong by Lesney, all-vinyl, fully jointed, bendable knees, rooted Dynel hair, sleep eyes in 1981, painted eyes in 1982, slimmer body, marked "GINNY" on head, "1978 VOGUE DOLLS INC//MOONACHIE N.J.//MADE IN HONG KONG" on back

8" $25.00 – 35.00

Ginny, 1984 – 1986, made by Meritus® in Hong Kong, vinyl, resembling Vogue's 1963 – 1971 Ginny, marked "GINNY®" on head, "VOGUE DOLLS// (a star logo)//M.I.I. 1984//Hong Kong" on back, porcelain marked: "GW//SCD//5184" on head, "GINNNY //®VOGUE DOLLS//INC//(a star logo) MII 1984//MADE IN TAIWAN."

8" $35.00 – 55.00

Ginny, 1986 – 1995, by Dakin, soft vinyl, marked "VOGUE®DOLLS//©1984 R. DAKIN INC.// MADE IN CHINA" on back; hard vinyl, marked "VOGUE//®// DOLLS//©1986 R. DAKIN and Co.//MADE IN CHINA"

8" $15.00 – 25.00

Ginny Baby, 1959 – 1982, vinyl, jointed, sleep eyes, rooted or molded hair, a drink

8" straight leg walker (SLW) Ginny w/trousseau trunk. $425.00. *Courtesy Richard W. Withington, Inc., Nashua, New Hampshire.*

Vinyl Ginnette. $225.00. *Courtesy of The Museum Doll Shop.*

and wet doll, some marked "GINNY BABY// VOGUE DOLLS INC."

12" $30.00 – 40.00
18" $40.00 – 50.00

Ginnette, 1955 – 1969, 1985 – 1986, vinyl, jointed, open mouth, 1955 – 1956 had painted eyes, 1956 – 1969 had sleep eyes, marked "VOGUE DOLLS INC"

8" $200.00 – 250.00

1962 – 1963, rooted hair Ginnette

8" $125.00 – 175.00

Jan, 1958 – 1960, 1963 – 1964, Jill's friend, vinyl head, six-piece rigid vinyl body, straight leg, swivel waist, rooted hair, marked "VOGUE," called Loveable Jan in 1963 and Sweetheart Jan in 1964

10½" $125.00 – 150.00

Jeff, 1958 – 1960, vinyl head, five-piece rigid vinyl body, molded and painted hair, marked "VOGUE DOLLS"

11" $85.00 – 100.00

Jill, 1957 – 1960, 1962 – 1963, 1965, seven-piece hard plastic teenage body, bent-knee walker, high-heeled doll, big sister to Ginny (made in vinyl in 1965), extra wardrobe, marked "JILL//VOGUE DOLLS//

MADEI NU.S.A.//©1957"

    10½" $175.00 – 225.00

Street dress $15.00 – 25.00

Special outfits $50.00 – 175.00

Jimmy, 1958, Ginny's baby brother, all-vinyl, open mouth, painted eye Ginnette, marked "VOGUE DOLLS/INC."

    8" $45.00 – 60.00

Little Miss Ginny, 1965 – 1971, all-vinyl, promoted as a pre-teen, one-piece hard plastic body and legs, soft vinyl head and arms, sleep eyes; head marked "VOGUE DOLL//19©67" or "©VOGUE DOLL//1968" and back, "VOGUE DOLL"

    12" $30.00 – 40.00

Miss Ginny, 1962 – 1965, 1967 – 1980, 1962 – 1964, soft vinyl head could be tilted, jointed vinyl arms, two-piece hard plastic body, swivel waist, flat feet; 1965 – 1980, vinyl head and arms, one-piece plastic body

    15" – 16" $35.00 – 45.00

Ginny Exclusives

Enchanted Doll House

1988, limited edition

                   $125.00 – 160.00

GiGi Dolls

1987, GiGi's Favorite

                   $75.00 – 95.00

1988, Sherry's Teddy Bear

                   $75.00 – 95.00

Little Friends, Anchorage, AK

1990, Alaska Ginny

                   $75.00 – 95.00

Meyer's Collectibles

1986, Fairy Godmother

                   $175.00 – 210.00

1987, Cinderella and Prince Charming

                   $175.00 – 210.00

1988, Clown

                   $75.00 – 95.00

10½" Hard plastic Vogue Jill. $200.00.
Courtesy of The Museum Doll Shop.

1989, American Cowgirl

                   $75.00 – 95.00

Modern Doll Convention

1986, Rose Queen

                   $150.00 – 200.00

1987, Ginny at the Seashore

                   $50.00 – 75.00

1988, Ginny's Claim

                   $55.00 – 80.00

1989, Ginny in Nashville

                   $90.00 – 110.00

1990, Ginny in Orlando

                   $75.00 – 95.00

1991, Ginny in Las Vegas

                   $75.00 – 95.00

1992, Poodle Skirt Ginny

                   $50.00 – 75.00

1993, World of Elegance

                   $145.00 – 60.00

Shirley's Doll House

1986, Ginny Goes Country

                   $75.00 – 95.00

1986, Ginny Goes to the Fair

                   $25.00 – 95.00

10½" Vogue Jan, vinyl. $150.00. *Courtesy of The Museum Doll Shop.*

1987, black Ginny in swimsuit
$25.00 – 95.00
1987, Santa & Mrs. Claus
$75.00 – 90.00
1988, Sunday Best, boy or girl
$45.00 – 60.00
1988, Ginny Babysits
$45.00 – 60.00
Toy Village, Lansing, Michigan
1989 Ashley Rose
$100.00 – 130.00
Vogue Doll Club
1990, Member Special
$75.00 – 95.00
U.F.D.C. (United Federation of Doll Clubs)
1987 Miss Unity $125.00 – 155.00
1988 Ginny Luncheon Souvenir
$110.00 – 140.00
Vogue Review Luncheon
1989, Ginny $200.00 – 250.00
1990 $90.00 – 110.00
1991 $75.00 – 95.00
1993, Special Christmas $50.00 – 75.00

1994, Apple of My Eye $50.00 – 75.00
1995, Secret Garden $50.00 – 75.00
Ginny Accessories
Book: Ginny's First Secret
$100.00 – 125.00
Furniture: chair, bed, dresser, wardrobe, rocking chair, each $60.00 – 75.00
Ginny Gym
$425.00 – 500.00
Ginny Name Pin
$35.00 – 50.00
Ginny Pup, Steiff
$200.00 – 250.00
Ginny's House
$900.00 – 1,200.00
Luggage set
$75.00 – 100.00
Parasol
$10.00 – 15.00
School bag
$50.00 – 75.00
Shoes/shoe bag
$30.00 – 40.00
Composition
Dora Lee, sleep eyes, closed mouth
11" $375.00 – 425.00
Jennie, 1940s, sleep eyes, open mouth, mohair wig, five-piece composition body
13" $300.00 – 350.00
Cynthia, 1940s, sleep eyes, open mouth, mohair wig, five-piece composition body
13" $300.00 – 350.00
Hard Plastic & Vinyl
Baby Dear, 1959 – 1964, 18" vinyl baby designed by Eloise Wilkin, vinyl limbs, cloth body, topknot or rooted hair, white tag on body "Vogue Dolls, Inc."; left leg stamped "1960/E.Wilkins." 12" size made in 1961
18" $275.00 – 325.00
Baby Dear One, 1962, a one-year-old toddler version of Baby Dear, sleep eyes,

Ginny as Miss Unity. $150.00. *Courtesy of The Museum Doll Shop.*

two teeth, marked "C//1961//E.Wilkin// Vogue Dolls//Inc." on neck, tag on body, mark on right leg

25"	$200.00 – 250.00

Baby Dear Musical, 1962 – 1963, 12" metal, 18" wooden shaft winds, plays tune, doll wiggles

12"	$100.00 – 150.00
18"	$200.00 – 250.00

Baby Too Dear, 1963 – 1965, two-year-old toddler version of Baby Dear, all-vinyl, open mouth, two teeth

17"	$200.00 – 250.00
23"	$300.00 – 350.00

Brikette, 1959 – 1961; 1979 – 1980, swivel waist joint, green flirty eyes in 22" size only, freckles, rooted straight orange hair, paper hang tag reads "I'm //Brikette// the//red headed//imp" marked on head "VOGUE INC.//19©60"

22"	$200.00 – 250.00

1960, sleep eyes only, platinum, brunette, or orange hair

16"	$95.00 – 125.00

1980, no swivel waist, curly pink, red, purple, or blond hair

16"	$45.00 – 60.00

Li'l Imp, 1959 – 1960, Brikette's little sister, vinyl head, bent knee walker, green sleep eyes, orange hair, freckles, marked "R and B//44" on head and "R and B Doll Co." on back

10½"	$50.00 – 75.00

Wee Imp, 1960, hard plastic body, orange saran wig, green eyes, freckles, marked "GINNY//VOGUE DOLS//INC./ /PAT.No. 2687594//MADE IN U.S.A."

8"	$250.00 – 350.00

Littlest Angel

1961 – 1963, also called Saucy Littlest Angel, vinyl head, hard plastic bent knee walker, sleep eyes, same doll as Arranbee Littlest Angel, rooted hair, marked "R & B"

10½"	$150.00 – 200.00

1967 – 1980, all-vinyl, jointed limbs, rooted red, blond, or brunette hair, looks older

11"	$35.00 – 55.00
15"	$25.00 – 40.00

22" Vogue Brikette. $225.00. *Courtesy of The Museum Doll Shop.*

Love Me Linda (Pretty as a Picture), *1965,* Vinyl, large painted eyes, rooted long straight hair, came with portrait, advertised as "Pretty as a Picture" in Sears and Montgomery Ward catalogs, marked "VOGUE DOLLS/©1965"

15" $45.00 – 65.00

Welcome Home Baby, 1978 – 1980, newborn, designed by Eloise Wilkin, vinyl head and arms, painted eyes, molded hair, cloth body, crier, marked "Lesney"

18" $45.00 – 65.00

Welcome Home Baby Turns Two, 1980, toddler, designed by Eloise Wilkin, vinyl head, arms, and legs, cloth body, sleep eyes, rooted hair, marked "42260 Lesney Prod. Corp.//1979//Vogue Doll"

22" $150.00 – 200.00

IZANNAH WALKER

1840s – 1888, Central Falls, Rhode Island. Made cloth stockinette dolls,

16" and 15" Izannah Walker dolls. $18,000.00 – 20,000.00. *Courtesy of Skinner Inc., Boston and Bolton, Massachusetts.*

with pressed mask face, oil-painted features, applied ears, brush-stroked or corkscrew curls, stitched hands and feet, some with painted boots. All dolls listed are in good condition with appropriate clothing.

Very good condition

17" – 19" $18,000.00 – 24,000.00

Fair condition

17" – 19" $8,000.00 – 12,000.00

WAX

1850 – 1930. Made by English, German, French, and other firms, reaching heights of popularity ca. 1875. Seldom marked, wax dolls were poured, some reinforced with plaster, and less expensive, but more durable with wax over papier-mâché or composition. English makers included Montanari, Pierotti, and Peck. German makers included Heinrich Stier.

Dolls listed are in good condition with original clothes, or appropriately dressed. More for exceptional dolls; much less for dolls in poor condition.

Slit-head wax, English, 1830 – 1860s, wax over composition shoulder head, hair inserted into slit on center top of head, glass eyes may use wire closure

14" $925.00 – 1,000.00

16" – 18" $1,000.00 – 1,100.00

23" – 25" $1,600.00 – 1,800.00

Poured Wax, 1850s – 1900s, baby, shoulder head, painted features, glass eyes, English Montanari type, closed mouth, cloth body, wig, or hair inserted into wax

16" – 18" $1,125.00 – 1,400.00

23" – 25" $1,700.00 – 2,150.00

English slit-head wax doll. $1,000.00.
Courtesy of The Museum Doll Shop.

Infant nurser, slightly turned shoulder head, set glass eyes, open mouth, inserted hair wig, cloth body, wax limbs, nicely dressed

26"	$1,320.00*

Child, shoulder head, inserted hair, glass eyes, wax limbs, cloth body

13" – 15"	$825.00 – 1,100.00
18" – 22"	$1,600.00 – 2,000.00
25" – 27"	$2,800.00 – 3,300.00

Lady

8"	$700.00 – 900.00
15"	$950.00 – 1,100.00

Bride, rose wax shoulder head, blue glass eyes, closed mouth, wig, kid jointed fashion body

15"	$1,650.00*

Wax over Composition or Reinforced, 1860s – 1890s

Child, ca. 1860 – 1890, early poured wax shoulder head, reinforced with plaster, inserted hair, glass eyes, cloth body

10" – 12"	$375.00 – 425.00
14" – 16"	$550.00 – 675.00
20" – 22"	$700.00 – 800.00

Child, wax over socket head, glass eyes

16" – 18"	$1,3500 – 1,500.00

Child, later wax over composition shoulder head, open or closed mouth, glass eyes, wig, cloth body

10" – 12"	$200.00 – 250.00
15" – 17"	$275.00 – 350.00
21" – 23"	$425.00 – 475.00

Molded hair, wax over composition, shoulder head, glass eyes, cloth body, wooden limbs, molded shoes

13" – 15"	$300.00 – 375.00
19" – 23"	$450.00 – 500.00

Alice in Wonderland style, with molded headband

16"	$625.00 – 700.00

Mechanical Baby, solid dome, wax over papier-mâché, painted hair, glass eyes, open mouth, papier-mâché torso with bellows mechanism

16" – 18"	$1,500.00 – 2,000.00*

Two-faced doll, ca. 1880 – 1890s, one laughing, one crying, body stamped "Bartenstein"

15"	$775.00 – 900.00

Three English poured wax dolls of the 1860s, doll on right is by Montanari. $1,700.00 to $2,200.00.
Courtesy of Skinner Inc., Boston and Bolton, Massachusetts.

25" English poured wax c. 1870, made by Lucy Peck. $2,800.00. *Courtesy of Skinner Inc., Boston and Bolton, Massachusetts.*

Bonnethead

Child, 1860 – 1880, with molded cap
 16" $400.00 – 500.00
Lady with poke bonnet
 25" $3,000.00
Too few in database for a reliable range.
Man, turned shoulder head, molded top hat, set eyes, cloth body, wooden arms
 17" $1,000.00
Too few in database for a reliable range.

14" wax over composition lady with wig. $1,000.00. *Courtesy Richard W. Withington, Inc., Nashua, New Hampshire.*

Wax crèche figure, 1880 – 1910, poured wax Christ Child, inset hair, glass eyes
 13" – 15" $350.00 – 600.00
Wax fashion doll, 1910 – 1920, wax head, wire armature body, by makers such as LaFitte et Desirat and others, usually on wooden base
 13" – 14" $500.00 – 900.00

Wax fashion lady, c. 1910s – 1920s. $500.00. *Courtesy of The Museum Doll Shop.*

NORAH WELLINGS

1926 to 1960, Wellington, Shropshire, England. The Victoria Toy Works was founded by Norah Wellings and her brother Leonard. Norah had previously worked as chief designer for Chad Valley. They made cloth dolls with molded heads and bodies of velvet, velveteen, plush, and felt, specializing in sailor souvenir dolls for steamship lines. The line included children, adults, blacks, ethnic, and fantasy dolls.

Baby, molded face, oil-painted features, some papier-mâché covered by stockinette, stitched hip and shoulder joints

10"	$275.00 – 375.00
15"	$425.00 – 600.00
22"	$775.00 – 900.00

Child, painted eyes

12" – 13"	$375.00 – 400.00
16" – 18"	$500.00 – 600.00
22" – 23"	$700.00 – 800.00
28"	$900.00 – 1,000.00

Glass eyes

15" – 18"	$700.00 – 850.00
22"	$1,000.00 – 1,300.00

Characters in uniform, regional dress, floppy limbed, painted eyes, Mounties, Sailors, Policemen, Scots, others

8" – 10"	$100.00 – 125.00
13" – 14"	$150.00 – 175.00

20" Norah Wellings boy in original box. $700.00. *Courtesy Richard W. Withington, Inc., Nashua, New Hampshire.*

Black Islander, glass eyes

13"	$150.00 – 200.00
16"	$225.00 – 300.00

14" Norah Wellings girl, painted eyes. $475.00. *Courtesy of The Museum Doll Shop.*

16" Black Norah Wellings child. $700.00. *Courtesy of The Museum Doll Shop.*

WOODEN

Wooden dolls have been made from the earliest recorded times. During the 1600s and 1700s they became the luxury play dolls. They were made commercially in England, Germany, Switzerland, Russia, United States, and other countries. By the late 1700s and early 1800s inexpensive German wooden dolls were the affordable doll of the masses and were exported worldwide.

English

William & Mary Period, 1690s – 1700, carved wooden head, tiny multi-stroke eyebrow and eyelashes, colored cheeks, human hair or flax wig, wooden body, fork-like carved wooden hands, jointed wooden legs, cloth upper arms, medium to fair condition

18" – 22" $36,350.00 – 46,000.00
Too few in database for a reliable range.

19½" English carved wooden, so-called Queen Anne, c. 1735. $16,200.00. *Courtesy of Skinner Inc., Boston and Bolton, Massachusetts.*

17½" English carved wooden, so-called Queen Anne, c. 1780. $5,000.00. *Courtesy of Skinner Inc., Boston and Bolton, Massachusetts.*

Queen Anne Period, early 1700s, dotted eyebrows, eyelashes, painted or glass eyes, no pupils, carved oval-shaped head, flat wooden back and hips, nicely dressed, good condition

14" $8,500.00 – 10,000.00
Too few in database for a reliable range.

18" $12,000.00 – 15,900.00
Too few in database for a reliable range.

24" $19,000.00 – 25,000.00
Too few in database for a reliable range.

Georgian Period, 1750s – 1800, round wooden head, gesso coated, inset glass eyes, dotted eyelashes and eyebrows, human hair or flax wig, jointed wooden body, pointed torso, medium to fair condition

13" – 16" $3,500.00 – 4,800.00
18" – 24" $6,500.00 – 8,000.00

1800 – 1840, gesso-coated wooden head, painted eyes, human hair or flax wig, original clothing comes down below wooden legs

12" – 15" $1,800.00 – 2,200.00
18" – 22" $2,800.00 – 3,200.00

German

1810 – 1850s, delicately carved painted hair style, spit curls, some with hair decorations such as "tuck comb," all wooden head and body, pegged or ball-jointed limbs

4½"	$450.00 – 500.00
7"	$625.00 – 725.00
12" – 13"	$1,300.00 – 1,400.00
17" – 18"	$1,900.00 – 2,100.00

Ca. 1800 doll with ball and socket joints at shoulders, elbows, hips, knees, and waist, with provenance

32"	$38,720.00*

1850s – 1900, all wood with painted plain hair style; may have spit curls

1"	$100.00 – 125.00
4" – 5"	$100.00 – 125.00
6" – 8"	$150.00 – 250.00
14" – 17"	$400.00 – 550.00

7¼" German peg jointed wooden doll, carved painted "tuck comb" in hair, c.1830s. $700.00. *Courtesy of The Museum Doll Shop.*

Wooden shoulder head, fancy carved hair style, wood limbs, cloth body

12"	$375.00 – 500.00
16", man, carved hair	$1,000.00
23"	$775.00 – 900.00

Bohemian, with red painted torso

8" – 10"	$175.00 – 225.00
14" – 16"	$250.00 – 300.00

1900 on, turned wooden head, carved nose, painted hair, lower legs with black shoes, peg jointed

11"	$60.00 – 80.00

Bébé Tout en Bois, 1900 – 1914, all-wooden doll made by German firms such as Rudolf Schneider, Schilling and others. Made for the French trade, child or baby, fully jointed body, glass eyes or painted, open mouth

15"	$450.00 – 550.00
18"	$625.00 – 725.00
23"	$825.00 – 925.00

Kokeshi, 1900 on, Japan, traditional simple turned wooden dolls made for native and foreign tourist trade, values can be higher for unusual design or known artists.

11½" carved wooden, c. 1820. $1,200.00. *Courtesy of Skinner Inc., Boston and Bolton, Massachusetts.*

32" wooden doll ca. 1800 – 1810. Sold for $38,720.00 at auction. A Bru Jne stands next to her. *Courtesy Richard W. Withington, Inc., Nashua, New Hampshire.*

12" Bébé Tout en Bois, German for the French market, c. 1900. $350.00. *Courtesy of The Museum Doll Shop.*

1850s – 1900
7" – 14" $900.00 – 1,000.00
1900 – 1930
7" – 9" $200.00 – 400.00

1950 to present
7" – 9" $50.00 – 150.00
Matryoskia – Russian Nesting Dolls, 1900, set of wooden canisters that separate in the middle, brightly painted with a glossy finish to represent adults, children, storybook or fairytale characters, and animals. These come in sets usually of five or more related characters, the larger doll opening to reveal a smaller doll nesting inside, and so on. Values can be much higher for unusual designer or known artists.
Set pre 1930s
4" $70.00 – 100.00
7" $115.00 – 150.00
9" $175.00 – 230.00
Set new
5" $12.00 – 20.00
7" $18.00 – 30.00
Political set: Gorbachev, Yeltsin
5" $20.00 – 35.00
7" $50.00 – 60.00

A pair of Japanese Kokeshi dolls, c. 1960s. $80.00 pair. *Courtesy of The Museum Doll Shop.*

Matryoskia, Semenov style, late twentieth century. $12.00. *Courtesy of The
Museum Doll Shop.*

Swiss, 1900 on, carved wooden dolls with
dowel jointed bodies, joined at elbow,
hips, knees, some with elaborate hair

12"	$475.00 – 575.00
16"	$625.00 – 725.00

Springfield, Vermont, Woodens,
Cooperative Manufacturing Co., 1873
– 1874, Joel Ellis manufactured wooden
dolls with pressed heads and mortise and
double tennon joints, with metal hands
and feet painted black or blue, painted
black molded hair sometimes blond. Similar
type wooden dolls were made by Jointed
Doll Co. under patents by Martin, Sanders,
Johnson, Mason & Taylor, a variety of head
and jointing styles were used on these dolls

Ellis, Joel (Cooperative Manufacturing Co.)

12"	$1,000.00 – 1,400.00
15"	$1,600.00 – 2,000.00

Jointed Doll Co.

11½"	$800.00 – 900.00

Fortune Tellers, wooden half or full doll
with folded papers with fortunes printed
on them making up the skirt

18"	$2,600.00 – 3,500.00

Too few in database for a reliable range.

Schoenhut: See that section.

11" Swiss wooden doll. $450.00. *Courtesy of
The Museum Doll Shop.*

15" wooden doll made by
Cooperative Manufacturing Co.,
designed by Joel Ellis. $1,600.00.
Courtesy of The Museum Doll Shop.

ROBIN WOODS

1980s on. Creative designer for various companies, including Le Petit Ami, Robin Woods Company, Madame Alexander (Alice Darling), Horsman, and Playtime Productions.

Price indicates mint complete doll; anything else would bring a lesser price.

Early Cloth Dolls, price depends on how well painted and quality of clothing and construction. The quality varies greatly in these early cloth dolls.

Children, very rare

Betsy Bluebonnet	$200.00 – 250.00
Enchanted Baby	$250.00 – 300.00
Jane	$250.00 – 300.00
Jessica	$200.00 – 250.00
Laura	$200.00 – 250.00

Children, rare, Mollie, Rachel, Rueben, Stevie $200.00 – 225.00

Children, common, City Child, Elizabeth, Mary Margaret, How Do I Love Thee
$35.00 – 50.00

Clowns, very rare, Aladdin, Sinbad, Wynter, Yankee Doodle $250.00 – 300.00

Clowns, rare, Cinamette, Happy Holiday, Kubla $200.00 – 250.00

Clowns, common, Bon Bon
$100.00 – 150.00

1986, Childhood Classics

Larissa
14" $35.00 – 45.00

1987

Catherine
14" $50.00 – 75.00

Christmas dolls, Nicholas & Noel, pair
14" $150.00 – 200.00

1988

Dickens
14" $75.00 – 125.00

Kristina Kringle
14" $75.00 – 125.00

Scarlett Sweetheart
14" $50.00 – 75.00

1989

Anne of Green Gables
14" $50.00 – 75.00

Heidi, red, white, blue
14" $75.00 – 150.00

Heidi, brown outfit
14" $50.00 – 75.00

Hope
14" $50.00 – 100.00

Lorna Doone
14" $25.00 – 50.00

Mary of Secret Garden
14" $75.00 – 100.00

Scarlett Christmas
14" $100.00 – 125.00

William Noel
14" $50.00 – 75.00

1990, Camelot Castle Collection

Bobbi
16" $35.00 – 50.00

Kyleigh Christmas
14" $50.00 – 75.00

Lady Linet
14" $25.00 – 35.00

Lady of the Lake
14" $100.00 – 150.00

Marjorie
14" $35.00 – 50.00

Meaghan (special)
14" $100.00 – 150.00

Melanie, Phebe
14" $35.00 – 50.00

Tessa at the Circus
14" $50.00 – 75.00

Tess of the D'urbervilles
14" $100.00 – 150.00

1991 Shades of Day collection

5,000 pieces each, Dawn, Glory, Stormy,

Joy, Sunny, Veil, Serenity, each
    14" $35.00 – 50.00
Others
Alice in Wonderland
    24" $50.00 – 75.00
Bette Jack
    14" $35.00 – 50.00
Bouquet, Lily
    14" $35.00 – 50.00
Delores
    14" $75.00 – 100.00
Eliza Doolittle
    14" $50.00 – 75.00
Mistress Mary
    8" $35.00 – 50.00
Miss Muffet
    14" $35.00 – 50.00
Princess & Pea
    15" $75.00 – 100.00
Rose, Violet
    14" $35.00 – 50.00
Rosemary
    14" $35.00 – 50.00
Sleeping Beauty Set
    8" $100.00 – 150.00
Tennison
    14" $35.00 – 50.00
Victoria
    14" $35.00 – 50.00
Robin Woods Limited Editions
Merri, 1991 Doll Convention Disney World, Christmas Tree doll, doll becomes the tree
    14" $100.00 – 150.00
Mindy, Made for Disney's Robin Wood's Day, limited to 300
    14" $75.00 – 125.00
Rainey, 1991 Robin Woods Club
    14" $35.00 – 60.00
J.C. Penney Limited Editions
Angelina, 1990 Christmas angel
    14" $100.00 – 150.00

Noelle, Christmas angel
    14" $100.00 – 150.00
Julianna, 1991, little girl holiday shopper
    14" $95.00 – 125.00
Robin Woods Exclusives
Gina, The Earthquake Doll, The Doll Place, Ann Parsons of Burlingame, CA
    14" $100.00 – 150.00

WORSTED DOLLS

1878 – 1900s, Emil Wittzack of Gotha, Thuringia, Germany. Woolen crib dolls with needle-sculpted features, bead eyes, chenille embroidered designs on bodies, some had bells sewn on them.
    7" – 10" $100.00 – 125.00
    15" – 18" $150.00 – 200.00

A pair of 8" worsted clown dolls. $115.00 each.
Courtesy of The Museum Doll Shop.

WPA, MILWAUKEE

1935 – 1943, Milwaukee, Wisconsin. Works Progress Administration project to provide work for artisans and home workers. Other states also ran doll making projects under the WPA.

Molded stockinette doll, cloth body, cotton yarn hair, painted features, tab hinged joint and hips

22"	$1,000.00 – 1,100.00
Black	$1,200.00 – 1,400.00

Flat face cloth doll, embroidered features, cotton yarn hair

11"	$450.00 – 475.00
14"	$500.00 – 550.00
16"	$650.00 – 750.00

22" Milwaukee WPA doll with molded stockinette face. $1,000.00.
Courtesy of The Museum Doll Shop.

16" pair of flat faced WPA cloth dolls. $650.00 each.
Courtesy of The Museum Doll Shop.

BIBLIOGRAPHY

Anderton, Johana Gast. *20th Century Dolls*. Des Moines, Iowa: Wallace Homestead Book Co., 1971.

_____. *More 20th Century Dolls, Vol. I & II*. Des Moines, Iowa: Wallace Homestead Book Co., 1974.

_____. *The Collector's Encyclopedia of Cloth Dolls*. Lombard: Wallace Homestead Book Co., 1984.

Angione, Genevieve, and Judith Whorton. *All Dolls Are Collectible*. New York, New York: Crown Publishers, Inc, 1977.

Bullard, Helen. *Crafts and Craftsmen of the Tennessee Mountains*. Falls Church, Virginia: The Summit Press Ltd., 1976.

_____. *The American Doll Artist*. Boston, Massachusetts: The Charles T. Branford Co., 1965.

_____.*The American Doll Artist*. Kansas City: Athens Publishing Co., 1975.

Cieslik, Jurgen and Marianne. *German Doll Encyclopedia*. Cumberland, Maryland: Hobby House Press, 1985.

Coleman, Dorothy S., Elizabeth A., Evelyn J. *The Collector's Encyclopedia of Dolls Vol. I & II*. New York, New York: Crown Publishers, Inc., 1968 & 1986.

_____. *The Collector's Book of Dolls' Clothes*. New York, New York: Crown Publishers, Inc., 1975.

DeMillar, Suzanne, and Dennis Brevik. *Arranbee Dolls*. Paducah, Kentucky: Collector Books, 2004.

Edward, Linda. *Cloth Dolls from Ancient to Modern*. Atglen, Pennsylvania: Schiffer Publishing, 1997.

Fawcett, Clara Hallard. *Dolls A Guide For Collectors*. New York, New York: H L Lindquist Publications, 1947.

_____. *Dolls A New Guide For Collectors*. Boston, Massachusetts: Charles T. Branford Co., 1964.

Foulke, Jan. T*he Blue Book of Dolls and Values Vol.. 2 through 14*. Cumberland, Maryland: Hobby House Press, 1976, 1978, 1980, 1982, 1984, 1986, 1987, 1989, 1991, 1993, 1995, 1997, 1999.

Grafnitz, Christiane. *German Paper-Mache Dolls 1760 – 1860*. Germany: Verlag Puppen & Spielzeug 1994.

Izen, Judith. *American Character Dolls*. Paducah, Kentucky: Collector Books, 2004.

_____. *Collector's Guide to Ideal Dolls*. Paducah, Kentucky: Collector Books, 2005.

Izen, Judith, and Carol Stover. *Collector's Encyclopedia of Vogue Dolls*. Paducah, Kentucky: Collector Books, 2005.

Jacobs, Flora Gill. *Dolls' Houses in America*. New York: Charles Scribner's Sons, 1974.

_____. *A History of Dolls' Houses*. New York: Charles Scribner's Sons, 1953.

Jensen, Don. *Collector's Guide to Horsman Dolls*. Paducah, Kentucky: Collector Books, 2002.

Johl, Janet Pagter. *The Fascinating Story of Dolls*. Watkins Glen: reissued Century House, 1970.

_____. *More About Dolls*. New York: H. L. Lundquist Publications, 1946.

_____. *Still More About Dolls*. New York: H. L. Lundquist Publications, 1950.

_____. *Your Dolls and Mine*. New York: H. L. Lundquist Publications, 1952.

Judd, Polly. *Cloth Dolls*. Cumberland: Hobby House Press,1990.

Judd, Pam and Polly. *Americas, Australia & Pacific Islands Costumed Dolls*. Grantsville: Hobby House Press, 1997.

King, Constance Eileen. *The Collector's History of Dolls*. New York: Bonanza Books, 1981.

Lavitt, Wendy. *American Folk Dolls*. New York: Alfred A. Knopf, Inc., 1982.

McFadden, Sybill. *Fawn Zeller's Porcelain Dollmaking Techniques*. Cumberland, Maryland: Hobby House Press, 1984.

McGonagle, Dorothy. *A Celebration of American Dolls*. Grantsville: Hobby House Press, 1997.

Merrill, Madeline O., and Nellie O. Perkins. *Handbook of Collectible Dolls Vol. I*. 1969.

Merrill, Madeline Osborne. *The Art of Dolls*. Cumberland, Maryland: Hobby House Press, 1985.

Mertz, Ursula. *Collector's Encyclopedia of Composition Dolls*. Paducah, Kentucky: Collector Books, 1999.

_____. *Collector's Encyclopedia of Composition Dolls Vol. II*. Paducah, Kentucky: Collector Books, 2004.

Mills, Winifred, and Louise Dunn. *The Story of Old Dolls and How to Make New Ones*. New York: Doubleday, Doran & Co., Inc., 1940.

Patino, Estelle. *American Rag Dolls*. Paducah, Kentucky: Collector Books, 1988.

Pardee, Elaine, and Jackie Robertson. *Encyclopedia of Bisque Nancy Ann Storybook Dolls*. Paducah, Kentucky: Collector Books, 2003.

Robertson, Julie Pelletier. *Celluloid Dolls, Toys & Playthings*. Paducah, Kentucky: Collector Books, 2006.

Revi, Albert Christian. *Spinning Wheel's Complete Book of Dolls*. New York, New York: Galahad Books, 1975.

Richter, Lydia. *Treasury of German Dolls*. Tucson: HP Books, 1984.

_____. *The Beloved Kathe Kruse Dolls*. Cumberland, Maryland: Hobby House Press, 1983.

Schiffer, Nancy. *Indian Dolls*. Atglen: Schiffer Publishing Ltd., 1997.

Singleton, Esther. *Dolls.* New York: Payson & Clark Ltd., 1927.

St. George, Eleanor. *The Dolls of Yesterday.* New York and London: Charles Scribner's Sons, 1948.

_____. *Dolls of Three Centuries.* New York and London: Charles Scribner's Sons, 1951.

Smith, Patricia. *Antique Collector's Dolls Vol. 2.* Paducah, Kentucky: Collector Books, 1976.

Sorensen, Lewis. *Lewis Sorensen's Doll Scrapbook.* Alhambra: Thor Publications, 1976.

Sutton, Sydney Ann. *Scouting Dolls Through the Years.* Paducah, Kentucky: Collector Books, 2003.

Theiriault, Florence. *Catalog Reprint Series.* Annapolis: Gold Horse Publishing, 1998.

Trotter, Gillian. *Norah Wellings Cloth Dolls and Soft Toys.* Grantsville: Hobby House Press, 2003.

Van Patten, Joan, and Linda Lau. *Nippon Dolls & Playthings.* Paducah, Kentucky: Collector Books, 2001.

Whitton, Blair. *Bliss Toys and Dollhouses.* New York: Dover Publications.

COLLECTORS' NETWORK

Alexander Doll Company
The Review
PO Box 330
Mundelein, IL 60060-0330
847-949-9200
fax: 847-949-9201
www.madc.org
Official publication of the Madame Alexander Doll Club, quarterly, plus two "Shoppers," $20.00 per year.

American Character
Tressy
Debby Davis, Collector/Dealer
3905 N. 15th St.
Milwaukee, WI 53206

Antique Dolls
Barbara DeFeo, Appraisals, Shows
Antique Dolls
PO Box 662
Bonita, CA 91908
e-mail: janara@pacbell.net

Linda Kellermann
11013 Treyburn Drive
Glen Allen, VA 23059
e-mail: lindas-antiques@erols.com

Antique and Modern Dolls
Rosalie Whyel Museum of Doll Art
1116 108th Avenue N.E.
Bellevue, WA 98004
206-455-1116
fax: 206-455-4793

Turn of the Century Antiques
1475 South Broadway
Denver, CO 80210
303-702-8700
www.turnofthecenturyantiques.com

The Museum Doll Shop
Newport, Rhode Island
www.dollmuseum.com

Auction Houses
Call or write for a list of upcoming auctions, or if you need information about selling a collection.
Alderfer Auction Company, Inc.
501 Fairgrounds Rd.
Hatfield,PA 19440
215-393-3000
fax: 215-368-9055
www.alderferauction.com

McMasters/Harris Doll Auctions
PO Box 1755
Cambridge, OH 43725
800-842-3526 or
740-432-4419
fax: 740-432-3191

Skinner Inc.
357 Main St.
Bolton, MA 01740
978-779-6241

Theriaults
PO Box 151
Annapolis, MD 21404
800-638-0422
www.theriaults.com

Richard Withington, Inc.
590 Center Rd.
Hillsboro, NH 03244
603-464-3232

Barbie Dolls, Mattel
Dream Dolls Galleries & More
Collector/Dealer
5700 Okeechobee Blvd. #20
West Palm Beach, FL 33417
e-mail: dollnmore@aol.com

Jaci Jueden, Collector/Dealer
575 Galice Rd.
Merlin, OR 97532
e-mail: jacidj@yahoo.com

Steven Pim, Collector/Dealer
3535 17th St.
San Francisco, CA 94110

Betsy McCall
Betsy's Fan Club
Marci Van Ausdall, Editor
PO Box 946
Quincy, CA 95971
Quarterly, $15.50 per year

Celebrity Dolls
Celebrity Doll Journal
Loraine Burdick, Editor
413 10th Ave. Ct. NE
Puyallup, WA 98372
Quarterly, $10.00 per year

Chatty Cathy, Mattel
Chatty Cathy Collector's Club
Lisa Eisenstein, Editor
PO Box 140
Readington, NJ 08870-0140
Quarterly newsletter, $28.00
e-mail: Chatty@eclipse.net

Composition and Travel Dolls
Effanbee's Patsy Family
Patsy & Friends Newsletter
PO Box 311

Deming, NM 88031
e-mail: moddoll@yahoo.com
Bi-monthly, $20.00 per year

Contemporary Doll Collector
Scott Publications
30595 Eight Mile
Livonia, MI 48152-1798
Subscription: 800-458-8237

Costuming
Doll Costumer's Guild
Patricia Gosh and Janet Hollingsworth, editors
5042 Wilshire Blvd
PMB573
Los Angeles, CA 90036
323-939-1482
fax: 323-939-3696
e-mail: patgosh@aol.com
Jhollwith@pacbell.net
Quarterly, $24.00
2 years, $44.00

French Fashion Gazette
Adele Leurquin, Editor
1862 Sequoia SE
Port Orchard, WA 98366

Deluxe Reading
Penny Brite
Dealer/Collector
Carole Fisher
RD 2, Box 301
Palmyra, PA 17078-9738
e-mail: rcfisher@voicenet.com

Dionne Quintuplets
Quint News
Jimmy and Fay Rodolfos, Editors
PO Box 2527
Woburn, MA 01888

Connie Lee Martin
Collector/Dealer
4018 East 17th St.
Tucson, AZ, 85711

Doll Artists
Jamie G. Anderson
10990 Greenlefe, P.O. Box 806
Rolla, MO 65402
573-364-7347
e-mail: jastudio@rollanet.org

Betsy Baker
81 Hy-Vue Terrace
Cold Spring, NY 10516

Cynthia Barron
7796 W. Port Madison
Bainbridge Island, WA 98110
206-780-9003

Charles Batte
272 Divisadero St. #4
San Francisco, CA 94117
415-252-7440

Atelier Bets van Boxel
De Poppenstee
't Vaartje 14
5165 NB Waspik, Holland
www.poppenstee.nl
e-mail: bets@poppenstee.nl

Cheryl Bollenbach
P.O. Box 740922
Arvada, CO 80006-0922
303-216-2424
e-mail: cdboll@aol.com

Laura Clark
P.O. Box 596
Mesilla, NM 88046

Ankie Daanen Doll-Art
Anton Mauvestraat 1
2102 BA HEEMSTEDE NL
023-5477980
fax: 023-5477981

Marleen Engeler
m'laine dolls
Noordeinde 67 1141 AH
Monnickendam
The Netherlands
31-299656814
e-mail: mlwent4.2@globalxs.nl

Judith & Lucia Friedericy
Friedericy Dolls
1260 Wesley Avenue
Pasadena, CA 91104
626-296-0065
e-mail: friedericy@aol.com

Originals by Goldie
8517 Edgeworth Drive
Capitol Heights, MD 20743
301-350-4119

Karen Hendrix
Santee, CA
e-mail: santeebird@cox.net

Lillian Hopkins
2315 29th Street
Santa Monica, CA 90405
310-396-3266
e-mail: lilyart@compuserve.com

Marylynn Huston
101 Mountain View Drive
Pflugerville, TX 78660
512-252-1192

Joyce Patterson
FabricImages
P.O. Box 1599
Brazoria, TX 77422
409-798-9890
e-mail: clothdol@tgn.net

W. Harry Perzyk
2860 Chiplay St.
Sacramento, CA 95826

Daryl Poole
450 Pioneer Trail
Dripping Springs, TX 78620
512-858-7181
e-mail: eltummo@aol.com

The Enchantment Peddler
Nellie Lamers
HC6 Box 0
Reeds Spring, MO 65737
417-272-3768

Peggy Ann Ridley
17 Ribon Road
Lisbon, ME 04250
207-353-8827

Anne Sanregret
22910 Estorial Drive, #6
Diamond Bar, CA 91765
909-860-8007

Sandy Simonds
334 Woodhurst Drive
Coppell, TX 75019
512-219-8759

Linda Lee Sutton Originals
P.O. Box 3725
Central Point, OR 97502
541-830-8384

lindaleesutton.com
e-mail: linda@lindaleesutton.com

Doll Manufacturers
Alexander Doll Company, Inc.
Gale Jarvis
Chairman & CEO
615 West 131st Street
New York, NY 10027
212-283-5900
fax: 212-283-6042

American Girl
8400 Fairway Place
P.O. Box 620190-0190
Middleton, WI 53562-0190
800-845-0005
www.americangirl.com

Collectible Concepts
Ivonne Heather, President
945 Hickory Run Land
Great Falls, VA 22066
703-821-0607
fax: 703-759-0408
e-mail: invonnehccc@aol.com

Susan Wakeen Doll Co., Inc.
P.O. Box 1321
Litchfield, CT 06759
860-567-0007
fax: 908-788-1955
e-mail: pkaverud@blast.net

Robert Tonner Doll Company
459 Hurley Avenue
Hurley, NY 12443
9 a.m. to 5 p.m. EST
845-339-9537
fax: 845-339-1259
e-mail:
customerservice@tonnerdoll.com

www.tonnerdoll.com
Vogue Doll Company
P.O. Box 756
Oakdale, CA 95361-0756
209-848-0300
fax: 209-848-4423
www.voguedolls.com

Doll Repairs
Doll Doc. Associates
1406 Sycamore Road
Montoursville, PA 17754
717-323-9604

Fresno Doll Hospital
1512N. College
Fresno, CA 93728
209-266-1108

Kandyland Dolls
PO Box 146
Grande Ronde, OR 97347
503-879-5153

Life's Little Treasures
PO Box 585
Winston OR 97496
541-679-3472

Oleta's Doll Hospital
1413 Seville Way
Modesto, CA 95355
209-523-6669

Gene
Ashton Drake Galleries
9200 N. Maryland Ave.
Niles, IL 60714-9853
888-For-Gene

Ginny
Ginny Journal
Suzanne Smith, Editor
P.O. Box 338

Oakdale, CA 95361-0338
877-848-0300 (toll free)
www.voguedolls.com
$15.00 dues

Girl Scouts
Girl Scout Doll Collector's Patch
Pidd Miller
PO Box 631092
Houston, TX, 77263

Diane Miller, Collector
13151 Roberta Place
Garden Grove, CA 92643

Ann Sutton, Collector/Dealer
2555 Prine Road
Lakeland, FL 33810-5703
e-mail: Sydneys@aol.com

Hasbro – Jem Dolls
Linda E. Holton, Collector/Dealer
P.O. Box 6753
San Rafael, CA 94903

Hitty
Friends of Hitty Newsletter
Virginia Ann Heyerdahl, Editor
2704 Belleview Ave
Cheverly, MD 20785
Quarterly, $18.00 per year

Hitty Artists
Judy Brown
506 N. Brighton Ct.
Sterling, VA 20164
703-450-0206

Ruth Brown
1606 SW Heather Dr.
Grants Pass, OR 97526

DeAnn Cote
5555 - 22nd Avenue South
Seattle, WA 98108-2912
206-763-1871
e-mail: DRCDesigne@aol.com

David R. Greene
255 Plainview Circle
North Little Rock, AR 72116
e-mail: greendesg@cs.com

Patti Hale
2301 Aazure Lane
Vista, CA 92083

JANCI
Nancy Elliott & Jill Sanders
2442 Hathaway Court
Muskegon, MI 49441
e-mail: janci@gte.net

Lotz Studio
Jean Lotz
P.O. Box 1308
Lacome, LA 70445
e-mail: lotz@gs.verio.net

Ideal
Ideal Collectors' Newsletter
Judith Izen, Editor
PO Box 623
Lexington, MA 02173
e-mail: Jizen@aol.com
Quarterly, $20.00 per year

Internet
eBay auction site
www.ebay.com

About.com Doll Collecting
Denise Von Patten
collectdolls.about.com
e-mail: denise@dollymaker.com

Internet Lists & Chat Rooms
AG Collector
For American Girl, Heidi Ott,
and other 18" play dolls, no selling,
just talk.
e-mail: ag-collector request@lists.best.
com

Barbie chat
e-mail: Fashion@ga.unc.edu

Doll Chat List
Friendly collectors talk dolls, no flaming
permitted, a great group.
E-mail is forwarded to your address
from host, no fees, to subscribe:
DollChatRequest @nbi.com then type
"subscribe" in body of message

Dolls n Stuff
e-mail: dollsnstuff @home.ease.lsoft.com

Sasha
e-mail: sasha-1-Subscribe@
makelist.com

Shirley Temple
e-mail: shirleycollect
subscribe@makelist.com

Preservation
Twin Pines
www.twinpines.com

Publications
Antique Doll Collector
6 Woodside Avenue, Suite 300
Northport, NY 11768

Collectors United
711S. 3rd Ave.
Chatsworth, GA 30705

706-695-8242
fax: 706-895-0770
e-mail: collun@Alltel.net

Contemporary Doll Collector
Scott Publications
30595 Eight Mile
Livonia, MI 48152-1798
800-458-8237

Doll Reader
Cumberland Publishing, Inc.
6405 Flank Dr.
Harrisburg, PA 17112
Subscriptions: 800-829-3340
e-mail: dollreader@palmcoastd.com

Dolls
170 Fifth Ave., 12th Fl.
New York, NY 1010
212-989-8700
fax: 212-645-8976
e-mail: snowy@lsol.net

Patsy & Friends Newsletter
P.O. Box 311
Deming, NM 88031
e-mail: sctrading@zianet.com

Klumpe Dolls
Sondra Gast, Collector/Dealer
PO Box 252
Spring Valley, CA 91976
fax: 619-444-4215
e-mail: klumpe@cox.net

Lawton, Wendy
Lawton Collectors Guild
PO Box 969
Turlock, CA 95381

Toni Winder, Collector/Dealer
1484 N. Vagedes
Fresno CA 93728
e-mail: TTUK77B@prodigy.com

Liddle Kiddles
For a signed copy of her book,
Liddle Kiddles. $22.95 post pd. Write:
Paris Langford
415 Dodge Ave
Jefferson, LA 70127
504-733-0676

Modern Doll Convention
Ruth Leif, president
22047 Timber Cove Road
Cazadero, CA 95421
e-mail: ruthstoys@aol.com

Museums
Arizona
Arizona Doll and Toy Museum
602 E Adams Street, Phoenix, AZ
Hours: Tue – Sat 10 – 4; Sun: 12 – 4.
www.artcom.com/museums/nv/af/
85004-23.htm

Colorado
Denver Museum of Miniatures, Dolls &
Toys
1880 Gaylord St.
Denver, CO 80206
303-322-1053
Hours: Tues. – Sat. 10 – 4; Sun.: 12 – 4
Closed Mondays and holidays.
www.coloradokids.com/miniatures/

Louisiana
The Enchanted Mansion, A Doll Museum
190 Lee Drive
Baton Rouge, LA 70808

225-769-0005
Hours: Mon., Wed. – Sat. 10 – 5. Closed Sun. and Tues.

The Lois Loftin Doll Museum
120 South Washington Avenue
DeRidder, LA 70634
Hours: Tues. – Sat. 10 – 4
www.beau.lib.la.us/doll.html

New Mexico
Land of Enchantment Doll Museum
5201 Constitution Ave.
Albuquerque, NM 87110-5813
505-821-8558
fax: 505-255-1259

New York
Museum of the City of New York
1220 Fifth Avenue @ 103rd St.
New York, NY 10029
212-534-1672
Hours: Open daily.
www.mcny.org/toy.htm

Margaret Woodbury Strong Museum
1 Manhattan Square
Rochester, NY 14607
716-263-2700

Ohio
Doll & Toy Museum
700 Winchester Pike
Canal Winchester, Ohio
Hours: Wed. – Sat. 11– 5
April – mid Dec.
home.att.net/~dollmuseum
614-837-5573

The Children's Toy & Doll Museum:
206 Gilman Street P.O. Box 4034
Marietta, OH 4575

740-373-5900
Hours: Sat. 1 – 4, May – Dec.
www.tourohio.com/TOYDOLL/

South Dakota
Enchanted World Doll Museum
615 North Main
Mitchell, SD 57301
606-996-9896
fax: 606-996-0210

Texas
Museum of American Architecture & Decorative Arts
7502 Fronden Rd
Houston, Texas 77074-3298
281-649-3811

Utah
McCurdy Historical Doll Museum
246 North 100 East
Provo, UT 84606
801-377-9935
Hours: Tues. – Sat., 12 – 6,
winter: 1 – 5

Vermont
Shelburne Museum
U.S. Route 7, P.O. Box 10
Shelburne, Vermont 05482
802-985-3346
Hours: Summer: 10 – 5 daily
www.shelburnemuseum.org

Washington
Rosalie Whyel Museum of Doll Art
1116 108th Avenue N.E.
Bellevue, WA 98004
206-455-1116
fax: 206-455-4793
www.dollart.com

Wisconsin
La Crosse Doll Museum
1213 Caledonia Street
La Crosse, WI 54603
Hours: Mon. – Sat., 10 – 5,
Sun. 11– 4
www.dollmuseum.org/
608-785-0020

The Fennimore Doll & Toy Museum and
Gift Shoppe
140 Lincoln Ave.
Fennimore, WI 53809
608-822-4100
Hours: May 7 – Dec. 14,
Mon. – Sat. 10 – 4
www.fennimore.com/dolltoy/

NADDA
National Antique Doll Dealers
Association
www.nadda.org

Nancy Ann Storybook
Elaine Pardee, Collector/Dealer
3613 Merano Way
Antelope, CA 95843
916-725-7227
fax: 916-725-7447
e-mail: epardee@jps.net

Oriental Dolls
Ninsyo Journal - Jade
Japanese American Doll Enthusiasts
406 Koser Ave
Iowa City, IA 52246
e-mail: Vickyd@jadejapandolls.com

Raggedy Ann
Rags Newsletter
Barbara Barth, Editor
PO Box 823
Atlanta, GA 30301
Quarterly $16.00

Robert Tonner Doll Club
Robert Tonner Doll Company
459 Hurley Avenue
Hurley, NY 12443
e-mail:
collectorclub@tonnerdoll.com

Roldan Dolls
Sondra Gast, Collector/Dealer
PO Box 252
Spring Valley, CA 91976
fax: 619-444-4215
e-mail: klumpe@cox.net

Sandra Sue Dolls, Richwood Toys Inc.
Peggy Millhouse, Collector/Dealer
510 Green Hill Road
Conestoga, PA 17516
e-mail: peggyin717@aol.com

Sasha Dolls
Friends of Sasha
Quarterly Newsletter
Dorisanne Osborn, Editor
Box 187
Keuka Park, NY 14478

Shirley Temple
Australian Shirley Temple Collectors News
Quarterly Newsletter
Victoria Horne, Editor
39 How Ave.
North Dandenong
Victoria, 3175, Australia
$25.00 U.S.

Lollipop News
Shirley Temple Collectors by the Sea
PO Box 6203
Oxnard, CA 93031
Membership dues: $14.00 year

Shirley Temple Collectors News
Rita Dubas, Editor
881 Colonial Road
Brooklyn NY 11209
Quarterly, $20.00 year
www.ritadubasdesign.com/shirley/
e-mail: bukowski@wazoo.com

Terri Lee
Daisy Chain Newsletter
Terry Bukowski, Editor
3010 Sunland Dr.
Alamogordo, NM 88310
$20.00 per year, quarterly

Ann Sutton, Collector/Dealer
2555 Prine Road
Lakeland, FL 33810-5703
e-mail: Sydneys@aol.com

Betty J. Woten, Collector
12 Big Bend Cut Off
Cloudcroft, NM 88317-9411

Videos
Leonard A. Swann, Jr.
SIROCCO Productions, Inc.
5660 E. Virgina Beach Blvd., Suite 105
Norfolk, VA 23502
757-461-8987
www.siroccovideo.com
e-mail: iswann@specialtyproducts.net

Vogue
Vogue Doll Co.
PO Box 756
Oakdale, CA 95361-0756
209-848-0300
fax: 209-848-4423
www.voguedolls.com/
e-mail: info@voguecolls.com

United Federation of Doll Clubs, Inc.
10900 North Pomona Avenue
Kansas City, MO 64153
816-891-7040
fax 816-891-8360
www.ufdc.org/about.html
e-mail: ufdcinfo@ufdc.org

Woods, Robin
Toni Winder, Collector/Dealer
1484 N. Vagedes
Fresno, CA 93728

LETTER INDEX

MOLD INDEX

22	Recknagel		100	Schuetzmeister & Quendt
23	Recknagel		101	Kämmer & Reinhardt
28	Kuhnlenz		101	Schoenhut
28	Recknagel		102	Unknown
31	Kuhnlenz		102	Kämmer & Reinhardt
31	Recknagel		102	Schoenhut
32	Kuhnlenz		102	Schuetzmeister & Quendt
32	Recknagel		103	Kämmer & Reinhardt
34	Kuhnlenz		103	Kestner
34.14	Kuhnlenz		103	Schoenhut
34.16	Kuhnlenz		104	Kämmer & Reinhardt
34.24	Kuhnlenz		104	Schoenhut
38	Kuhnlenz		105	Kämmer & Reinhardt
41	Kuhnlenz		105	Schoenhut
44	Kuhnlenz		106	Kämmer & Reinhardt
44	Recknagel		106	Schoenhut
45	Recknagel		107	Kämmer & Reinhardt
60	Unis France		107	Schoenhut
60	SFBJ		107W	Schoenhut
69	H. Handwerck		108	Kämmer & Reinhardt
71	SFBJ		108	Schoenhut
79	H. Handwerck		108W	Schoenhut
81	H. Alexandre		109	H. Handwerck
83/100	Unknown		109	Kämmer & Reinhardt
83/125	Unknown		109W	Schoenhut
83/150	Unknown		110	Wislizenus
83/225	Unknown		110W	Schoenhut
85	H. Alexandre		111	Unknown
88	H. Alexandre		112	Kämmer & Reinhardt
89	H. Handwerck		112X	Kämmer & Reinhardt
90	H. Alexandre		114	Kämmer & Reinhardt
91	H. Alexandre		115	Kämmer & Reinhardt
95	H. Alexandre		115a	Kämmer & Reinhardt
98	Koenig & Wernicke		116	Belton
99	H. Handwerck		116	Kämmer & Reinhardt
99	Koenig & Wernicke		116a	Kämmer & Reinhardt
100	Unknown		116a	Kämmer & Reinhardt
100	Belton		117	Belton
100	Kämmer & Reinhardt		117	Kämmer & Reinhardt
100	Schoenhut		117A	Kämmer & Reinhardt

117N	Kämmer & Reinhardt		137	Recknagel
117X	Kämmer & Reinhardt		138	Recknagel
118	Kämmer & Reinhardt		138	Kley & Hahn
118A	Kämmer & Reinhardt		139	H. Handwerck
119	H. Handwerck		140	Hertel Schwab
119	Kämmer & Reinhardt		141	Hertel Schwab
120	Belton		142	Hertel Schwab
120	Goebel		142	Kestner
121	Kämmer & Reinhardt		143	Kestner
121	Recknagel		144	Kestner
122	Kämmer & Reinhardt		145	Kestner
123	Kämmer & Reinhardt		146	Kestner
123	Kling		147	Kestner
124	Kämmer & Reinhardt		148	Kestner
124	Kling		149	Hertel Schwab
125	Belton		149	Kestner
126	Kämmer & Reinhardt		150	Bonn or Kestner
126	Recknagel		150	Arnold, Max Oscar
127	Belton		150	Hertel Schwab
127	Hertel Schwab		150	Ohlhaver
127	Kämmer & Reinhardt		150	Simon & Halbig
127N	Kämmer & Reinhardt		151	Hertel Schwab
128	Unknown		151	Simon & Halbig
128	Kämmer & Reinhardt		152	Hertel Schwab
128	Kestner		153	Simon & Halbig
128	H. Steiner		154	Belton
129	Kestner		154	Hertel Schwab
130	Bonn or Kestner		154	Kestner
130	Hertel Schwab		154	Kley & Hahn
131	Kämmer & Reinhardt		155	Unknown
131	Hertel Schwab		155	Kestner
131	Kling		156	Unknown
133	H. Steiner		156	A. Hülss
133	Kley & Hahn		158	Kley & Hahn
134	Hertel Schwab		159	Hertel Schwab
135	Kämmer & Reinhardt		160	A. Heller
135	Kley & Hahn		160	Kestner
135	Kling		160	Kley & Hahn
136	Unknown		161	Kestner
136	Hertel Schwab		161	Kley & Hahn
137	Unknown		162	Kestner
137	Belton		162	Kley & Hahn

540	Simon & Halbig		701	A. Marseille
546	Kley & Hahn		701	Kämmer & Reinhardt
549	Kley & Hahn		711	A. Marseille
550	A. Marseille		715	Kämmer & Reinhardt
550	Simon & Halbig		717	Kämmer & Reinhardt
554	Kley & Hahn		719	Simon & Halbig
560	A. Marseille		720	Simon & Halbig
562	A. Marseille		728	Kämmer & Reinhardt
567	Kley & Hahn		729	Simon & Halbig
568	Kley & Hahn		739	Simon & Halbig
570	A. Marseille		740	Simon & Halbig
570	Simon & Halbig		749	Simon & Halbig
571	Kley & Hahn		750	A. Marseille
585	Bähr & Pröschild		758	Simon & Halbig
586	Bähr & Pröschild		759	Simon & Halbig
587	Bähr & Pröschild		769	Simon & Halbig
590	A. Marseille		775	Kämmer & Reinhardt
600	Marottes		778	Kämmer & Reinhardt
600	A. Marseille		784	Alt, Beck & Gottschalck
600	Simon & Halbig		790	Bonn or Kestner
602	Bonn or Kestner		790	A. Marseille
602	Bähr & Pröschild		791	Bonn or Kestner
604	Bähr & Pröschild		792	Bonn or Kestner
612	Bergmann		800	A. Marseille
619	Bähr & Pröschild		830	Unknown
620	Bähr & Pröschild		833	Unknown
620	A. Marseille		852	Simon & Halbig
624	Bähr & Pröschild		870	Alt, Beck & Gottschalck
630	Alt, Beck & Gottschalck		880	Alt, Beck & Gottschalck
630	Bähr & Pröschild		881	Simon & Halbig
630	A. Marseille		886	Simon & Halbig
639	Alt, Beck & Gottschalck		890	Simon & Halbig
639	Simon & Halbig		890	Alt, Beck & Gottschalck
640	A. Marseille		900	A. Marseille
641	Bähr & Pröschild		905	Simon & Halbig
642	Bähr & Pröschild		908	Simon & Halbig
678	Bähr & Pröschild		911	Alt, Beck & Gottschalck
680	Kley & Hahn		912	Alt, Beck & Gottschalck
686	Bähr & Pröschild		914	Schoenau & Hoffmeister
698	Alt, Beck & Gottschalck		915	Alt, Beck & Gottschalck
700	A. Marseille		916	Alt, Beck & Gottschalck
700	Kämmer & Reinhardt		919	Simon & Halbig

927	A. Marseille	1040	Simon & Halbig
927	F. Schmidt	1044	Alt, Beck & Gottschalck
927	Simon & Halbig	1046	Alt, Beck & Gottschalck
929	Simon & Halbig	1049	Simon & Halbig
938	Alt, Beck & Gottschalck	1059	Simon & Halbig
939	Simon & Halbig	1064	Alt, Beck & Gottschalck
940	Simon & Halbig	1069	Simon & Halbig
949	Simon & Halbig	1070	Koenig & Wernicke
950	P.M.	1070	Kestner
950	Simon & Halbig	1078	Simon & Halbig
966	A. Marseille	1079	Simon & Halbig
969	Simon & Halbig	1080	Simon & Halbig
970	A. Marseille	1099	Simon & Halbig
971	A. Marseille	1100	Catterfelder Puppenfabrik
972	Amberg, Louis & Sons	1109	Simon & Halbig
973	Amberg, Louis & Sons	1112	Alt, Beck & Gottschalck
974	Alt, Beck & Gottschalck	1123	Alt, Beck & Gottschalck
975	A. Marseille	1127	Alt, Beck & Gottschalck
979	Simon & Halbig	1129	Simon & Halbig
980	A. Marseille	1142	Alt, Beck & Gottschalck
982	Amberg, Louis & Sons	1159	Simon & Halbig
983	Amberg, Louis & Sons	1160	Simon & Halbig
984	A. Marseille	1170	Simon & Halbig
985	A. Marseille	1180	F. Schmidt
990	Alt, Beck & Gottschalck	1199	Simon & Halbig
990	A. Marseille	1200	Catterfelder Puppenfabrik
991	A. Marseille	1210	Alt, Beck & Gottschalck
992	A. Marseille	1222	Alt, Beck & Gottschalck
995	A. Marseille	1234	Alt, Beck & Gottschalck
996	A. Marseille	1235	Alt, Beck & Gottschalck
1000	Alt, Beck & Gottschalck	1246	Simon & Halbig
1005	Averill, G.	1248	Simon & Halbig
1006	Amusco	1249	Simon & Halbig
1008	Alt, Beck & Gottschalck	1250	Simon & Halbig
1009	Simon & Halbig	1253	F. Schmidt
1010	Simon & Halbig	1254	Alt, Beck & Gottschalck
1019	Simon & Halbig	1256	Alt, Beck & Gottschalck
1020	Muller & Strasburger	1259	F. Schmidt
1028	Alt, Beck & Gottschalck	1260	Simon & Halbig
1029	Simon & Halbig	1262	F. Schmidt
1032	Alt, Beck & Gottschalck	1263	F. Schmidt
1039	Simon & Halbig	1266	F. Schmidt

1267	F. Schmidt	1469	Simon & Halbig
1269	Simon & Halbig	1478	Simon & Halbig
1270	F. Schmidt	1488	Simon & Halbig
1271	F. Schmidt	1489	Simon & Halbig
1272	Simon & Halbig	1498	Simon & Halbig
1272	F. Schmidt	1890	A. Marseille
1279	Simon & Halbig	1892	A. Marseille
1288	Alt, Beck & Gottschalck	1893	A. Marseille
1294	Simon & Halbig	1894	A. Marseille
1299	Simon & Halbig	1897	A. Marseille
1302	Simon & Halbig	1898	A. Marseille
1303	Simon & Halbig	1899	A. Marseille
1304	Alt, Beck & Gottschalck	1900	E. Heubach
1304	Simon & Halbig	1900	A. Marseille
1305	Simon & Halbig	1901	A. Marseille
1308	Simon & Halbig	1902	A. Marseille
1310	F. Schmidt	1903	A. Marseille
1322	Alt, Beck & Gottschalck	1906	Schoenau & Hoffmeister
1329	Simon & Halbig	1907	Recknagel
1339	Simon & Halbig	1909	Schoenau Hoffmeister
1342	Alt, Beck & Gottschalck	1909	A. Marseille
1346	Alt, Beck & Gottschalck	1909	Recknagel
1348	Cuno & Otto Dressel	1909	Schoenau & Hoffmeister
1349	Cuno & Otto Dressel	1912	A. Marseille
1352	Alt, Beck & Gottschalck	1912	Cuno & Otto Dressel
1357	Alt, Beck & Gottschalck	1914	A. Marseille
1357	Catterfelder Puppenfabrik	1914	Cuno & Otto Dressel
1358	Alt, Beck & Gottschalck	1914	Recknagel
1358	Simon & Halbig	1916	Simon & Halbig
1361	Alt, Beck & Gottschalck	1924	Recknagel
1362	Alt, Beck & Gottschalck	2015	Muller & Strasburger
1367	Alt, Beck & Gottschalck	2020	Muller & Strasburger
1368	Alt, Beck & Gottschalck	2023	Bähr & Pröschild
1368	Averill, G.	2023	B. Schmidt
1368	Simon & Halbig	2033	B. Schmidt
1376	Schuetzmeister & Quendt	2048	B. Schmidt
1388	Simon & Halbig	2052	B. Schmidt
1394	Unknown	2072	Bähr & Pröschild
1394	Borgfeldt	2072	B. Schmidt
1402	Averill, G.	2092	B. Schmidt
1428	Simon & Halbig	2094	B. Schmidt
1448	Simon & Halbig	2095	B. Schmidt

2096	B. Schmidt		7644	G. Heubach
2097	B. Schmidt		7657	G. Heubach
2500	Schoenau & Hoffmeister		7658	G. Heubach
2966	Armand Marseille		7661	G. Heubach
3200	Marottes		7668	G. Heubach
3200	A. Marseille		7671	G. Heubach
3841	G. Heubach		7681	G. Heubach
4000	Schoenau & Hoffmeister		7686	G. Heubach
4515	Muller & Strasburger		7711	G. Heubach
4600	Schoenau & Hoffmeister		7759	G. Heubach
4700	Marottes		7847	G. Heubach
4700	Schoenau & Hoffmeister		7850	G. Heubach
4843 - 4883	Kewpie		7911	G. Heubach
4900	Schoenau & Hoffmeister		7925	G. Heubach
4900	Schoenau & Hoffmeister		7926	G. Heubach
5500	Schoenau & Hoffmeister		7972	G. Heubach
5636	G. Heubach		7975	G. Heubach
5689	G. Heubach		7977	G. Heubach
5700	Schoenau & Hoffmeister		8191	G. Heubach
5730	G. Heubach		8192	G. Heubach
5777	G. Heubach		8221	G. Heubach
5800	Schoenau & Hoffmeister		8316	G. Heubach
6688	G. Heubach		8381	G. Heubach
6692	G. Heubach		8413	G. Heubach
6736	G. Heubach		8420	G. Heubach
6894	G. Heubach		8429	G. Heubach
6897	G. Heubach		8552	Unknown
6969	G. Heubach		8556	G. Heubach
6970	G. Heubach		8661	Limbach
6971	G. Heubach		8676	G. Heubach
7246	G. Heubach		8682	Limbach
7247	G. Heubach		8686	G. Heubach
7248	G. Heubach		8723	G. Heubach
7268	G. Heubach		8764	G. Heubach
7287	G. Heubach		8774	G. Heubach
7345	G. Heubach		8819	G. Heubach
7407	G. Heubach		8950	G. Heubach
7602	G. Heubach		8995	G. Heubach
7603	G. Heubach		9027	G. Heubach
7604	G. Heubach		9055	G. Heubach
7622	G. Heubach		9056	G. Heubach
7623	G. Heubach		9355	G. Heubach

9457	G. Heubach		10532	G. Heubach
9573	G. Heubach		11010	G. Heubach
9578	G. Heubach		10016	Unknown
9693	G. Heubach		11173	G. Heubach
9743	G. Heubach		15509	Unknown
9746	G. Heubach		22674	Unknown

MARKS INDEX

Alabama Baby

Alabama Indestructible Dolls Marks:
"MRS. S.S. SMITH//MANUFACTURER AND
DEALER IN// THE ALABAMA
INDESTRUCTIBLE DOLL// ROANOKE, ALA.//
PATENTED//SEPT. 26, 1905."

Alexandre, Henri

Alt, Beck, & Gottschalck

Arranbee Doll Co.

ARRANBEE//DOLL
Co. or R & B

Arnold, Max Oscar

Art Fabric Mills

Art Fabric Mills Marks:
*"ART FABRIC MILLS, NY,
PAT. FEB. 13TH, 1900" on
shoe or bottom of foot.*

Averill, Georgene

Tag on original outfit reads:
"BONNIE BABE COPYRIGHTED
BY GEORGENE AVERILL MADE
BY K AND K TOY CO."

COPR GEORGENE AVERILL
1005/3652 GERMANY

BÄHR & PRÖSCHILD

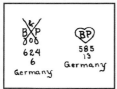

BERGMANN, C.M.

C.M.B
SIMON & HALBIG
Eleonore

BARBIE®

1959 – 1962
BARBIE™
PATS. PEND.
©MCMLVIII
BY//MATTEL, INC.
1963 – 1968
MIDGE™©1962
Barbie®/©1958
BY//MATTEL, INC.
1964 – 1966
©1958//MATTEL, IN.
U.S. PATENTED
U.S. PAT. PEND.
1966 – 1969
©1966//MATTEL, INC.
U.S. PATENTED//
U.S. PAT. PEND//
MADE IN JAPAN

BRU

Fashion-Type Mark:
*Marked "A" through "M," "11" to
"28," indicating size numbers only*

Bru Jne Marks:
*"BRU JNE," with size number on
head, kid over wood body marked
with rectangular paper label.*

Bru Jne R. Marks:
*"BRU. JNE R." with size number on
head, body stamped in red, "Bébé
Bru," and size number.*

Bébé Breveté Marks:
*"Bébé Breveté"
Head marked with size number
only; kid body may have paper
Bébé Breveté label.*

BARRIOS, E.

E 3 B
E. 8 DEPOSE B.

Bye-Lo Baby

© 1923 by
Grace S. Putnam
MADE IN GERMANY
7372145

Catterfelder Puppenfabrik

C. P.
208/34 S
Deponiert

1100
Catterfelder Puppenfabrik
2

Century Doll Co.

CENTURY DOLL C°.
Kestner Germany

Chuckles mark on back:
"CHUCKLES//A
CENTURY DOLL"

Chase Doll Company

"CHASE STOCKINET DOLL"
on left leg or under left arm.
Paper label, if there, reads
"CHASE//HOSPITAL DOLL//
TRADE MARK// PAWTUCKET,
RI// MADE IN U.S.A."

Columbian

"COLUMBIAN DOLL,
EMMA E. ADAMS,
OSWEGO, NY"

Danel et Cie

E. (Size number) D. on head.
Eiffel Tower "PARIS BEBE"
on body; shoes with "PARIS
BEBE" in star.

Dressel, Cuno, & Otto

Heubach•Köppelsdorf
Jutta-Baby
Dressel
Germany
1922
10

E.D.

EDEN BEBE
PARIS

Eegee

Trademark, EEGEE,
or circle with the words,
"TRADEMARK //EEGEE//
Dolls//MADE IN USA"
Later changed to just
initials, E.G.

Effanbee

Some marked on shoulder
plate, "EFFANBEE //BABY
DAINTY"
or "EFFANBEE //DOLLS//
WALK, TALK, SLEEP"
in oval

Fulper Pottery Co.

GANS & SEYFARTH PUPPENBABRIK

```
Germany
  G. & S
    3
```

GAULTIER, FRANCOIS

GESLAND

E. GESLAND
B^TE S. G. D. G.
PARIS

GIBBS, RUTH

RG on back shoulder blade
Box labeled:
"GODEY LITTLE LADY DOLLS"

GLADDIE

Gladdie
Copyright By
Helen W. Jensen
Germany

GOEBEL, WM. AND F. & W.

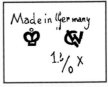

GREINER, LUDWIG

GREINER'S
PATENT HEADS.
No. 0.
Pat. March 30th, '58.

GUND

"A Gund Product, A Toy of Quality and Distinction." From World War II on: Stylized "G" with rabbit ears and whiskers. Mid 1960s – 1987: Bear's head above the letter "U." From 1987 on: "GUND."

HANDWERCK, HEINRICH

HANDWERCK
5
Germany

HANDWERCK, MAX

Max Handweck
Bebe Elite
286/3
Germany

283/28,5
MAJC.
HANDWERCK
GERMANY.
2¼

HARTMANN, CARL

Globe Baby
DEP
Germany
C 3 H

HARTMANN, KARL

HASBRO

1964 – 1965
Marked on right
lower back:
*G.I. Joe TM//COPYRIGHT 1964//BY
HASBRO ®//PATENT PENDING//
MADE IN U.S.A.//GIJoe®*

1967
Slight change in marking:
*COPYRIGHT 1964//BY HASBRO
®//PATENT PENDING// MADE IN
U.S.A.// GIJoe®*
*This mark appears on all four
armed service branches, excluding
the black action figures.*

HERTEL SCHWAB & CO.

HEUBACH, ERNST

HEUBACH, GEBRÜDER

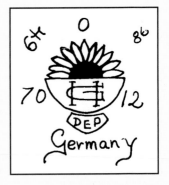

HORSEMAN, E.I.

"E.I. H.//CO."
and "CAN'T
BREAK 'EM"

MARY HOYER DOLL MFG. CO.

"THE MARY HOYER DOLL" or "ORIGINAL MARY HOYER DOLL"

HÜLSS, ADOLPH

IDEAL NOVELTY AND TOY CO.

"IDEAL" (in a diamond), "US of A: IDEAL NOVELTY," and "TOY CO. BROOKLYN, NEW YORK," and others.

JUMEAU

E.J. Bébé
1881 – 86
6
E.J.

KAMKINS

Heart-shaped sticker:
"KAMKINS// A DOLLY MADE TO LOVE // PATENTED//FROM// L.R. KAMPES//STUDIOS// ATLANTIC CITY//N.J."

KÄMMER & REINHARDT

Germany
1126 - 21

KESTNER, J.D.

F made in Germany 10
243

KEWPIE

KRUEGER, RICHARD

"KRUEGER NY//REG. U.S. PAT. OFF/
/MADE IN U.S.A." on body
or clothing seam.

KLING & CO., C.F.

KRUSE, KÄTHE

KUHNLENZ, GEBRUDER

KNOCH, GEBRUDER

LENCI

KONIG & WERNICKE

K&W
HARTGUMMI
555 0
GERMANY

LIMBACH, A.G.

MARSEILLE ARMAND

Armand Marseille
Germany
390
A. 4. M.

Queen Louise
Germany
7.

Made in Germany
Florodora
A 5 M

MAY FRERES CIE

On head:
MASCOTTE
On body:
Bébé Mascotte Paris
Child marked:
Mascotte on head

MORIMURA BOTHERS

Mark for Morimura Brothers,
Japan 1915 on:

OHLHAVER, GEBRUDER

.Revalo.
Germany

PETITE ET DUMONTIER

P 3 D

RABERY & DELPHIEU

Mark: R.3. D

RECKNAGEL, THEODOR

357

ROHMER

SCHMITT & FILS

Shield on head, "SCH" in
shield on bottom of
flat cut derriere.

SCHMIDT, BRUNO

SCHMIDT, FRANZ

1310
F.S.&C

or
S&C
ANVIL MARK

SCHOENAU &
HOFFMEISTER

SCHOENHUT & CO., A.

SCHUETZMEISTER & QUENDT

2·01

Germany

S.F.B.J

23
S.F.B.J.
236
PARIS
4

SHIRLEY TEMPLE

Shirley Temple//
IDEAl Nov. & TOY on
back of head and
SHIRLEY TEMPLE on
body. Some marked
only on head and
with a size.

SIMON & HALBIG

1079
HALBIG
S&H
Germany

S&H. 1249
DEP
Germany
SANTA

Germany
S H 13-1010 DEP.

STEIFF, MARGARETE

Button in ear

STEINER, HERMANN

Made in
Germany
HermSteiner
18
0

SWAINE & CO.

THUILLIER, A.

A . 14. T

WOLFE, LOUIS & CO.

152
L. W. & Cº
12

SYMBOL INDEX

INDEX

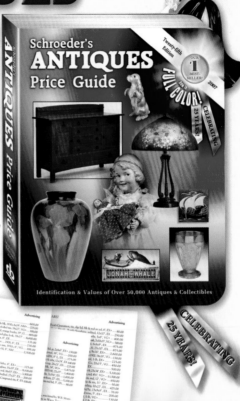

THE SOCIAL REBEL

in American Literature

PERSPECTIVES ON AMERICAN LITERATURE

Robert H. Woodward and James J. Clark
General Editors

THE
SOCIAL REBEL
in American Literature

———•———

EDITED BY

ROBERT H. WOODWARD
San Jose State College

JAMES J. CLARK
San Jose State College

THE ODYSSEY PRESS

NEW YORK

Copyright © 1968 by Western Publishing Company, Inc.
Published by The Odyssey Press
A Division of Western Publishing Company, Inc.
All rights reserved
Printed in the United States
Library of Congress Catalog Card Number: 68–21801
A 0 9 8 7 6 5 4 3 2 1

ACKNOWLEDGMENTS

Acknowledgment is gratefully made for permission to reprint the following material:

Daniel Aaron. From *Writers on the Left,* © 1961, by Daniel Aaron. Reprinted by permission of Harcourt, Brace & World, Inc.
Sherwood Anderson. From *A Story Teller's Story.* Reprinted by permission of Harold Ober Associates, Inc. Copyright © 1924 by B. W. Huebsch. Renewed 1951 by Eleanor Copenhaver Anderson.
James Baldwin. From *Notes of a Native Son.* Reprinted by permission of the publisher, Beacon Press, copyright © 1955 by James Baldwin.
Randolph S. Bourne. "For Radicals" from *Youth and Life.* Reprinted by permission of Houghton Mifflin Company.
Henry Steele Commager. From *The American Mind,* by Henry Steele Commager, pp. 247–250, 257–262, 267, 273–276. Reprinted by permission of Yale University Press.
Malcolm Cowley. From *Exile's Return* by Malcolm Cowley. Copyright 1934, © 1962 by Malcolm Cowley. Reprinted by permission of The Viking Press, Inc.
John Dos Passos. From *Three Soldiers.* Copyright 1921 by John Dos Passos. Copyright Renewed 1949 by John Dos Passos. Published by Houghton Mifflin Company. From *The 42nd Parallel.* Copyright 1930 by John Dos Passos. Copyright Renewed 1958 by John Dos Passos. Published by Houghton Mifflin Company. From *Nineteen Nineteen.* Copyright 1932 by John Dos Passos. Copyright Renewed 1960 by John Dos Passos. Published by Houghton Mifflin Company.
Joseph Freeman. "The Tradition of American Revolutionary Literature" from *American Writers' Congress,* Henry Hart (ed.). Reprinted by permission of International Publishers Co., Inc. From *An American Testa-*

ment by Joseph Freeman. Copyright 1936, © 1964 by Joseph Freeman. Reprinted by permission of Holt, Rinehart and Winston, Inc.

Allen Ginsberg. "America" from *Howl and Other Poems*. Copyright © 1956, 1959 by Allen Ginsberg. Reprinted by permission of City Lights Books.

Albert Halper. From *The Foundry* by Albert Halper. Copyright, 1934, 1962, by Albert Halper.

LeRoi Jones. "The Screamers." Copyright © 1963 by LeRoi Jones. From *The Moderns*, published by Corinth Books. Reprinted by permission of The Sterling Lord Agency.

Jack Kerouac. From *On the Road* by Jack Kerouac. Copyright © 1955, 1957 by Jack Kerouac. Reprinted by permission of The Viking Press, Inc.

Martin Luther King, Jr. "Love, Law and Civil Disobedience" from *Rhetoric of Racial Revolt* by Roy L. Hill, published by Golden Bell Press, Denver, Colorado.

Sinclair Lewis. From *Main Street* by Sinclair Lewis, copyright, 1920, by Harcourt, Brace & World, Inc.; copyright, 1948, by Sinclair Lewis. Reprinted by permission of the publisher.

Norman Mailer. "The Patron Saint of MacDougal Alley." Reprinted by permission of G. P. Putnam's Sons from *Advertisements for Myself* by Norman Mailer. © 1959 by Norman Mailer.

H. L. Mencken. "Duty" from *Prejudices: Third Series* by H. L. Mencken. Copyright 1922 by Alfred A. Knopf, Inc. and renewed 1950 by H. L. Mencken. Reprinted by permission. "The Icononoclast" from *A Mencken Chrestomathy* by H. L. Mencken. Copyright 1924 by Alfred A. Knopf Inc. and renewed 1952 by H. L. Mencken. By permission of Alfred A. Knopf, Inc.

Henry Miller. "Epidaurus and Mycenae" from *The Colossus of Maroussi*. Copyright 1941 by Henry Miller. Reprinted by permission of New Directions Publishing Corporation.

Michael Millgate. From *American Social Fiction* by Michael Millgate. Reprinted by permission of the publisher, Barnes & Noble, Inc., and the author.

C. Wright Mills. "On the New Left." Reprinted with permission from *Studies on the Left*, Volume II, No. 1 (1961).

Kenneth Rexroth. "The Students Take Over" from *The Nation*, Vol. 191 (July 2, 1960). Reprinted by permission of Kenneth Rexroth.

Upton Sinclair. From *Boston*. Reprinted by permission of Bertha Klausner International Literary Agency, Inc.

John P. Sisk. "Beatniks and Tradition" from *The Commonweal*, Vol. 70 (April 17, 1959). Reprinted by permission of Commonweal Publishing Co., Inc.

John Steinbeck. From *In Dubious Battle* by John Steinbeck. Copyright 1936, © 1964 by John Steinbeck. Reprinted by permission of The Viking Press, Inc.

Mark Twain. "The War Prayer" from *Europe and Elsewhere* by Mark Twain. Copyright 1923, 1951 by The Mark Twain Company. Reprinted by permission of Harper & Row, Publishers.

PREFACE

ALTHOUGH AMERICAN SOCIETY is noted for the high degree of conformity that it imposes on its members and for the materialistic values that seem often to take precedence over human ones, it is a significant fact that much of the serious literature of America has since its beginnings been one of criticism, dissent, rebellion—a double-sided mirror that reflects not only social practices but also the underlying ideals and aspirations of America. The theme of social rebellion is a fundamental one—perhaps the fundamental one—in American literature. This collection of comment on the role of the social rebel in American life and of literature reflecting the course and direction of his rebellion is designed primarily for use as a controlled-research casebook that will allow the student sufficient material to formulate and to document his own conclusions about "the subversive tradition" in American literature.

In a volume of this size we could not hope to cover adequately the multifaceted body of literature of social rebellion. We have, therefore, emphasized the recurrent tendencies that seem to us the most significantly American ones—those reflecting the continuing moral revolution against the stringent restrictions of a puritan heritage, those stemming from the democratic faith in the individual and the belief in his inalienable rights, and those in opposition to the economic structure of American society. We have had to be satisfied merely to glance at literature of dissent that is less locally American— utopian literature and the literature of bohemia, for example.

The volume contains two principal types of selections. The first section, "Perspectives," contains several authoritative assessments of or germinal statements about the literature of rebellion and the role of the rebel. These essays make generalizations and observations that can be supported—or argued—by the second type of selections, usually works of imaginative literature expressing important features of the theme of social rebellion. The organization of the three literary sections permits a chronological overview that suggests major lines of development or evolution of particular aspects of the theme.

We have kept editorial additions to the minimum necessary for effective use of the volume in courses in American civilization, American history, American literature, and English composition. The introductions to the four divisions provide only brief generalizations about the selections that follow. At the end of the book are questions intended to provoke discussion and suggest topics for papers. The volume concludes with suggestions for further reading and notes on the authors. Bibliographical information about each selection appears in a footnote, and the original pagination is shown within brackets. The number before the virgule (/) indicates the end of the original page; the number after it signals the beginning of a new page. If in the original a word is divided at the end of a page, the page number has been placed at the end of the word.

We wish to express our appreciation to two of our colleagues, Nils T. Peterson and Graham C. Wilson, for their suggestions and interest; to E. R. Hagemann, University of Louisville, and the staff of the San Jose State College Library for their cooperation; and to Vivien Nylen for her assistance in the preparation of the manuscript.

ROBERT H. WOODWARD
JAMES J. CLARK

San Jose State College
San Jose, California

CONTENTS

THE SOCIAL REBEL

in American Literature

I

Perspectives

IT IS PERHAPS an ironic feature of American literary history that social protest literature has had a long and respectable past, that society would find acceptable the kinds of criticism which frankly attempt to subvert the values of that society. Thomas Jefferson saw the political need of "little rebellions" to keep society healthy, and, to bear out Jefferson's hopes, America's history is a chronicle of the activities of those who sought to instigate "little rebellions," the list of the instigators including famous as well as infamous names. There was the not-so-respectable Thomas Morton in the 1600's, the pious John Woolman in the 1700's, James Fenimore Cooper, Emerson, and Thoreau, to name only the best known of the critics in the early 1800's. Since the days of Emerson and Thoreau the list has progressively increased, the American critics of America speaking loudly and persistently, sometimes, it would appear, even obsessively—the English critic Michael Millgate regrets the American writer's "inescapable self-consciousness" about his society—but speaking frankly and openly, sparing no one and no institution. The American writer has been amused by or has criticized capitalism, commercialism, Puritanism, the middle class or *booboisee*, Main Street and Madison Avenue, and even himself, and in so doing has prepared a body of literature that is marked certainly by a great deal of variety and often by an impressive degree of literary excellence.

From this literature has emerged a figure, the social rebel, a person who chose in some way to oppose the world he lives in. He is the antagonist, the adversary. This rebel may be the writer himself —a Thoreau, Whitman, or Ginsberg—or he may be a fictional representation, a Huckleberry Finn, or Tom Joad of *Grapes of Wrath*, or John Andrews of *Three Soldiers*. In general these writers or characters may be viewed as social rebels rather than revolutionists; they are members of a society that is ever changing, that, in addition, has in its structure the political and social ingredients to ferment new

1

changes. They serve generally a useful purpose in a watch-dog capacity, exposing the corrupt and awakening the conscience of a busy and practical country: Mark Twain's Huckleberry Finn uncovered the hypocritical moral pretensions of a nation when he befriended a Negro named Jim; in his two-year stay at Walden Pond Thoreau made a quiet protest that capitalism and commercialism have yet to answer effectively; Sister Carrie dreamed her way past an entire culture of Puritan restrictions and inhibitions; Jack London's Martin Eden in his suicide revealed an ultimate defiance of the whole ethic of money success; Fitzgerald's flappers introduced jazz and Freud to a shocked nation, revealing the flaws of the involved Puritan and Victorian fabric of social morality. The contemporary writer-rebel, history may record, is providing an equivalent useful social purpose in reminding a conformist culture about what John P. Sisk calls the "dream of utopian freedom and innocence to be found in a commitment to instinct and feeling." All of these writers or their creations have succeeded in some measure in changing social attitudes. How profound the changes have been or will prove to be perhaps creates a separate question. Commager, for instance, argues that the social criticism of the 1920's was largely ineffectual, that "the economic hide was too thick for the barbs of the satirists." And it has been often noted by many other critics that the middle class commercial culture is able to absorb seemingly alien philosophies with no perceptible harm to its own character—that it is able to use bohemianism, for instance, for its own commercial purpose. The importance of the changes may be a matter of controversy, but the fact of the confrontations of rebel and society is not. The confrontations are a matter of record, and they therefore can be examined and analyzed.

In his article on American writing Millgate raises a basic question: what are the reasons for the American artist's seeming antipathy toward his culture? To answer his question, he suggests that the problems facing the American artist are unique (as opposed to the problems faced by the English writer), the American artist having to come to terms with the "peculiar difficulties presented by the vastness, newness, shapelessness, and instability of American society." Commager, interested also in the American artist's problems of identity with his culture, suggests that the artist "took seriously the promise of American life, expected to realize the American dream," and therefore he was critical when the ideal seemed distorted. Other critics have singled out the corrupting influences of commercialism, or the process of dehumanization in modern industry that leads to the alienation of the individual man from a realistic commitment to his work or to his fellow man.

Another simpler explanation to help account for these many criti-